What Men Know That Women Don't

How to Love Women Without Losing your Soul

Other books by Rich Zubaty:

The Corporate Cult

Surviving the Feminization of America

Water People

Wisdom

What Men Know That Women Don't

How to Love Women Without Losing Your Soul

Rich Zubaty

completely revised, rewritten, globalized
and updated from the original
1993 classic edition:

Surviving the Feminization of America

Co-published by

Virtualbookworm.com
College Station, Texas

and

Zubaty Publishing
[formerly Panther Press (IL)]
Kaunakakai, Hawaii

2001

photos by M. Noyce
Capitol drawing by Hord Stubblefield
turtle and fish drawings Dan Burgevin

Orders:

Virtualbookworm.com Publishing
PO Box 9949
College Station, Texas 77842

Toll free phone/fax: 1-877-376-4955

Email: **orders@virtualbookworm.com**
info@virtualbookworm.com

Web Site: **http://www.virtualbookworm.com**

Zubaty Publishing
PO Box 1442
Kaunakakai, Hawaii 96748

Email: **richzubaty@hotmail.com**

Rich Zubaty Web Site:
http://www.geocities.com/Athens/Oracle/5225/

ISBN: 1-58939-039-3 (book)
ISBN: 1-58939-040-7 (e-book)
ISBN: 1-58939-041-5 (CD)

Library of Congress Cataloging-in-Publication Data
Zubaty, Rich, 1948–
  What men know that women don't : how to love women
without losing your soul / by Rich Zubaty ; preface by Bill
Kauth.
    p. cm.
  Includes bibliographical references.
  ISBN 1-58939-039-3 (pbk. : alk. paper)
  1. Sex role—United States.
  2. Man-woman relationships—United States.
  3. Men—United States—Psychology.
  4. Masculinity—United States. I. Title.
  HQ1075.5.U6 Z836 2001
  305.3—dc21   2001003551

Published in the United States of America

9 8 7 6 5 4 3 2

Acknowledgements:

   This book could not have been published without the creative, editorial, and technical contributions of **Craig Moberg**.
Thanks to **M. Noyce** for proofreading, brainstorming, and all-
around inspirational support. A special thanks to my elders in
men's work, **Roy Schenk** and **Bill Kauth**, for encouraging my
efforts and furthering my personal evolution in the best tradition of elders. And thanks also to **Rich Angell** for staying a true
friend through the best and worst of times.

For Aaron and Rebecca

May the Truth
Follow You Home

Table of Contents

THE WITCH

I have cut the plantain grove
I have taken off my clothes
I have learnt from my mother-in-law
How to eat my husband

I have grown weary
Weary of eating rice

India:Santal [1]

Preface

Rich Zubaty barbecues sacred cows for breakfast.

I LIKE BOOKS THAT challenge me and this is the most ex-cruciatingly provocative book I've ever read. It's astoundingly hard to describe because it's so completely original in its basic premise.

Imagine this scenario: The masculine and feminine roles in life have been disturbed – swapped – turned up-side down. Men are acting more like women and women are acting more like men – each acting out the other's weaker nature. And women in general witlessly participate in an unholy alliance with big government and big corporations to commercialize our society.

Heresy, blasphemy – sacred cows are diving for cover. Well, hang on to you psychic seat belts, because Zubaty makes a damn good case for such radical unorthodoxy.

When the first edition came out in 1993 Rich Zubaty was harassed and threatened, his distribution was sabotaged and suppressed by feminist sympathizers – misshelving in libraries and bookstores, intimidating distributors, lost orders, etc. To censor what? His homely theory that we *might* be happier, more content creatures if we got closer to our essential gender natures? *Ergo, we need to find out what our essential gender natures are!* Does that sound threatening or subversive? Apparently to some humorless lock-steppers it was. Seems like Ms. mommy pseudo-nature gets cranky with theories that don't fit with proper party propaganda.

What kind of uncivilized guy would draw this kind of fire? Let me introduce you to…Zubaty! I read the first version of this book 8 or 9 years ago. I loved and hated it so much that I called him immediately. We went fishing together and bonded as men around two things (besides fishing). First, the powerful little word "meme" (more on that in this book), and second, the need for men's initiation into an aware healthy masculinity.

What you need to know about his history, in one paragraph, goes like this. Smart enough for a full scholarship to the U. of Chicago, he blew it off to get involved in the youth protests of the 60s, married a beautiful woman, had two kids, built homes for a living and even put his wife through law school. She promptly sued for divorce, took the kids, the house, the car, and left him with the bill. Unwilling to knuckle under to this "no options" state of affairs, he began his pilgrimage in search of truth. He went to India, where he sat with Bede Griffiths (an east/west mystic) until his travel visa ran out, then to a monastery in Thailand, on to South Seas islands, back to the States to hang out with the Benedictines, and eventually Mexico where he wrote his first book.

He painted houses, took odd jobs, lived on food stamps, crashed with friends and seemed able to survive almost anywhere in the world. All the while he kept reaching out to the son and daughter who had been poisoned against him and taught to fear him. Little by little his son came around – he's still waiting 12 years on his daughter.

Over the years I came to appreciate Zubaty as a truly un-common and uncivilized man. (I mean this in a good way.) He's a one-of-a-kind original. Having lived in so many cultures it's like he's sort of a trans-civil being. A neo-primitive. Like he'll never be tamed. **A wild mustang of the psyche.** Each of us has our beauty and gift to the world, and Zubaty brings the passion and juiciness of a man truly living life fully.

This book is uncivilized; he says stuff so far beyond impolite it sears your brain. Admittedly it's an angry book. He *owns* that. And certain things in it infuriate me – so much so that I want to smash it against the wall. But other parts of it make me stand up and laugh. And yet other parts of it lift me off on a mental/spiritual moonshot.

He butchers sacred cows you didn't even know you had on a pedestal until you see them tottering toward a crash. If he doesn't ruffle your feathers regularly you're not paying attention.

I'll be reading along, laughing, and suddenly he pisses me off. I shout, "he's nuts" and feel like tearing the book apart. Then magically in two pages something begins to make sense. He manages to convince me there is at least *some* truth to his latest outlandish proclamation.

And that's the point. He wants us to think about a *way of thinking* we have rarely tried before ("new memes")! The point is *not* to agree with him...but to actually *think critically*. A skill that is fast being homogenized by the mavens of corporate culture – those slick promoters who have a tremendous investment in keeping us as mentally dull as they can so we let *them* do our thinking for us.

Yes, it will challenge you. This book is a hard, though loving swat up-side the head for us new age, religion-morphing, feminist-trusting, know-it-all, oh-so psychologically evolved types.

And even if I still don't buy all of it I have to admire each amazing elucidation (say that 3 times.) There is no way to read this book and remain a dittohead, parroting some ignorant charismatic vampire. **This is anarchy for the soul.** You actually learn to question the authority of damn near everything you have ever learned. Then create your own opinion. And it becomes *your creation!* Not something you heard from mom, or school, or the radio/TV. It's your *own* creation based on information *you* gathered in your *own* life. And because you created it, it might change again as you gain further life experience. That's the way we grow. And to me, evolving into more complex beings is the very *definition* of joy. This goofy book will trigger your joy – over and over again – if you can just keep from throwing it against the wall!

Zubaty will tease and prod and poke you and joke you, and slap you around. And he'll keep doing it for hundreds of pages.

Who says non-fiction writing can't be passionate, funny, and at times, maybe even angry?

If nothing else his writing style – wise-cracking, caustic, enlivened by spontaneous metaphors – is a cold beer in the parched desert of most non-fiction writing. This book will make you learn and make you laugh.

Bill Kauth
Ashland, Oregon
June 2001

Bio:

Bill Kauth co-founder of the New Warrior Training Adventure (20,000 graduates) and The Warrior Monk Training Intensive and author of *A Circle of Men: The Original Manual for Men's Support Groups* (published 1992: St. Martin's Press, still in print)

Prologue

WHAT MOST MEN WANT to know is how come we live in a society that *appears* to be run by men, but *feels* like it's run by women? The answer is pretty simple. The men who run modern society – the politicians, businessmen, educators and priests – are men who think like women. They are men who espouse and advance female values. Why do they do this? Because women have more purchasing power, more voting power and more cultural power than men. Women control the marketplace, the polling place and the content of our schools, churches and media. The "secret of success" of the modern "successful" man is that he sold his soul to women and female values. Our society is being run by men who think and act like women. That's why we have so many problems. The Patriarchy is, in fact, a Matriarchy. Female values rule.

Most men already know this, but they haven't been able to "put it into words". Putting it into words helps us to see the situation more clearly and devise strategies to pull the plug on this global Wal-Mart of the human psyche. It's high time for men to be men again, and this book takes a flying leap in that direction.

Since the first print edition of this book came out in 1994 I've received thousands of responses from readers detailing what they "learned" in these pages. To my amazement what they "learned" were quite often things that are *not* in this book. A 70-year-old grandmother told me how reading this book reminded her of fishing with her father around small islands near Seattle, spending the night in a cabin with no electricity – only kerosene lamps – and what a wonderful memory that was for her. A great number of men and women told me reading the book helped them understand why their marriage fell apart, and how to do it better next time. One young man told me this book gave him "permission" to *feel* his pent-up anger against women – which was the first step in allowing him to release that anger without causing harm to himself or others. The boyfriend of a young Dutch woman said his girlfriend should pay me $1000 for bringing up something in these pages (?) which enabled her to understand and forgive her father. I guess therapy didn't work.

The point is, the readers who got the most out of this book are the ones who brought *themselves* to the book. They let these words bounce around inside their heads long enough to catalyze their own thoughts and feelings and opinions into new realizations. The results have amazed me beyond belief. I poured my heart out on paper – and other people poured theirs back. This is not your normal, dispassionate, objective nonfiction book. This book was written with gobs of passion.

The people who accuse me of being angry have never seen me *really* get angry. If they had they would understand that this book is an attempt to vent my passion and frustration in a constructive manner. Without the passion (anger?) this book would never have been written.

Moreover, I believe that most of us, in this feminized society we inhabit, have lost the ability to distinguish passion from anger. We were all taught by mommy how to be polite, how to apologize for burping or farting, and how to discuss our feelings without "losing our temper". That's feminized crap. That's how mom taught us to act so we could make a good impression on the judge or get a nice job at a corporation. Well guess what? As far as I'm concerned a judge has to EARN my respect. He has to do something to warrant being addressed as "Your Honor". He doesn't just garner that respect by wearing a black dress and looking down at me from a high chair. And I don't *want* to work for any corporation that's wrecking the environment, oppressing workers, and making me suppress my feelings. By extension, that means I don't want to work for *any* corporation. Corporations are not the best way to organize business – they're the worst. Corporations are not the most efficient way to organize our lives, they're the least efficient. So there's plenty to be angry about, and anyone who tells you you shouldn't be angry is killing off your Male Soul. They're talking at you from that little "mommy" they carry around inside their heads. The best thing you can do is laugh in their face. That might wake them up. Rationality and objectivity are not admirable traits. They're evidence of having sold your soul in order to "get along" in the world. Mommyism. Don't be afraid of anger. Don't suppress passion. The trick is to learn how to channel anger and passion constructively.

After some 200 radio shows, a dozen TV shows, and twenty print articles I've been forced to hone my ramblings down to some two-minute soundbites. My simple thesis is this:

Feminists are corporate whores.

For over 30 years feminists have demonized men, undermined the family, and ridiculed religion. Male values, family values and religious values have been marginalized, made fun of, dismissed as passé. In the vacuum created by the hemorrhage of these historically cardinal values corporations rushed in and flooded our brains with their core values: wealth, celebrity, and the "free trade" smorgasbord of things to buy. But since, as their root strategy, corporations *design* themselves to appeal to the endemic shopping compulsions of women, what we are left with is an incestuous, self-perpetuating cycle of greed. Feminists feed corporations and corporations feed feminists. Feminists don't care if corporations ship our jobs overseas and build Third World sweatshops. They only care if there are equal numbers of women on the boards of directors. Feminism is not a grassroots movement of oppressed women. It's a multi-billion dollar a year "INFORMATION INDUSTRY" that has infected our schools, government, factories and families with high-paid workers oozing an academic pus of wrong "facts", misplaced priorities, bad ideas and self-righteous rhetoric.

* * *

Ever since we were walking around in wet diapers all of us have been drenched in a never-ending rain of corporate propaganda – on the TV, in the papers, on the streets, everywhere we look, everywhere we listen. At the same time, thanks to the haughty drumbeat of feminist ideologues screeching at us from every available electronic soapbox, we have been deprived of the masculine values, family values and church values which could have balanced the seesaw of modern culture. Feminists sold our heads to huge corporations with a whistle and a blowjob. They got jobs. So what? The trade-off was that our lives are now being bought and sold by impersonal, non-accountable, corporate behemoths. We have lost all sense of what a man is, what a family is, and what Faith is. In other words, we have lost all sense of the Meaning of Life.

The solution is simple.

We need to regenerate a male-flavored spirituality.

We need to move men, families and Faith to a reinvigorated prominence in our lives. Forget feminist schemes, Forget corporate scams. And don't forget that big government *means* big business these days. The two are equivalent. Or, as Gerry Spence says, big government and big corporations are like two screwing dogs who got stuck together. When one pulls, the other follows. Crude. But sublimely accurate.

And what's the first step in recovering from this feminist/corporate/big government nightmare? We need to get our thinking straight. Right now we've got it all backwards.

Men and women have swapped mental roles. Men have become more like women. Women have become more like men. Men are submitting to their "female" side. Women, to offset this vacuum of masculinity, have begun acting out of their "male" side. It's not good. In fact, it's a disaster. Men do not make good women and women do not make good men. We are both operating out of our weaker natures. Men have no aptitude for the finer nuances of domesticity. Women do not understand the finer nuances of the "hunt". We have crippled ourselves. We're eating soup with a fork. We've tied our families into knots.

The feminization of human society began 8000 years ago when we abandoned hunting and gathering for the joys of agriculture. The "King" was the first feminized man. He wore dresses, garnished himself with jewelry, perverted the hunters into soldiers to guard his castle full of stuff, and all in all, behaved just like a woman. He was rich and powerful – which women admire. And he set a feminized, materialistic standard for what men should be like.

Our lives are inside out. Here's what we got backwards:

Women are more materialistic than men. *Mater*, the Latin word for mother, is the root word of *mater*ialism. Women own 65% of America's wealth according to *Forbes* magazine. Seven times more retail space is allotted to women's personal items than to men's. Women make 85% of buying decisions. Women have naively entered into an unholy alliance with corporations to provide themselves with more jobs and more stuff. The corporate conquest, the *mater*ialist mindset of modern society, may be blamed directly on female greed, female self-seeking and female *mater*ialism.

Men are not the cause of war. Greed, *mater*ialism, and self-seeking are the causes of war. The 20th century witnessed an exponential increase in women' rights including the right to vote. And an exponential increase in war – two World Wars and hundreds of equally deadly lesser conflicts. These facts are NOT unrelated. Female greed, *mater*ialism, and self-seeking are the major causes of war. Men are obligated to fight war. Women are not. But women adore the security, luxury and technical "time-saving" gadgetry produced in a military economy. Female values are the cause of war. **Women are the cause of war.**

* * *

Men are more spiritual than women. Every human society has acknowledged the Earth Mother and the Sky Father. Woman is down, into the earth, grounded, *mater*ialistic. Man is up, into the sky, dreamy, creative, spontaneous, seeking that invisible God. It is a travesty and oppression of male nature to claim women are more spiritual than men.

Women are not Morally Superior to men. Women are not always kind, caring, and sharing. Sometimes they're mean and conniving and manipulating. Psychological stereotyping has done a *profound* disservice to men by casting women as nurturing and men as aggressive. Female business barracudas and politicians are ruthless beyond belief to most men's way of thinking. My kind, caring, sharing side is not my female side; it's my kind, caring, sharing side! My mean, manipulative, aggressive side is not my masculine side; it's my mean, manipulative, aggressive side! Sadly, due to our societal blindness to the fact that women are *not* morally superior to men, women get away with perpetrating far more than their fair share of tragedies and outrages. If a man hits a woman we want to toss the bastard in jail. If a woman hits a man we want to know what he said to piss her off.

Women think "Fidelity" is a city in Pennsylvania. Throughout human history women, being physically weaker, have honed their skills at lies, deceptions, and masquerades. But we, simple-minded saps that we are, succumbing to their smiley, solicitous mannerisms, have subconsciously elevated them onto a pedestal of Moral Superiority. It's a crock. Women know what other women are like. It's us dopes who deny the moral sliminess of women. We think we "need" some image of feminine purity. We crawl on our bellies through the grease pits of life clinging to some icon of "mom". Well chumps…here's the low-down. When it's a man's word against a woman's word, best to believe the man.

Men are more intuitive than women. Our art, our science, our mathematics – our entire society – is the product of male intuition. For millennia men have grabbed abstractions out of the sky and struggled to bring them into physical form – "intuiting" the possibilities. "Women's intuition" is little more than analytical extrapolations driven by negativity – perennial predictions of doom. Few women are spending any time thinking about why the universe is now expanding faster than it has been for the past 10 billion years. But every one of them can produce detailed scenarios of how "everything is going to get worse".

Women are more analytical than men. Later I'll launch into a discussion of who's more "logical", but it's obvious to anyone that women analyze the bejesus out of the tiniest details of every situation. Men take a wider view and see a larger, albeit foggier picture.

Men are more skilled in relationships than women. Women talk a lot about relationships. Men DO relationships. Men are team players. That's how Columbus crossed the Atlantic. That's how men got on the moon. Watch a basketball game – darting, dribbling, signaling with a bobbed head, motioning with an eye-twitch, passing to the place where the guy is *supposed* to be – leaping, catching, shooting, scoring. Male relationship happens faster than the speed of talk.

Men have deeper feelings than women. Women have more emotions, men have deeper feelings. Women gush about this or wail about that. Men hold their feelings deep down inside them. Occasionally masculine feeling explodes into the open – virtually all of our art and music and literature are products of masculine feelings. But mostly men are afraid to show their feelings – afraid because they've been shamed. Shamed by the very women who claim they want men who are "not afraid" to express their feelings. But when men put caution aside and tell their women how they really feel, inevitably, in one way or another, the women respond with, "You shouldn't feel like that." *i.e.* "You shouldn't have those feelings." *i.e.* "Shame on you, you big lout". And it's all accomplished with such sharing, caring, solicitousness that, from a very young age, men learn to see this for what it is: another female manipulation. When you reveal your feelings to a woman she'll use them against you somehow. It's like we're always in court, and the opposing attorney is drilling us with a deposition while she's cooking us spaghetti. Scary. Who do you trust? Other men? You must be kidding.

"Equality" is meaningless. Is a bee equal to a sparrow? Is a whale equal to a squirrel? The term is meaningless. And anyway, feminism was never honestly about Equality. Feminism was about MORE STUFF FOR WOMEN. Women don't want to mine coal or get drafted into war. That's too much Equality for them. Just let them have some office job so they can stay comfortable and buy more stuff. Forget that they live 8 years longer than us. Ignore the fact that 19 out of 20 people who die on the job are men. Or 4 out of 5 suicides are men. Or 80% of the home-less are men. That's the other side of Equality, and they don't want to hear about it.

"Create programs for men? Men already have everything – don't they?...Me?" she titters. "Sign up for the draft? Drill oil? You must be kidding. I'm not equipped for that. That's not the kind of Equality I mean."

Feminism is a disaster. For 8000 years the world has been becoming progressively more feminized. We've lost sight of our true gender natures. 100 years ago the feminists were trying to get women and kids out of the factories to make stronger families. The current feminist movement wants to put them back in – and *destroy* the family. Insidious. Misguided. Evil.

Men are not the oppressors of women. The simple proof of that is that **Women are not oppressed.** Women are not now, and never have been "oppressed". Women have the right to vote with NO concomitant obligation to be drafted in time of war to protect their right to vote. Personally, I don't see how they got the one without being forced to assume the other. They have power without responsibility. The only way Democracy got reborn in the modern world was because men fought and died battling the power of kings and their corporations to seize this right. But women gained it by fighting what? A "courageous" ideological struggle? It's Twinkies. Philosophical oatmeal. Nor are women expected to perform heavy labor – laying bricks, pouring asphalt, fixing cars. They live in houses they don't build, drive cars they can't fix, eat food they don't grow. This is oppression? In fact, women are *coddled*, not oppressed. Women are strident and pushy and obnoxious in ways men never can be because we'd get punched or shamed or arrested, and they won't – since they're *just* women.

If someone came up to me tomorrow and said, "I got a great deal for you. You'll never have to fight in war or do heavy labor again...All you have to do is sign away your right to vote." I'd say, "Where do I sign?" That's all I NEED government for. Keeping me out of war and protecting me from oppressive labor conditions. I don't *need* to vote if those rights are guaranteed. That's fair. But apparently it's not fair enough for women. They can vote but they need not fight nor pour concrete. That's a perversion of the word Equality. The entire feminist movement is built on the phony proclamation that "women are oppressed". Pull that out from under them (as I have on various radio shows) and their naked ego and raw greed flap like pantyhose in the wind. And what do they do then? Scream. Scream like little girls. Try to shame me any way they can. **The Achilles' Heel of feminism is the unprovable proposition that women are oppressed.**

Feminism has, in fact, created an **Aristocracy of Women** – a select club of people who, by virtue of birth alone, do not have to fight in war or pound nails. And, as if that privilege wasn't enough, they've browbeat politicians into instituting government fast-tracks so they can attain the highest positions of power and authority in society – judges, senators, CEOs, media mavens.

Feminism is government by coffee klatch. Feminism, by its very nature, dissociates opinions from action. It's easy to vote boys into war, or write a column about how bridges should be repaired, as long as you never have to be the one to fight or do

the work. Feminism divorces ideas from action. Feminism destroys masculine soul. **Feminism annihilates Love.**

Time to recapture our true natures. Time to bury the
hatchet in the gender wars by rediscovering who we really are,
where our true strengths lie, and what we honestly expect out of
life. It's either that, or we'll all be permanently assigned to a
corporation at birth. Destruction of the family – social disintegration, ethical collapse – leads directly to corporate colonialism – the usurpation of all money and media and education and
government and means of production – all thoughts and dreams
and aspirations – by huge economic entities, servicing the
"needs" of women – which "needs" were put there by corporations in the first place! That amounts to *de facto* Economic
Slavery. Soul murder. The Dark Ages again. A snake biting its
own tail.

The unintended consequence of feminism, the feminization
of human society – the destruction of the family – has been the
corporate conquest of our brains and our bodies and our lives.
Corporate Colonialism. No, that's not what the girls meant to
have happen. But it happened. So let's call it a mistake. A big
mistake. Forgive each other. Trash the whole thing. And move
on. Our enemy is NOT women. It's Corporate Colonialism.
But we can never win this war when one half of the human race
is blindly selling out to the other side. We need the women to
wake up. Feminists are frauds. In a society as crippled by stress
and frustration as ours – after 30 years of women having things
their way – it's clear that women don't have the answers. They
don't have any inborn natural knowledge of what is good and
what is right. Time to dig deeper. I'm tired of living in a "female
friendly" world that has become oppressive to both men and
women.

**By destroying the family feminism threw the door open
for the corporate conquest of our lives.** By marginalizing
family and church values, a vacuum was created whereby corporate values became ascendant. Our kids' brains are boobed
out.

* * *

The first edition of this book, titled *Surviving the Feminization of America*, was an iconoclastic cruise missile aimed at men and women in the United States of America. It only took a few months for me to realize I'd made a BIG mistake. Men in England, Canada, Australia, New Zealand, Holland, France and Germany were quick to tell me they had the exact same problems in their countries: women and corporations were taking over their lives. An unholy alliance between Feminism, Big Government, and Big Corporations was squeezing the life-blood out of them. As often happens, BAD ideas that originate in the USA seem to scatter like viruses infecting other countries and cultures.

Though I've tried to revise this book to give it a more international character, that's a difficult thing to do in retrospect. However, despite the fact that many of the examples I use to illustrate my points are drawn from the USA and Canada, it won't take much imagination to identify the Political Blowhards, Corporate Vultures, and Feminist Foghorns in your own country who – like brainless sponges – have sucked up the rotten milk of Feminist and Global Corporate propaganda, and are squeezing it down our throats. Women and Global Corporations are witless, oblivious conspirators in an international offensive to demonize, emasculate, and ultimately co-opt the productivity of men. They wish to see huge transnational structures in place which will monitor and determine every detail of what we think and do. It's a war. What's at stake is the very life or death of the Male Soul. We have no choice but to engage them on every frontier. Without that, we cease to exist. This book has some proven value in clarifying these complex issues. I believe it can make you feel better about yourself, and even help you invent your own personalized strategies for dealing with this feminized/globalized soul-destroying mess. The bottom line is: It's OK to be a Man. Everything else starts with knowing that.

Rich Zubaty
Flathead River Indian Reservation

Western Montana
May, 2000

And here's how the book started off 8 years ago:

* * *

This book is meant to be read by men who don't read a lot. They might read a few pages, put it down, think about it when they're fixing their car or watching football, and then pick it up again. Therefore, important themes are restated and repeated throughout – sort of like a good novel. This is jazz writing, a Blues Book, where themes are stated, embellished, left entirely behind, then revisited and restated, again and again until the end. It's not stream of consciousness, it's just blues.

I'm a novelist, not a journalist. I lay out a few licks of suspense, some flourishes of confusion, a host of seedy characters with obscure motives, and try my very best to coax all these together in such a way that you will draw your own meaning from them. I am not a disciple of any particular religion or philosophy. I'm not trying to convince you of anything other than penetrating the veil of cowshit we inhabit. Look on through to the other side. It will not be possible to find a couple of things you disagree with and thereby reject this whole book. There is just too much here – too much evidence, too many opinions, too many observations – and you'll only be cheating yourself if you bail out halfway through the trip. If you don't like one chapter, skip on to the next. This book has more changes than a drunk has excuses. I guarantee it will change the way you look at things.

I haven't spared the emotion either. Emotion is what wrote this book. That's something else you won't find often in non-fiction. But something remarkable happens regarding the emotion just past midway through the writing. It's real. As in any good story, the main character goes through a change, and that is really what the story is all about.

In deference to academia I want to apologize that a good number of the source *materi*als are not cited. I don't remember where I heard the stuff – but I didn't make it up. A dedicated researcher with privileges at a university library will be able to track them down. The hundreds of footnotes I have made are indexed numerically at the back of the book. That's the most I can do with them right now. Since I can't find a publisher to read this manuscript, much less publish it, it looks like I'll have to put in some hard hours house painting to raise the money to publish it myself. We live in an age of woman-think, *de facto* censorship. If you don't believe that – skip to the next chapter. But let me remind you of one thing. Our congressmen go to work every day inside a domed Capitol building that is, in form and fact, a big tit.

Oaxaca, Mexico
February 1993

Introduction

**THE SAGE BATTLES HIS OWN EGO
THE FOOL BATTLES EVERYONE ELSE'S**
— Sufi Proverb

IN ORDER FOR A MAN to survive in the modern world it is imperative that he understand two things:

1) **Women do not want what they say they want**
2) **Women do not know what they want**

This is not as desperate a situation as it seems. It does not mean that we needn't love women. It means that we needn't be hurt by them anymore. Our war is not against women. Our war is the classical spiritual battle against the dragon of the ego, the undifferentiated reptilian self, that came to life licking swamp air and looking around to get laid. And now, 50 million years later, TV is selling wet dreams to the scaly-skinned beast in all of us through the illusory mindscape of those men I call MANHOLES — the men who think like women. These manholes defend and propagate female values at the price of drowning the masculine soul. They are traitors to all men; and it will surprise you to come to know who these manholes are and what stations they occupy.

But first of all, who am I?

I'm just another jerk who believed the lie. American society told me that if I went to college, got a career, got married, had kids, bought property, pumped some money into a bank account, and joined a religious community, I could have security. Security means freedom from fear, a somewhat common human urge, I think.

Then one afternoon I was awakened from a nap by a bearded, bald, pot-bellied guy pacing around in my living room like a nervous panther. He was reading out loud from some loose sheets of paper as if he were auditioning for a play. I rubbed my eyes and slapped my head. The process-server said, "I'm sorry," as he handed me a sheaf of documents entitled DISSOLUTION OF MARRIAGE, and as I took them from him I crossed some threshold of existence and entered a new earthly incarnation. Everything I had known and loved and worked for over a period of twelve years was removed from me in that instant. I felt like I'd been pillaged by Cossacks. I was allowed two weeks to get out of the house I had built for my own family with my own hands and my own money. Nazism? No. Communism? No. Feminism. A new outbreak of an ancient social virus set free to ravage human society everywhere on earth.

So, I discovered, security was not to be found in anything that anyone had been telling me for the past 39 years. I felt betrayed; not just by my wife, not just by the law, but by the whole damn mindscape.

I slogged through a year and a half of divorce proceedings successfully fending off insane accusations by my ex that I had been a child abuser. This legal ploy effectively allowed her to remove the kids from my presence, and by the time I disproved these charges to the court's satisfaction it was too late. My children were lost to me – poisoned against me, afraid to be with me. In America, the divorced parent who gets the kids, gets the house, gets the money. You don't own your house. Your kids do. So that's why the women go after the kids. That's how the monster works.

Anyway, I lost four houses, a boat, cars, a truck, my business, and my kids to lawyers, lies, and legal monstrosities. I finally whittled the number of possessions in my life down to those that would fit into one large suitcase, plus whatever T-shirts and underpants I could tuck behind the keys of my battered Smith Corona typewriter, and I set off on a spiritual odyssey of grandiose intentions. I wanted to learn how to live without fear. The *right* way, not the American way.

First stop India, where I stayed at Dom Bede Griffiths' Shantivanam, the Forest of Peace, a Camaldolese monastery/ashram in southern Tamil Nadu. Here, at last, I took refuge from America, immersing myself in the bright colors and reedy sounds of Hindu culture. At daybreak, as I read Krishnamurti under a tree on the bank of the River Cauvery, I watched the local women herd their water buffaloes down the slick mud, splashing into the current and up onto green grassy islands for the morning's grazing. A tall, black-skinned, withered old man I nicknamed "The Heron," wearing what looked like a cloth diaper under his groin and another wrapped around his head, waded along the bank scaring tiny fish into a net he had draped over a bush on shore. A barefoot two-year-old boy passed by holding one end of a stick. The other end of the stick was clasped in the fist of a grizzly-bearded blind man who balanced an awkward bundle of firewood on his head as the boy guided him over the crunchy leaves through the eucalyptus grove back to town.

Slowly, very slowly, the molecules between my ears began to reorganize themselves. My brain started resonating at a new frequency. And finally, Bede Griffiths told me the most important thing I ever learned in my life. The discord in this life, said Bede, stems primarily from the fact that people tend to confuse psychic phenomena with spiritual phenomena. We must learn to distinguish the psychic from the spiritual, advised Bede, or we will spend our lives wallowing in a psychic swamp.

Psychic events, I discovered, are mind events, ego events, arts like psychology and astrology and palmistry, which relate to what shape my ego is in today – what are the stars predicting for me today? – ego stuff.

Spiritual events, on the other hand, are beyond the ego, beyond the sights and sounds and visualizations and verbalizations we use to construct our world. Psychic teachings come from parts of California and New York and India. Spiritual teachings come from sitting quietly in a chair or watching babies sleep. Psychic events are sensual; spiritual events are outside the senses. And I might as well spit it out right now: psychic events are essentially feminine and spiritual events are overwhelmingly masculine. Women who break their minds out of the psychic swamp are few and far between. There are measurable biological, psychological and social reasons for this perceptual discrepancy and much of this book is devoted to examining these reasons.

Before your brain explodes let me quickly state that two of the greatest spiritual leaders of all time, Mother Teresa and Peace Pilgrim, have recently been amongst us. These women did the work of annihilating their egos. Mother Teresa left Albania as a young girl and was never allowed back in to see her mother or sister again. Peace Pilgrim changed her name, sloughed off her past, and walked 25,000 miles for peace, possessing ONLY what she carried in her pockets! But generally, women confuse their psyche (ego) with their spirit; they look for the "goddess within" and blur the boundary between the two realms. This fact constitutes an awesome difference between the sexes with profound implications for human society. When a woman is talking about "spirituality", she is almost always referring to psychic phenomena. This book will examine why that is so.

I'm not writing this book to stroke male egos or polish any behinds. I'm writing it because I think there is a chance we can reverse the global trend toward ravaged homes and broken families if we make some attempt to figure out what is truly going on between the sexes. The biggest crisis in global culture is NOT the economy, or the warmongers, or corporate welfare; it is the dissolution of the family – so distressingly ubiquitous that we ignore it. It's not news and they don't even talk about it on *60 Minutes*. No society in all of history has tolerated half of their children growing up without their fathers. What kinds of idiots are we? We can't let this go on.

We need some new perceptions to work with; we need metaphors that make some kind of sense; we need values that are grounded in observable reality, not canned ego-fantasies or freeze-dried myths. There would be no point in addressing the spiritual realm – that would just be another escape from reality – if it were not for the increasingly obvious scientific evidence that our world emanates from a zone of virtual particles which have been fleetingly spotted by physicists but which remain virtually hidden from our senses. There is a hidden world of energy that secretes our world – what physicist David Bohm calls the Implicate Order – and this hidden world represents a neutral ground from which we can view the psychic trappings and linguistic deficiencies of our culture. This Implicate Order of virtual reality is a sort of spiritual ground. We know it's there, but we don't know much more than that.

The physics is fascinating and it points to a hidden world, but why bring any of this up? Because it is my belief that what we are facing in the battle of the sexes is a spiritual problem, not a political problem. We can't solve this thing by marching around waving placards or shouting slogans or passing new laws. We need to shovel our way out of this mess by employing a commonly accepted value system – one that people choose to live by, not one that must be enforced. And spiritual zones are the very places where values originate.

Some people are gun-shy talking about God, that overused and abused word. I was an atheist for 20 years and now I've come to believe in a Life Force that stimulates all things to grow and reproduce. A value system is nothing less than the agenda of this Life Force, hidden from our senses, yet observable in a million manifestations all around us every moment of our lives.

In Asia today, as in ancient Greece, the hidden world is represented by a panoply of gods which are drawn to represent archetypal human values: compassion, humility, severance of attachment. Somehow, the very strangeness of these gods makes their attributes more accessible to the Westerner. That's why I was in Asia.

When my visa for India expired I went to study Buddhism in Sri Lanka and then at Wat Suan Mokh in southern Thailand. Practicing Buddhism in Thailand was like weaving underwater, so fierce was the clash between the noisy, commercial, feminine Thai culture and the ascetic stillness of Theraveda Buddhism.

And little by little, as I tripped through these ancient civilizations and exotic mindscapes that have remained culturally intact since thousands of years before Christ, a new filmstrip of physical reality emerged in my mind.

I have been forced to conclude that virtually everything in this world is the outright opposite of what we were taught it is. Thousands of years ago our minds slipped off the ends of the earth and we started missing the point in a big way. And right at the top of my list of misperceived things, in fact the essence of the problem, are the supposed attributes of men and women. The reason that men and women don't get along, the reason the divorce rate in America is 60% and half the kids are growing up without dads, is that somehow, over thousands of years, men and women have swapped mental roles and each are acting out of character weaknesses which have been wrongly perceived as the inherited strengths of that sexual model. Essentially, we've got it all backwards.

For example: we were all raised with the notion that men are rational and women are intuitive. This reminds me of Aristotle's statement that objects of different sizes fall at different speeds. Sounds logical. But not for 2000 years, until Galileo hiked to the top of the Tower of Pisa, did anyone bother to drop two rocks and check it out. The rocks hit at the same time, even though they were different sizes. Acceleration, gravity, is a constant. So let's drop two rocks out of the windows of our inner reverie and see what we can find regarding men and women and intuition.

Men have been responsible for almost every single creative leap, almost every single passionate insight or wild deduction ever achieved by the human species. Don't take my word for it. Look at the history of art and science and religion. The knee-jerk feminist response to this is to say that men have repressed women for millennia. Excuse me! I'm a creative person and I know you do not repress the creative impulse. It overtakes you. If you want to be an astronomer, you look at stars; if you want to be an artist, you fool around with paint and clay; and if you want to be a spiritual leader, you renounce *mater*ial attachments and fly outside your ego. It takes nothing to do any of these things other than the impulse to do them. You don't need approval or encouragement to be an artist or a writer – you need a piece of paper and a pencil.

Women have not been without their own merit. Women have been responsible for order and method and almost every attempt to control and subdue nature. The very notion of manufacturing is a female invention, from clay pots to looms to planting kernels of corn – *i.e.*, manufacturing food.

What preposterous idea am I suggesting? Women are not now and never have been intuitive or creative? That's like saying the Pope is a woman. That's like saying corporate jocks are feminist enforcers. Where do I get such mad ideas?

From history, that's where.

Ten thousand years ago, when a man woke up in the morning, he grabbed his spear and walked out into the forests and prairies. There he listened to the birdcalls, smelled the air, touched animal tracks. He sat in itchy bushes waiting for game, scanning the treetops hoping to spot bees returning to their hives full of honey…And he prayed.

He prayed to the Deer God to sacrifice one of its own to feed the human tribe. He prayed to the Monarch of Pheasants and the Father of Fish. And most of all he prayed to the Great Mystery, the Great Spirit, that secreted all these forms because even then men knew that God is not nature, God MAKES nature.

This man was humble and vulnerable and dependent on the awesome power of nature, and he prayed to be in harmony with these incomprehensible forces. He was not in the business of sitting at a desk counting beans, naming feelings, labeling or sorting things. He couldn't even talk out loud to the other guys he was with for fear of scaring off wary prey. He was operating from a deep intuitive well, trying to seduce nature, trying to coax a livelihood from it. This wasn't about killing. It was about praying. Praying to the Deer God – preying on deer. Does this sound at all rational to you?

Meanwhile, back at the tent, his wife was five months pregnant. She was manufacturing garments out of animal and/ or vegetable fibers to be ready when the baby arrived in four months. She had solidified her position in the hierarchy, the pecking order, the bureaucracy, the *de facto government* of the tribe, and was organizing other wives and older children into work gangs outfitted with seed kernels and sharpened digging sticks and sending them out into the bottomland to plant corn so there would be flatbread to eat in six months. She was dominating and controlling everything she possibly could within her restricted domain. That was her nature, her approach to life. And that is precisely what women, corporations and government try to do today.

The highly touted Great Earth Mother of recent popular rediscovery and adulation was a control freak – the prototype of modern government and modern corporations – an anal retentive, female, control mindscape.

It is known that on the 21st of June and the 21st of December virgin boys were castrated and bled to death for her edification and honor. They were fed to the Mother, sacrificed to her, their blood poured onto the dirt of the fields to enrich the anticipated harvest. This was the cult of the Great Earth Mother that pushed out the Deer God and accompanied the emergence of agriculture. She was brutal. She was an odious witch.

And that's why men took religion back. That's how the so-called Patriarchy began. Men were sick and tired of having their balls cut off. Literally! Abraham had to be willing to sacrifice his son Isaac before God could be convinced of his loyalty. That was the mindscape of that era – the feminist, Astartian mindscape. Then Jesus came along and said, "I am the sacrifice. You don't have to sacrifice flesh – the boy or the ram who represents the boy – anymore." And through his crucifixion he both fulfilled and put an end to the cult of Astarte, the Great Mother Earth.

Jesus had a nomadic disposition. He was no great fan of agriculture. When asked about work he replied, "Who feeds the birds of the sky and clothes the flowers of the fields?" Jesus was not a farmer. He was a fisherman. A resurgence of the male energy that motivated pre-agricultural man. Just as early men prayed to the Deer God and ate deer meat, so the cult of Jesus bid devotees to pray to Him and eat His body and drink His blood! That's the Male Religion, an uninterrupted mental module from the cave paintings of Lascaux, France in 15,000 BC right through to last Sunday's mass anywhere on earth. That's why Christianity has been so successful. So-called "primitive" people can relate to it. It talks to them. The God you pray to feeds you his own body.

We cannot see gravity but we can see the effects of gravity. We cannot see the Life Force but we can see the effects of the Life Force. That's the Invisible God that men and male spirituality seek – what Native Americans call the Great Mystery and Judeo-Christians call God the Father – a benevolent force that is not seen except through its deeds. Jesus was the son, the offspring of Zeus, the Deer God, the Mystery made flesh – most recent in a long line of hidden gods who sent an emissary to dwell in the flesh.

So, agriculture, planting, the sedentary existence, subduing and controlling the earth, were inventions of the Great Earth Mother, whoever she was. And soon enough men were being enticed out of the forests and set to work in the fields. Pussy power? You bet. The guys who went off to be men, to do God's work, didn't get laid, and in their stead emerged the manholes, the men who think like women, the men who espouse female values, the men who built castles and lived in mansions surrounded by wealth.

You think I'm making this up? Listen to the story of Enkidu from the Sumerian epic of *Gilgamesh* – it tells it all. And remember, Sumeria was the center of the Fertile Crescent, the first farm.

Enkidu was a man who grazed with the gazelles and slurped at the watering hole. He hung out with the animals. He was the Wildman; he was nature. He was us. Gilgamesh, the king, heard about Enkidu and sent a temple prostitute from the Goddess Astarte to seduce him. She waited near a water hole until the herd of gazelles that Enkidu traveled with came to drink. Then she bared her breasts and enticed him away from the animals and made love to him for six days and seven nights. After that Enkidu tried to rejoin his animal friends but they turned and ran away. Enkidu was now joined to the female urges and aspirations and it scared them. "No matter," said the prostitute. "I'll take you with me to the temple city of Ishtar (Astarte) and there you will have a good friend, Gilgamesh." (The first king. The original manhole.)

Whereas the first men were nomads who lived close to nature, with agriculture came the stockpiling of wealth (cities) and the need to defend the fertile bottomlands (organized warfare) and the rulers who would administer the accumulated wealth of the Earth Mother – Kings.

Yes, kings. Kings are men who wear dresses, a type of garment which is certainly not suited for tracking lions or chasing deer. Kings are men who enjoy sedentary lives amassing jewels and shiny minerals in the manner of women. Kings tax farmers for their supposed protection, bicker over territory, and raise armies of boys who fight for glory as the king and his women watch from a hillside. Kings were the first manholes. Kings institutionalized female values.

And all around the king, comprising his court, sprang up counselors and strategists and accountants to advise him on operating his empire. This academic society of individuals who gained food and housing for producing nothing more than abstract intrigues crystallized into a gang of lords whose power and lifestyle were envied and aspired to by every lad in the kingdom. And so it came to pass people started believing that what constituted manhood was the accumulation of wealth and power.

Meanwhile, in places like Africa and the American Northwest, the citizenry didn't buy into this Astartian plot. What did they do? They did what Jesus advised. They did what the Deer God advised. They lived amidst nature. They did not set upon nature with the purpose of subduing it. To this day the average Australian aborigine – the one who hasn't yet been seduced out of the outback by the temple prostitutes of *mater*ialism – still works only twelve hours a week. That's all that's required for him to provide for his family. The rest of his time is spent making art and dance and music, the very things that keep him harmonizing with his natural world.

To the Native American of the Pacific Northwest the man accorded the greatest prestige was the one who, at the annual Potlatch ceremony, gave the most away! He gave away the most salmon, the most honey, the most furs, and he gave away the most prayers; for everyone understood a real man could always get more of what people needed and therefore he had no need to hoard any of it! This is masculine thinking. Sharing is the *essential* part of masculine nature. This is what MAN is all about: the faith that his rapport with nature and with his God will continue to provide what is best for him. This is *not* rugged individualism. This is rugged spiritualism. Here is a belief, a choice, made in favor of the notion that the universe is essentially a good place. This is the Male Choice.

Do you ever listen to women talk? Do you get the idea that the foundation of their belief system is that the world is essentially a good place? Or do you get the feeling from them that life is a constant battle of things to be manipulated and arranged? The king was the first manhole. The corporate male is the latest incarnation of men who have bought into women's values. Have you ever heard of anyone pray for a rise in the Dow Jones? Have you ever heard of anyone pray for a BMW? Not likely. People instinctively know what the Deer God is listening for. You can pretty much cut the cake separating male from female aspirations according to whether the item in question is something people would pray for or not. The king – the feudal corporation – is a product of feminine/agrarian/ manufacturing type of thinking. The king embodies a belief in scarcity and the hoarding of wealth. People who devote their lives to making money should be ashamed of themselves.

I understand more than most that we cannot march 8,000 years back in time. I also understand that it is imperative for the very survival of the world that we attempt to recreate some balance between the masculine and feminine poles. It's my opinion that the tragedy of modern times – the past 8,000 years – is that the masculine pole has been deserted. It's time to relocate the center of gravity of the human personality far, far back onto the male end of the spectrum. Buddha, Jesus, some Sufi mystics – all of them tried to bring the male spirit back to life, but their messages were reinterpreted in the context of agrarian, mercantile nations. The message was perverted. Now fundamentalists talk about the Christian Work Ethic. THERE IS NO CHRISTIAN WORK ETHIC.

We don't have the faintest idea what it means to be men anymore. Our male models are reconstituted women. They are the men women like, not the men God likes. Our planet is overpopulated, the thrust of our lives is the accumulation of wealth; intuition, the basic brain mode of the male psyche, has been attributed to women. We talk about farming the oceans as if that were a good thing. The mystics and seekers who embody essential male virtues of trust in life have been castigated as effeminate wimps and the aggressive, manipulating, controlling, female-influenced captains of industry we regard as male prototypes. What a fuck up! Men have been yanked out of nature and put on shift work – historically, characteristically women's work.

Eight thousand years ago women didn't want men's jobs; they were too dangerous, they were too subtle, and women were not physically or temperamentally suited to chasing wildebeests or fighting lions. Then, in Sumeria, the Fertile Crescent, men were brought in to do the women's work of farming the fields. And recently, starting 140 years ago, men were taken completely out of nature and sent in to the office and the factory where they manufacture and sell more items to make women's lives easier. Thus, men have been maneuvered into doing work that historically, for 2.2 million years, had been women's work: farming and making pots.

Children were removed from the daily companionship of their dads where they exchanged energy sowing, reaping, fishing, repairing wagon wheels, investigating bird's nests and hollow logs; and they were shunted off to school where they were raised, by and large, by women. Gone is praying to the Deer God; enter the computer terminal. Terminal means "end" and of all the dead ends humankind has created for itself, staring at computer screens all day long has got to be one of the grandest. Have you ever seen a subtle computer terminal? Has anybody ever got anything out of praying to a Macintosh?

The computer is the single greatest feminizing force in society today. Machines that are "user friendly" are electro-plastic seductresses. We already have *too much* information. We need to use what we've got. We don't need to worry about how much calcium or zinc we're getting in our diets; we need to annihilate our egos. We don't need more education. That's more feminist propaganda. Right now, during a so-called economic boom, there are four men for every three jobs in this country. More education can't solve that. The most we will get out of more education is a reshuffling of colors and sexes and more white guys out of work. Traditionally this has been working out because white guys haven't complained about the relentless erosion of their rights and opportunities. Those days are over. You can have only so many chemical engineers working at McDonald's, only so many philosophers painting houses, before you start bumping up against real problems. We don't need more education. We need more spirituality – more of a sense of how to live happily with less.

And what do we have now? Manholes are tripping all over each other vying to build a society along parameters that are pleasing to women – and the hell with the Deer God. That's called selling your soul for a piece of ass and that has never worked for long. Believe me, I've tried it. Men don't need to do what women want; men need to do what the Deer God wants. By the time every woman on earth has an automatic dishwasher to pop her dirty dishes into as she rushes off to the office, the entire earth will be a ravaged burning volcanic pimple, denuded of trees, stripped of minerals, toxic to life. Curbing women's lust for *mater*ial objects is the ONLY important agenda of civilization.

The last decades have seen a big push of women entering the work force. Why not? They don't have to beat clothes on rocks like women in most of the rest of the world; they don't have to keep wood fires burning all day long to cook beans. And what's more, it hasn't taken women very long to figure out that they can do men's work because, after all, now men's work is mostly all women's work. No more chasing antelope with pointed sticks, now it's: counting, sorting, buying, selling, talking on the phone. Stamping auto parts and delivering mail in cute little jeeps have nothing to do with praying to the Deer God. Let's get real. These are not now and never have been men's jobs. We have no aptitude for them. Working as a lawyer, sifting through case histories and talking a lot to the judge is not a man's job; it's a woman's job. Working as a doctor, a healer, is not a man's job. Women are much more sensitive and suited to the requirements of that kind of work. Our priests wear gowns, our judges wear robes, and our ex-wives wear jeans. Manholes steer our commerce and adjudicate our laws and all the while real men are browbeaten for how unfair they've been to women.

Women live 10% longer than men in most countries on earth; in America that amounts to almost eight years. Slaves do not live longer than their oppressors. By that criterion alone, it is clear that men have been enslaved by women. Whenever there is an oil rig fire to be put out, or a skyscraper to be erected, or explosive charges to be removed, or paint fumes to be inhaled, 999 times out of 1,000 you will find a man doing the work. Clean work is done by women: teaching, appraisals, bureaucratic stuff, media positions, computerized access to information, mastery of facts and opinions – ALL these jobs are controlled by women and manholes. When there is a war to fight, men are sent to fight it. Women help some, but men are the ones in the tanks and the trenches.

Boys, we have choices. We can say "NO" to the relentless systematization of life. We can crack the vicious cycle of feminist propaganda which is telling us that everything will work out fine if we just get more organized. That's prison they're talking about. We're already TOO organized…A female friend once chided me that the whole point of the Industrial Revolution was for men to make more things for women to buy. That's right from the horse's mouth.

We vote with our bodies. It doesn't matter what we think, what opinions we hold. That's urban crapola. It matters what we do. If we vote to sit in front of computer terminals all day, we are voting with our bodies as to what shape human life will take. We are voting against nature and against the Deer God, and it doesn't matter what we think about seals or dolphins.

Don't do it.

Spend some time seeking the Deer God.

Obviously I'm not talking about some specific deity. It is the seeking itself that is the deep experience; casting your nets over the horizon beyond the shores of logic, steering your consciousness into intuitive space. DON'T get hung up on a particular god; that's the psychic trap. Seek the transcendence. Annihilate logic. Emptiness is form and form is emptiness, as the Buddhists teach.

And while we're at it, let's puncture another toxic myth right now: that women are not logical. Inevitably the female system relies on logic. Logic is what I call the "bicycle sprocket with missing teeth". By that I mean that logic pulls straight and true for a quarter turn on the wheel of life, then hits a broken spot and skips four teeth; it pulls again for an eighth turn then snaps over a few teeth, then pulls fine for a turn and a half, slips a half turn and catches again. This is the same phenomenon Kurt Vonnegut calls the "cuckoo clock in hell". The cuckoo clock in hell keeps perfect time for twenty minutes then skips four minutes, keeps perfect time for 47 minutes then skips eleven, keeps time for six minutes then skips sixteen. The point is that logic launches its canoe midstream in the river of life making perfect sense stroke for stroke, point upon point, along a stretch of scenic shoreline until it reaches a cataract where the paddlers pull out the canoe and portage around the obstacle – thereby creating a rationalization. Within a limited context, logic may ring true but removed from that context, it is nothing more than the convoluted babbling that leads to fanaticism. More logic, like more information, is not going to solve our problems.

Pursuit of happiness is primarily a female goal. Pursuit of the mysteries of life is primarily a male goal. Men know you cannot pursue happiness. When you pursue happiness directly, it eludes you. It is impossible to grasp. The historian Alexis de Tocqueville pointed out this defect in the U.S. Constitution more than a century ago. You can't chase happiness, he said. It doesn't work. You can offer yourself in service to the heavenly King, the Grail King; you can submit to the mysteries of the universe, the Life Force; you can surrender your will to your God and your reward, if you are lucky, might be happiness. But happiness is not something you can get. It is a gift that must be received. Happiness is something you are given. David Steindl-Rast teaches that gratefulness does not come from happiness as most people believe. You don't get happy first and then become grateful. First be grateful for the good and the bad and the fact that you are here to experience all of it. First be grateful and then happiness will be given to you.

Very few people in this feminized society of ours seem to understand this. That's why we are the richest, unhappiest country on earth. It's a shame. Women and manholes go to work for themselves (or those bodily extensions they call their children – through whom they live vicariously). They serve a higher power only in so far as it furthers their goals. Loyalty is unknown in the workplace. That is an incredible development, or shall I call it a devolution.

And on top of that we are brainwashed with the false philosophy that we can buy happiness every time we turn on the tube. Advertising is not dumb. Advertising is evil. It's porno-graphic. By James Joyce's definition, any art which instills desire in the viewer is pornographic. That's advertising – pornography.

The contemporary path to power requires hoarding, not generosity. Women flooding the workplace bring with them the hoarding instinct. We are being daily overrun by female values in courts, in the media, at work. Women in business are barracudas imitating the corporate lifestyle of the very men who disgusted the world during the 1960s by their duplicity and their body counts and their media manipulations. I know. I was one of the guys who fought the Vietnam war by getting chased around by the FBI for a couple of years and when I resurfaced above ground again, I found that all the jobs refused by the "Hell no, we won't go" guys, and forfeited by the guys who actually did go, had been filled by women and manholes. Dow Chemical, which was frying the forests with Agent Orange and Vietnamese farm kids with napalm, is today being advertised as a place where young female chemists can go to get a job that "let's you do great things". These are mental atrocities. Haven't we seen enough chemical companies advertised by campaigns to save eagles? Haven't we seen enough oil companies advertised by footage of baby seals? Do you imagine for one moment that these are MALE ideas?

Recently I have been made aware of the Federal Government employing teams of female lawyers to promote their rapacious land use policies on Federal Lands (that means land that is supposed to belong to you and me). Obviously having cadres of pert, handsome women defending geothermal drilling or clear cutting of forests has had some subliminal charismatic impact on the success of these ventures. Hasn't anyone figured out yet that female lawyers are lawyers, not women?

Women who use paper diapers are raping the environment and I don't care how they feel about whales or seals or caged minks. We vote with our bodies. What we think does not matter. It is what we do or do not do that matters. I guess that's why I have so little patience with female gossip. Women think that because they are talking about something, they are doing something about it. They're not. It's just wind. Men speak an average of 2,000 words a day and women speak 7,000. What are they talking about?

In case you can't tell, I choose not to be shamed; and I don't like apologizing for being a man – for thinking like a man, feeling like a man and dreaming like a man; for stinking like a man and laughing like a man and singing like a man. My life cannot be "understood" by the courts, by the newspaper publishers, by the bastions of institutionalized feminist values. The authorities are the King's men – an army of feminist enforcers – pussy-whipped politicians cruising for votes, funding women's clinics and shelters and support groups while they squeeze the last juice out of the very men who fought and risked and died to make this the most egalitarian society the earth has ever known. And have we been repaid with even a modicum of understanding? No. We are ridiculed on TV, taken for granted at home, and openly despised in the print media. I have not read a single article on divorce that was not cast from the slant of the poor, suffering women. Enough media distortion. Our families are dying!

We have to stop them. If it means shutting down the cities and blockading the highways to get their attention, we'll have to do that. If that doesn't work, we'll have to set the girls back to canning their homegrown tomatoes and scavenging their own cooking wood, using cloth diapers and wiping their behinds with old newspapers. That'll get their ear. When real men stop going to work, the information processors won't have any information to process. That's the one curious fact about a network – somebody actually has to do something or else it's just an electronic fantasy. Show the women how to use shovels and drive garbage trucks. They want power? Let them take responsibility for the jobs that HAVE to be done, not just this information processing cowshit. Yes. This is just what it sounds like: the long-awaited, long-predicted Male Backlash. And they ain't seen nothing yet.

You want to know what has happened to us men? Look at Native Americans. The decay and dissolution we see in them is the exact same thing that has happened to all of us. What we are seeing on the reservation is a speeded up version of what Western society has done to all men – killed off the visionaries and turned the rest into a bunch of alcoholic businessmen. What they have gone through in the last 200 years is what we have gone through over the last 2,000. Their sustaining myths have been disemboweled, their attention drawn to pickups and snowmobiles and VCRs. Those whose spiritual connectedness is most sensitive and subtle are the very ones who are most susceptible to the ravages of alcohol and business and materialism.

Let us recognize that Mater, the Latin word for mother, is the root of materialism. I don't think it is possible to read too much into this. Mother is everything for our senses that is comfortable and good and hearty and material. We, in the West, are being smothered in mother.

Women are people-oriented and men are object-oriented. That's why we see so many women buying crap in the malls and so many boys playing team sports. Have you ever been in a bachelor apartment? There's a stereo, one sheet, and a plastic spoon/fork from Kentucky Fried Chicken. Wait 'til the poor sucker gets married. Let's clear the air on this. WOMEN are object-oriented. MEN are people-oriented.

Well, what about the patriarchy?

The Torah, the Five Books of Moses, better known as the Old Testament, is the historical record of a tribe of nomadic goat herders who keep trying to cease their wandering and settle down where they can establish farms and cities which are then destroyed because of their intractable possessiveness, whereby they are forced to rediscover God and move on again. Sound familiar? It's virtually the theme of Western Civilization. It is the quintessential clash between the male and the female. So now the feminist *mater*ialists have created a new Israeli state which has turned away from spiritual values so rapidly that it is either going to drag all of world Jewry down with it or they are going to cut it loose. What does history tell us? Israel has to change prodigiously, has to rediscover its God, or the people will cut it loose.

The same with America.

Feminists are fond of ranting about the Jewish Patriarchy. God spoke to the Jewish men of the Promised Land because the women were already listening. Superficially Judaism might appear male-dominated, but only someone who has never been inside a Jewish household could accuse Judaism of being a patriarchy. My ex is Jewish. My kids are Jewish. Morning *minyan* is the only place men can go to get away from the women and that's only because the women are still in bed. Judaism is a Matriarchy disguised as a Patriarchy. Jewish women obey no one – not their husbands, not their God. They are in many ways the mold for the type of women American society is producing. I can't help it if these statements strike you as racist, sexist or fanatic. I call 'em as I see 'em. It's a free country. I have a right to my opinions. There is enough feminist propaganda. These things must be said. Judaism is a system for enforcing female values and the hell with goat herds. Christianity has borrowed the righteous, elitist cultural views of the Old Testament – and that's not what Jesus had in mind.

We can bash the Pope and bash the Fundamentalists and bash the Eucharist but we can't bash the Jewish Mother? Sorry. The truth knows no sacred cows.

But what about those other guys? What about the Catholics? In the Catholic Church, the most available forgiving figure is Mary, not Jesus. Catholics pray more to Mary than to Jesus. It took six hundred years for Mary to creep back into the Catholic observance, and can you guess who Mary is? Mary is Astarte, minus temple prostitution. Mary is a JEWISH MOTHER. Catholics refer to their church as the Mother Church. Does the Pope wear a dress and garnish himself with jewels?

Protestants feel left out? Give it a few hundred years. It's beginning to look to me as if the entire history of religion of the past 3,000 years has been some futile attempt to move *mater*ialism, motherialism, out of the center and off to the periphery. We haven't succeeded yet, but neither have they. Despite the intricate machinations of Astarte, something within us still wants to pray to the Deer God.

If we don't recognize the enemy and identify the problems, we will continue being subverted by our wives, colonized by the Mother, and castrated by Astarte. Women have the majority and they have the vote. If they can't get it together on that kind of head start, they really do have emotional problems.

Any man between the ages of 25 and 45 has been discriminated against often enough in the job market to know that women in this age group, far from being oppressed, are in fact receiving preferential treatment from the WWII codgers who are still holding onto their executive suites by trading away the jobs of younger men to satisfy affirmative action quotas. These are the manholes. These are the enemy.

We now live in a country where 60% of marriages end in divorce and half the kids are being brought up without dads. This is not men's fault. This is women's fault. 85% of divorce actions are filed by women. This does not mean that 85% of men are assholes. It means that 85% of women are profoundly unhappy with life.

Five percent of the people and 75% of the lawyers live and work in the United States. What does that mean? It means that we in America, in lieu of a functioning value system, are attempting to litigate values. We are trying to pass laws to enforce morals. Haven't we learned anything at all from the holy books? Haven't we learned anything from the collapse of communism? Values do not come from mumbled prayers or out of the barrel of a gun. Values are something we choose. Values are something we agree to live by, and when we don't uphold them, we can surely anticipate a punishment, from God or from Life. The penalty is paid in Karma. We don't need religious enforcers or legal enforcers. We need people who live the teachings. We all know what the teachings are but we rarely see anybody living them. That's the problem.

When a woman divorces her husband, he doesn't work for her anymore. A lot of women don't seem to be able to get this straight. They want the kids and the house and the money; they want bozo out of the house, but they want him to keep paying the bills. What kind of feminist outrage is this? One hundred years ago, in a divorce, the man got the house and the kids, and the woman walked. That was the only option.

Is it not true that religious laws have a lot to say about wives being obedient to their husbands? Why would you think every single religion on the earth, in every existent culture, including the 120,000-year-old aboriginal culture, has strictures regarding this? Is it possible that the cultures that never took steps to curb the raw ambition of their women are not around any longer? Don't you imagine that some extinct culture in the last 120,000 years experimented with the total emancipation of women?

We get married in a church and divorced in a court of law. I think if we get married under the laws of the church, we should live by them and get divorced under them. If marriage is primarily a legal and financial arrangement, let's not obscure that with non-enforceable platitudes spoken at an altar; let's make it clear from the start. Let's get married in court...Now doesn't that sound wrong to the ear?

We cannot possibly obey two different value systems. God's law says: don't lie, don't cheat, don't steal, don't commit adultery. Man's Law, as it is practiced before the courts today, says: don't get caught lying, don't get caught cheating, don't get caught stealing, don't get caught committing adultery. You can say whatever you want to in a court of law and, as long as no one can disprove it, you've slipped one past Scylla and Charybdis. The willful separation from Karma, from God's Law, doesn't even enter the picture. This is not a value system. Don't expect courts to enforce values. They can't do it.

What the courts are permitting to happen to the children in this country is an abomination. The only other country I know of where the children are circumstantially removed from their fathers is South Africa (1993) where the black miners are compelled to work hundreds of miles away from where their families are allowed to live. This insures that no tradition will be handed down from father to son, thus culture and history can be manufactured by whites assuring a maximum amount of female values and dependencies. The situation is no different for children in the U.S. We, in the country ruled by laws, not men, have created a system of emotional abuse, wage slavery, and disenfranchisement from the most basic human need – seeing our own kids – equaled only in the bastion of apartheid, a system designed to destroy continuity between generations and allow domination by a weaker, trickier race.

So that's what we are up against. Our kids are being raised by women and the laws in this country have become polluted with feminist propaganda. Equal employment opportunity has become a necessary evil in light of the preponderance of feminine jobs which are now being made available in the "information age". Gone is buffalo hunting; enter computerized bean counting. Equality in employment is an acceptable situation, BUT ONLY in so far as men are allowed equality in reproduction. Yes, you heard that right. We want COMPLETE EQUALITY IN REPRODUCTION, no ifs, ands or buts about it. That means that the kids are not just hers. The children are 100% mine and

100% hers. That means that I, as the father, have a completely equal say in everything to do with the children, including their births and how they are educated and what church they go to. These are sacred, constitutional rights which the father possesses until being CONVICTED of some heinous crime against his own children, by a jury of his peers, in a court of law. That's what the Constitution says: we're innocent until proven guilty. And we are tired of hearing this noise about how the courts are just trying to protect the children. *Most* child abuse is *committed by mothers* against 2-3-year-old boys! In order to protect a few hundred kids from a few hundred maniacs, we are destroying the paternal bond between tens of millions of kids and their fathers. This is an outrage.

Pro Choice?

What is it?

Pro Choice is supposed to mean that I, as the father, as the sperm, as one-half of the chromosomes, have exactly one-half the right and responsibility to decide what is going to happen to my unborn baby.

However, in our time Pro Choice has been resurrected right out of *Animal Farm* double-think to mean removing the biological father from any choice whatsoever in determining the life of his unborn child. Pro Choice has gone way beyond being an issue about unborn fetuses. Pro Choice has become the Female Manifesto – a one-sided, sexist attempt to remove men from decisions regarding the birth of their own children at a time when women are demanding equal rights in the job market. Let them have the jobs; I want the kids.

"Our bodies, our business," they proclaim. But just make sure the check gets here on time.

I'm not going to argue the merits or demerits of abortion. And just to clarify some other issues, I want to say (1) I believe the earth has too many people. (2) Abortion is not an acceptable method of birth control. (3) If you took all the people on earth and moved them to the United States, we would still have HALF the population density that England has today!

What I am getting at is that the Pro Choice movement has nearly succeeded in entirely removing God and Man from having any say-so regarding reproduction. They are setting themselves up as goddesses again, granting themselves the power over life and death. They want to control the kids, they want to control the money, and they want to control the men. I'm sorry, but it's time to draw a line in the sand. This can't go on. I feel like the boy watching the pageant of the Emperor's New Clothes in the *New York Times* and even the supposedly conservative *Chicago Tribune*. I *can't* be the only one who sees this.

Women who take matters of who lives and who dies into their own hands are co-opting God. This is not their decision alone to make. They can decide not to have sex; *that* is their boundary. And, of course, in the few actual cases of rape where this becomes an issue, where no man comes forward to assume the responsibility of raising the child, then the choice to abort belongs to the woman alone.

The fact is, when men and women are equal, women are more equal than men because they control reproduction. Ultimately, the main thing that gives a man meaning and purpose in his sorry life, the thing that gets him up in the morning and off to work at some stink-ass job, is the time he spends being enriched by his kids. Kids do that for men. They make us happy to be alive. Where does this society get off ripping that away from us and still expecting us to perform?

No society can long survive that tears this paternal bond apart. Feminists have gone too far and tens of millions of people are suffering for it. Nothing less than the continued existence of American society is at stake. Feminists worship at the altars of their own egos. The only god they serve is their own appetite. Implicit in the Pro Choice idea that a woman owns her own body is the assumption that people needn't live within a value system that is any larger than their own egos. That is a recipe for disaster.

I have met some number of ten thousand recovering alcoholics who told me, "I discovered God and stopped drinking." I have never met a single person who told me, "I discovered secular humanism and stopped drinking." Female logic is not going to help us with spiritual problems. For that we have to pray. I don't know anyone who knows why praying works. What I do know is that it is scientifically observable and statistically demonstrable that praying *does work* to relieve human suffering. People who pray live healthier, more stable lives than people who don't. Don't take my word for it. Just look around you. Praying makes us reach out and become part of something that is greater than ourselves.

Praying is what men do, silently on our knees, or splattered with mud dancing around a fire in the woods at night. We pray. And we don't have to apologize for being men or for how we pray any longer. Even Eric Clapton prays, on his knees, every night. What a MAN.

Men know a lot of things women can never know. I have no doubt it is the same for women. Marriage was intended to achieve a golden mean between the practicality of women and the soaring inspiration of men. Men have always been the dreamers, the poets, the artists, the imaginers. Men don't talk as much as women, not because they are insipid, but because they perceive reality differently. Men do not see the same things. We look for essence more than form. We look for hidden truths while women look for hidden motives. We tend to see the world as a satisfying whole whereas women and manholes see it as a terrifying disarray of broken parts. For us daily life is a semi-transparent watercolor unfolding in four dimensions – a fluid, amoebic hologram pulsing in and out of itself as it touches hidden fingers of energy. For women daily life is a problem to be solved. Men cast their nets into the sea of life, over and over again, mostly coming up empty. But eventually they bring in buckets full of many-colored fish, and women gather on the shore to sort them and haggle over the price.

That's how the world works, from the Gulf of Mexico to the Gulf of Siam – not how you see it on TV where the men are stumbling, bumbling, inarticulate, incompetent fools who can't even answer the phone without dropping it on their foot. The media bosses in this country are manholes. They've got theirs. They're out for Nielsen votes. The presidents of CBS, NBC, ABC, MGM and other media Cossacks who wield power vastly out of proportion to their accountability to the rest of us should be held up for re-election by popular vote, not by stockholder vote, every four years. Never before in history have so few wielded so much power, over so many, so irresponsibly. If this is the best we can do in the country of laws, not men, I want to go back to the country of men. At least then I'll know someone is operating out of a value system.

And what mental landscape have the media moguls wrought? American women are the freest, unhappiest, least secure women on earth. Why is that? I think it has something to do with the gods they serve. In truth, their children are as much a part of their bodies as their arms and legs and when I listen to their appeals about how much they have sacrificed for their kids' sake, I get the same sick feeling in my gut that I get when someone explains to me how rough it is being a Hollywood celebrity. Women manipulate the bananas out of their kids, especially their sons, creating vicarious existences to supercharge their own dull egos – and they have the nerve to call that nurturing. What they call nurturing I call psychological child abuse and yet a tidal wave of psychological literature will refer to women as the nurturing half of the species. If men are not nurturing, where do all of the apples and corn come from? How do we get bread and chicken and honey? Who started this conspiracy of cowshit that labeled us as aggressive and not nurturing? We *are* the Great Father Earth. Men *make* the stuff of life; women and manholes administer it and haggle over it. And how do they get the inside track on co-opting us of our labor?

School.

School is the place you go to learn all the things that are exactly the opposite of what you need to know to succeed in life. Life requires cooperation and giving of your time to other people and to yourself. School teaches you to compete for grades. It teaches you to repress your feelings for the sake of studying – sitting in the same chair straining over the same book for hours and hours. School tells you to sit quietly and not talk to other people and pay attention. Before your second year of that kind of mental abuse, your values have been subverted to the extent that you believe getting an "A" on your arithmetic exam is more important than writing a letter to your estranged dad, because school gives you a grade and Dad doesn't, and your whole measure of your self-worth has become dependent on the high water mark of your external achievements. John Gatto, 1991 New York School Teacher of the Year, said – shortly after he quit teaching – that he was tired of teaching kids how to fit into a society that he didn't care to live in anymore.

No one, but no one, in the modern American school, is guiding the kids in the means to connect their inner self to a transcendent reality. Going to school used to *mean* going to church. That's where you went to learn to read so you could study the holy book which told you everything you needed to know about how to live a successful life in your given culture. That was school. Now you learn computers. Now you go to a place where you find out William Shakespeare was a great man, but you don't even hear the names of Jesus or Buddha or Moses or Mohammed or Krishna or Ahura Mazda or Black Elk. What kind of education could anyone possibly get in a place that ignores the major players in the growth and development of human civilization, but where students are trained to hang on the sensuous and undeniably compelling words of a possibly pseudonymous 16th Century actor? What is this place? They've got good computers. I suppose that will make the kids into competent travel agents and legal secretaries. But certainly there is more to life than being trained as wage slaves – serfs in a corporate fiefdom.

When the modern system of compulsory education was introduced in Massachusetts less than 150 years ago, there were civilian riots and the National Guard had to be called in to implement the plan. Why? Because nobody wanted the government brainwashing their children. Do you think that was a paranoid concern? Do you think it is any coincidence that the rise of compulsory education has marched in lock step with the Industrial Revolution? No. It's the same feudal machinery at work. And doesn't it seem even just a little bit insane to you that the thrust of schools and education seems to be job training rather than how to live a fulfilled life? How can the bent of our whole educational system be job training? How did corporate thinking take over our schools?

We've let our ethics rot like a half a baloney sandwich left in a clarinet case in a long-forgotten corner of the music room. In case you think I'm a religious fanatic, let's listen to economist E. F. Schumacher recounting the ideas of G. N. M. Tyrell in his book, *Small Is Beautiful*:

> Tyrell has put forth the terms "divergent" and "convergent" to distinguish problems which cannot be solved by logical reasoning from those that can. Life is being kept going by divergent problems which have to be "lived" and are "solved" only in death. Convergent problems, on the other hand, are man's most useful invention; they do not, as such, exist in reality but are created by a process of abstraction. When they have been solved, the solution can be written down and passed on to others, who can apply it without needing to reproduce the mental effort necessary to find it (*i.e.*, $E = mC^2$). If this were the case in human relations – in family life, economics, politics, education, and so forth – well, I am at a loss how to finish the sentence. There would be no more human relations but only mechanical reactions; life would be a living death. Divergent problems, as it were, force man to strain himself to a level above himself; they demand, and thus provoke the supply of, forces from a higher level, thus bringing love, beauty, goodness and truth into our lives. It is only with the help of these higher forces that the opposites can be reconciled in the living situation.
>
> The physical sciences and mathematics are concerned exclusively with convergent problems. That is why they can progress cumulatively and each generation can begin just where their forbearers left off. The price, however, is a heavy one. Dealing exclusively with convergent problems does not lead into life but away from it…[a phenomenon I call the Fix-It Philosophy or Information Enema].
>
> The true problems of living – in politics, economics, education, marriage, etc. – are always problems of over-coming or reconciling opposites. They are divergent problems

and have no solution in the ordinary sense of the word. They demand of man not merely the employment of reasoning powers but the commitment of his whole personality...[we can assassinate the latest Islamic madman, but that will just spawn four more to take his place].

The most powerful ideas of the nineteenth century [evolution, natural selection, class struggle, Freudian subconscious, relativism, applied science] have denied or at least obscured the whole concept of "levels of being," and the idea that some things are higher than others. ["Everything is relative" is the cry of secular humanism.] This, of course has meant the destruction of ethics, which is based on the distinction of good and evil, claiming that good is higher than evil. Again, the sins of the fathers are being visited on the third and fourth generations who now find themselves growing up without moral instruction of any kind...The resulting confusion is indescribable. What is the guiding image in accordance with which young people could try to form and educate themselves? There is none, or rather there is such a muddle and mess of images that no sensible guidance issues from them...

In ethics, as in so many other fields, we have recklessly and willfully abandoned our great classical-Christian heritage...We have no ideas to think with...Who knows anything today of the Seven Deadly Sins or the Four Cardinal Virtues? Who could even name them?

The task of our generation, I have no doubt, is one of metaphysical reconstruction...[this is an economist saying this!].

The problems of education are merely reflections of the deepest problems of our age. They cannot be solved by organization, administration or the *expenditure of money*... We are suffering from a metaphysical disease, and the cure must therefore be metaphysical.[2]

From another quarter, the brilliant words of Rainer Maria Rilke:

...try to live the questions themselves...Don't search for the answers, which could not be given to you now, because you would not be able to live them. And the point is to live everything. *Live* the questions now. Perhaps then, someday far in the future, you will gradually, without even noticing it, live your way into the answers.[3]

Well. This is no Fix-It Philosophy. This is called Living in the Paradox. This is the Deer God at work.

The best things in life are free.
Nothing you can buy is worth having.
The real work of life is praying to the Deer God.

Platitudes, you say? Impossible ideals? Foolish sentiments? At least once a week I am pinioned by a critical stare and assaulted by a phrase that is such a monument of homespun horseshit I have come to believe it is *the* central rationalization of feudal/corporate society. "That may be fine for you," says the carrier of the Dow Jones Industrial Mythology. "But if everybody lived like that the whole world would collapse."

My response, practiced over thousands of identical confrontations, is simple and direct: if *half* of the people in the world thought like me and lived like me then we would consume *half* as much oil and copper and lumber and paper, *half* as much electricity and tin and rubber, pollute *half* as many lakes and rivers; and we could close down *half* our nuclear plants and toxic waste dump sites.

I don't believe that the world has the option of doing anything except starting to think like Peace Pilgrim and E. F. Schumacher and Jesus Christ, and then actually voting with their bodies and making something of these beliefs. We have too much of everything except inner peace. More computers, more information, more education are not going to help. Schools are job training arenas geared toward teaching students corporate skills. They do not teach human values but corporate values. The public school system should be shrunk in favor of private institutions which rely less on machines, computers, and teaching corporate skills.

Decades ago Schumacher said that the pursuit of wealth – *mater*ialism – does not fit into the world because it contains no limiting principles. Freedom means freedom *from* things. Freedom from automobiles and ironing boards and computers. Hands to my ears, mouth hanging open, I watch the explosion of information processing like an aquarium keeper watching the piranhas in a feeding frenzy – they won't stop until the victim is bones. There are no limiting forces. The very things that are supposed to save us time colonize our lives. Remember the days before beepers and cellular phones? Can anyone explain to me exactly what has been improved by everyone having to be on call 24 hours a day just to keep their stupid little business competitive with everyone else's? We need to institute elementary school classes which teach kids the fine art of turning the TV off, turning the computer off, turning the dishwasher off. And we have to show them the example by actually extending our own hands and turning the damn things off ourselves. Also we should swiftly and graciously accommodate and give moral support to those who do just that, instead of accusing them of advocating the end of civilization. The people who are learning to live happily with less are the cutting edge of the future. We need economic systems based, not upon growth, but upon sustainability.

I like to tell people, especially people in other nations, that America is not a country, it's an idea. It's a baby, only 200 years old. Cultures like India and China have been around for thousands of years and one of the things we stand to learn from observing them is that the "slow" people are the ones who survive the centuries of overcrowding. It is the monk, the hermit, the wandering *sanyassin* who provide a cool refreshment in the parched lives of overly busy people. Willfulness and aggression are biologically edited out of the populations.

An Indian tradition that has endured for millennia is that of the *sanyassin*. A man goes to school, gets trained for a job, gets married and raises his family. When the last child leaves the house, the man gives all his possessions to his wife, including the house, takes up an orange robe and a wooden begging bowl, and walks through the world "seeking" – praying to his concept of the Deer God.

He may continue this work for decades and, even in a country renowned for poverty, he will not perish from malnutrition. Socially his evacuation opens up a job at the bottom of the employment ladder for another young man who is launching his family – a situation which is clearly the opposite of what we have in this country where the WWII codgers are still clinging to employment and sucking benefits out of a younger generation which can't even find steady work. It's an outrage. And it is certainly a contributing factor to the stress of double income families and the divorce mess.

The WWII generation remains the most rapacious generation the world has ever seen. Those guys are getting automatic Cost of Living Adjustments to their unearned income while young families are struggling to make it on two paychecks and real wages have not gone up in twenty years. I'm sorry everybody, but this is calling a spade a spade. It's got to stop, and it's got to stop now. Per capita this group has used more iron and copper and wood and oil than any other group of people in history ever has or ever will. Their greed knew no limits, and we are following in their footsteps. This is not a political problem. This is a spiritual problem. It requires a spiritual solution – living with less.

The Bahai Faith has a wonderfully stated objective at the core of its beliefs: Bahais endeavor to seek spiritual solutions to economic problems. Now that, in my opinion, is beautiful. That is the kind of stuff we need to hear. Therein lies some key to the future of this planet. I've asked some influential Bahais exactly what they meant by this and they sort of waffled out from under the question, but that's OK. It's not an easy question to answer. This is a divergent problem, a problem that can only be lived through. Seek a spiritual solution to your economic problems. NOW. Not tomorrow. That is our life's work. We need to work on it a little bit every day.

Spirituality means that there is more to life than our bodies – and that big gland between our ears – tell us there is. Modern physics has discovered, through a phenomenon they call virtual particles, that there is a realm which is hidden from our senses and from those machines we use to extend the range of our senses. Virtual particles appear out of nowhere, live a brief life as particles (wads of energy) in this world, and then go back to nowhere – which is actually somewhere but we don't know where it is. We can't find it. The mystic has been shutting off his conscious mind and putting himself in contact with this realm for many thousands of years. And that contact, for some scientifically observable, yet elusively metaphysical reason, ushers into the life of the mystic the very fountainhead of security – freedom from fear. We are, in this text, contemplating an economic system which is not based on fear of scarcity, but instead, upon a belief in the natural abundance of life. Not communism. Not capitalism. Godism. Deer Godism. An ancient theme in the real life of real men. The God you pray to feeds you his own body.

If you thought this book was going to be limited to a tirade against women, you must be confused by now. See here. I am not advocating a political program. That won't work. That just plays right into the mouth of the beast that feeds the illusion that all we have to do is fix up the world and everything will be good. It won't. One hundred million years from now there will still be unhappy people who live an ego-driven, self-consumed existence, and peaceful people who have done battle with their egos. This is not a genetic thing. Every human being that gets born is going to have to ride this horse. To imagine differently is to slip back into the grip of Astarte.

Things will change the instant we change our thinking about them. We don't have to strategize for months or years; enlightenment is right here, right now. The Kingdom of the Father is all around us if we will but see it. It is a man's deepest instinctual capacity to see the world through God's eyes – to look for God's will, the will of the Life Force. It is natural, not unnatural, to understand that we are not the center of the universe, but that we are connected to the center of the universe – it is right here. The God we pray to feeds us his body. Welcome to the Prince of Peace. Welcome to the Deer God.

* * *

Before Astarte and her agricultural plotters a man never had to fear hunger because he could always say a prayer, pick up his bow, and go shoot a rabbit. Now they call that trespassing! Back then he didn't need a Social Security number, which is really a Pay-Your-Tax-Or-Get-Arrested number. No one asked him if he could work a computer – they wanted to know if he could pray, if he had some sway with the gods, some intuitive connection. He didn't have to climb barbed wire fences, or ask permission from a farmer, or buy a hunting license, or buy a pheasant stamp, or purchase a firearms permit in order to be eligible to buy shotgun shells. No. He just went out and got food. He knew where the bananas were, where the honey was; he knew the pools where the big fish liked to hang out. He was a part of it all. We were a part of it all.

And somehow, the Great Earth Mother made all this into trespassing. The king sold out to female values and started fencing everything in and employing soldiers to protect it. The Anatolian Goddess, according to Joseph Campbell, was worshipped from 7000 B.C. to around 100 A.D. In early statuettes she was a plump fertility goddess, Reubenesque, the shape of a ripe pear. By the end of the Roman Empire she was a bathing beauty with a crown on her head. The crown represented the walled city, the fortress. And today we can find the Anatolian Goddess in the *New York Times* any day of the week selling perfume and lingerie and urban excitement. Chic. The farm girl goes to the big city and finds love.

The hunting club is the fundamental primate institution, immediately apparent in bands of foraging chimpanzees, sport fishing tournaments, and sorties to the moon. Primates, indeed most mammals, tend to segregate themselves according to sex. Males and females don't hang out in the same groups because they don't operate on the same wavelengths; they are not keying on the same conscious or subconscious symbols. The tragedy of the modern workplace, dominated by women and manholes operating out of their shared philosophies of hoarding and scarcity, is that real men quickly become alienated. The hunting club, which is how we used to work, has reverted to the drinking club, which is how we obliterate our alienation. So who's running the show? The people who spend all their time convincing us we need to want more of everything. Pornography. E. F. Schumacher has plenty to say about this:

> The cultivation and expansion of needs is the antithesis of wisdom. It is also the antithesis of freedom and peace. Every increase of needs tends to increase one's dependence on outside forces over which one cannot have control, and therefore increases existential fear. Only by a reduction of needs can one promote a genuine reduction in those tensions which are the ultimate causes of strife and war...
> "War is a judgment," said Dorothy L. Sayers, "that overtakes societies when they have been living upon ideas that conflict too violently with the laws governing the universe...Never think that wars are irrational catastrophes: they happen when wrong ways of thinking and living bring about intolerable situations." Economically, our wrong living consists primarily in systematically cultivating greed and envy and thus advancing a vast agenda of totally unwarrantable acts. It is the sin of greed that has delivered us over into the power of the machine. If greed were not the master of modern man [read woman and manhole] – ably assisted by envy – how could it be that the frenzy of economism does not abate as higher "standards of living" are attained and that it is precisely the richest societies which pursue their economic advantage with the greatest ruthlessness? ...It is only necessary to assert that something would reduce the "standard of living" and every debate is instantly closed. That soul-destroying, meaningless, monotonous, moronic work is an insult to human nature which must necessarily and inevitably produce either escapism or aggression, and that no amount of "bread and circuses" can compensate for the damage done – these are facts which are neither denied nor acknowledged but are met with an unbreakable conspiracy of silence – because to deny them would be too obviously absurd and to acknowledge them would condemn the central preoccupation of modern society – work – as a crime against humanity.

The neglect, indeed the rejection, of wisdom has gone so far that most of our intellectuals have not even the faintest idea what the term could mean. As a result they always tend to cure a disease by intensifying its causes...allowing cleverness to replace wisdom...But what is wisdom? Where can it be found? Here we come to the crux of the matter: it can be read about in numerous publications but it can be found only inside oneself. To be able to find it one has first to liberate oneself from such masters as greed and envy. The stillness following liberation – even if only momentary – produces insights of wisdom which are obtainable no other way.

They enable us to see the hollowness and fundamental unsatisfactoriness of a life devoted primarily to the pursuit of *mater*ial [motherial] ends, to the neglect of the spiritual. Such a life necessarily sets man against man and nation against nation, because men's needs are infinite and infinitude can be achieved only in the spiritual realm, never in the *mater*ial...infinite growth is not possible in a finite realm.[4]

Have you seen the photos of the earth from space? What we have down here folks is definitely a finite realm.

What we are hearing is E. F. Schumacher, an economist, talking about spiritual solutions to economic problems: disarming greed and envy and acquisitiveness and hoarding to produce real wealth; shackling our motherial nature, exactly what the so-called patriarchal religions have been trying unsuccessfully to accomplish for 4,000 years.

It is becoming astoundingly clear to me that solving the malaise of the modern male is on a parallel course with rescuing the environment, hobbling the women's movement, exploding the bubble of greed that tells us a healthy economy is based upon constant growth rather than on a sustainable pattern of utilization of resources, and rediscovering our way into the natural mysteries which inform every moment of our lives.

Joseph Campbell was fond of pointing out that life lives by killing and eating itself. Early man recognized this cycle and sanctified it with a covenant between plants, animals, and people. The yearly renewal of this covenant became the focus of their worship. In the highly feminized Greek religion male initiation rites enacted the death of the ego. The initiate entered the earth as a seed guided by two goddesses, one of whom was Semele, the seed (semen), mother of Dionysus, the grape. (So here, by the way, we have the grain and the wine associated in a death and resurrection ritual, thousands of years before Christ.) After a sojourn in the underworld, the world of the dead, the initiate was thrust back up into the world of light, the world of Apollo. The individual ego, the seed, was dissolved in death and the crest of many seeds burst forth into the sun – the initiate was reborn, manifold, opened to all creation. Is that not what Easter is all about?

Jesus taught that the Kingdom of the Father will come about through the death of the ego, the death of the self-centered life. That thought, in the exact form, is at least 50,000 years old and probably many times older. It was known to Chinese and Indians and Greeks. It is a fundamental human truth experienced in the same manner in nearly identical rituals by cultures scattered across the globe with only the scantest opportunities for contact with each other. Life comes from death. Your physical life comes through the death of your ancestors. Your spiritual life comes through the death of your ego. When Joe Campbell said there was only one myth, this is what he was talking about. We need to be *constantly, hourly* reminded to drop our egos. That's what spiritual instruction is for.

Women do not want what they say they want
Women do not know what they want

Women want spiritual leadership out of the prison of themselves

And, guys, if we can't give it to them, 300 years from now the only men left will be Chippendale strippers and bottles of sperm in somebody's fridge. The marriage ceremony will consist of saying three Hail Marys and receiving a dildo and a plastic tube of semen.

Let's just be men again. Unisex is a wonderful symbol of spiritual union but it has no place in physical reality. Men and women are not the same. They never will be. We need to expend some effort realistically appraising the differences between them. There is nothing wrong with trying to be politically correct as long as this is done in the context of trying to be spiritually correct. The former without the latter is just another dildo.

The women are right. Religion was invented to contain female greed and *mater*ialism and self-seeking egomania. When the crowned Goddess transformed herself into the walled city, the mindscape of religion preserved the last remnants of the male hunter/seeker instinct. What we hunt is within us.

When I was getting divorced by my ex, I went to a marriage counselor who told me about the marriage pyramid as described, according to him, in the Old Testament. "At the top," he said, "is the peak experience, your common spiritual life." He formed a triangle with his fingertips and lowered his hands in front of his chest, tracing the imaginary sloped sides of the pyramid. "Next comes your spouse, then your kids, then your job...Was your marriage built like that?" he asked me.

No. How could it have been? During eighteen some years of education culminating at the University of Chicago, no one had ever bothered to tell me how a marriage was made. I'd learned all kinds of crap about algebra and the Peloponnesian War but nothing about how to have a family. Left to my own devices, I'd ended up running my family in reverse, priorities arranged in precisely the wrong order. First came my work, then came my kids, then came my spouse, and in a distant last place came the Deer God. Is it any wonder it didn't work?

Spiritual awareness is an active appreciation for other realms of existence which somehow makes life on this earth in this body more bearable. It is a journey to the inner reaches of outer space; a trip outside ourselves which brings us to the center of ourselves. According to Joseph Campbell, life requires life-supporting illusions. Human beings are gifted with creative imaginations which tend to manufacture poetry at about one percent the rate they manufacture fear and worry. It's worth it, but it's rough to live with, and we need a little help.

At some moment in life, although there is no objective, conclusive, logical proof one way or the other, it is necessary to make a decision that there is meaning and purpose in the universe. In actuality, this is the only choice we ever make: to choose God or not choose God. But the G-word is a loaded word so we can try to approach it another way. We are all cells in the body of humanity, and it is as if we all bump and ooze our way through each day performing as lung cells or liver cells or bone cells, as the case may be. And then one day, the realization comes to us that we really *are* part of a vast organism, the motives and operations of which are impossibly beyond our comprehension. Can your bone cells or heart cells comprehend that you are reading this right now? No. And yet, one day we get the almost mystical feeling that we really are part of the whole thing. And once we have thus chosen for God or *sunyata* or the Force, our only function becomes to surrender our will to it and come into harmony with that higher perception.

Dag Hammarskjold put it this way: "I don't know who – or what – put the question. I don't know when it was put. I don't even remember answering. But at some moment I did answer 'yes' to someone – or something – and from that hour I was certain that existence was meaningful and that, therefore, my life in self-surrender has a goal…From that moment I have known what it means 'not to look back', and 'to take no thought for tomorrow'."[5]

A man must obey his God, a woman must obey her man, children must obey their parents. This is the way of the world. I'm not making this up. Men's Rights, Women's Rights, Children's Rights are all a cruel fraud. Our choices are to be willful or to surrender to a higher ideal. Surrender is *always* the hardest choice. If your company is polluting a river, there is no way you can continue working for that company; that's surrender, that's the hard choice. Every society on earth except ours employs the God-man-woman-child hierarchy and in those societies – some of which have been around for thousands of years – the divorce rate hovers around 1% rather than 60%.

Add to that the powerful statistic that second-time marriages in the USA shoot up to a 75% failure rate, and it is plain that nothing more is being understood the second time around. Face it, folks, the ego way, Sinatra's way, "my way", is the shortcut to marital disaster.

Children need not be obedient to a woman who shows no obedience to her husband. Wives need not be obedient to a man who shows no obedience to God. That is the escape clause in God's law. Men without a spiritual life end up being despised. Yes, despised. Our job is to pray. It always has been. Pray to the Deer God, pray to Allah, pray to the Heavenly Father, pray to rocks and stones. Just pray. That is what our women and children need from us. Just pray.

Chapter One

Biology and Physiology

WHEN YOU BEGIN LOOKING into the areas of biological differences between the sexes two facts leap off the page and slap you in the face:

1) **We are *all* women.**
2) **Our brain is a gonad, a sex gland.**

The brain, often lumped in with the other organs, is, in fact, a gland. Actually it is a communion of glands which secrete and respond to vast numbers of chemical and electrical fields that suffuse the entire body. In current scientific mythology the brain has been likened to a computer. In past ages it was described as a cantaloupe, a fishing net, and an encyclopedia, according to the extant state of technology. It's my guess that the computer analogy will prove to be no more accurate than the fishing net and indeed the image of trawling the oceans of the subconscious dredging up prehistoric fish is probably a much more refined and accurate notion of what the brain actually does.

But one thing we have found out for sure: whatever the brain does, it does not do it the same way in men and women. The differences in brain sex first emerge in the womb.

Joseph Chilton Pearce has provided a remarkable purview of how the brain works.

66

Says Pearce:

There's a fascinating function in the brain they call the "target cell function". When the brain first starts forming in utero, it doesn't form as a structure but forms as a homogenized mass, a kind of "soup" of random cells. When this "soup" reaches a certain critical mass, key target cells mysteriously appear. Those target cells send out a signal for the other cells to link up with them...The other cells begin throwing out dendrites and axons trying to link up with their target cells...Optical cells link up with the optical target cells, and the whole optical system forms in an incredibly brief time. The auditory cells do the same thing, and so forth ...These target cells that appear are indicators of our own higher structure.[6]

During the first few weeks the fetus which emerges from the soup, including its gonads, appears to be unisex. But then something remarkable begins to happen – something with astounding implications for human society. Between the 8th and 12th weeks a fetus with male chromosomes begins to produce testosterone and other androgens which "differentiate" its masculine genitals, and later, its brain. A fetus with female chromosomes, because it is exposed to much less androgen, continues to develop along female lines.

A person's prenatal hormonal experience appears to be an especially strong influence on later behavior. From those controversial corridors of animal research comes conclusive evidence that a male rat will act like one only if it has gotten the right amount of androgen, starting at the right time, and for the right duration, in the course of its development. If he hasn't received the proper amounts of hormones at the proper times he will act like a female, even if he looks like a normal male.

Conversely, Robert Goy says the evidence is "indisputable" that excessive prenatal exposure to male androgen can produce male gender-role behavior in females. And, Roger Gorski's UCLA team found that when testosterone is withheld by castrating rat pups their brains look like those of females.

What does it all mean? It means that, all things being equal, we would all come out female. It means that a male baby's Y chromosome induces the mother's undescended testicles to manufacture testosterone and other male androgens that shape a male fetus' gonads and brain and launch him on a life course which is incomparable and literally inconceivable to the female of the species; and this process begins in the first weeks of existence as a zygote.

But most importantly, it means that males are not born, they are *made*.

They are made by hormones which enlarge and reform the normal model brain creating a greater right-brain capacity, and vastly different perceptual skills. And they are made by the sport and war and government and literature and legends of the older men whose duty it is to initiate the younger men into the formation of those values which beget and sustain human life. Men do not just happen.

Women reach puberty, their breasts enlarge, they bleed between their legs, and life tells them that they are mature females. They can hardly fail to get the point. The female initiation in many tribes is simply for the pubescent girl to sit still and meditate silently on her condition. With men, the transitions, though noticeable, are hardly that distinct. Men must be activated, by hormones and by the society of men. Men must be made, and if they're not what you get are men who act like women.

Sex has been called the original sin of some amoebas. Strictly speaking, sex is not necessary for reproduction. A great variety of very long-lived microbes reproduce asexually and there is even one species of lizard called the whiptail which is entirely female: it lays eggs that hatch without ever being fertilized. It is conceivable that we could all reproduce by parthenogenesis like whiptail lizards except for one thing – Nature doesn't want it that way. Nature has gone to great lengths to produce the male – that spontaneous, intuitive, athletic, sexually aggressive carrier of a complementary gene package – that one which is more erratic, more creative and more vulnerable than the female.

Why did Father Nature go to all that trouble? My guess is that it has something to do with speeding up evolution. Father Nature perceived that without this spontaneous erratic male influence the unfolding of life would be deadened and ossified, and society would have little chance of adapting to ice ages, floods, microbial epidemics and other terrestrial cataclysms. We would drown in our own pee. Therefore, enter the male, who is definitely talented at moving society forward.

However, there emerged weak links in this speeded-up evolution, for by introducing the Y chromosomes to trigger male hormone production, Father Nature left the male zygote exposed to certain inherited maladies. In a female the X chromosome supplied by the father duplicates the genetic information on the X chromosome supplied by the mother. Thus, if there are potentially debilitating genetic anomalies in one of the female's X chromosomes, the other X chromosome may cancel the effects (XX). But the male embryo has no such protection (XY). What's written on his sole X chromosome rules the day. Among the X-linked troubles a man is more likely to inherit are color blindness, hemophilia, leukemia and dyslexia.

So what does Father Nature do to offset the inherited vulnerabilities of the male? For starters, he makes a lot more boys than girls. How? The Y carrying sperm has a sharp pointed head while the X carrying sperm is rounded. Thus, Y sperm enter the egg more readily and this allows for proportionally more males than females to be conceived. Between 130-150 males are conceived in the womb for every 100 females. Some Hassidic Jewish communities have recorded male/female birthrates as high as 132/100, but on the average about 105 boys are born to every 100 girls. So out of an initial 150 male fetuses some 20 to 50 boys never make it out of the womb to try breathing air. What happens to them? They are stillborn due to some degree of genetic/hormonal dysfunction.

By the age of twenty there are 98 boys per 100 girls and over sixty-five there are only 68 men per 100 women. Over the age of one hundred, 90% of the survivors are female. It is common knowledge in America that women live about 8 years longer than men, but it is not common knowledge that this is a recent inversion. For the past 10,000 years or more, until around 1840, females lived 10% shorter lives than men – that is the current ratio in reverse. Is there any doubt who is profiting from the Industrial Revolution?

Which is the weaker sex? Which are the most vulnerable and the most in need of protection? Our men are going the way of the African elephant. It isn't that we are not hardy. The problem is that our habitat is being destroyed. Our territory has been fenced and plowed under, our ivory sold for earrings, our children poached to serve institutions of higher something or other. We are being squeezed out by feminist values. There is scarcely a real man left alive.

If we can get so excited about preserving elephants, by God, let's get just as excited about preserving men. Few images are as pathetic to my eye as that of the domesticated elephant, rocking side to side neurotically to sublimate his stir-craziness: a huge, dignified, intelligent animal, controlled by an impish creature wielding a stick and tossing it peanuts. We've created parks for wild elephants; maybe we'll have to establish some game reserves for men – human nature sanctuaries, monasteries of maleness, museums of the soul.

Despite what the National Organization for Women would have you believe Father Nature wants there to be men, wants there to be differences between the sexes, wants human life to express itself according to two natures. Therein lies the essence of choice which is the basis of cultural evolution. Man is the creature who occupies the greatest variety of climates and terrains on this planet. Unlike every other animal, we choose our environment; we select the thoughts and motivations that will occupy us. In service to Allah or the Deer God or the Life Pattern or whatever you want to call it, we co-create our world.

Our brain is a sex gland. It has biologically prepared the ground for us to utilize our powers of discrimination. Sex means choice. Why else would the brain come in two flavors: male and female. We don't have male lungs or female intestines. Something very deep is at work here.

* * *

It is known that the right hemisphere of the brain is the region associated with imagery, music, imagination, art, pure math, creativity, insight, the spiritual realms, and INTUITION. The left hemisphere processes language, logic, applied mathematics, scientific skills, the physical world, and REASON. It has been shown that the right brain is bigger in men than in women. That is, men are naturally endowed with a *greater* physical brain capacity for embracing the *spiritual and intuitive* dimensions of life. Clearly this is the exact opposite of what we have been led to believe.

Men's brains are, on average, 15% larger than women's – about twice the difference in average body size between the two.[7] But male brains don't start out bigger. A mature human brain is too big to pass through the mother's birth canal. It gets as big as it can inside mom then BLAM!, it squirts out into the world with its spindly arms and legs attached. A deer can walk within hours of being born; we're so undeveloped we can't even open our eyes. Our brains (and bodies) are born prematurely and the parameters of this physical phenomenon necessitate extensive growth spurts and sexual differentiation *after birth*. The brains of human babies are the same size until two or three years. After that male brains grow faster and larger until age six when full brain size is reached. Many researchers agree that this pattern reflects the fact that the basic format of the brain is female, and that format is modified and enlarged when the male hormones kick in.

This does not mean that men are "better" than women. It does mean that men are different than women, and that difference, it's clear to me, is something that is being obscured in our *mater*ialistic society. It is possible that men's brains can do most of the things that women's brains do, *plus* do something else. This "something else" is precisely what I will be attempting to identify in this book. This "something else", or rather, the lack of it – in a society that is being increasingly defined by females and female values – is where I believe we will find the root cause of the malaise of modern man.

Says Pearce:

We have three separate brains in our head. On the lowest most physical level is the reptile brain, which we share with all animals, reptiles and amphibians, and which incorporates bodily movement, motor skills, sensory impressions, survival of self and species – issues of food, sex and territorial impulses. Then there is the old mammalian brain, which mankind shares with all mammals, and which governs relationship, emotions, the immune system, self-healing, learning and memory, biorhythms and bonding. [Notice please that these are in great part "female traits".]

The third brain, the neocortex, involves creativity and intellect, and is quite large in humans, particularly the male who has the greater brain capacity in this species.

In a fully functioning human, there is a perfect integration and balance between the three brain systems: the R system, or reptile brain, involves itself only with physical activities; the limbic structure, or old mammalian brain, is concerned only with feelings and emotions; and the neocortex relates to what we usually call "thinking". Thinking is not limited to reasoning but also includes intuitive, creative thought.

When the connections between the three brains are not properly established, thinking often gets short-circuited, reverting to emotionalism. Emotionalism, territorialism, survival-of-the-species response, and even violent activity are the product of constricted neural functioning between the three brains.

Is it possible that a brain with less overall capacity will spend more of its time grooving in the tried and tested reptile and limbic realms? Is it possible that a brain with less overall capacity will "short-circuit" more readily – cut out of the neocortex and run back to first base, back to the secure emotional formulas of mammalian antiquity? I'm not going to be the one to stick my balls in the lioness' jaws trying to prove this one, but I'll tell you what – I think so. I think this is worthy enough of a suspicion that a Titan booster rocket worth of economic fuel should be poured down the throat of those queries to establish what we can establish scientifically. Science aside, it's time to look out the window of our inner reveries and admit that women are more prone than men to emotional, manipulative, she-bear-protecting-her-cubs sort of responses. They go on the defensive sooner, stay on longer, and don't know the meaning of the word "overkill". They spend the greater part of their lives operating out of the mammalian brain. "Thinking", which includes both logic and intuition, has little to do with what they spend their time doing. If it did, Oprah could never have been on the air so long.

It is a fact that teenage girls whose mothers took male hormones during pregnancy have overall higher IQs.[8] It is a fact that testosterone makes the brain less likely to fatigue. And it is a fact, according to Ruben Gur, that women's brains that are asleep show as much neural activity as men's brains that are solving a difficult problem. Women are always "thinking", processing something. They have trouble shutting their brains off – which is just what the guru advises us to do if we want to experience inner peace. Their heads are caught inside the washing machine from hell – the one that never clicks off. It lurches from wash to rinse to spin dry and back to wash again, endlessly processing the outer garments of life with detergents and fabric softeners, desperately bleaching the threads of existence until some goofball comes along and kicks the goddamn plug out of the wall. That goofball is us.

It is not only in brain size but also in the actual physical composition that great differences have been detected between males and females. According to Kathryn Phillips, male brains – with fewer connections across the corpus callosum (the thick bundle of nerves connecting the brain's right and left hemispheres) – are more lateralized than those of females. This increased lateralization, so the theory goes, allows for greater right brain performance.[9] In her opinion this accounts for males' superior performance in visuo-spatial skills; and in my opinion it tips us off to a quickening of intuition, creative association, and spiritual connectedness within the male psyche. The Landing Strip of the Gods is in our heads, not somewhere off in Peru. That's one of the things men know that women have a rough time with. Women think it's more important to visit Jerusalem or Chartres than it is to annihilate their own ego. They constantly try to physicalize, reify, the abstract experience.

Greater right brain performance in boys is corroborated by Moir and Jessel who say that while both sexes are equal in their performance in two dimensions, boys four years old and up perform better in three dimensional mindscapes. Men are more at home in multi-dimensional space. Some of us can experience the notion of ten dimensional space. The very thought fries most women's circuits.

Everyone seems to know that girls are better with language than boys. They learn to talk sooner and have a greater vocabulary. Language is an area that has been well studied. By monitoring patterns of blood flow employed during language exercises it was found that men use two distinct left brain locations to process words whereas women seem to employ additional locations in both lobes of the brain. The additional areas utilized by women lie behind the primary visual and auditory regions so one might argue (as does Cecile Naylor) [10] that women have an additional imaging function during the language process. The area in question, located in the right hemisphere, is involved in the emotional comprehension and expression aspect of the language. In other words, women are more adept at tacking words onto emotions, images and sounds.

In men, as language impulses move toward speech, only Broca's area, a zone in the left frontal lobe, is engaged. In women, Naylor found, "almost every area in the cortex, left and right hemisphere, has some relationship with Broca's area during the task, as if there were many independent things going on between Broca's and lots of different regions. [This suggests] that women are recruiting areas of the brain that enable them to use more strategies than men."

Are women more adept at plotting and scheming than men? Are they more devious in problem solving? Do they tend to rationalize away the warts on the face of their fondest fantasies? Do they "improve" the truth?

You'll have to search your own heart for the answers to those questions, and anyway I don't want to get shot; but the research seems to be suggesting that men are just plain not as biologically equipped to do this. Thank goodness that these studies were performed and these conclusions arrived at by a couple of women or they might never have been published in this era of woman-think.

Kathryn Phillips winds up her presentation by saying that women, with theoretically increased bilateralization, excel at verbal skills because, with more cross-communication, they have decreased focus on the right hemisphere. They don't use their right brain independently of the left. It has been shown that gifted children use their right brain significantly more, often to the point of ignoring the left. Einstein and Edison didn't even speak until they were five – three years later than the average girl. What were they thinking about? All the things that our world has come to be made of. What word could they have used to describe a light bulb or nuclear fission to a person who had never seen either? That would have been like Jesus talking about protons and neutrons to a bunch of goat herders. It's not done.

Kathryn Phillips has demonstrated to me that women have less of an ability to live in separate halves of their brains. Moir and Jessel say that men use their right brain when working on an abstract problem while women use both hemispheres. In one way you could say men are more naturally schizophrenic. I won't argue with that, and neither will the intake personnel at any mental health clinic. On the other hand, Sandra Witelson suggests that greater separation of brain spheres in males makes it easier for them to do two things at once – easier to do what the guru do – live in the paradox. Women are handicapped in the sense that if they can't put a word on it *they don't see it*! All the psychic garbage aside, unless an image or a feeling or a sound can be named, it can hardly be noticed at all by a woman. According to the Taoists, knowledge shreds the world, wisdom makes it whole. Naming everything is exactly what tears the world up into ten billion shattered parts.

No wonder there are so few women artists and spiritual leaders, and so many psychics and realtors and lawyers. Art shatters physical perception (I'm not talking here about watercolors of horses and barns) and spirituality transcends and transforms the *mater*ial, mother-ial world. Art and spirituality, by definition, defy verbal description; they evoke sensations that are outside our normal repertoire of phonic symbols. Shortly I will show that females have better fine-hand motor skill aptitudes than men and that's why you see so many of them in arts and crafts classes making baskets and ceramic butterflies, but creative giants like Marc Chagall and Pablo Picasso could scarcely be accused of exercising fine motor skills. What they can be credited with is poking a maniac's peephole into the mind of God.

By contrast, the psychic realms – everything from palmistry to psychiatry, astrology, Jungian archetypes, "light bodies", logic and legislation – are feminized intellectual attempts to quantify life with verbal images: What do the stars have in store for me today? What happened to the Earth Goddess? How do we define child abuse? Statistically, married women have their first affair at four years…It's all a bunch of psychic ego-garbage.

Words are not facts or truths. Words are symbols: broken, bumbling, desperate attempts to capsulize fragments of physical or metaphysical reality. Words are the very things which create the dualities, the rip in the fabric of unity among all things, that spiritual teachers constantly warn us against. Krishnamurti said, with good reason, that words are violent. They tear up perception. Deborah Tannen claims men speak 2000 words a day and women speak 7000.

I love words. I work with them habitually. But they're just metaphors, black smudges on white paper. They must never be confused with reality, just as the flag of the United States of America must never be confused with the United States of America.

Women, living in both sides of their brain, seem to have a problem with this. They are given to logicizing: constructing rational-sounding sentences which are essentially word association games. Mention the word "hose" in a sentence about boats and you're just as likely to end up talking about stockings. Men get frustrated to hell conversing with women because women think nothing of skipping off the topic at hand to track down some word association. It's not a question of their being irrational, though that's what they're most often accused of.

The problem is one of being too literal. When the conversation wanders into an area which is unfamiliar to them, rather than just *listening*, they will leap out at some random word and jerk the whole thread of thinking back into some groove that is familiar to them. It must be very difficult trying to learn anything at all when your basic response to a situation is throwing words at it and straining to capsulize it in preconceived pat phrases.

Maharishi has said that life is 100% Unity and 100% Diversity – probably the most direct statement of truth I have ever run across. He bids us to live in this fundamental paradox. This sort of koan opens a doorway in most men's minds, a vista on greater things. Most women go into spasms of dissociation when this thought ricochets around inside their skulls trying to find a solid place to land. But there is no solid place in this entire universe of energy bubbles. Drop a pellet from a black hole and it would fall through the earth as if the earth were air. Such is the scientific reality of this enormous paradox we inhabit, which men – from 2.2 million years of sitting silently behind a bush waiting for a zebra – have absorbed into the vastness of their right brains.

For a woman to break out of her psychic stew of verbal props must be as frightening as leaping off a bridge into a misty bottomless canyon. It is not part of her experience; she has nothing to hang on to. Women are biologically disposed to expressing life with words. It is not a fault *per se*, but neither should men feel inferior because we don't reduce the vastness of our right brains into words that women understand. That's expecting an elephant to fly. We're not made for that. We have other strengths.

Men are given to operating out of either one side of their brain or the other. There are many things that men see and experience and feel that do not fit readily into words. It doesn't mean they're dumb. It doesn't mean they're dullards with speech. It means they are receptive to different things. If I tell my kids, "I happened upon a moment of Buddha consciousness standing on a street corner", my son will say, "What's Buddha consciousness?" and my daughter will say "What street corner?" I love my daughter more than all the raindrops that fall on the

Pacific Ocean in 1000 years, but notice from her answer that one could easily be mistaken into assuming that she knows exactly what Buddha consciousness is and she just needs to pinpoint where to find it, when, in fact, she knows nothing about it at all and therefore the words don't even stick in her head. This is language? This is "communication"? I'm not convinced most women have any idea at all what communication is. They don't expand their vistas. They throw words at each other while clinging to their prejudices. They're not fast learners.

Yes, this is a stupid example. My daughter might never say that at all. But the point I am trying to make is that her way into the situation is through what she knows, or might know. My son's way into the situation is through what he doesn't know. She wants to establish what she knows. He wants to establish what he doesn't know. When pressed, she will express the opinion that whatever she doesn't know is wrong or bad or dangerous (this is what they call women's intuition. More on this later.) My son is interested in the hidden miracles and opportunities present in that which he doesn't know. He wants to learn. She wants to establish where she is.

Can you see them 50,000 years ago? She wants to know if the firewood is dry. He wants to know what that black shadow lurking on the cliff is. Maybe a monster. Maybe his friend, blinded in an orgy of too much sex, stumbling back to camp with directions for how to find the lost tribe of nymphomaniac women – who never complain about anything – on the other side of the mountain. He is not going to shoot the lurking shadow with his arrow until he finds out for sure.

What a pair they make: the protector and the seeker. A bit of genetic genius going on here. Let's enjoy the difference.

It has often been said that Knowledge may be taught but Wisdom must be experienced. One belief commonly shared by the sages of all time is that Wisdom cannot be imparted in words. Silence is where Wisdom comes from. Sharing with a woman most often means responding to her questions. Sharing with a man means being quiet and just being with him, absorbing the silent wisdom of the universe that pervades every moment. You want us to talk? Fine. Give us equal time in silence and I'm sure something wonderful will come of it.

Men have gone to fabulous impossible lengths to create ritual space where gossiping and murmuring are not permitted. "Be still and know that I am God", are the watchwords. The purpose of a ritual is to annihilate time and to transport us outward, upward, into the transcendent realm of the Deer God. Life cannot be expressed in words, only in silence. News cannot be expressed in silence, only in words. The belief that the sacredness of life can be rendered in words is the endemic disease of our cultural era.

Verbal applications are only one aspect of hemispheric differentiation between the sexes. Diane McGuinness presents a fund of information regarding left brain/right brain, female/male differences. The left brain, she says, is more highly involved than the right in developing skilled performance, especially that requiring fluent sequential action such as dance, gymnastics, imitative art or technical piano playing. Girls are more elastic and outperform boys in these skilled sequential activities. They're better at sewing and better at tying shoes. They're better because they rely more on their left brain – the logical, rational side of the brain – which, reasonably enough, seems to order sequential actions. Boys are better at catching baseballs because they have readier access to the less logical, spatial-relationship qualities of the right brain. A boy who throws with his right catches with his left. A boy who wants to make the basketball team must learn to dribble with his left hand. Though it flies in the face of classical Darwinism, there is no doubt in my mind that, as Robert Ardrey posited in *African Genesis*, the use of a tool creates a feedback loop with that portion of the brain which is involved with the operation of that tool. It would not surprise me to find, with the number of girls now playing baseball and basketball, that these girls have augmented their right brain capacity. I think it's a study that needs to be done.

To support her conclusions about fine motor skills McGuinness cites a study by Lomas and Kimura who found that speaking interfered dramatically with finger-tapping sequences, especially of the right hand (which, of course, by some quirk of physiology, is coordinated by the left brain). The results might indicate that fine motor control in humans is localized in the left brain. Or it might not. It might be that flipping your concentration back and forth from one lobe of the brain (to perform a manual task) to the other lobe of the brain (to speak) diminishes your concentration in the opposing lobe. For men, at least, I suspect this is nearer the mark. How do you like it when your wife is talking to you as you try to hang a picture? How do you like it knowing from experience that your chances of bludgeoning your thumb with the hammer rise 1000% with every word she utters. Talking to a man who is working is a form of violence that puts him in danger of bodily harm. Men on construction sites don't talk to a guy who is pounding a nail or sawing a board. If he's doing something wrong they might shout out, "Wait!", get him to stop, and then talk it over. They don't want to see him push his thumb through the whirling razors of a table saw.

Lomas and Kimura found girls more skilled with their right limbs whereas boys were better with their left. Experiments with 5-6 year old girls performing heel and toe tapping exercises reveal that they are remarkably more dexterous with their right foot. This indicates girls are considerably more biased toward left hemispheric activation – the logical organizational locus.[11]

I still don't understand what sinister forces have been operating to convince us that men are more "logical" than women. The evidence to the contrary is all around us. Who are the ones in your work place who keep everything organized? Who are the ones who come up with the brainstorms to invest in Hawaiian real estate or convert bankrupt sausage factories into yuppie condos? Who are the ones who stand slack-jawed, staring up an elephant's asshole, amazed at the sheer amount of shit up there, and wondering how to turn a buck on it?

Forgive me, excuse me. Back to the dry tortillas of scientific method. The first drafts of this chapter were so parched I had to try something. "Just the facts ma'am", says Dragnet detective Joe Friday somewhere down in my reptile brain. OK, OK, just the facts:

Diane McGuinness found that when the speed of motor sequencing is combined with a verbal or visual task, such as cross-referencing two scrambled lists, female ability is pronounced. Essentially girls move words into images and images into words much more easily than boys. Men are poorer at identifying word-sounds and are particularly disadvantaged at creating a visual image of a word they hear. Seventy-five percent of the reading disabled population is male.

Diane McGuinness concludes, on the basis of available data, that females are more attentive to speech sounds, more accurate in decoding speech, more fluent, have better skills in temporal sequencing and exhibit noticeable superiority in fine motor fluency. Girls have a decided advantage in learning to read. They make better typists and better neurosurgeons.

There have been 4,000 experiments performed to rate verbal skills and 8 performed to rate math skills. Got any idea who's scoring the grant money?

Finally, Diane McGuinness goes on to tantalize us with her perception of how the female tactic unravels. She says females tend to persist in adopting verbal problem-solving strategies even when they are inappropriate, such as when learning algebra or geometry.

McGuinness views mathematics as a language devised for dealing with the world of objects – clearly she hasn't touched on black holes or ten-dimensional space yet – that's why men are better at it (the old man-and-his-objects bias again). In fact, mathematics, to anyone familiar with it, is the epitome of abstraction, bordering on phantasm. Where did we get this idea that mathematics has something to do with physical reality? Some woman measures out a half a cup of flour and concludes that is what math is good for? Projecting rocket trajectories around Jupiter? Yeah, great, that's applied mathematics. What it took to get there from here was centuries of abstraction.

Mathematics, she says, is related to syntax and not phonetics. I have some trouble understanding this academic psychobabble but I guess she is saying that in mathematics it is the relationships between the symbols, not the symbols themselves, which matter. Syntax regards the relationship of the words in a sentence, or the numerals in an equation. Is Diane McGuinness saying that men are better at intuiting relationships than women? If she used clear, simple English I would know for sure but it is beginning to look to me as I write this that we have shattered another toxic myth: women are not more attuned to relationships than men. In fact, men are more perceptive of relationships in all things. Women are victims of their biology and their innate willfulness. Men, with more compartmentalized brains, have a whole different vista on the relationships between things *and* between people. Men don't worry too much about what they are feeling because they know that, just like the tides, those feelings will pass. Feelings are not any sort of constant, or anything substantial to run your life on. We don't like talking about emotions any more than we like talking about clothes. You have them. So what? They're not the basis of a life well lived. A life geared toward "feeling good", for men, is the express train to addiction.

Next McGuinness says that it is difficult to "talk" mathematics or even communicate mathematical concepts in conventional language. Funny that she reflexively views this as a problem with mathematics rather than as a problem with language. It's difficult to talk about God or the Life Force in conventional language too. Is that God's problem? Here is the female bias at work in the woman who is so brilliantly pointing out the female bias. That's not bad, it's good. It picks up on the underlying biology at work. To her, mathematics, because it doesn't fit into words, is somehow less graspable.

In 1967 Sherman suggested that one of the reasons why girls may have difficulties in both spatial ability and mathematics is that they rely too heavily on verbal problem-solving strategies. She ascertained that researchers who investigated visuo-spatial problem-solving often asked their subjects how they solved the problems. Females, who repeatedly scored lower than males, were far more likely to describe their strategy as one of labeling (naming) parts of the figure and comparing them with one another. Males were much more likely to report that they made the diagram "move" inside their heads. That is, they rotated the three-dimensional object inside their mind. Females may be forced back on verbalization due to an undeveloped capacity for visualization, or they may lack visual skills since they opt for verbal solutions because these have worked for them in the past. They think words work for everything.

McGuinness finds that 25% of severely dyslexic boys are mathematically gifted, suggesting that there is a trade-off between verbal activity and spatial-mathematical ability. It turns out Henry Ford had very poor language skills. It's a good thing he wasn't laughed out of school or we might all be walking to work.

McGuinness concludes that the key sensorimotor skills involved in reading, writing, and spelling are almost identical to the perceptual and motor abilities that differentiate males and females, implying that there are biological and genetic reasons why girls and boys develop different sets of abilities in cognitive tasks – i.e., our brains are different so we think different.

Diane McGuinness has been admirably objective in her analysis of these biological/verbal interfaces, and I do admire her and her work greatly, but I cannot resist injecting that anyone who assumes the world is supposed to be a rational place finds it very easy to prove all men are idiots. For example, observation tells us that a tree is green. However, science tells us that the leaves of a tree are absorbing every color – black, blue, red, yellow – to utilize in photosynthesis and, in fact, the only color which is *not* being absorbed, the color which is bouncing off the leaf into our eye, is the color green. So, a tree is every color *except* green. See how funny things get, see how easy it is to be deceived about the true nature of things, when we rely too heavily on the input from our senses. This is not even spirituality, it's just science, though by now I'm sure you can tell how fascinated I am by how these realms move together at a deeper level. That is the problem with the literal approach; if we rely only on sense data, which women tend to do, it can really goof us up.

In addition to the corpus callosum and the language loci, the hypothalamus, a lusty little gland perched on top of the brain stem in the reptile brain area, displays obvious gender differences. Often referred to as the Third Eye, or the Sixth Chakra in the Hindu metaphor, the hypothalamus operates in a primal emotional zone somewhere between reptilian and mammalian consciousness producing rage, hunger, thirst, and desire, including sexual desire. Charlotte M. Otten says the hypothalamus functions both as a nerve structure and an endocrine gland...It can be stimulated by the central nervous system or by chemical feedback from the bloodstream. It is the nexus of primitive sense stimuli and feedback.[12]

Two areas in the hypothalamus show sex differences. One is a group of neurons that acts as a built-in clock controlling circadian rhythms and, in women, ovulation. Also, a cell group in the preoptic area is twice as large and has twice as many neurons in heterosexual men as it does in women and homosexual men! Men have different body rhythms and different visual apparatus than women or homosexual men. We feel and see differently! Is this a surprise?

The significance of this last finding for understanding sex differences is hard to overestimate. What Simon LeVay, of the Salk Institute for Biological Studies is saying here is that a person with a male body and a female hypothalamus is going to be female. He/she will possess the male reproductive function, but he/she is very unlikely to reproduce because he/she regards life as a female – an unmade male. In sexual orientation, that sex gland in the brain, the hypothalamus, is capable of overriding the behavior of the entire physical prototype.[13]

It has been found that women who endured a great amount of stress during pregnancy (such as pregnant women who lived in London during the bombing of Britain by Germany during WW II) and women who took barbiturates during their pregnancy (which were prescribed by medical idiots) both gave birth to disproportionately high numbers of homosexuals. In other words, the normal and proper secretions of male androgens during pregnancy were inhibited by stress or downers to the extent that normal male brain formation did not take place.

Male homosexuals do not take the same hormone ride which formulates the heterosexual male. They have the Y chromosome, but they don't experience the requisite numbers or quantities of hormonal baths which form the male brain. Their brain physiology is closer to that of the female prototype of the species. They are born, not made. This should come as a great relief. Parents relax! It's not your fault. Your kids aren't going to "turn into" homosexuals unless they have the biological components in place. Just avoid stress and downers when you're pregnant. Homosexuality is not a cultural phenomenon – as I spent most of my life believing. It is primarily a hormonal event, not even genetic, so there's no imputed shame there either. It's no one's fault. It's not bad. It just *is*.

In XXY males, who possess an extra female chromosome, a confused genetic message giving contrary instructions to the gonads creates a situation in which not enough masculine hormone has been dispatched to the developing brain to make it match its male body. These men tend to be shy, hesitant, unmade males.

Turner's Syndrome Kids – kids born with only one X chromosome – are so entirely female they are born without ovaries so they have no opportunity whatever of secreting "male" androgens (like testosterone, which is found in both men and women, and which is the main sexual activator in our bodies). These kids are disproportionately *protective of objects* like toys and dolls and they adore jewelry and rings. Here is the unopposed female instinct, *Mater*, at work. Kids who don't have a trace of male hormones in them *instinctively* hoard objects. They shun sports, they love to go shopping. Why would this simple observation come as a surprise unless we had all been brainwashed into believing that boys love objects and girls love people. It's hokum. But it's dangerous! It's how they got us out of the forest and into the factory.

Sandra Witelson proposes that the brain is a mosaic of areas that may respond to sex hormones at various times during early development...Typical male or female hormone levels would produce a typical male or female brain, but unusual levels of sex hormones at any given time may switch the development of susceptible brain areas. This could cause different areas in the same brain to undergo different sexual orientation. You might have a female sexual preference with male emotional wiring or vice versa. Receiving the exact amount of hormones at the exact times is the critical factor.

Says Witelson:

Depending on levels of timing, sex hormones could influence handedness, sexual orientation, emotional composition, or other characteristics. Researchers suspect that an excess of testosterone before birth (secreted by the mother's undescended testes) enables the right hemisphere to dominate the brain resulting in left-handedness.[14]

Moir and Jessel admitted in their book *Brain Sex* that they were baffled by the revelation that lesbians are four times more likely to be left-handed than straight women. Isn't it obvious? Take the blinders off. The right brain is male. An overload of testosterone in the womb produces left handedness, which is right brainedness. We are the poets. Intuition is our secret garden. Silence is our soil. Sex our rain. We reap music in the wind and art in the sun and verse from the moon. Our fruits are nothing less than the bread of life.

"Just the facts ma'am."

A brain hormone (GnRH) released by the hypothalamus affects ovulation, menstruation, and the onset of menopause. Also, according to Sergio Ojeda of the Oregon Primate Research Center, "It is clear now that the onset of puberty is a brain-driven event." It is initiated by the hypothalamus in the absence of gonads.

Similarly, we used to think that the depletion of eggs in the ovaries caused the onset of menopause but that doesn't seem to be the case. Ovaries from old rats have been put in young rats and they became fertile again, whereas young ovaries put in old rats didn't switch on again. According to Phyllis Wise of the

University of Maryland School of Medicine in Baltimore "...hypothalamic function changes in mid-age and this may play an important role in the loss of fecundity and cyclicity (in women)." Men, however, can produce sperm into their nineties.

The hypothalamus-pituitary in men tries to keep hormonal blood levels more or less constant, whereas in women these combined glands purposely induce vast fluctuations effecting menstruation and wild mood swings – unless they're pregnant. Women are biological victims of a chemical gloom. It's nature's way of prodding them toward the imagined terrors of pregnancy. Their chemistry evens out and they get peaceful when they get pregnant.

Prehistoric woman, say Moir and Jessel, with a shorter life span and more pregnancies than modern women, could expect 10 menstruations in her life. Modern women can expect 400! We have to put up with 40 times more shit from our women than biology ever intended, and they expect us to believe that *we* are the problem. Contrary to toxic rumor, pregnant women are the happiest, most centered, women in the world. Women were intended to spend the great part of their young lives pregnant, not working in offices. It's a biological fact. Blame God, not us. You don't want to get pregnant? Fine. Don't sabotage my life with your chemical gloom. Women's chemistry is women's chemistry, not my chemistry. I can work around it, but I don't have to wallow in it. You can't defy biology and then blame me for the ensuing problems and grief. Says London psychiatrist Glenn Wilson, feminists want men to behave more like women. That's biological violence. When we look at a 60% divorce rate, the plague of wimpy men, and the spiritual poverty of modern women, it should be clear to us this cannot endure.

So they should all stay pregnant? No. There are too many people already. Until biology catches up, over the next several millennia, there is only one thing that will work. Surrender to your Goddess. Hand off your cramps and your nausea and your irritability to a higher power. If it works for alcoholics it will work for menopausal women. Surrender your pain to something big enough to handle it, and don't take it out on your husband or boyfriend. The angst of non-pregnant women is shredding our civilization.

Testosterone is the key sexual activator in both sexes. Women passing through menopause often find their sex drive and demands increasing. This starts around 32, not 48, as some dumb folk wisdom has led us to believe. It's not when women finally stop menstruating that matters, it's when their bodies begin the transition that has the greatest impact. Look at any 32-year-old woman. She's nuts. Her hormones are changing, she's worried about how she looks, she feels desperate and she's not sure why – so what does she do? She blames it all on *him*! *He* is not taking care of her needs. *He* is inadequate. It is all *his* fault. Hormonal insanity.

As the levels of female hormones subside her ratio of testosterone rises and her libido increases. She wants more sex or better sex or something! She doesn't know what she wants. The bush league scorekeeper in the dugout of my brain tells me that 32-year-old women have the hardest time staying married. What could we do? Remove their adrenal glands so their libidos collapse? Hardly. I think we're back to the spiritual approach. Without some spiritual trip, without some method whereby women can remove themselves from themselves, there is no way to pull the plug on their emotional haunted house. I have lived on every continent except Africa (and Antarctica) and I have never seen a society in which the women were as aspiritual and *mater*ially obsessed as American women. 2.2 million years of human evolution has shown us that women need some manner of spiritual surrender to soften the biological edges in their lives, but we in America blithely refuse to acknowledge this.

Women score as high or higher than men in verbal aggression. During and after menopause, they no longer produce the amounts of female hormones that were circulating through their bodies to offset their male hormones, so they grow beards and become aggressive. Is this news or what? Why don't they ever report on this kind of stuff on *60 Minutes*? Why don't we learn it in grade school for Christ sakes?

In their 60s, while women become more bad-tempered and selfish; men, with declining testosterone, become gentler and learn to value intimacy and silliness. Look at grandma and grandpa. She's always bitching and all he wants to do is goof around with the grandchildren. Welcome to the human experience. We get to have it all in one lifetime. Isn't it wonderful!

Say Moir and Jessel, men of all ages have a higher threshold of anger and frustration. This, they claim, is a result of less structured thinking, planning, expectations. Men don't get angry or frustrated as easily because nothing in the right brain makes logical sense anyway so why would the world be logical or predictable. Men are the creative unit. Creativity is born of chaos – free association, relationship – right brain work.

Men apply for ninety-nine percent of all patents. Genius may have a lot to do with the greater male facility for single-mindedness – separation of the brain spheres – say Moir and Jessel. We can stay in our right brain, our intuitive brain, for lengthy periods of time, as long as no one jerks us out of it by asking us where we put Bobby's muddy shoes. Talking is a form of mental abuse – violence – perpetrated against men, by women, on a constant, unremitting, incognizant basis day in and day out.

It's time to draw a line in the sand. You want to gab? Call your girlfriend. You can't just conquer space in my brain without stopping to consider what an invasion it is of my privacy and my humanity. I have a right *not* to talk. We can talk – when I'm ready. You cannot clobber me with incessant chatter. It is violence against my person.

If you don't have the compassion to understand that, understand this: the chatter between both halves of the female brain is precisely what makes women less decisive. What men are good for is making decisions. And why we are good at it is that our "thinking" is not clouded by words. We separate issues, visualize alternatives, and act on them. Our mind is not a phonic stew.

Understand that we love you – *but we don't want to talk about it*. Not right now. You don't want us to beat you over the

head with clubs. That's fair. We don't want to talk. This is
exactly the same thing. Reticence is not a defect of the male
character. It's a strength!

Men have a deep, hormonally driven vitality – ambition –
that clicks on at 13. Women at middle age experience a spurt of
ambition as their testosterone ratio rises. That's why so many
of them start careers and businesses at that age. Say Moir and
Jessel, you can remove obstacles but you cannot inject ambition.
For every woman who *wants* to be a neurosurgeon there are ten
men. Thank biology for that. I don't want to make love to a
bearded woman and I don't care if she *is* a neurosurgeon.
Removing obstacles is one thing. But for a woman to feel guilty
because she didn't become an astronaut or a brain surgeon is
stupid. Astronauts and neurosurgeons are graded on a curve.
The ten smartest people with the most grace under pressure are
chosen. We cannot ignore the biology at work in competitive
arenas.

By now some scholar must be chomping at the bit with the
heady perception that the culprit is really the white male system
and once we change the rules of the system women will rise to
their natural level of authority and competence. Moir and Jessel
have the perfect retort for that. Would you let your mother fly
on an affirmative action airline? Would you? Men aren't making
the rules up there. Gravity is. You want as much competence
between your ma and the cornfields of Iowa as you can possibly
muster. Any job that doesn't have to be done right is perfect
territory for affirmative action. For any job that *has* to be done
right you better find someone who is capable of doing it with
one arm blown off and a flying saucer lodged in his knee. This
is no legal abstraction we inhabit. This is gravity.

Male *homo sapiens* has the longest, thickest erect penis of
the 192 species of apes. It is no secret that men want sex all the
time and that women, unlike other mammals, are not prone to
service them for only two weeks in spring, but indeed are sexually
available all year round, even when they're pregnant. How come?
Because the human childhood is so long, and keeps getting
longer. It used to be over at thirteen – grade school. Then we

invented high school, then we invented college, then we invented graduate school. A healthy man only has to work hard an hour or two a day to feed himself. The men in the Mexican fishing village I'm living in right now go fishing from 6 to 9 every morning, three hours, that's it. There is no way a man could be induced to spend all day underground in a coal mine, or all day laying bricks, if he wasn't getting SEX.

Women are the reproductive unit of the species but men are the creative unit of the species. The human male has a giant brain and a giant penis; they are both a liability and an asset. Men stick around to raise the kids and will work like slaves as long as they're getting laid. Women control male energy with sex. That's the biological game we're playing here folks. Men who are not getting laid are not going to stick around and pay the bills and I don't care what modern divorce law says. The duration of modern childhood has become an oppression of men. The son who used to be available to help dad cut wood and catch food is still in school for fifteen more years! It is a genuine outrage that we have arrived at the societal consensus that the purpose of a man's life is to pay other people to raise his kids. He'll do it, as long as he's getting enough sex. Take that away and American culture is left peeing on its foot. We'll go back to being stags, working two hours a day, screwing who we want, and let somebody else pay the bills. Human males are biologically evolved to crave sex – that's what keeps the nuclear family together. It's the price we pay for keeping our kids in schools for 25 years instead of having them begin doing some productive activity starting at age 12. No amount of feminist politicking is going to change this. Condition men to crave sex less and they're not going to stick around. Refuse to give them sex, and they're not going to stick around. Either way you have it, the feminist agenda, as I have come to know it in my lifetime, spells death to the nuclear family. And for the starry-eyed idealists who think that that is a "workable" alternative, I say, go to Jamaica, go to South Africa, read up on Sparta, where the women owned *everything* and the men were bred as machines to go to war and defend *mater*. Tear apart the family and human culture ceases to have meaning or direction.

Another sow in a tuxedo is female promiscuity. The real reason human females are sexually active all year long is that they are biologically driven to expand the gene pool – have sex with men other than their workhorse husbands or boyfriends. Elk only have to watch over their women a month or so in fall to ensure their genes disseminate. Human males have to watch over their women all year long. We can't do it. Women are not naturally faithful creatures and it is a travesty to acculturate men with the notion that if they are good to their wives their wives will be faithful to them. That's extremely unlikely. A DNA study done in a block of English row houses revealed that one out of three children could NOT have been the biological issue of their alleged fathers. Face it men. Women screw around. Even if you treat them right they screw around. It's not your fault. You don't have to bear the shame in silence and isolation – thinking it's only you – torturing yourself with desperate imaginings that if you had just *done* this or *said* that she wouldn't have yanked off her panties for someone else. Cowshit. She STILL would have done it. Women are not loyal creatures and the sooner men learn that the more bearable life becomes.

Now hear this: you need not be shamed by your wife's infidelity. It's not you, it's her. It's *her* problem. Her nature. Cement a good relationship with your kids, keep some cash socked away in an account she doesn't know about, and *expect* that someday your wife will run off to "find herself" – move to the Rockies, or shack up with a Rastafarian beach bum. If you're prepared for it you can survive it. If you're blind-sided, like most of us, it becomes an emotional disaster. She'll still claim monetary support from you, but you'll no longer be entitled to any kind of emotional support from her. Divorce is a *tsunami* for men because we don't see it coming. We don't *plan* for it. Women are clever; women are two-faced. The closer they get to divorce the smoother things will appear to be running because they're making plans behind your back. Be ready. And remember, her infidelity is not your fault. Not your shame. Shame on her for being so shallow and duplicitous.

* * *

This is a right-brain book and I make no apologies for that. This is jazz writing, not the rambling funk of stream-of-consciousness, but a form in which themes are stated, embellished, digressed upon; only to be restated, embellished and digressed upon, again and again. This is a Blues Book. No more pandering to east/west coast editors who think that a book that is not logically constructed is somehow a lesser book. I'm not writing this to please women. I'm writing it to tell the truth as I see it, and to squeeze some fresh juice into the brainpans of men. We need it. We've all gotten too nuts, and maybe somewhere in the trumpet blasts and bass runs and keyboard flourishes of the next several hundred pages a melody will appear, something that touches our minds and lifts us up to a place where rhythm has meaning in the song of the stars, and where we feel the pulse of our Emergency Room culture reviving and gathering strength for another run at life.

"Just the facts ma'am."

OK.

Apart from the gonads and brain, which are my main areas of concern, there are numerous less remarkable instances of sexual dimorphism (differences). I'll try to zip through them quickly without bringing on the whole band so you may be apprised of their existence and evaluate them as you wish.

Men are attracted by visual sex stimuli; that's why women dress pretty; that's why the biggest consumers of pornographic books and videotapes are men.

Women are primarily stimulated by aural sex stimuli; that's why they scream and cream over rock performers; that's why singers and jive talkers get laid a lot.

The kidneys and liver also display degrees of sexual dimorphism with male kidneys being larger. The male kidneys don't have more cells but the cells they have are larger. In the liver, sex differences affect enzyme production for metabolism of various drugs, steroids and toxins.[15]

Body metabolisms work differently in the sexes. Generally women gain weight more easily than men, but they also have the ability to process fat (lose weight) more efficiently and safely than men, until older age, when they fight a harder battle with obesity. Women store fat in their breasts, hips and thighs. In fact, they need to store a minimum amount of fat in order to begin and maintain normal menstrual cycles and thus be able to reproduce. Women who do not maintain a certain minimum fat ratio will not menstruate or ovulate – that's why they used to like it when we came back to camp dragging a fat seal or a couple geese. That's why female sprinters don't get periods. The mature woman carries about twice as much fat per pound as a man, but a man carries 1.5 times more muscle and bone.

Due to the female hormone, estrogen, which works to keep women's bodies in peak childbearing condition, women have certain built-in health advantages – including more pliable blood vessels to accommodate more blood during pregnancy. This reduces the risk of arteriosclerosis, hardening of the arteries. After menopause estrogen production drops off, but only slowly do the blood vessels become more rigid. This is one of the main reasons why women have half as much coronary disease as men.

Women spend 40% more days sick in bed but live 10% longer than men.

Males under 50 are more likely to suffer from allergies and hiccups.

Boys are three times as likely to be nearsighted, dyslexic, or left handed.

Females appear to have a better sense of smell and seem to be more sensitive to taste and touch. That's why they wash the bed sheets when they're still clean. That's why they like to be stroked while they're munching chocolate.

Females hear higher-pitched sounds and suffer less hearing loss than men. They move sounds into words easier. That's why the current educational system, with its reliance on lectures, greatly favors females. A patriarchal system of education would require students and teachers to *do* things together.

Women have more visual acuity in low-light conditions and, curiously, they seem to have a special sensitivity to the color red. Women have wider peripheral vision (like a deer) because they have more of the receptor rods and cones behind the retina.

Men have more visual acuity in normal or daylight conditions and (like a lion) their vision concentrates on depth perception. Males are quicker to identify a figure or figures in depth using a process called "binocular fusion" which is carried out by the visual cortex of the brain. That's why men are better drivers.

Have you ever gone hunting? I don't get out there as often as I did when I was a kid but I can tell you one thing: I have never seen a buck or a turkey or a cock pheasant thrust his chest out at me like a calendar painting as if to say, "Shoot me." It doesn't happen like that. The most the hunter sees of his game is a flash of fur behind a tree or a blur of wings behind a bush. The entire sport occurs by judging speed, direction, species and sex within tenths of a second using the scantest visual information. My ex-wife was a fine marksperson, but she couldn't hit a moving barnyard chicken to win a free Toyota.

Women have a genetic edge in combating certain illnesses. X-linked immunoregulatory genes give women a clear advantage in resisting infectious diseases. Five immunoglobulin deficiency diseases occur solely in males indicating these disorders probably arise from mutant genes on the single exposed X chromosome. Lymphoma and leukemia are associated with low antibody production.

* * *

On the other hand, women are more susceptible to autoimmune disorders which involve formation of antibodies against the tissues of one's own body.

Women are more prone to contracting rheumatoid arthritis.

Males have proportionally more red blood cells and more hemoglobin. This certainly has something to do with better endurance in sport and war.

Men get more gout, ulcers and cirrhosis of the liver.

Women are generally found to be more anxious and less jocular than men, say Moir and Jessel.

Men have twice as many fantasies as women. That's the right brain at work again.

Ruben Gur has found that women pick up emotional signals with much less effort than men. He determined this by measuring blood flow to the brain while testing his subjects to interpret certain emotional cues. This is the sole example of what we call "women's intuition" that I have run across in my two years of research. It exists, but it exists within the limited parameters of "reading emotions." More on women's intuition in the next chapter.

Age has an unequal impact on men and women. Men lose brain cells three times faster in old age. As men age the *corpus callosum* withers, decreasing communication between both spheres of the brain, even more so than in youth. Responding to language – chatter – requires an obnoxious, annoying amount of mental effort, especially if the old guy is approached in a moment of right brain reverie. That's why grandpa never listens to grandma and why grandma is always yelling at him to pay attention. She thinks he's deaf, but he's just off in a different part of his brain. Old age becomes a war of the sexes to see whose brain content is going to dominate the home front. Sadly, if grandpa is not permitted to build a hogan of his own out behind the chicken coop he will be trampled by an invading army of words. He waves the white flag and sets up camp by that lake inside his mind that he remembers from when he was a boy. It is one of the forgotten jobs of this society to protect old men from the cheekiness of old women.

James Dabbs of Georgia State University found that men with high testosterone have more divorces. Then he found that men prone to violence and drug abuse and getting in trouble have high testosterone levels. Then he found that the trial lawyers who defend these criminals have testosterone levels that are only slightly lower than the bad actors themselves. Then he found that women lawyers have higher testosterone than housewives. Any surprises here? Why don't we measure grandma's and grandpa's testosterone levels and see what we get? Clearly there is a supertanker worth of research left to do in the endocrine ocean.

While we're at it let's throw in some conflicting reports just to show how half-baked scientific method can be. In *The Male Experience* James Doyle says that testosterone levels affect a man's emotional state especially with respect to depression. The more testosterone the more depressed men report feeling. Says Doyle, no correlation was found between testosterone and anxiety or hostility.[16]

Then, along come Moir and Jessel in Brain Sex who say that Sport doesn't work off male aggression – it actually increases the levels of testosterone. High testosterone, they say, has been associated with high incidence of auto accidents, crime and *aggression* (hostility?).

Who's right? It seems to me there must be other hormones or other factors at work here which simply aren't being studied yet. Time to throw some money at these queries.

Sylvia Hewlett has observed that now, with more women working, most women are in worse economic shape than their mothers. Say Moir and Jessel, a study of work patterns in California caused the authors to gasp at the pervasiveness of women's concentration in "organizational ghettos" – left brain jobs. I gasped when I read somewhere that more than 52% of all managers are women and less than 1% of roofers, carpenters and house painters are women. Women gravitate toward bean-counting and manipulating other people. Men gravitate toward jobs which require a lot of action and not much talking. This is not the "patriarchy" at work, this is deep biology.

The French psychologist Jean Piaget wrote that he did not find a single girls' game that has as elaborate an organization of rules as the boys' game of marbles. Boys launch into incredible rounds of discussion to set rules of fair play that don't even enter girls' minds. Girls do not play by rules and that is what boys resent. When two people make a pact to be monogamous one of them can't merely rationalize away an affair – a violation of the rules – the way women seem to do. Given the assumption that you are unhappy does not lead to the conclusion that you need to fuck some other guy. By boys' sandlot standards, girls are not honorable.

Believe it or not, real business runs on honor. In a proper business arrangement, two people win. One doesn't get reamed while the other prospers. People enter into a business contract because they both expect to get a reward. I have too many fish, you have too many oranges, we trade, we both supplement our diets. That's how this has been working for 2.2 million years. The sheer number of self-seeking manholes who have swooped in on our business arrangements have distorted this simple process beyond belief. And now women have come up with the heady perception that, "I can do that." Yeah. They can. That's how they have been doing business for eons. The thing is, real business is played on a level playing field. People who don't abide by that don't even get in the same room with the people who are playing the real game. It's not a question of male or female *per se*. It's a question of honor. It's not that business is bad. It's greed and self-seeking and she-bearism that are bad.

Biology and psychology seem to blur their frontiers and fade into each other at this point. The she-bearism that appears to be a deep biological program in women seems to be a culturally acquired taste in manholes. Maybe they got it from their moms. But wherever it comes from we cannot permit our society to devolve to the point where we assume that business is a one-sided, get-everything-I-can-for-myself proposition. We are doomed if we do.

Women have the capacity to do outrageous things, erase them from their minds, and then bristle with indignation that anyone would even suggest that they had behaved so unsociably. Manholes, corporate jocks who seem to drink a lot, are prone to the same behavior. This is, in fact, a kind of sleep. These people are sleeping their way through life. It can be summed up in one word – Denial.

Denial is refusing to see your own part in the problem. It is railing about the guys cutting rain forests in Brazil while you diaper your baby with a paper diaper. It is pretending that computers use less paper than typewriters. It is selling shoes that fall apart or medicines that people don't need. Women and manholes seem to have blinders in their brains to erase unpleasantness. I wish the medical and psychological researchers would get to work on this one. Just what does it take for us to be conscious human beings? Just what does it take to surmount a pattern of living which, for the most part, puts us to sleep?

To wrap up Chapter One:

The biological and physiological differences between men and women are vast. Hormonal influence is prodigious. A man is made by hormones.

Men have greater overall brain capacity than women, particularly right brain capacity – which is the intuitive, creative side of the brain.

Gender specific research must be performed to determine everything from how different medicines affect men and women differently, to what is grandma's testosterone count anyway?

Homosexuality can, at last, be accepted for what it is – a biological phenomenon. Homosexuality is no reason to give someone a job, and no reason to withhold a job from someone. TV cameramen and graphic arts should not be dominated by homosexual hiring biases, and the Army should not be forbidden to them. They give us some arts, we give them some army. That's fair.

But most of all we need to appreciate the significance of the fact that the brain is a sex gland. Considering that, except for the fleeting presence of minute amounts of a handful of hormones, we would all be born female, it is clear that the drive of the human species to differentiate sexes has deep biological importance and implications. Men are not genetic accidents, not a roll of the chromosomal dice. Men do not just happen. Men are not born. Men are made.

Chapter Two

Psychology
Schooling
Praise Addiction
Female Propaganda

A QUICK LOOK AT the psychological differences between men and women reveals several curiosities:

1) Men and women do not mean the same thing by "I love you."

2) If men are more "object oriented" and women are more "people oriented" why do women spend so much time shopping and why do men play team sports?

3) Women manipulate the macaroni out of men using praise.

The workings of the human mind are vast and amorphous and not entirely understood by anybody. But Michael Hutchinson in *The Plague of Intolerance*[17] provides us with a workable model for understanding the how and why of our mental constructs and thus affords us a valuable jumping off point into the miasma of opinions, pseudo-science, and myth we use to try to understand the opposite sex. According to Mr. Hutchinson, as scientists have studied nongenetic transmission of information in recent years, they have come to realize that certain information patterns seem to carry with them self-replicating messages. It is almost as if these packets of information carry with them a hidden command: "Pass me along!" Or, in a more highly evolved form: "It is your duty to spread this information." Anthropologists and evolutionary biologists have been struck by the similarity between genes – which are molecular bundles of self-replicating information – and those other, apparently non-molecular, bundles of self-replicating information. Seeking an analogy to the word *gene*, British biologist Richard Dawkins in 1976 coined the word *meme* (rhymes with "theme"), which he defined as a self-replicating information pattern that uses minds to get itself reproduced. According to Dawkins, examples of memes are: tunes, ideas, catch-phrases, clothes fashions, ways of making pots or of building arches. (And concepts such as Feminism or Discrimination.) Just as genes propagate themselves in the gene pool by leaping from body to body via sperm or eggs, so memes propagate themselves in the meme pool by leaping from brain to brain via a process which, in the broad sense, can be called "imitation". If a scientist hears, or reads about, a good idea, he passes it on to his colleagues and students. He mentions it in his articles and his lectures. If the idea catches on, it can be said to propagate itself, spreading from brain to brain.

As a concept, memes are a little subtler than gravity but certainly more apparent than "democracy". We recognize memes through their consequences – the real effects they have had on civilization.

Says Hutchinson:
      The evolutionary value of memes is clear. The ability to pass on complex bundles of information, such as the right way to chip a tool out of a piece of rock, make pottery, hunt down different types of animals, or find water or edible plants, was an enormous advance over the potentially lethal method of trial and error. Memes freed humans from "hard-wired"

biological programs by enabling us to "think" about reality, to consciously choose to override genetic drives – choosing celibacy, say, in response to religious memes, or choosing to obey the dictum *Thou Shalt Not Kill*. [Or adopting the meme that women are equivalent to men in every way except for how they have been raised.] Since the capacity to transmit memes has such a high survival value, individuals with that capacity would tend to become more common in the gene pool, while those whose brains did not have the capacity would tend to disappear. The result is that our brains have been molded by the forces of natural selection to ensure that we have a highly developed receptivity to memes.

Indeed, N. K. Humphrey, a colleague of Dawkins, argues that memes should be regarded as living structures, not just metaphorically but technically. When you plant a fertile meme in my mind, you literally parasitize my brain, turning it into a vehicle for the meme's propagation in just the way that a virus may parasitize the genetic mechanisms of a host cell. Others have been struck by the similarity between viruses and memes. Like viruses, memes are infectious. Whereas viruses use cells to get themselves copied so that they can infect other cells, memes use minds to get themselves copied so that they can infect other minds – memes use minds to reproduce. They are "infectious information". For this reason students of memetics speak of the "germ theory of ideas".

Memes have an enormous impact on our lives – from such statements as "the curved surface on the top of an airplane's wing creates lift" to "There is only one God and Mohammed is his prophet". Memes are a vessel of interface between mind and body and Hutchinson's explanation for the mechanism of meme propagation is nothing less than stunning.

Says Hutchinson:
Because sex is the key to the process of gene propagation, the forces of evolution have ensured that humans would want to engage in this activity by providing them with a reward for doing so. When humans have sex, neuroscientists have

discovered, their brain and nervous system reward them (or "reinforce" that behavior) by releasing large amounts of extremely pleasurable neurochemicals. Among these are the euphoria-producing endorphins, known as the body's own opiates.

Memes are spread through a similar process: The activity of implanting a meme in someone's brain is a lot like having sex with that person. The similarity is one that humans have long recognized, at lease unconsciously. It is no coincidence that we speak of "seminal" ideas and "disseminating" information; that teachers speak of their students as fertile minds; that certain ideas are spoken of as being "seductive" and others as barren or sterile.

But the relationship is more than just metaphorical. Neuroscientists have recently discovered that the places in the human brain that produce the most endorphins and that contain the *largest* concentration of endorphin receptors are those involved most intimately with learning, which is to say, with receiving new information – new memes! We get an opium buzz when we learn something new, that's why a lot of writers and intellectuals become alcoholics or druggies – they get hooked on the buzz.

Scientists have even mapped the "reward pathways" or "pleasure centers" of the brain and found them tightly connected with the learning centers and pathways.

Says Hutchinson:

It's a truth we have all experienced: we are presented with new information, a new idea, that doesn't quite make sense, doesn't quite fit into our brain. We resist it or we play around with it. Then, suddenly, bingo, it slips in; we understand. The light bulb goes on in the brain. *Aha!* The new idea or information makes sense, and we are filled with a flood of pleasure, a sensual feeling of satisfaction as our body flows with warmth. We have just received a new meme, and our brain is rewarding us by releasing large quantities of endorphins and other pleasure-producing neurochemicals.

And after we have received the meme what happens next? We want to spread the meme. We have all experienced something that seems tremendously important to us – that we must eliminate nuclear weapons, or that abortion is murder [or Our Bodies Our Business, or all men are rapists]. We become alert, looking for likely individuals around us to whom we can transmit this crucial meme. When we find one – or a whole crowd of them perhaps – we transmit the whole bundle of information. If the listeners' minds are fertile, which is to say susceptible or receptive, they are inseminated by the meme. They cry *Aha!*, they cheer, they agree with us. They are infected by the meme and immediately want to transmit it to others or help us to transmit it to others by contributing to our cause, signing petitions, attending demonstrations, purchasing our record or book. The meme has been propagated. We are filled with a rush of pleasure, satisfaction, a sense of having fulfilled a mission, as our brain pours out rewarding neurochemicals.

It is this sense of mission and its sensual reward that compels ideologues, preachers, actors, artists, entertainers, writers [and feminists] to devote enormous energies to speaking or performing from every soapbox, stage, pulpit and podium they can find. This is the reward that keeps many school teachers passionately engaged in what are otherwise pitifully underpaid and difficult jobs. This is the erotic reward so many people find to be better than sex. Meme-spreading – hormonal intoxication.

Meme spreading is "idea orgasm", a mental concept that induces a physical response in our brain's pleasure centers, but is not necessarily keyed to anything else we do. Haven't we all met people who crinkle their nose at pork but admit they love bacon, or gush about saving whales while they douse their yard with petrochemicals, or rhapsodize about rain forests while they change their baby's paper diaper. Haven't we all done it ourselves? It's called hypocrisy – not walking the talk – and our lives are riddled with it.

Culture is comprised of memes. In fact, that's what culture is: an assortment of memes. Memes are what we maxi-brained mammals have to work with, and the whole point of this book is to introduce some new memes to American culture because the old ones aren't working. Women and men are not equal. The divorce rate is 60%. The American family exists only in cereal commercials and novels from the 1930s. We don't have one moment to waste getting our thinking straight on male/fe-male issues. I'm thrilled to hear that certain new experiments in education are posing imaginary relationship difficulties to young boys and girls, and asking them to offer solutions or approaches to the problem based upon the varying sexes of the participants in the problem.

It's time for us to wrestle with some concepts which may not seem just or fair, but which may, in fact, be the truth. I don't want to live in a world run by Japanese, and I don't want to live in a world run by women – and for the same reasons. Computerized meme-spreading has organized the world vastly beyond my ability to appreciate what is happening. Life is NOT better when it is more organized. Life is better when people leave each other alone. That is the male meme. We don't need to nurture the planet. We need to leave it alone.

Communism and Feminism are soul brothers. Both are systems devoid of God. Both are programs for organizing society on the basis of glorious egalitarian philosophies but which, in fact, benefit only an elite group of people – the party bosses or Feminist Media Celebrities. No woman's life has been improved by going to work a "job" for forty hours a week. The richest country in the world should be perfecting meaningful ways to NOT work – and what are we doing? Sitting around computer terminals, hacking information, burning out our eyeballs and irradiating our gonads. Father Nature doesn't like that. And what is all this information about? Who cares? More information is not the solution to our problems. Living with less, instead of TALKING about living with less, is the solution to our problems. The Third World has told us they'll stop cutting down their forests when we turn off our air conditioners – and that's the point, isn't it? We cannot have infinite expansion on a finite planet.

So how have the memes that invaded our minds managed to perpetuate themselves? Michael Hutchinson takes us to a deeper level of the problem.

Says Hutchinson:

The central law of meme evolution, as in gene evolution, is survival of the stable. Our intellectual universe is populated by memes that have survived, or maintained their stability, through their power to make copies of themselves by leaping from mind to mind. This power is related, first, to their tolerance for competing memes: memes that carry intolerance messages regarding competing memes will soon carve out a larger evolutionary niche in the meme pool than will memes that contain tolerance messages. For example, a meme that carries the message that it is the absolute Truth, that this Truth must be propagated, and that any memes carrying competing messages are false and must be eradicated, would have evolutionary advantages.

In addition, the survival of memes depends on their ability to replicate themselves without copying errors, that is, on their *predictability*. To maintain their stability, memes must be intolerant of error, violation, or mutation; alterations become heresy.

Memes that generate incorrect copies of themselves – that get "misunderstood" each time they leap from mind to mind – would, like the message passed along in the child's game of "telephone", tend to degenerate rapidly and disappear from the meme pool.

So there is a curious irony here. The very evolutionary breakthrough that liberated us from slavery to our genetic programs – our skill at manipulating information – simultaneously shackled us to another master. In freeing ourselves from the domination of our genes, we became subject to the domination of memes. That's why we're pig-headed – all of us. That's why we resist changes in our thought and why we get intoxicated with causes.

Men and women hold competing memes. Gender diversity begins way back in our biology and expresses itself through our play and work. Neither male nor female meme system can be considered right or wrong in and of itself. Each deserves the honor and respect of the opposing system because human life is dependent on the constant interplay of these competing systems weighing and reevaluating changing circumstances. As I said earlier, "work" in the modern world has become largely feminized. There are few jobs women cannot do as well as men – although women routinely shun dirtier, heavy labor jobs. And yet the overall thrust of performance is bound to be different if you have a woman rather than a man doing the job. The female product is going to be much better researched and more detailed, more analytical, more logical. The male product is likely to be a creative mess supported by intuitive hunches that are correct more often than not. Most jobs today issue from logic. Intuition is not in high regard in the classroom or at the computer terminal. But the person who is gauging the likelihood of rain before he plants 500 acres of corn has to fall back on an educated hunch. If you're redesigning a modern city from the ground up, get a female architect. If you're designing a city under the sea, get a man. What are we saying? That women are not creative? Then why are art classes comprised of 80% females? Because women, biologically endowed with superior fine motor skills, have an easier time controlling brushes. For drawing horses or flowers these are perfect attributes. But if you are trying to capture the soul of a Bolivian shaman, better take along a man.

Margaret Mead said it best: Women are essentially the same all over the world. The problem in any culture is to figure out what to do with the men. When, as in the American ghetto, the system dispenses economic power through women (AFDC), men become obsolete. They posture like proud peacocks seething with anger and hostility toward other men and toward the very women who support them with love and foodstamps. This same scenario, the disempowerment of males resigned to a feminist regime, could easily erode American Jewish males if they did not run off to the synagogue or B'nai B'rith – the havens of the "patriarchy", the place where the guys go to get away from the women...Simplistic examples? Possibly. But allow the meme to settle in. There is something important to understand about how religious life gives men a rallying point. The shattered cultures, the cultures where the priests are the spokesmen for women's values, are the cultures in the gravest danger. Priests in dresses marching around inside stone castles scaring children – it's not good enough. Nowhere in the Bible do we hear about Jesus laughing. Buddha laughed, Krishna laughed, Zeus laughed. Jesus did too. Over thousands of years "civilization" has been geared to eroding our male birthrights – crushing male spirituality. As Fr. Richard Rohr says, religion is the safest place to avoid God. God teaches self-surrender and religion teaches self-control. It's time to rediscover and reinvent what it is to be a man. I promise you the priests and the courts aren't going to do it for us. All of us have been infected with feminine memes.

Says Hutchinson:
Our susceptibility to infection by memes is at an all time high. A key cause for this has been the enormous increase in anxiety and powerlessness being experienced as a result of forces such as environmental devastation, economic confusion, metastasizing poverty, and the proliferation of nuclear weapons. In addition, our resistance to meme infection has been dampened by a quantum leap in the speed and effectiveness of meme vectors or means of transmission. Virtually every person on the globe can now be exposed, directly, quickly and repeatedly, to virulent memes by radio and television. Computer networks, telephones, portable audiocassette players, fax machines, photocopiers, VCRs, automobiles, vast highway networks, and jet travel also contribute to the spreading potential of memes. Nothing in evolutionary history has equipped humans to deal with the sheer quantity of infective memes they are exposed to every day. It is like a long-isolated tribe suddenly exposed to invaders carrying a huge assortment of virulent germs to which the natives have no resistance.

When I was a kid all the faces on TV were men. Now they're all women and manholes – even sportscasters. We are being hourly bombarded with gossip and snippets of information about how to do things that nobody is actually going to do. We've been bestowed the Fix-It-Philosophy, that if the President just does this or doesn't do that everything is going to be wonderful or awful. The media is guilty of government by gossip, and who are they serving? The people who do the shopping. The women.

So here's the answer to the question that every man wonders about:

Q. How come we live in a society that APPEARS to be run by men but FEELS like it's run by women?

A. Because, like viruses, FEMALE MEMES have invaded our psyches. Men's psyches, women's psyches, children's psyches. We live in a world designed by and for female values – female memes.

Empowerment is surrender. What? Yes. That's it. Empowerment is surrender. That is one of the fundamental paradoxes of life, and, says Richard Rohr, truth without paradox is not truth. If you want to be empowered as an attorney you surrender to the metaphysical whimsy of preparing for the Bar Exam. If you want to be empowered as a mother you surrender to the needs of your child. The ego-driven locomotives of the feminist movement have never understood these simple life principles.

Sally Quinn, writing in the Washington Post, Says:
Is it possible that feminism as we have known it is dead? I think so. Like communism in the former Soviet empire the movement in its present form has outlasted its usefulness.
The feminists, and by that I mean the people who spoke for the movement, were never honest with women. They didn't tell the truth. They were hypocritical. Not surprisingly, when Steinem used to say, "A women needs a man like a

fish needs a bicycle", the women who believed her felt ashamed and guilty.

Betty Friedan wrote *The Second Stage* several years ago, a courageous book espousing the concept of motherhood. This was something which, unbelievably, had gotten lost on most of the feminists who thought having babies was not the politically correct thing to do...

(Among normal women) there was always the suspicion that, like the commissars who preached sacrifice to their comrades and bought their caviar at the party store, feminist leaders were publicly telling mothers of three it was great to leave their husbands and be independent – and then secretly dressing up in Frederick's of Hollywood for their guys. It was the hypocrisy that turned off mainstream women...

Whoever the new leaders are, whoever emerges to speak to the real issues confronting most women, will not succeed unless they are willing and able to acknowledge and address the basic question – the "human factor".

Sally Quinn understands memes. She knows that it often takes extremists to kick off a movement, but she also knows that a maturation, a ripening, is required to sustain any agenda. We are, all of us, in search of a new gender meme – the meme that informs us with the right to be different, the right to be human. No sense being locked into either feminism or machismo, and yet, if we don't appreciate the basic differences between the sexes we are expecting apples to taste like peaches. Our perceptions are clouded by warped memes.

We are wounding some of the most vital people in our society – Men – by impressing them with false memes. Men are becoming incredibly dysfunctional. Society stabs us in the press, bulldozes us in divorce court, ridicules us on TV. The heroes that were held up for us turned out to be junkies like John Lennon, or pill addicts like JFK. We are seeking affirmations for the living values of our culture and not finding them.

Who or what are we up against?

Says Ruth Benedict in *Patterns of Culture*:

Those who function inadequately in any society are not those with certain fixed "abnormal" traits, but may well be those whose responses have received no support in the institutions of their culture. The weakness of these aberrants is in great measure illusory. It springs, not from the fact that they are lacking the necessary vigor, but that they are individuals whose native responses are not reaffirmed by society. They are alienated from an impossible world.[18]

Think about it. Who in our government or churches affirms the right of a man to walk naked over the prairie shooting rabbits with his homemade bow and arrow? No one. We've created entire industries to raise children and make pots and deliver water, all formerly female occupations, and no one but no one in the church or the government or the business community even considers the spiritual and psychological value of creating wildlife refuges for men. It's not part of the meme.

We are all seeking affirmation and somehow some insidious meme monsters have convinced us that affirmation is a paycheck. SICK! The money meme. Portable greed. The perfect shopping tool. Forget pointed sticks, give the girls money.

Minorities and women have convinced America that the wrong people have the money. That may or may not be so, but that IS NOT the problem with this country. The problem is that we worship money. It's a disease. The ghetto rioters in Los Angeles in 1992 had better food, medical care, transportation; more freedom and more entertainment than 95% of the people in the world. They were shrewd enough not to burn down the Post Office which is where the welfare checks came to. So what was their problem? Aggravated desires. Lusting after all the stuff they saw on TV. The advertising meme. Pornography.

I watched it happen in Tonga. A simple, wholesome yam and fish economy invaded by VCRs and within five years the violence and alcoholism and sheer greed of the people has become frightening.

Empowerment is surrender. How do you empower yourself? Give up trying to control the events of your life, says Gurudev, speaking out of 5000 years of Hindu wisdom. Life is about something more than pursuing ego-driven self-interest. Those are not my rules. Ask any shaman. Those are Life's Rules. Check out every culture that ever existed. The wholesale pursuit of self-interest was considered a crime in most of them.

Feminism is a *mater*ialistic pipedream, like communism. It doesn't work except on paper. It's only agenda is power, the lust to exert control. There is no thought of operating for a greater good or serving a Higher Power other than the Great Body of Feminism, *Mater*, the *Mater*ial. Doesn't anyone ever risk telling these college girls that liberated women are *no* happier and often much more miserable than traditional women? Capitalism doesn't work. Communism doesn't work. Feminism doesn't work. What works? God works. The spiritual life is proven over 5000 years or more to bring inner peace.

You don't like the word "God"? I can't fault you for that. No concept in human history has been more abused. The Chinese teach of Yin and Yang. The Greeks discourse on form and matter (*Mater*). In Indian philosophy *prakriti* is matter, the physical, the feminine; *purusha* is spirit, consciousness, masculine. If you don't like to think about God think about this: the purveyors of spirit and consciousness and form and yang energy have always, in every culture, been men. In cultures separated by thousands of years and thousands of miles the vessels of the spirit were always men.

And what kind of culture did we grow up in? The men were removed from us. In an article by Janet Saltzman Chafetz we detect the beginnings of the cultural confusion.

Says Chafetz:
Female babies learn to do things by copying mom. Given the relative absence of male figures during his waking hours the male toddler is hard-pressed to find out what he is supposed to do...Dick must identify with a cultural definition of masculinity that he pieces together from peers, media, and a series of "don'ts" from his parents...Dick has to make the mental effort to comprehend what he is supposed to be...And...

Males develop greater problem-solving abilities because of this early mental exercise. Moreover they become more concerned with internalized moral standards than females, who rely more on the opinions of others.[19]

It is surely a significant observation that boys develop internalized moral standards more readily than girls. I'm glad it was a woman, describing the process of being raised by women, who came up with this one. Absence of the father, incomprehensible complexities from the mother, drive the young man out onto the ball field to make sense out of life. Fish swim and boys play games. On the playing field he is away from mom's manipulations. If he does something good his mates cheer, if he does something stupid they yell at him. To the extent that boys listen to their peers more than they listen to their dads every American boy is responsible for reinventing society. It is an awesome responsibility – a rudderless ship. The ones who find a higher meaning make it across the sea of Change. The ones who get stuck in *mater*ialism do not.

America expects too much of its boys. According to poet Robert Bly, the love unit most damaged by the Industrial Revolution is the father-son bond. Fathers are the ones with the Spirit, the ones who dispense a vision of how to live – not what you are going to be when you grow up – that's mom. And fathers are the ones who, through job commitments and divorce and feminized education, are being ruthlessly excised from the family unit.

The school used to *mean* the church, the temple, the mosque. Boys went to school to learn how to read the holy language so they could read the holy book so they could learn how to live the values revered in that culture. School was where boys went to learn how to be men from men.

And what is school like now? School is where boys go to be shamed by women. School is where boys go to learn how to be men from women in the absence of God or religion or clear value systems. When I talk about feminization and secularization and *mater*ialization of society I am talking about the same thing. These processes are equivalent.

According to Patricia Cayo Sexton in *The Feminized Male*:

The feminized male, like Kennedy assassins Lee Harvey Oswald and Sirhan Sirhan are "nice" guys; quiet, controlled, dutiful sons – whose male impulses are suppressed or misshapen by overexposure to feminine norms...

Though run at the top by men, schools are essentially feminine institutions from nursery through graduate schools ...Women set the standard for adult behavior and favor those who are polite and clean.[20]

And what of the male teachers? Undeniably there are many fine men and there need to be more in a country where 85% of all teachers are white women, but, a man who is less than a man can be more damaging to boys than a domineering mother. And the chance of hiring feminized men in schools is fairly high because those eligible and willing are those who made it through a feminized school system in good standing without conflict or failure.

Methods of school instruction require little more than passive receiving and repeating. Learning is passive and feminine. The boy sits, listens, reads, writes, repeats and speaks when spoken to. School bores some boys and feminizes the others. They are rewarded for hewing to female norms. Boys who are boys have a troubled time in school...[21]

Most boys have friends and hang out in groups.[22] Gangs of boys are 300 times more common than gangs of girls.[23]

Boys clubs seem to know more about how to educate boys than teachers, schools, or child study experts.[24] Boys learn by doing. They solve problems by being "in" them. Boys are united in flocks. It is almost impossible for them to avoid teamwork. Girls seldom get together in groups above four whereas for boys a group of four is almost useless.[25]

Says Jules Henry in *Culture Against Men*, in boys' groups the emphasis is on masculine unity; in girls' cliques the purpose is to shut out other girls.

School is the place where boys go to be shamed by girls. It's *never* happened before in history. Schools set boys to competing with girls in subjects like handwriting where girls have, as we have seen, a biological fine-motor advantage. Girls aren't required to pass baseball, where boys' visuo-spatial aptitude gives them the advantage, but boys have to pass handwriting.

On a Sioux Indian reservation, Says Sexton:

> The misconduct condemned by authorities is a badge of honor for the boys...By the time he finishes eighth grade the Sioux Boy has many fine qualities: zest for life, curiosity, pride, physical courage, sensibility to human relationships, experience with the elemental facts of life, and intense group loyalty and integrity – *none of which were learned in school.* Nor has the school managed to teach any of its values: a narrow and absolute respect for "regulations" and "government property", routine, discipline, diligence.[26]

What is the future of these vital human beings? Menial jobs and alcoholism, while women and manholes plot their grief on computer screens. We are making the American man and the Native American man obsolete.

We are killing off the very people who led their families across the land bridge from Asia 12,000 years ago as well as the men who took the ancient Greek ideal of Democracy and made it live again in a New World after 2000 years of dormancy. We have been invaded by the meme which asserts that the more organized society is the better it is. The better for whom?

Women and manholes.

College is the haven of middle class culture and feminized behavior, says Sexton. Boys who survive college are the ones who have been successfully feminized:

> A preschool boy grabs toys, attacks others, ignores teacher requests, wastes his time, asks for unnecessary help, laughs, squeals, jumps around excessively, is more tense at rest, stays awake in naps, breaks toys, rushes into danger, and handles sex organs more than girls. [No doubt the periodic onslaught of male hormonal secretions has something to do with this hyperactivity.] The preschool girl is more likely to avoid play, stay near adults, dawdle at meals,

suck her thumb, avoid risk, fear high places, refuse to eat, twist her hair, and be jealous.[27]

An obvious feminist bias in the classroom is the meme that a physical blow is sinful or uncivilized whereas humiliating people and assaulting them with verbal blows and shame is perfectly OK. Any male would rather be punched than shamed. The punch goes away, the shame doesn't.

Male suicides outnumber female 70% to 30%. The suicide rates for women and non-white men remain consistently low throughout life…In mental institutions boys outnumber girls 3 to 1.[28]

Considering there are 200 miscarriages of boys to every 100 miscarriages of girls, there are more males brain-injured at birth, and that blindness, deafness and epilepsy are commoner in boys, it is amazing there are any men left at all. Real men are as rare as bald eagles and just as worthy of saving.

Says Sexton:

Schools have feminized boys mainly because society turned education over to women and feminized men after 50,000 years of letting men do it. The ensuing secularization and ignorance of male values is appalling. For instance, girls typically see no dishonor in "brown nosing" and usually even fail to see it for what it is [a military expression for shoving your nose up the captain's you know what]. The boy code regards most forms of apple polishing as unmanly. The male code of honor also tends to discourage many forms of cheating and to favor conduct that is open, honest, and above board…Many schools and academies are dehumanizing and unmanly places. Boys who succeed in them often do so by grossly violating many codes of honor and the norms of boy-culture.[29]

And then, in an astounding leap of prophecy, writing in 1969, Ms. Sexton announces, "The computer looms ahead as a feminizer of males. Computer programming and operating are essentially clerical jobs" – bean counting. Says she, "Many males who seem shriller than the most shrike-like women I have known are attracted to the business."[30]

Computers operate logically. They are a system for organizing columns and amounts and bits of information – like recipes and measuring spoons and bags of different flour. Get it. That's the underlying assumption of all this computer madness – that life is some kind of recipe and all we have to do is just get the information right and everything will come out just fine, just like a cake. Life is not a cake! Life is not a problem to be organized. Life is a mysterious paradox to be experienced in all of its sacredness and fullness. You can't do that by working at the same desk collating the same information for 30 years. You have to get out and get dirty once in a while.

I have just spent one week trying to get some information out of the Washington bureaucracy and after following up on one phone number after another phone number to another phone number to a fax number, I finally was issued the same phone number that I had been given to start the whole pointless loop. These people are getting paid for this! It's beyond comprehension that all these female voices could be getting paid all this money to provide all this useless information.

The Information Age is the Feminist Age, make no mistake about that. Sorting, counting, organizing information, has always been a female *forté*. The idea that we are going to live in a society where everyone just spends their day passing information around to everybody else is obscene. Who the hell is going to do anything? How is anything going to get done? Property can be bought and sold without realtors. Disputes can be settled without lawyers. But for paint to appear on a wall someone has to actually pick up a brush. To fix the hole in the roof someone has to get up on the roof. What this country needs to light a fire up its wazoo is a one-week strike by anyone who considers himself a "real" man. That would be more devastating than Hurricane Andrew and the San Francisco Earthquake all rolled up into one. Just one week of real work not getting done. Out with the manholes, up with the men.

* * *

And why don't we do it? Why won't we men revolt for one week? Because men are addicted to praise.

Esther Vilar in *The Manipulated Man* Says that the manipulation of men begins when they are born:

> Mothers, with some fantasy cut-out in their heads of what boys are like, and suffering from the deficiencies of their husbands, set about to make junior a perfect little man. He is such a "good little boy" when he learns to pee pee inside the round white hole and resists smacking the cat with his toy bulldozer. Mothers love their daughters, but they wax with pride over their sons. They immediately set about trying to make them into everything the husband is not...

> The mere fact that a man is accustomed from his earliest years to have women around, to find their presence "normal", their absence "abnormal", tends to make him dependent on women later in life. Dad is a character that comes and goes, but mom is the rock in junior's life. He learns from her that taking directions from women who act like they know what they are doing is normal. It is almost impossible to under-estimate the psychological power of this early social dynamic. A man's whole notion of security and safety throughout life comes from giving himself to this dependent relationship. Like an imprinted gosling he spends his whole life looking for a certain shape to attach himself to.[31]

We spend our marriages trying to wrest the same affirmation from our wives that we got from our moms, way back when, before we could even "think". Our wives accuse us of trying to get them to mother us and it's true, we are, that's how we were trained. I know a phone-sex vendor in Chicago named Valerie Craft who stated unequivocally that her entire business consists in comforting men in the manner of their mothers. Astounding! But not really.

Says Vilar:

One of the most useful factors in conditioning a man is praise. Its effect is better and much more long-lasting than say, sex, as it may be started early and continued throughout a man's life. Furthermore, if praise is applied in the correct dosage a woman will never need to scold. Any man who is accustomed to a regular and conditional dosage of praise will interpret its absence as displeasure.[32]

Most jilted male lovers and husbands have an explosive mental meltdown at their beloved's infidelities, which is vastly out of proportion to what they are being deprived of. It feels to them as if they are being torn away from their mother's bodies, and indeed, that's just what is going on down deep in their psyches. They are losing the basic unit of security, the emotional lifeline ingrained in them when they were still peeing in their pants. That's why men rage and want to beat people up when their lovers leave them. That's why most breakups involve women leaving men rather than men leaving women. Why would a man leave? After years of adolescent drunken degradation and self-abuse he has an hour-glass-shaped praise-giver back in his life again. That's normal. That's how it's supposed to be. That's what mom showed him.

Says Vilar:
   Training by means of praise has the following advantages: it makes the object of praise dependent (in order for praise to be worth something it has to come from a "higher" source, thus the object of praise exalts the praise-giver to a superior level); it creates an addict (without praise he no longer knows whether or not he is worth something – automatic existential shame – and he forgets the ability to identify with himself); praise increases his productivity (it is most effectively meted out not for the same achievements but for increasingly higher ones). Only mothers and wives, not other men or women, dispense the hugs and praise that men so crave. A boy, like a monkey, will repeat the actions that called forth endearments and, if at any time recognition is not granted, he will do everything in his power, bar nothing, to regain it.

* * *

He will climb mountains or work in coal mines or eat shit,
allowing himself, like a junkie, to be totally shamed. And, says
Vilar, the happiness he feels when praise is restored will already
have assumed the proportions of an addiction.[33]

Shame, that deep feeling of worthlessness and helplessness,
is precisely the result of withheld praise. Regarding my own
mother I've always referred to it as "withdrawal of love". Even
now, 43 years after the fact, she can set off an awful, depressing,
manic, physical grinding in my stomach simply by withdrawing
her love. Clearly she trained me to respond that way eons ago,
before I had any sense of how anything works. In its way, it is
sheer brutality. This is the meaning of Jesus' admonition that
we must learn to hate our mother and father if we expect to find
God – find inner peace. Dependency training is like teaching a
puppy to come on the word "go" and then sending him off on a
walk with a total stranger. The entire phenomenon of praise,
and shame, and withdrawal of love is a very distorted garbling
of signals imprinted in babies' heads. God says surrender your
ego. Mom says hang onto your ego so I can continue to use it to
shame you into doing what I want. Who do you want to believe?
God or mom?

Men have huge unaddressed issues with their mothers – and
they'll kill themselves with drugs, alcohol and bad marriages
rather than confront them. Men always blame the problem on
dad – dad didn't do this or dad didn't do that – but the real
problem is mom. Mom is the one who trained you to mistrust
dad. Mom is the one who trashed dad to your face – behind
dad's back, while he was gone from the house, working his ass
off to support you – so she could bind you more closely to her
needy self. Mom is the one who imprinted you with her flawed,
ego-driven worldview and her vicarious dreams of success. Mom
is the one who controlled you with praise and shame. Mom is
the one who resents your wife for usurping her decades- long,
praise-dispensing leverage over you. What do football players
shout on TV? "Hi mom!" Here I am! Look at me now! I did
what you said! See me! Praise me.

Do you wonder why so many more men than women drink
and abuse drugs? Here is the substance of addiction. We were
strung out on praise early in life and without regular doses of
praise we hurt so bad and feel so useless we have to try to kill
the pain somehow. Ah, that first glass of beer, that first joint,
how it took the pain away!

Responsible older men used to be available to initiate younger
men away from this bondage to women. Without the mental
breakdown that accompanies initiation men remain enslaved to
female praise. It's a fact, and an outrage. We are letting them
rent free space in our heads.

And what do we do for young boys today?

In the Catholic Church we dress them up in gowns like women
and have them eat flat bread. My son, who was bar mitzvahed,
got to put on a symbolic hat and read some Hebrew. What we
should do is take them out into the woods and splash them with
mud and make them kill a chicken with their bare hands – and
then tell them the chicken is their MOTHER! Shame on us for
allowing our society to become so sanitized, so womanized,
that an idea like this seems brutal and without merit. We are all
wearing feminist blinders fixed to our heads with a loving pat
from our mothers.

Says Vilar:

During the first two years of life a mother does not
discriminate between boys and girls. The female infant is
submitted to the same form of manipulation as the male until
the principles of potty training and personal hygiene are
absorbed, but from that moment on, the education of the
two sexes follows very different paths. The older the girl
grows, the more highly conditioned she becomes to the art
of exploiting others, while a boy is increasingly manipulated
into becoming an object of exploitation.[34]

Girls are given dolls and boys are given train sets. While
boys are learning to keep the wheels on the track girls are
scolding and praising their dolls just like mommy does to
them. Thus, the boy will become adept at manipulating the
physical world and the girl will become adept at manipulating

him into manipulating it for her. Why should she bother to learn how to change a tire when half of the earth's population is knowledgeable and eligible to be manipulated into doing it for her?

Watch children play:

A boy is bending over his dump truck in a sandbox making BRRR-BRRR noises, lost in a powerful, satisfying meme of the *moment*. A little girl comes over and sits on the edge of the box. She smoothes her curls and begins telling him that someday they are going to get married and live together in a big house and have a little baby, and they'll each have their own car, his so he can get to work, and hers so she can go shopping and pick the baby up from daycare and—

He picks up a handful of sand and throws it at her. She runs off screaming to "teacher" that he hit her for no reason. What has she done to him?

1) She has destroyed the sacredness of the moment by involving him in some futurist plot which instinctively revolts him and threatens his freedom of action.

2) She has yanked him out of the imaginary world of his right brain and thrust him into a left-brain verbal construct that leaves him gasping for meaning. She is not considering a single one of his intimate needs in her plot, and his gonads have not yet started raging to the extent that he actually buys into this shit. Finally he needs to shut if off. He throws sand, which no boy makes much of an issue about. She accuses him of wife abuse and he isn't even five years old yet. Women are always trying to get men to be sensible – that's *their* problem.

As time passes she will gain skill and become subtler in her approach, and once he no longer has mommy at hand to affirm him with praise he will be a walking wound in search of a bandage, a weary eagle looking for a safe place to land.

* * *

Says Vilar:

> No matter what labor saving devices arrive a woman's demands on life will always be *materi*al, never intellectual, *never spiritual*.[35]

Our lives are replete with technical marvels: automatic dishwashers and microwave ovens and hot running water and electric garage door openers. Can it be said that life is any less hectic or more profound, that we have created room for deeper artistic or spiritual pursuits – contemplation perhaps? Is it true that in the absence of beating clothes on rocks and carrying water jugs on our heads we have meditated more on the essence of creation? No. We just chase around faster and faster trying to keep up the payments on all our labor saving gadgets.

Women who move from South America to North America are shocked. South of the border they had other people who came in and did their cooking and cleaning and washing – they paid another human being who took on this tedious part-time work and received a small amount of money, and the Señora forgot about it. Up here the Señora is the one who has to jam the clothes into the washer and dash off to the store and be back in time for the kids and then pop something in the microwave and rush through dinner so she can rush off to work to pay for all these OBJECTS. No. I'm not advocating slavery. I *am* advocating paying other human beings instead of machines to do our work whenever possible; it is *always* the preferred way to go. Fuck machines, hire people.

But back to Esther Vilar:

> Someday it will dawn on man that woman does not read the wonderful books with which he has filled his libraries, and though she may well admire his marvelous works of art in museums she herself will rarely create, only copy.[36]

In ancient societies women worked harder than men providing daily needs, while men studied the stars and built pyramids and made religious art which put them in contact with the forces of life. Then came the Industrial Revolution, when families were removed from the land, and men were yoked with the sole responsibility of providing for the family by manufacturing the pots and processing the cooking fuel that women used to provide.

And what have women done? Put us on the moon? Put us in touch with God? No. They militate for more rights to go to work to buy more objects. Western Civilization suffers from a disease called Shopping. It's a cancer, malignant melanoma of the soul.

Who is left to relate us artistically and spiritually to the deeper reality?

It is known that Australian aborigines work 12 hours a *week*. It is believed that the men who made the cave paintings in Lascaux, France circa 15,000 B.C. worked about 20 hours a week. What did they do the rest of the time? Invent culture. They made art – religious art – art that informed them of the cycles of life and the mysteries of creation. Art that gave them a sense of the sacredness of their world, and that showed them their rightful place amidst the majesty of nature. Is anyone doing that today? Anyone at all? Art to academic in-crowders is a nitpicking discussion of gloppy techniques. They actually believe that art is about how the medium is applied, rather than the human quest for understanding that unfolds the whole process of describing the world through objects. Art is transcendent. And now we watch sociological animal movies on TV that might just as well have been made on Venus for all our ability to relate to them intimately.

We have lost the sense of the sacred in our lives. Women were entrusted with the education of children and what do we have? The objectification of learning. A bunch of stupid rules. If we cannot resurrect the wherewithal to relate ourselves through our art to the world we live in we are doomed to extinction. We don't need more things. We don't need more psychobabble from the mouths of secular humanists. We need images and sounds compelling enough to resuscitate our slums into neighborhoods, to penetrate suburban alienation and the cult of ownership, to inform our children with the sacredness of creation.

But is this how we raise our boys?

Says Vilar:

A male child is constantly praised for everything except playing with miniature human beings. He builds model bridges, dams, and canals; takes toys apart to see how they work; shoots plastic pistols, and practices on a small scale all the things he will need later in life when he is providing for a woman. The more initiative he shows the more he is praised. Woman wants him to develop to the point where he knows more than she does about all the disgusting things she never intends to do. His knowledge must be superior to hers in everything concerning work, for woman cannot survive without man. For woman, man is really a kind of machine, if rather an unusual one. Her ideal, if she could define it, would be a robot capable of thought.[37]

Long before a man is in a position to choose his own way of life he will have formed the necessary addiction to praise. He will be happy only when his work brings him praise and, because he is an addict, his need will increase – and with it, the type of achievement praised by women. Without cheerleaders there would be no football players. When women shun warriors men don't go into the Army. Women love money because they love shopping – power over objects – and they love men who give them the money to have this power. If suddenly women decided they liked tinkerers or fishermen, we would be amazed at the number of miter boxes and fishing reels sold within one week. A man cannot find meaning in life unless he is making an effort to please some woman, even if it's only a babe in a commercial.

Says Vilar:

The male need for affirmation could, to an extent, be satisfied by another man, but as each man is working feverishly in the interest of his own addiction he has no time to help others. Indeed, man exists, as it were, in a state of constant antagonistic competition with other men. It is one of the reasons he loses no time in getting his own private panegyrist, one whose praise will be his exclusive right, someone who will always be waiting at home to tell him when he has been good and just how good he has been. It appears to be only by a stroke of chance that woman is best suited to this role but, in fact, she has been preparing all her life [since way back in the sandbox] waiting to assume it.

It is rare for a successful artist or scientist, for instance, to be able to conquer his addiction to the extent that he is satisfied by another man's praise. If he does so, it is really only women he has managed to escape – never the craving they instilled in him in the first place.

[All this business of glory and honor comes from mom, not dad. Women are the molders of ego.]

Once a particular field of work has brought a man success and financial security, it is uncommon for him to test his abilities in another sphere...his supply of praise might be dangerously reduced. Like Miro and his dots-and-lines technique, Johann Strauss and his waltzes, and Tennessee Williams with his plays about psychotic women, he will stick firmly to his successful technique. The risk of him attempting to be the measure of his own success is too great for him to take.[38]

A lawyer who suddenly decides to write a suspense novel doesn't have a breath of a chance of success without the support of his wife. But John Grisham had a wife who supported and encouraged him. When people talk about the "woman who stands behind the man" what they mean is that even if she did not lift one finger to help him, at least she held in check her vast repertoire of tools with which she could have sabotaged his delicate, uncertain, creative leap. It's not easy for a woman, with limited right brain and no creative disposition, to resist critiquing and manipulating her spouse into more logically productive activity. There are no more than a handful of women alive who can see their way to supporting men's follies when the paycheck stops coming in. Our whole civilization is hooked on a money mentality and it takes a deep spiritual trust in life to relinquish *mater*ial goals to serve male memes, even when you know that the possible rewards could be enormous.

A man is generally delighted to find that his wife is taking up painting or weaving or writing because this means that she has less time for shopping or manipulating him, or arranging romantic trysts. Who cares if the dirty dishes pile up? If she's happy she's not going to torment him.

Says Vilar:

The work of a household of four is easily done in two hours each morning and women live beyond their means at men's expense. [This was true in America throughout the 50s and 60s and then the other shoe dropped.] Left with the leisure time to create great inspirational works, freed from the drudgery of manual labor, liberated from eons of oppression, American woman decided to repair once and for all the pettiness of her life, the vacuousness of her own creation.

Living in some comfortably situated ranch house, surrounded by children, dogs, other women, by every possible kind of labor-saving device, equipped with television sets and second cars, she needled her husband about what a lucky man he was, what a fulfilled life he led while she, "as a woman", was constrained to lead a life unworthy of a human being. She said *this* to the man who had paid for all that trash with *his freedom and his life* – and he believed her!

So? Faced with endless opportunities for creative expansion, the reality of a leisure life that makes men drool, she, woman, made the decision to go to work in the service economy so she could have *more* money. Dig ditches? No. Paint cars? No. Some kind of office work manipulating electronic digits and flying pieces of paper to other desks, sifting through numbers like so much flour.

A society turned belly-up from over-consumption of everything and just what we didn't need was more people going to work in more offices consuming more paper and electricity and gas. In twenty short years of the service economy we have raped the environment and seen the wage scale plummet due to a surplus of workers. DINKS, Double-Income-No-Kids have inflated the prices of real estate and automobiles to the point where *not working* is no longer a real option for married women. Our technical marvels brought us to the edge of a whole new horizon of existence and what happened? We got transported back 8000 years, sucked down into a vortex of *mater*ialism by self-serving feminist revolutionaries. So now they've got jobs. So what? The real ones laughing are the huge corporations. Suppressed wages, more consumers (every family needs two cars now). Global flag-waving, gutter politics. Fat City for the Fat Cats.

What we call the "work ethic" is activity which has no fundamental rest, says Fr. Bede Griffiths in *River of Compassion*.[39] Once we let action take over our lives we are bound by our actions. There is no room for new memes. They are not tolerated. The engine churns onward. It cannot be controlled. And this is what has happened with the entire industrial system. It has released forces which simply control men, reducing them to slaves of the machine. We have lost any sense of the stillness at the center of our lives – except when we are drunk. We are working ourselves into a furor and entertaining ourselves to death.

We dropped the golden ring. We had it. Then we dropped it. A window of opportunity opened in the sixties and was quickly filled with female job hunters after the same old shit. The men told Dow Chemical "we won't go" and so the women went – scabs, strike-breakers, traitors to the very humanist ideals they would have us believe they espouse.

We are wage slaves. All of us. We are separated from the sources of production of everything from food to fuel and thus dependent on a feminized capitalist system to provide it, just as long as we go to work. Forget about raising your own pigs or burning wood – we have covenants and ordinances against that. It amazes me to hear Americans mock Third World dwellers without for a second understanding that these people have more food laying around in their own backyard than they could eat in a year. That's wealth. That's security. It's going to take a lot of ascetic power to keep ourselves from driving off the cliff of our workaholism. But we must find the stillpoint at the center. We cannot have infinite expansion in a finite world.

Says Vilar:

Women invent rules, manipulate men to obey them, and in this way dominate men – but in no way apply the rules to themselves. The "weaker" sex is not bound by honor, justice, or fairness. [A woman's right to change her mind means her right to change the rules of the game while you're running between second and third base. They don't play boy-rules.] Honor and etiquette have no place in women's lives, they live by subterfuge, deceit and innuendo.

Woman is not a Goddess. She is a breathing bag of protoplasm – spiffed up with pink panties and blue eyeliner. She is earth, not sky. Down, not up. Her children are as much a part of her body as her arms and legs, and when she claims to have sacrificed everything for her family it is akin to saying she did everything she possibly could for her thighs and hips.

I had to laugh at Susan Faludi and Gloria Steinem on the cover of the March 1992 *TIME* holed up in an attic like the Weather Underground posing as guerrilla feminists. Good theater, girls, but I *still* crash in rooms like that and it's not a game, not a pose. Who are these women? Neither of them has ever bothered to have kids. Who do they speak for? The Female Ego?

Says Vilar:

Women really are callous creatures – mainly because it is not to their advantage to feel deeply. Feelings might seduce them into choosing a man who is no use to them, *i.e.*, a man who they could not manipulate at will. Listen to the conversation of young lovers in the park. It is ALWAYS about the female trying to convince the male to do, or not do, something. The first thing a woman wants to know is whether she can manipulate the man. That is the beginning of the relationship, the beginning of "I love you."

But she knows, at the same time, that it is absolutely necessary for "woman" to enact the role of a sensitive being, or man would become aware of her essentially cold, calculating nature.

So, she analyzes the shit out of details of posture or attire or word-usage to field a gross offensive against the suspicion that she might only be thinking about herself.

Says Vilar:
Since her emotions are always faked and never felt, she can keep a clear head. You can take advantage of someone's feelings only if you are not involved yourself. Therefore, she turns her partner's emotions to her own profit, only taking great care to make sure he believes she feels as deeply as he himself, perhaps even more deeply. She must make him believe that she, "as a woman", is much less stable, much more irrational, much more emotional, than he is. Only thus may her callous deception remain undetected.

In fact, Eleanor E. Maccoby in *American Psychologist*, reports there is evidence that men fall in love faster and report feeling more deeply in love than do women early in intimate relationships…and Sheldon (1989) reported that when girls talk they appear to have a double agenda: to be nice and sustain social relationships, while at the same time working to achieve their objectives. In the same article Ms. Maccoby refers to Gottman and Levinson (1988); and Kelley *et al* (1978), when stating that there is evidence that men, on average, are more conflict-avoidant than women.[40]

Come on. Does any of this come as a surprise to anyone? Men fall in love more quickly and more deeply than women. Women talk out of both sides of their mouths; they always have two things going on when they talk. Men like to avoid arguments more than women. Open your ears. Walk into any bakery or butcher shop, close your eyes, and listen! Through double-signals, deception, and feistiness women create discord that they expect men to repair, "to show me you love me." This is not helpless emotionalism; this is analytical manipulation run wild. Baffle them with cowshit. And men, the deep lovers, put up with it.

Says Vilar:

A macho man does not weep or laugh very loud; he never shows surprise; he does not show when he is making an effort; he does not even sing when he is happy. Therefore, if a man notices all these emotional reactions in a woman, she strikes him as being free and spontaneous and it never occurs to him that he has been conditioned by a woman not to express his own similar feelings. As a result he assumes she is much more sensitive than he is. What an advantage a man would have if he only realized the cold, clear thoughts running through a woman's head while her eyes are brimming with tears.[41]

Let us begin *now* to relocate the center of gravity of the human personality far, far back onto the male end of the continuum. By the unequivocal admissions of Esther Vilar, a woman, a physician, born in Argentina and practicing medicine in Germany at the time of her writing; and from the research of Eleanor E. Maccoby; and from our own lifetimes of observation; let us recognize and establish and conclude that *men feel things more deeply than women!* The only remarkable thing about any of this is that we would expect it to be any different. A Female Meme has been telling us for centuries that women are more emotional than men, but who are the passionate artists? Who are the passionate musicians? Who are the passionate inventors? Men, men, and more men!

We don't put words on our emotions. We don't cry as often as we should. Our words get stuck in our throats and our tears get stuck in our eyes, but the emotions, nonetheless, run deep. Very, very deep.

Women are emotional faucets. A woman can insult the intestines out of her husband, brush on some eyeliner, go to a dinner party, and have a wonderful time, meanwhile leaving the poor man writhing in pain all night. And why does he keep coming back for the abuse? Because he needs the praise that mom taught him to need. And he needs sex.

Says Vilar:
The need for sex is so strong, and its fulfillment gives man such intense pleasure [and an endorphin release at the center of his brain] that one suspects it may be the primary reason for his enslavement to women. His longing for subjection may even be a facet of his sexual make-up.[42]

Valerie Craft, the phone-sex vendor, certainly agrees that it is. The sheer number of cross-dressers she handles astounds her. "They all want to dress up like mommy", says Valerie.

Says George Gilder in Sexual Suicide:
Women control not the economy of the marketplace but the economy of Eros: the life force in our society and our lives. What happens in the inner realm of women finally shapes what happens on our social surfaces, determining the levels of happiness, energy, creativity, and solidarity, in the nation. Conventional male power, in fact, might be considered more the ideological myth. It is a ploy designed to induce the majority of men to accept a bondage to the machine and the marketplace, to a large extent in service to women and the supposed interests of civilization. Female power comes from what women offer or withhold. The woman can grant a man the sexual affirmation that he needs much more than she does; she can offer him progeny otherwise permanently denied him; and she can give him a way of living happily and productively in a civilized society that is otherwise *oppressive to the male nature*.[43]

When men and women are equal, women are more equal than men because they control reproduction. Gilder goes on to suggest that it may have been the desire for love – to gain the wherewithal for marriage – that precipitated the Industrial Revolution. Does anyone doubt that? Why would a sensible man, concerned with his own health and sanity, go off to work in a coal mine or a stinking, smoking steel mill five days a week? Who convinced us this was living? Who benefited from it?

Women with babies.

We have been enslaved by praise and sexual promise.

Says Vilar:

The basis of our economy is a barter system. Therefore, someone demanding a service must be able to offer something of equal value in exchange for it. But as a man must fulfill his sexual desire, and, since he tends to want to possess exclusive rights over one vagina, the prices have risen to an extortionate level. Monogamy was not conceived by man. That was the barter system at work. He was allowed exclusive rights to one vagina, but only one vagina. And who dispensed these rights? Women, supported by their enforcers, the clergy [manholes of the Church]. This made it possible for women to follow a system of exploitation which puts the most ruthless robber barons to shame. It is the female partner in any relationship who exploits the male: for to be female means to be undersexed. Thus, not needing sex, women can wield it as a weapon, dispensing it or withholding it according to what they can receive.[44]

Says George Gilder:

Differences in sexual compulsiveness (need) means that a woman's decision to pursue "illicit" sex represents a more significant violation of love. It indicates a more deliberate repudiation of the values of the ordered sexuality on which the social system depends...To uphold the double standard is merely to recognize the greater responsibility borne by women for the sexual perquisites of a civilized society. It is to acknowledge the greater sexual power and responsibility inevitably exercised by women.

Says Vilar:

Just as a woman denies herself depth of emotion, she denies herself a sexual appetite: how else can a young girl tell her boyfriend she loves him but refuse him her body? What is she talking about? What does she mean by love? Thanks to her mother's advice, a girl will suppress her desires even in puberty for the sake of capital to be gained later.

And then came abortion – where even mistakes could be fixed. The Abortion Issue has virtually nothing to do with killing unborn babies. It is a raw power grab by middle-class women. Ghetto dwellers don't want abortions because when they have babies they receive AFDC and other government handouts. Have enough babies and they can move out of mom's and get their own place.

According to a friend of mine who works in a Florida State HRS (Public Aid) office, young pregnant girls come in and sit across his desk glowing with anticipation and the certain knowledge that they have "arrived" as he explains to them how much money they will get while they are pregnant, and how much they will get once the baby is born. These girls don't want abortions. They want money.

The women who battle for abortion rights are the ones least likely to need an abortion. For them, this is a political power issue. They want control. They want to control their lives and their destinies, not in the service of a God or a Life Force or a Higher Power, but according to what they feel is beneficial to themselves – whatever strokes their egos and "empowers" them. They want to remove men from any decision-making regarding the bearing of children. These types of women were known to the ancient Greeks as Amazons.

Certainly abortion is warranted in some few instances of rape, or where clear danger to the mother or child is present, but this cannot be used as a blanket political rationalization to grant power over a fetus' life or death. When men and women are equal, women are more equal than men because they control reproduction.

And on top of that, in America and Europe, men's libidos are constantly being aggravated and stimulated. Soda ads, short skirts, magazine covers, beer commercials, ruthlessly stimulate his sex. His relentless exposure to things feminine keeps him in a constant state of sexual arousal – a testosterone nightmare of cruel pervasiveness which is not known in "primitive" societies.

But man, himself, is never dressed in such a way as to awaken sexual desire in the opposite sex, and considering his craving for sex and the examples set by cock pheasants and peacocks, this is a very curious circumstance. Who made these rules? Women? Or manholes?

> Says Vilar:
> It is very much the contrary with woman. By the age of twelve she is already disguised as bait. The curve of breast and hip are exaggerated by tight-fitting clothes, and the length of leg, the shape of the calf and ankle, are enhanced by trans-parent stockings. Her lips and eyes beckon, moist with make-up; her hair with gleaming tints. And to what purpose if not to stimulate the male.[45]

Stimulate him to do what?

Work. What else?

Vilar says that "I love him" means he is an excellent workhorse. Is she 100% right? Of course not. But she is right enough to encourage us to relocate the center of gravity of the human personality far, far back into the male realm. The female perception of life is *deadly* to men and great for women and babies. We need more balance in this. Fewer wars, fought over fewer mineral and petroleum resources, to satisfy fewer *mater*ialistic desires.

Men are stupid to imagine that women think the same way they do, or even that they have men's interests in mind. They don't. That's what gets us into trouble. When a man says "I love you" he's thinking about what he can give her. When a woman says "I love you" she's thinking about what she will get. It's a perfect match, as long as you understand what's going on.

> Says Vilar:
> Women keep men in a continual state of sexual excitement so they will demand the reward again and again. One of the

results of this female system of sex rewards is that a man with strong sexual needs must be more obedient to women than others: look at the advertisements for dynamic, enterprising, energetic, enthusiastic young men, so much in demand in business. What are such men, in fact, but sexually dependent psychopaths who have set their standards in women too high? Why else would a man use all his energy and imagination to sell tires or toothpaste? Only for this reward? The whole world outside his office window beckons him with the promise of adventure; yet so strong is his sex drive that he forgoes all that is out there and instead buys himself a women with his hard-earned money.[46]

She praises him, she affirms him, she takes his money, and he's addicted to it. This is the manhole. The man more committed to female values than indeed, even women are. He is compliant to any demand as long as he gets laid. Give him a blowjob and his ethics disappear. He is a traitor to the male bond, the pride of hunters. He is a modern alienated man and he has been *made*, manufactured, by modern woman to service her demands for even more *mater*ial convenience, or else! We have allowed it to happen to us. It is not women's fault, *per se*, and anyway we can't expect them to change. They never have. They probably never will. They're still pursuing the same *mater*ialistic goals in the same *mater*ialistic ways they have been following for 2.2 million years. It's not their fault. They're born like that.

Women are, by no means, lesser creatures. As we have seen, biologically, they are the fundamental unit of the human species.

Says Vilar:
    A woman only says she is worth less than a man. She doesn't really believe it for a second. Women allow men to revel in their supposed powerlessness. Women let men work for them, think for them, and take on their responsibilities – in fact they exploit men. Since men are strong, intelligent, and imaginative, while women are weak, unimaginative, and stupid, why isn't it men who exploit women?

Could it be that strength, intelligence and imagination are not prerequisites for power but merely qualifications for slavery? Could it be that the world is not being ruled by experts, but by beings who are not fit for anything else – by women? And if this is so how do women manage it so that their victims do not feel themselves cheated and humiliated, but rather believe themselves to be what they are least of all – masters of the universe.

How?
Praise?

The world runs like it does for the benefit of women and children. Men cleave to their agendas. No man wakes up and asks, "What do I want to do today?" He says, "What do I have to do today?" He is an emotional junkie starting each day by servicing the agenda of the praise-givers and sex-bestowers. He has no center in his own life that has not been infiltrated by his sex partner. He is a servant, a trained performer, pursuing the gratification that his mother and his wife have hooked him on. Why do you suspect mothers-in-law and wives don't get along? They're both competing for the same praise/manipulation territory in their son's/husband's brain.

Here is how Esther Vilar begins her book *The Manipulated Man*. The first chapter is called The Slave's Happiness:

The lemon-colored MG skids across the road, and the woman driver brings it to a somewhat uncertain halt. She gets out and finds her left front tire flat. Without wasting a moment she prepares to fix it: she looks toward the passing cars as if expecting someone. Recognizing this standard international sign of woman in distress ("weak female let down by male technology"), a station wagon draws up. The driver sees what is wrong at a glance and says comfortingly, "Don't worry, we'll fix it in a jiffy." To prove his determination he asks for her jack. He does not ask if she is capable of changing the tire herself because he knows – she is about thirty, smartly dressed and made-up – that she is not. Since she cannot find her jack he fetches his own, together with his other tools. Five minutes later the job is done and the punctured tire properly stowed. His hands are covered with grease. She offers him an embroidered handkerchief, which he politely refuses. He has a rag for such occasions in his toolbox.

The woman thanks him profusely, apologizing for her "typically feminine" helplessness. She might have been there 'til dusk, she says, had he not stopped. He makes no reply and, as she gets back into the car, gallantly shuts the door for her. Through the wound-down window he advises her to have her tire patched at once and she promises to get her garage man to see to it that very evening. Then she waves and drives off.

As the man collects his tools and goes back to his own car he wishes he could wash his hands. His shoes – he has been standing in mud while changing the tire – are not as clean as they should be (he is a salesman). What is more, he will have to hurry to keep his next appointment. As he starts his engine he thinks, "Women!" One's more stupid than the next. He wonders what she would have done if he had not been there to help. He puts his foot on the accelerator and drives off – faster than usual. There is the delay to make up. His car skids slightly on the slick road surface.

After a while he starts to hum to himself. In a way, he is happy.

I don't think there is a man alive who has not been through this exact scenario. We could add up at least some 100 million flat tires that were *not* changed by women. Women make us happy by getting us to do things for them. We love to do things for them. They make us feel needed and worthy and not shamed. And they do it by exploiting us. That's OK. There's nothing really wrong with it. But by God, it's important for us to understand what's going on here. Working women want to bring home a paycheck so that they can pay men to fix their cars and their faucets and their roofs, and not have to be beholden to a husband to get the job done. But the point is, how much women's work can this society absorb? How much can we dish out for appraisals, and education, and news, and gossip, and generalized information peddling in order to pay for the nuts and bolts of our existence? The answer is: certainly a lot less than we are dishing out right now. Our society doesn't work.

Instead of expecting women to get married we have now rigged it so that they can do basically meaningless, unnecessary jobs, get a paycheck, and pay men to do their dirty work. And men are happy to do it, because they have child support and alimony checks due to some other woman if they want to stay out of jail. We are caged animals. We're not getting laid. And we're still making everything happen. It cannot last.

Are we beginning to get the picture here? Women don't beat clothes on rocks anymore – like they still do throughout *most* of the rest of the world. I've been there. I've seen it. Women do not work with asbestos or tar. Machines do their housework. They live longer than men. They get paid to do "information" jobs. They fire their husbands and get other men to do the husband's work. This is the biggest scam in the history of humanity! Women work less and get more than they ever have in the entire history of life on earth – and they're not happy about it.

According to Vilar:

Women live an animal existence. They like eating, drinking, sleeping – even sex, providing there is nothing to do and no real effort required of them. The female allows the male to serve her in bed just as he does in every other sphere of life. Men suspect that women tend to exploit them during intercourse and have developed a certain fear of female sexual appetite...Since the discovery of oral contraceptives this fear has reached almost hysterical proportions.

In truth, reliable oral contraceptives, (invented by a man, naturally) have robbed man of the only triumph left to him in his state of sexual subjugation. Previously, woman was always to a certain extent at his mercy. Now she is suddenly, totally, in control. She can have as many children as she wishes. She can select the father, rich if possible. If she has no intention of having children she can indulge in intercourse as often as it appears advantageous to her. And beneath it all she still contrives to create the myth of feminine depth of feeling and vulnerability.

A woman will feel happy when she has an orgasm – but a cocktail party or buying a new pair of aubergine-colored patent-leather boots rates far higher.[47]

The standards of the Church are always the standards of women. Jesus Christ and Gandhi are idealized states of manhood which normal men – because of their slavery to their instincts, sustained by media and women – are never able to achieve. These demi-humans confirm men's suspicions that all qualities truly worth worshipping are feminine.[48]

If Jesus came to earth to be a man he had to get laid, and he had to laugh. Or else he wasted the whole trip. Eighteen years out of the middle of his life – from 12 to 30 – are missing from the record books. Someone buried whatever they found out about him a long time ago. Mahatma Gandhi was a wife beater. How about that? Even the saint of non-violence had his limits when it came to yapping wives. We have only been given part of the story – the female part.

Says Vilar:

Men are made to feel guilty for being over-sexed. Yet, in reality, neither women nor their chosen police force, the clergy, are really interested in man's sexual drive. The taboo did not have to apply to this particular instinct. They merely chose it because it is man's greatest and purest pleasure. Had he derived as much pleasure from smoking rope or eating mushrooms woman would have equated these with sin. The point is to keep him in a constant state of sin (fear) and thus open to manipulation. Moral authority can only be the product of moral inadequacy – somebody else's moral inadequacy.

This is one of the reasons why the catalogue of sins varies according to age. For a small child the taboo is lying, stealing toys, not listening to mom and pop. For an adult the taboo is the sexual drive – wanting to jump in bed with the neighbor.[49]

Yet, how can men recognize these sins when they know neither the rules nor the system in whose name they were established? How can they believe in something that does not exist, or feel ashamed of a pleasure that does not hurt anyone? [And right here, Esther Vilar, for all her compelling observations, stays true to female form – how could it be any different? – and treats spirituality as a product, a logical input from our chronically limited natural senses. But don't be mistaken. I LOVE her for it. At least it's honest.] For anything that deals with religious beliefs is contrary to the rules of reason and consequently, has to be instilled at an age when a sense of logic is as yet undeveloped. If possible, this should take place in a building whose absurd architecture and design equal the absurdity of that which is preached in it, thus making it all a little less incredible. And the purveyors of this illogical thinking should, if possible, look different from other people. If children are taught by men who dress like women, for example, or who adopt some other form of masquerade, their pupils' bewilderment and awe will be all the greater, and their respect for these figures will never entirely leave them.[50]

Women have taken great care to ensure that their lobby, the clergy, are always men. First, because the female image might be damaged if they represented their own interests – men might think them calculating – and second, because they know men rate feminine intelligence rather low, which is why they can only influence a man's emotions. Advice from another man, and one respected from childhood, is much more likely to be listened to and taken. Although this advice always benefits women (a priest will advise a man to stay with a woman he doesn't love or support children he never wanted) it does not reflect hostility on the part of this holy lobby toward "normal" men, but is a direct consequence of that lobby's financial dependence on women.

Women could easily survive without the Church (they only need it for the training of men and children, or as a setting for the display of specialized wardrobes), but the Church would be ruined without the support of women. Children can be trained and today are often raised without the Church's help. It is entirely possible that women one day might give up the nave of a church as the most effective background for a white dress. They might even consider a registrar sufficient to subdue a nervous bridegroom. If this became the fashion, people would see churches for what they really are – relics of a long-dead age. And they would withdraw their financial support, both public and private, which in the last analysis has always been provided by men. It is man who pays his own tormentors. So when we hear someone say what magical power the Church has, since it still draws people to it after many hundreds of years, the circumstance has obviously been misunderstood. It is not the Church which possesses a magical power – it is women. All such institutions have long since become mere tools in the hands of women, and it is unlikely they will ever do anything other than fulfill women's expectations.

God bless this woman. She shoots the priests right in their behinds. The Church has no room for male spirituality. The Church is a feminist institution and so is the synagogue.

Mystics from St. Francis of Assisi to St. John of the Cross to Teillhard de Chardin to the Quietists (whose approach to spirituality was to sit around being quiet and listening to God) have never been welcomed by the Church bureaucracy. Monasteries like Melk in Austria, supposedly devoted to poverty, control vast tracts of land, gold, jewels, gourmet restaurants, cellars crammed with the finest wines, and tuition-generating schools.

Says Vilar:
Ultimately, the victims of this feminist cadre in the driver's seat of the purportedly patriarchal religious are not the members of the various religious communities themselves. The monks and priests only want to live a peaceful, undisturbed life, away from women (at the expense of

masculine men – just like women). But they have become a kind of Mafia used by women to terrify children, enslave men, and put a brake on progress. These men are forced, under threat of boycott, to appear in ludicrously effeminate clothes, to intone grotesque songs loudly, and to tell horror stories even to sometimes intelligent audiences. All this despite the fact that these stories, by which they make such abject fools of themselves, have long been discarded by modern technology and stand in obvious contrast to all they have been taught as students at the university.[51]

In the previous paragraph Esther Vilar has made several points for me at once. She confirms the feminist control of religion and annihilates these institutions with logic, another female weapon. She exposes priests as manholes who live off the wealth created by real men. And she notices, along with us, that what is missing in all this is a spiritual pursuit that is of and for men. Men, the carriers of the Spirit throughout the ages, have been put to work with tractors and shovels to create the wealth which is garnered by women and priests. It's like a science fiction nightmare. But it's real.

Men have been hobbled by female institutions and mocked and ridiculed when they go off into the woods for a weekend to play drums and get in touch with themselves. Manholes in the media make fun of this, afraid to face the extent of their own feminization, afraid of the merest hint that they are devoid of male spirituality. Meanwhile, Jungian analysts gather around us in the woods trying to sell us archetypes based on prehistoric crapola. To the high priests of psychobabble it's just something else to sell, just another way to make a buck without getting dirt under their fingernails. We escape from them long enough to bake in a sweat lodge and howl at the moon and retch out all the symbolism and memes, to arrive in a purely intuitive place, a male place, a homecoming of the soul. But as soon as we throw aside the tent flap the analysts are in our faces again, telling us what we just learned; putting it into words; feminizing it for us within seconds. Manholes.

Male spirituality is *still* alive, despite all the forces trying to kill it off, and despite all the forces trying to sell it to us. Male spirituality is for free. You don't need to pay anyone for it. It's not for sale. The logicizing and computerizing and *Jung*ification of our world have taken their toll, but there is still room for the man who has the courage to pray to a flower, or hunt a pheasant, or create a poem, or swim in a muddy pond. They have not killed us off yet.

Says Vilar:

Modern Theology, of course, is useless for conditioning purposes now that it has renounced the carrot-and-the-stick principle. Women needed those moth-eaten tales of heaven and hell, of devils and angels, of paradise and judgment day. Death is only a useful means of manipulation if it is a door leading to eternal happiness or eternal damnation. Into which of these two realms this door might lead is dependent on a kind of a point system, scored according to earthly achievement, and calculated by women. If life everlasting can be won with faithfulness and slavery it falls in with the interests of women.

Women themselves are, of course, quite unmoved by all of these myths. They go to church only if and when they want to. Their consciences do not bother them either way.

Esther Vilar, speaking as a woman and a mother, has popped the bubble of female intentions and demonstrated to us how women use the church and the synagogue as their enforcers. She made these observations in 1972 and they are still very true today, judging from how my ex has raised our kids.

But nowadays we see a lot more of a certain kind of woman I call the "self-consumed woman". The self-consumed woman is young and pretty and may or may not have children. Her vision is always set on some distant spot located over the horizon which is somehow never attainable, and she is seething with frustration right now because of that. Hang out on a college campus. The place is full of women like this.

If she is married to a carpenter she is having an affair with a sculptor. If she is married to a sculptor she is having an affair with a carpenter. It doesn't matter. She is never happy and heedlessly drags her lovers and family down into this pit of anxiety with her. She thinks nothing of trashing other people's minds with her problems. There is no pleasing this woman because her only knowledge of satisfaction is self-gratification. She is the one who wants to save the world because, having equated herself with the world through New Age memes, she assumes that is the best way to save herself. These people are dangerous and probably should be knocked up or sent into the army. Her life mission is to be a journalist or a lawyer, never a carpenter or a truck driver. She obeys no Higher Call and her word is worthless because, though she strives to be logical and accurate, at the core of it all, she is lying to herself. She is consumed with her "Self".

Says Vilar:

In contemporary society, where all labor is divided, each man must be able to work with, and rely on, the other. If men were to take to lying when the moment seemed opportune, say in matters such as train schedules, freighter's capacities, or the amount of fuel left in an airplane's tank, the effect on our commercial system would be disastrous. Within a very short time there would be complete chaos.

Women, however, can lie with a clear conscience. They are not involved in the process of work, so their lies will harm only one person – their husbands. And if the deception is not discovered it is not a lie at all – it is "feminine guile". The only crime which does not come under this heading is physical unfaithfulness, which a man will not forgive… Women talk openly about guile and hand it out as advice to their daughters and why not? It is quite justified since all their comfort depends on it, for they are frequently forced to exploit the same man – first the mother's husband and later, if the mother moves nearby to be near the kids, the daughter's husband. Their whole future depends on whether these men come to heel.

...If a mother tells her child not to lie because it is "bad", he will automatically have a guilty conscience if he does. [Shame.] She does not even need to be specific about his "badness". The child believes her implicitly, is dependent on her, and relies on what she tells him. He believes she would never lie. This is nonsense, of course, for mothers constantly tell their children the most bare-faced lies.

The meme I find emerging here is one of self-service. Men are slaves to women and women serve themselves. For all the talk they make of the sacrifices they endure for other people, and for their children, the female meme is devoted, like all memes, to perpetuating itself through other minds. Woman is the fundamental human unit and woman believes in herself and her agenda with such deep-rooted intolerance for other memes that she is outright shocking. Men are often embarrassed by the strident self-serving their wives engage in. It's just plain embarrassing to watch a person who is so self-consumed. Women do have a right to their opinions. *But men have a right to their opinions too!*, and that is precisely what is being eroded in modern society. How many more TV commercials can they make of the sensible woman explaining to the abstracted man about the right soap to buy or the right food additives to purchase in his breakfast cereal?

Says Vilar:
The ideal of any trainer would be to bring an animal to the level where it is capable of training itself...The world of pop songs is one example of man's efforts at self-manipulation. The best example of conditioning, however, is to be found in the advertising industry. In advertising man does not idealize women from any masochistic tendency. It is purely a question of survival. Only his exploiters, women, have sufficient time and money to consume all his products. To supply the woman inhabiting his ranch house with purchasing power he has no choice but to cultivate legions of other women who enjoy spending as much as his wife does...Then they will buy his goods and keep his wife in

pocket money. This is the beginning of a vicious cycle – a cycle which turns faster and faster until he cannot keep up with it anymore and someone else has to take over [bypass boogie]. There is no getting off and running away.[52]

Ah, the good old days, 1972, when one man working could support his wife and seven kids on one paycheck. Gas was 30¢ a gallon, people still washed dishes in the sink, and the wages in the building trades were the same then as today, exactly the same. And what happened? The empowerment of women. The poor, the oppressed, the discriminated-against, the held-back – the self-consumed woman – threw off her shackles and thrust herself into the race for economic power with such a fury that the pants fell off our economy, the prices of everything quadrupled, and the wages stayed the same, so now it takes four people working to make what one man could make in 1972. When are we going to call this for what it is? We don't need more job training. We are the most over-educated species on this planet. We have two people for every existing job. Education is an illusion. You want to shuffle more minorities and women into the existing jobs? Nothing could please me more. Or let the corporations ship ALL the jobs overseas – that's where we're headed. But let's accept the fact that there will be fewer men working, and because of that fact alone we need to reassess what exactly it is that a man is supposed to do out here. Take the jobs. We don't want them. We're not gonna march. We're going to go hunting and fishing and pray a lot. Just don't call us when the toilet breaks or the roof starts leaking. Get away from the computer screen, grab a ladder out of the garage, and go up on the roof to check it out. We're busy doing other things. We're busy fishing. We're busy praying.

The unemployment statistics we're fed are a joke. In the past 30 years 30 million women and 30 million immigrants have entered the work force. Plus we lost 3 million manufacturing jobs. The number of employed men has fallen from 85% to 74% – one out of four men are out of work. So much for your "official" 5% unemployment figures. The "official" policy of the United States Government is Low Wages. Let me say that again: The Official Policy of the U.S. Government is Low Wages! Bastards like Robert Rubin, Alan Greenspan, and President Clinton – Republicrats – crossbreeds between Republicans and Democrats – who pound their chest about how they represent the "working people", have sold us all down the drain. They have purposely, intentionally, kept the job market flooded to keep wages down. The productivity of American workers has risen 30% in the last ten years, and real wages have not risen a penny. All the profits are siphoned off to Wall Street where the Money Barons snicker, buy private jets, and toss some small change back at the hungry dogs in Congress and the White House. In one dirty deal *AmWay* founders Richard and Helen DeVos contributed $1 million to the Republican National Committee, and then received a $16 million tax break written directly into the tax code. $15 million profit subsidized by U.S. taxpayers? To buy off our own politicians? Is this the *Am*erican *Way*? *AmWay*? You bet your ass. Corrupt beyond belief. The Federal Government spends $400 billion a year on Corporate Welfare and $40 billion on welfare for human beings. And for that largess we get jobs? Jobs? Where? In China?

Who are we kidding with these same old laments about job training and education and becoming computer literate? Truck drivers need to make a Living Wage. Farmers need to make a Living Wage. Carpenters need to make a Living Wage. We can't survive without trucks and food and houses, no matter how many computers we churn out. These people need to make enough money to LIVE! To pay their bills. To raise their kids. And we *need* them to do what they do for us. Our priorities are fucked!

Just the facts ma'am.

These ARE the facts, dipstick.

Well then…back to the facts about women.

OK…We earthlings are wallowing in a spiritual crisis of profound dimensions. A brief survey of history will convince any skeptic that every enduring civilization was built on the bones of a strong spiritual base. Government is a soy-meal hotdog bought and devoured by corporations – and we're tossed the hard tip of the bun. No help there. Science is not enough because science, without ethics, leads to the cannon ball, the atom bomb, and the death laser.

We don't need more stuff. We desperately need people who are willing to live with less stuff. An end to feminine manure-spreading. An end to corporate-driven consumption. An end to *mater*ialism. We need some man to take off his clothes and walk stark naked into a N.O.W convention holding a sign that says FIX YOUR OWN TOILETS! We need people to lead us into the simplest values at the core of life. Dump the Feminist Meme. It's a disease of willfulness and consumerism. It's merely somebody's selfish dream to lay waste to the environment in order to provide themself with their own pile of consumer garbage. It's killing the planet and it's killing the men. It's ridiculing the meaning of life under the guise of justice and equality. Yes, you have an equal right to fix your own toilets. Go do it.

The dis-ease that we're experiencing today has been going on for some time.

Says Vilar:

Every few years a wave of indignation sweeps over the male ranks as a result of this expensive fostering of the female craze for consumption. Men have been blinded by the stereotyped image of woman as victim of male exploitation to such an extent that they do not realize that they themselves are, in fact, the sufferers.

A study by Robert Shapiro and Harpreet Mahajan of the University of Connecticut from 1964-1988 found that men consistently support women's rights 3% more often than women do, including abortion "rights".[53]

Says Vilar:

Men maintain that women's naive and gullible, *i.e.*, stupid, natures are exploited by advertisers for the purpose of increasing sales. One day these men will get around to asking themselves who is really being exploited. Is it the creature whose innermost wishes are sought out, coddled and fulfilled? Or is it he who, in his desire to retain the affection of the woman, seeks out, coddles and fulfills them? It has always been one of man's greatest aims in life to fulfill woman's innermost desires, in fact, to anticipate her every wish, as contemporary fiction still puts it. They have achieved their goal: there is practically no female desire left undiscovered and probably very few which could not, if necessary, be fulfilled.

Woman's image is no longer created by women but by advertising. Advertising says that woman is witty, intelligent, creative, imaginative, warmhearted, practical, and capable. This image of woman, created by man to sell his goods, is repeated incessantly with the help of mass media throughout the Western Hemisphere; and each day it is being reinforced. How could anyone dare to admit, even to himself, that in reality women are unimaginative, stupid, and insensitive? It would obviously be too much to expect of women – and it is an admission that men, to retain their coping mechanisms, cannot afford.[54]

Man is caught in a trap of his own making. While outside the struggle for money is becoming fiercer and fiercer, at home his wife is growing more and more moronic, and from day to day his house fills up with more junk and knick-knacks...Men, who in fact prefer the plain and functional, every day find themselves more deeply entangled in the undergrowth of superfluous ornamentation and all kinds of embellishments. In their living rooms the porcelain cats, barstools, candelabra and imported rugs pile up...and if they look for a place to put their razor in the bathroom they have to shove aside shelves full of thousands of creams and dyes and cosmetics.

It is interesting to note that nearly the only products sold are those of benefit to women. Men, historically depicted as the object-oriented half of the species, in fact need and want very few *mater*ial things. A few wrenches, a fishing pole, a couple good books can keep a man occupied for years. Not so with women. Their life means the manipulation of objects. None has been served better by the electric motor or the gasoline engine than the women who now control mega-power with the flip of a switch. From garbage disposals to garage door openers to station wagons to telephones, the cybernetic revolution has benefited [and "empowered"] women far more than men. And are they happy about it? Are they even cognizant of it?[55]

Advertising for men consists of some guys hiring half-naked girls to cause other guys to have erections which cannot be relieved by buying the advertised product, but only can be relieved by buying a woman at the customary price.

Playboy magazine represents one of man's best efforts at conditioning himself. Sandwiched between luscious pairs of naked breasts are excellent articles of a highly theoretical nature to diminish his erections. All of this padded with offers of expensive cars, liquors, smoking jackets, and other unnecessary clothing.

Most adult men live in a state of permanent hell, an emotional slavery enforced by their conditioned fears [which fester untreated in an atmosphere devoid of male spirituality – the historically proven tool for easing fear]. The happiness of women is not only primitive, but obtained mostly at other people's expense.[56]

Yes, now we're getting somewhat of a complete picture. Female happiness usually occurs at someone or something else's expense. More rights for women means less rights for men. More kitchen apparatus means more miners in Peru spending their lives underground in damp ratholes contracting TB. More paper diapers means less trees. Two cars in a family means less oil, higher prices for it, and more pollution in Mexico and Malaysia and Kuwait. Not growing her own vegetables means more petrochemicals sprayed on more commercial crops. More divorces – more broken children. More education – more college educated waitresses, and house painters. Everything on this earth is interconnected and women have a blind spot when it comes to understanding this and moving with this.

In *Fire in the Belly* Sam Keen says, men can't be comfortable in intimacy with women because we have never been comfortable in being distant from them. From mother to wife to daughter we are addicted to their affirmation and approval of us. Most modern men have never learned the joy of solitude. [Contemplation.] We have failed to define our identity, our purpose, our *raison d'etre* apart from our relationship with WOMAN. As Howard Thurman said, we have gotten the questions we ask ourselves in the wrong order. Before asking what our life journey should be, we ask if she will go with us and where she wants to go. And having sold our soul for her approval we are ill at ease...The urgency men feel about sex, intimacy, marriage, and getting things right with women is precisely what creates the anxiety that forces us into relationships in which we betray our manhood and do violence (to ourselves and) to women.[57]

And, as if the male/female dynamic alone wasn't enough of a mess let's toss a couple of kids into the stew.

Says Vilar:

It would be mistaken to maintain that only women are interested in having children. Men want them too. Children are one of the two or three excuses by which they justify their subjugation to women. Women, on the other hand, need children to justify their laziness, stupidity, and lack of responsibility. Both sexes, therefore, exploit the child for their own ends.

Man has a need to explain his enslavement to a particular woman and this is simple. She is, after all, the *mother* of his children. Since woman is the excuse for his subjugation he can only have one at a time (in every industrial culture man is monotheistic, *i.e.*, monogamous); more than one (god) woman at a time would make him insecure, lead him to question his own identity, and throw him back into the state of freedom he is constantly trying to escape. Stripped of a meaningful God responsive to his maleness he is afraid to confront his own life.

Questions about the meaning of life do not interest woman. Since she does not think abstractly the problems of existential anxiety do not touch her. All she needs is an excuse for making one particular man work for her long after he ceases to want to go to bed with her. This excuse is provided by bearing his children.

When a man engenders children he gives a woman hostages in hopes that she will exploit him forever. It is the only thing that gives him some sort of stability [in a godless age] and the only way of justifying the senseless slavery to which he has been conditioned. When he works for his wife and child...he is working for a system which embraces everything in this world that is poor, helpless, and in need of protection [a deep male meme] and which, so he believes, really needs him.

Thanks to his wife and child, man has acquired an excuse, an artificial justification for his wretched existence, for his subjugation. He calls this holy unit his "family". Woman accepts his services in the name of the "family", accepts the hostages he entrusts to her, and proceeds to carry out his desires by binding him ever more tightly to her and blackmailing him until he dies.[58]

And if he doesn't perform in ways that suit her she withdraws his reason for working and for living – the "family". Here is the docile little darling wielding the sledgehammer of DIVORCE. She knows all about it because her friends have all been through it. She threatens him, regularly, with all the power of the courts behind her, brandishing the very real menace of never allowing him to see his kids again – but still having to pay all their bills. No man ever wants to get divorced. When he looks at divorce he is looking at losing his kids, his house, his money, *and* losing his affirming vagina. When a woman views divorce she is looking at keeping the kids, keeping the house, getting most of the money, screwing who she wants, and getting the old man to send her a check every month – or getting him tossed in jail and ruining his business and his livelihood in perpetuity. Who did this to us? Who set up women as the arbiters of what is good and what is right in this world?

Man's advantage in having a family lies in the fact that he appears to lead a more meaningful life, says Vilar, and that he is able to become a slave forever – and the woman has all the other advantages. As if that isn't skewed enough the women and manholes who run the State Bureaucracies collect money outright from the Federal Government *and* deduct a portion from the father's check every time he sends in his child support payment. They make money off our pain. It's beyond belief. These political armadillos are enforcing laws that destroy families, sending us the bill for it, and making their own mealy income out of the holocaust of destroyed homes. And we're letting them get away with it because we're afraid they won't let us see our kids – and they won't. In what demon's name did we cede such power to these beasts?

Says Vilar:

But society has convinced us that women are the nurturing half of the species. Although orphanages throughout the world are full of appealing, needy children, and although the newspapers and TV report daily on the number of little Africans, Indians, or South Americans who are starving to death, a woman would rather give a stray cat or dog a home than a deserted child. And yet she pretends to love children. [She loves children who are connected to a paycheck.]

As far as the "suffering" and "sacrifice" of having children, many women feel healthier, both physically and emotionally, when expecting a child and it is becoming fashionable to admit it.[59]

And, by the time the children start school, most of even a prolific woman's work is done.[60]

Betty Friedan, in her Second Feminist Agenda, (*The Second Stage*), argues passionately for the importance of families.

Says Friedan:

Women must now confront anew their own needs for love and comfort and caring support, as well as the needs of children and men, for whom, I believe, we cannot escape bedrock human responsibility.[61]

However, Ms. Friedan also thinks it is a national disgrace that we don't have national public nursery schools for 2-3-year-olds like France, Australia and Israel.[62] What kind of double-think is this? How can you espouse family values out of one side of your mouth and then turn your babies over to the state to be raised? We need national daycare about as much as we need national dog kennels. More kids will be deprived of their moms for what? So mom can get a job at Wal-Mart or Citigroup? State-sponsored Corporate Colonialism and State-supported Feminism marching hand in hand into the future creating an ever more comfortable world for women, and an ever more onerous world for men. According to poet Robert Bly the angst of modern society is caused by children being separated from their dads, and now Friedan wants them separated from their moms too. For what? So the moms can meditate? Find God? Or just flood the service job market and hold down wages even lower? Everything is interconnected. If you have too many people working no one gets paid enough. Is this stupid or what?

There was a market in Bangkok I used to frequent to buy noodle soup and I recall two old women, sitting in stalls ten feet apart, selling the identical noodle soup, all day every day, and all night every night. They were always there! I wanted to tell them, "Look, why doesn't one of you go home for 12 hours and let the other one have all the business and then, after 12 hours, the one who stayed here can go home; you can switch, AND YOU CAN BOTH HAVE A LIFE!" They don't get it. It's like a missing meme or something.

Says Vilar:

Most men will never admit the depth of their wives' stupidity. They agree that women are not terribly clever, but grant them "intuition" or "instinct" instead. And they like to call this "feminine instinct" as opposed to that of an animal.

Unfortunately this famous feminine instinct is really nothing more than a euphemism for statistical probability. Women interfere and give opinions about everything and, since they are so stupid, they don't realize they are making fools of themselves. According to the law of averages, their forecasts will be correct now and again. In any case, most of their predictions are negative or vague. Banalities such as: "It can only end in disaster", or "I'd steer clear of that if I were you", or "Your so-called friends will only let you down in the end", are meaningless. Anyone would be safe in making such generalizations but men don't talk as much, so less of this stuff comes out of their mouths...And if, occasionally, women do see more clearly than men it is only because their feelings, unlike those of men, are never involved.[63]

One day a Man's Intuition said:
"Let's tie a note to this pigeon's leg and send a message home."

His Wife's Intuition said:
"It'll get lost."

One day a Man's Intuition said:
"I'm going to stretch this string on that bowed branch and use it to shoot a small spear."

His Wife's Intuition said:
"You'll hurt one of the kids."

One day a Man's Intuition said:
"I'm going to carve some paddles so I can row my raft offshore."

His Wife's Intuition said:
"You'll just drown."

If civilization relied on Women's Intuition we would still be living in caves munching cold seeds and listening to them complain about that!

Walt Disney, the artist who "defined" the visual age we live in, was cursed with an "intuitive" wife. When he wanted to invest all of his money into making the first color cartoon she threatened to leave him. When he wanted to make the first feature length cartoon she blustered about divorce. When he wanted to throw everything he had behind a theme park to be called "Disneyland" she enlisted the help of Walt's brother to try and stop him. What a visionary! I think Walt would pee out his ears if he saw what a corporate monstrosity his creations have spawned today, but my point here is that every one of his new ideas set off a fierce drubbing from his wife's "intuition." He didn't cave. Neither should you. Don't argue with them, but just don't listen to them. They have no vision. They are dispassionate, calculating logicians, co-opting forces and creative movements far beyond their ability to understand, and attempting to absorb them in the female meme.

Says Vilar:
Woman's silliness is but the natural result of her attitude toward life.

They know better than we that logic is the bicycle sprocket with missing teeth: it pulls fine for a quarter turn, then skips a few teeth, then pulls for a half turn, then slides around a couple times. Logic and mathematics do not explain nor predict life. If they did we would be able to predict the weather for more than a couple days in advance. Chaos – movement into the unknown, constant creativity – is the axle of the sprocket on which our physical world turns. Life looks for new things, all by itself. The female nature suppresses that quest.

Says Vilar:
Women are not interested in most things that do not have a "female" tag on them. Since the range of subjects likely to interest women is necessarily limited, editors are frequently at a loss for copy. As a result they have to fall back on so-called male themes – and since men's interests are so wide there are plenty of them. These go through a complete

metamorphosis to suit female readers, the main rule of which is quite simple: each article must create the impression that it is basically a report about women. For example, an account of a former heavyweight champion must read: "Women ruined me." If a composer is interviewed for an article he must say at least once that a melody is "like a pretty girl – only not quite so beautiful."

With skill, even the most unlikely subjects can be camouflaged to appeal to women. One can arouse their interest in the defense budget, providing one dresses up the report as an account of the family life of the Secretary of Defense. Women will read articles on foreign countries if the passage begins: "I married an Israeli" (Japanese, Saudi, Peruvian) provided the wife in question comes from the same background as her female readers...Politics interest women only in so far as they involve women's issues. The first political action of any man who seeks power is to marry a photogenic wife.[64]

There are many women who take their place in the working world today...One might even get the impression that women's nature has undergone a radical change in the past decades. Today's young women appear to be less unfair than their mothers. They seem to have decided not to exploit men any more but to become, in truth, their partners.

This impression is deceptive. The only important act in any woman's life is the selection of the right partner. Consequently, she will look for a man where he works or studies, and where she can best observe and judge the necessary masculine qualities she values. Offices, factories, colleges and universities are, to her, nothing more than gigantic marriage markets.[65]

Yes, yes, we are bombarded with media images of independent women but who are they independent of? Man? God? Who do they serve? Their own senses? Their own appetites? Let us remember that although the stories of the Amazons – women who lived on an island without men – were a myth, that is, they didn't exist in the physical world; what these stories represent is a slice of the human psyche, a meme, that surrounds us every single day of our existence. We in Western Civilization are deeply, biologically, socially, religiously suspicious of self-consumed women, and have been for thousands of years. Did the ancient Greeks know what they were talking about? Look around you. Is this society of "liberated" women working? Are kids raised without dads not being raised by Amazons?

Says Vilar:

> The particular field chosen by any young woman as a hunting ground will depend to a large extent on the level of income of the man who has previously been her slave, in other words, her father. The daughters of men in the upper income brackets will choose colleges or universities. These offer the best chance of capturing a man who will earn enough money to maintain the standards she has already acquired…Girls from less well-off homes will have to go to factories, shops, offices or hospitals…None of them intend to stay in these jobs for long. They will continue only until marriage – or in cases of hardship, pregnancy. This offers women one important advantage: any woman who marries nowadays has given up her studies or her job "for the sake of her husband" – and "sacrifices" of this nature create big time obligations. The man is eternally bludgeoned with what she gave up for him and what a rotten choice that was. And it was *all his fault!*[66]

> If a woman leaves the university with a ring on her finger she has earned her degree…If she breaks off her studies and marries a university lecturer she has achieved the same level as him without exerting herself. That doesn't work the other way around for men. The wife of a factory worker is treated with greater respect than he is, and not as somebody who, at best, would be employable on the assembly line in the same factory. As a wife she always has the same standard of living and social prestige and has to do nothing to maintain them – as he does. For this reason the quickest way to succeed is always to marry a successful man. She does not win him by

her industry, ambition, or perseverance – but simply through an attractive appearance.

As soon as the woman has caught her man she "gives up her career for love" – or at least that's what she will tell him…Who knows, he thinks, she might have become a famous surgeon, prima ballerina, brilliant journalist, and she has given it all up for me! He would never believe that she preferred to be the wife of a famous surgeon, to have his income and prestige without having either the work or the responsibility. Therefore, he resolves to make her life at his side as comfortable as possible to compensate for her great sacrifice.[67]

But, it is only the beautiful women who can become emancipated. Plain Jane settles for what she can get. She does not command an array of options in the marketplace.

Yet, the complaint of the liberated one is always the same: even as an emancipated woman one is simply not given the same chances as a man. It would never occur to this one that she, not man, is the cause of this unequal state of affairs – she, woman, with her total lack of interest, her venality, her unreliability, her ridiculous masquerades, and above all, because of her merciless manipulation of men, is the author of this state of affairs.[68]

The husbands of so-called emancipated women are usually extremely unhappy. An emancipated woman is far from being a help to her man. She exploits him even more than the others. He is there simply to provide some sort of launching pad for her to pursue her career or hobbies or the raising of her children. The higher she rises the more restlessly she drives him. If his position is relatively low, every time she gets an advancement or a promotion it will be a traumatic experience for him. He lives in constant fear that she will one day overtake him, and she will. After all, she's not worried about paying the bills; that's his job. She's aiming somewhere above and beyond that. And on top of it all, he suffers constant agonies of jealousy about the strange men she meets every day because she will have affairs with them if they somehow advance her emotional career.

The man who has married the self-consumed career dynamo feels superfluous, and he is; his whole existence seems pointless because she no longer seems to need him. He's looking for some poor helpless thing to protect [in the manner of the male meme that is 2.2 million years old]. The one true happiness of the slave – the only happiness left to the manipulated man – is now denied him.

A woman of this type does not even make her children happy. After all, she is entertained more by her stupid work than by her children. But she is not going to give them up.

And when she divorces her husband she is certainly not going to share the children or allow him to influence their upbringing. Everything he tells them will be ridiculed and diverted. He will have no influence as a father.

Says Vilar:

Woman frees herself from her imaginary "chains" at regular intervals: spiritual ones being unknown to her, she interprets them literally. At the turn of the century it was the corset that went, in the seventies the bra. But their stupidity, their inanity, their ridiculous behavior, their mendacity and lack of feeling, and their tedious and abysmally stupid chatter are still there. Women have never taken steps to get rid of these.[69]

No matter how much the woman is earning she will not let the man take her place in the house, nor will she take on the responsibility of earning the family's livelihood. Her income is reserved for luxury purchases and special activities or clothes for her and her children. She does not countenance helping *him* with *her* money...

There is not a country in the world where men are worse off than in the US...A factory worker's wife lives a life that is luxurious compared to the life of the factory worker himself...In no other country with a comparable standard of living are jobs so tenuous.[70]

In no other country with a comparable rate of unemployment are the demands made by the standard of living as high. The difference between a "success" and a "failure" is nowhere so clearly defined as in the US. Added to these external difficulties is the fact that no other man is so thoroughly manipulated as the American male. The adult American male is manipulated so expertly that there appears to be nothing he would not willingly endure, and indeed, he is exploited without scruple. In no other country do mothers so pitilessly train the infant male to perform. No other society exists where the male sex drive is exploited for money so unscrupulously. Nobody except the American woman so shamelessly professes a creed of profit under the guise of love.

This does not mean that American women are cruel. This simply means that American women, more than other women, fail to consider men as fellow human beings.

And American men prefer to see themselves in this role: a man's salary is the yardstick of his worth. America is the only place where a badly paid professor is a bad professor, and an unsuccessful writer is a bad writer. For the Latin American male, masculinity is still associated with sexual potency. For the American male, however, the association is directly with money.

The American man knows that happiness comes only through women, and women are expensive. He is ready to pay that price. As a young adult he pays in advance, as a grownup he pays in installments, and as a corpse he is cashed in for a fortune. A man from another country realizes this as soon as he sees a flourishing divorce paradise like Reno, or the thousands of his fellow men sitting in jail for overdue alimony payments…A 1972 poll showed that *more* American men than women believe that women are suppressed, and fifty-one per cent of American men believe that the situation of American white women is as bad as that of the American black man.

The American man, more than any other man, mistakes his wife's lack of intellectual ambition for modesty, her stupidity for exceptional femininity, her giving up responsibilities for love. More than any other man he is able to close his eyes to the evidence of his own exploitation.

In America, man is manipulated with much less inhibition than in other countries, hence, women should be even easier to unmask. But the American man does not want to see or know. It seems appropriate to him that in the TV show his children are watching the father is portrayed as a fool, the mother as a star. Wasn't his own mother a star? Wasn't his own father a fool? That a Mafia of women's groups controls all cultural life seems unavoidable to him. Who else has the time? Somebody has to take care of culture...The fact that a majority of psychiatric patients are women, while men have a higher suicide rate, is his evidence for the value of psychoanalysis. He thinks it fair that for generations men have become crippled war veterans, while generations of women do not even know what a hand grenade looks like. Man is stronger and the stronger goes to war.

Since the American woman is the highest paid wife she, of course, wants something in return for her money. Of all women she leads the most comfortable life. More often than her sisters of other nationalities she lives in her own house, drives her own car, goes on vacation, does her work with the help of machines, and uses ready-to-cook food. She has a fully automated household, a bus takes her children to school, and they are gone most of the day. She can take up a job, take up a hobby, or take up a lover.

America has the highest divorce rate and the chance that an infant will grow up without a father is greater than in any other country in the world...American fathers pay the highest alimonies, and since non-payment can be punished by imprisonment, he pays promptly...Even his old age insurance rates are the highest.

One might assume that a prerequisite for the high profit achieved by American woman's femininity would be top performance in other areas, but for the connoisseur, she is neither a good cook nor an experienced lover.

The American woman is no worse than other women. She is only ahead of them. Her unscrupulous tactics for exploitation would not be so dangerous if they were not being constantly idealized by a powerful TV and film industry. As the latter creates the image of Western Woman, her behavior is being copied, and as her standard of living is constantly raised, the fate of her husband automatically becomes the fate of men in other countries.

Why, one might ask, did this uprising of women start in America, of all places, where women are obviously better off? The explanation is simple: exactly for that reason.[71]

The woman who supports a healthy man and his children all her life is practically unknown and this concept even sounds funny to the brain. Women supporting men? Preposterous to the Westerner, but life as usual in most of the rest of the world. Men are sporadic producers, but when they score they score big. They bring back an elephant or they bring in a giant paycheck. Women are the rock, the earth, the center. They hold down the home fort. Historically, women brought in the grain to sustain life; men brought in the fatty game that raised the woman's fat content to the point where she would ovulate and reproduce. Woman brings home the bread. Man brings home the bacon.

Says Vilar:

Intellectual women have not dealt honestly or objectively with the friction between the sexes. They insist that American women are more pitiable and suppressed and exploited than the male brain can ever imagine. These women have claimed a rather dubious fame for their sex; instead of being unmasked as the most cunning slave traders in history, they have undersold women and made them the object of male charity: man the tyrant, woman the victim.

Betty Friedan, Kate Millett, Germaine Greer...each a repetition of the last. They went head over heels in their effort to come up with evidence of male infamy, but they wrote nothing truly worth mentioning on their real subject – women. They copied the male idea about women without recognizing that *that idea was put there by women!,* and thus they became the object of their own manipulations!

So these are the reasons yet another women's liberation movement has failed: the enemies they fought were really their friends, and the real enemies, their own egos, remained undetected. Everybody from the *New York Times* to the *Christian Science Monitor*, from Kissinger to McGovern, from Jane Fonda to Nancy Reagan, lauded the liberationists. [But 30 years later Jane Fonda scratched her acting career because she said Ted Turner was not the kind of husband you left to go on location; he wants you around all the time.] No hard-hat men took to the streets to demonstrate against the liberationists the way they demonstrated against the peaceniks. Why? Because it was another case of female masturbation. Another issue that completely misses the mark. For American society to work women do not have to change men, women have to change themselves.[72]

So says Esther Vilar in 1972 and there we were two decades later asphyxiating under a 60% divorce rate, the biggest riots of the century had recently immobilized Los Angeles and shocked the world by the sheer upwelling of greed and craving – *mater*ial addiction – fueling them. Rodney King goes out one evening to rob a liquor store and a year later they are burning down the city in his honor, to service their own cravings. This is really sick stuff. You wouldn't torture your dog by putting his food in a cage so he could smell it all day long, but not get at it; why do we – why does our media – do this to human beings all day long every day? Tantalize their ears and eyeballs with fantastic vacations, and delivered food, and expensive clothes and pricey cars. Have you ever watched TV when you were on a diet? Your stomach starts making telepathic phone calls to Pizza Hut and McDonald's. It's pornography – feminized corporate ethics which will withhold no tool of seduction in their unholy mission to prod you to buy something. And the arbiters of ethics are the self-consumed women who dominate our schools and shovel their skewed, uninitiated, self-serving philosophies into the minds of helplessly restricted boys. It's obscene.

As Robert Bly has said, the young man of the last 20 years has become more thoughtful and more gentle, but he has not become more free. He has gotten *none* of the things promised him by the Feminists. He has been sucked into a Feminist Meme.

Says Vilar:
     Just as their predecessors, the suffragettes, Women's Liberation saw most of its demands fulfilled immediately. Why? The "outrageous inequalities" in the law had, after all, been established by men to protect women.

Real wages have plummeted in this country over the past twenty years. Ross Perot has said that the 1992 dollar is worth 18 cents compared to the 1952 dollar. The flood of baby boomers entering the job markets have brought us the right of a waitress to work double shifts, the right of a woman mechanic to carry heavy equipment, the rights of women to climb telephone poles, pay alimony, fight in wars.

But, Says Vilar:
     The army of suppressed women awaiting the moment of liberation simply never *mater*ialized. As soon as the first American women had climbed a telephone pole, the first female plumber, construction worker, and furniture mover had been photographed and the photos printed in newspapers all over the world, the uproar died down. Why should it have gone any further? After all, it's not much fun to repair water pipes, to lay bricks, or to lug furniture. Unlike men, women can choose whether they want to do drudgery or not. It is logical that most of them decide against it. And given a choice they will also avoid military service and going to war. Women think of themselves as pacifists [never admitting the clear consequences of their *mater*ial lusts] and wars are imputed to the madness of men [to please women?] despite women's right to vote.[73]

Isn't it possible, even likely, that WW II was really caused by women, who, with their newfound right to vote, could not manage to contain their *mater*ial lusts. If women don't want wars then they shouldn't want more "things", because wars are fought for "things".

With incredible skills of perception and prognostication Esther Vilar anticipated a significant historical consequence. At the time of her writing a countermovement within Women's Lib protested: "We don't want men's jobs. If all women start working now we will have an economic crisis." But women went to work in service jobs and now we're getting 18 cents on the dollar. Two people working can scarcely make ends meet. This is wage slavery. The Feudal Meme trying to reassert itself. Corporate/ Feminist Feudalism.

Vilar goes on to point out another mental gap: how come a "liberated" woman won't willingly go to work to support her husband and children. We're not talking about "house husband" here. Having a man at home is a good thing for shoveling driveways, fixing pipes, painting walls, and repairing roofs. The average working man has no time for these jobs so he hires someone to cover these bases for him. But let's switch the roles for a moment and assume the woman is going off into the job market every day, the man is at home maintaining the real property, and so, the woman uses part of her paycheck to cover *her* bases – *i.e.*, hiring a maid to clean the house and wash the clothes and be there when the kids get home from school. As wrong as this may sound to the ear it is the true obverse of the traditional gender roles. Not men doing women's work, but women paying someone out of pocket to get their work done. This is true role reversal. The man gets to spend a lot of time with the kids and work on the real property. The wife gets to go to work somewhere to pay *all* the bills including domestic service. The husband "manages" the maid just as the wife used to "manage" the roofers; but the wife pays the whole tab.

I have not yet met the woman who would gladly serve as the sole support of her family. Men go to work out of kindness and love for women. Women do not go to work out of kindness or love for men. Their idea of working is to bring more disposable income into the family for gifts and toys, or so that they can purchase a more ostentatious house – and that is what has dri-

ven the price of an average house over $100,000. It's simple
economics. Banks loan money on what people are willing to
pay, and two people can pay more than one, so an object which
should cost no more than $50,000 ends up costing $100,000.
Those are the stark facts about what working women have done
to the US economy. We produce nothing more than we did before and take two people to do it. Had they had the dignity and
grace to go to work and leave their husbands home this need
never have happened, but, as is clear to all of us, this is not part
of the Feminist Meme. Women do not want equality. They don't
want to do what men have been doing for the past two hundred
years of the Industrial Revolution. Work in a steel mill? Pull
people out of burning buildings? Pour cement? Ick! They expect
to stand on our backs and have equality.

Says Vilar:

For women, work has to be *fun*, and to make sure it is,
the employed wife needs a working husband, or at least,
some child support trickling in. If the wife goes to work she
will usually make some demands and one of these demands
will be that she can choose her work and quit any time she
feels like it. She takes her newborn to a daycare center and
would quit working rather than allow her husband to stay
home with the kid.

Women's Liberation has failed. The saga of the under-
privileged woman is an invention – and against an invention
one cannot stage a rebellion. In a country where man is
exploited as unscrupulously by woman as in the USA, a
movement that fights for yet more of women's rights is
reactionary. But, as long as the screaming for female equality
does not stop, man will never get the idea that he is actually
the victim of this farce.[74]

Sam Keen in *Fire in the Belly* has composed a list of
characteristics of women and men, culled from articles in
feminist anthologies that specifically identify themselves with
"nonviolence" and "spirituality". Listen to this:

Women developed agriculture
— Men invented war and technology

Women worship nurturing ecological goddesses
— Men worship destructive divisive gods

Women cooperate
— Men compete

Women are empathetic
— Men are insensitive

Women are person-oriented
— Men are thing-oriented

Women are egalitarian
— Men are hierarchical

Women share power
— Men manipulate and dominate

Women are the saviors
— Men are the problem

Says Keen:

When any people wishes to dehumanize and *sanction the conquest*, domination, or destruction of another people, they inevitably revert to a standard repertoire of images and metaphors. In constructing the face of the enemy, they always portray him as: aggressor, atheist, barbarian, liar, feelingless automaton, sadist and rapist; as greedy, beastly, death-oriented, and conspiratorial. It is distressing to realize how many of these epithets have been pressed into service by the ideological feminists in the recent war between the sexes. As these feminists reconstruct history, the reign of "patriarchy", which is to say all modern history, becomes the story of invasion by barbarian hordes (male), the worship of false gods (male), the practice of profane technology [male?], the destruction of a spiritually superior class (women) by their spiritual inferiors (men), and the rape of all things feminine.[75]

This type of demonic theory of history renders men responsible for all the ills of society, and women remain innocent. It's diseased – infected with female memes.

Women and manholes are the logicians, the *mater*ialists, the consumers, the manipulators. Men are the intuitive, the spiritual, the non-hierarchical team players. What a spectacular whitewash of our mindscapes has been the Feminist Meme.

Keen shows how this memetic virus penetrated our psyches by looking into its collusion with the civil rights movement.

Says Keen:

Early on, many feminists borrowed the categories and buzzwords oppressed minorities and colonial peoples used in their fight against racism and imperialism, to press their case against the "patriarchy" [what we know as the men who wear dresses]. All men, by definition, became guilty of sexism, and all women were victims…But, there is one certain mark of oppression. Oppressors have greater access to comfort and health care, and thus live longer than their victims. In technologically developed nations since early in the 20th century women have outlived men by an average of 8 years. Blacks, as an oppressed minority, have shorter life expectancies than WASPs. It is an insult to the oppressed of the world to have rich and powerful women included within the congregation of downtrodden merely because they are female.[76]

What woman ever died for feminism? What are Gloria Steinem and Betty Friedan doing on the back of the bus with Medgar Evers and Martin Luther King Jr.? This is a media monstrosity as phony as talking soup cans – the Feminist Meme – spreading like a virus and intolerant of other gender paradigms. Have you ever heard a feminist laugh about anything other than the incompetence of men? Feminists are humorless, intolerant, constantly on the defensive, and downright scary.

How many men have you met who are automatic apologists for harm done to women by men who lived *hundreds* if not *thousands* of years ago? This is neurosis. A preposterous attempt to rope us into a Collective Guilt. I am not to blame for witch hunts in New England or wartime rapes, just as women are not individually to blame for the fact that 19 out of 20 people who die on the job are men, or that they live 8 years longer than we do. These guys, these apologists, are some kind of blinded worms who have lost their male identity. They are the "naive men" Robert Bly talks about. They have received nothing from feminism but destroyed families and yet they support it. This is mental illness on a massive scale.

Says Vilar:

A female reader of *Psychology Today* wrote in to say, "It's better to let them think they are king of the castle, lean and depend on them, and continue to control and manipulate them as we always have."

Man has been manipulated by woman to the point where he cannot live without her and therefore will do anything she asks of him. He fights for his life and calls it "love", drowning in a whirlpool of praise addiction.

To a woman love means power, to a man enslavement. "For the sake of love" woman will do things that are only of advantage to herself, while man does only those things that will harm him. For both sexes love is a fight for survival, but the one survives only by being victorious, and the other only by being defeated. It is a paradox that women can make their greatest gains during moments of utter passivity and that the word "love" endows them with the halo of self-lessness, even at the moment of their most pitiless deception of man.[77]

Surrender to win. That's how they do it. The old spiritual approach focused away from God and onto man. It's as old as clay pots. The drama of the vulva.

Says Vilar:

As a result of "love" man is able to hide his cowardly self-deception behind a smoke screen of sentiment. He is able to make himself believe that his senseless enslavement to woman and her hostages is more an act of honor, it has a higher purpose. He is entirely happy in his role as slave [as long as he gets laid twice a week]. But the more man tries to ingratiate himself with her the more demanding she will become, the more he desires her the less desirable she will find him; the more comforts he provides for her, the more indolent, fat, stupid and inhuman she will become – and man will grow ever lonelier as a result.

Only woman can break the vicious cycle of man's manipulation and exploitation, but she will not do it. There is absolutely no compelling reason why she should. It is useless to appeal to her feelings because she is callous and knows no pity. And so the world will go on, sinking deeper and deeper into this morass of kitsch, barbarism, and inanity called Femininity. And man, that wonderful dreamer, will never awaken from his dream.[78]

Whew!

So ends our book report on Esther Vilar's *The Manipulated Man*. It is powerful, disturbing, inflammatory, and prophetic. Are men lonelier as a result of this Feminist Meme, this concocted estrangement from women? I am. And I think I speak for a lot of men when I admit it.

Esther Vilar's analysis is not 100% correct, but it is true enough in its perceptions to boot the center of gravity of the human emotional personality far, far back onto the male side of the playing field. We make a lot of noise about finding "balance" in life and what that means for us right now is loading this container of heavy emotional components, this Male Meme, onto the scale of the human personality so it too can be weighed in the balance. Right now we are working with a scale whose fulcrum is rusted and corroded with female memes. Drop this Male Meme into place and it's going to shake everything loose. The brain-power of Western Civilization has been suffering from a lobotomy affecting its ability to discern the simplest gender traits, traits that are clearly observable, all around us, every day. Women are intuitive? Men are object-oriented? It's a travesty. Junk in, Junk out.

And what is the outcome of all this manipulation? Who is the cause of the angst? Says Keen, most women claim to want good, solid, dependable men, but when they have one, after a time, they come to regard him as boring. The very traits they claim to prize in theory will become the fodder for later resentments. The very clay they molded into the design they wanted has become cold in their grasp. They have killed it. Why? Because they do not know what they are doing besides serving their own *mater*ial appetites. Their willfulness is made out of woman and nothing more. Not God, not man, not eternity. Woman has made man a thinking robot neurotically dependent upon her injections of praise. Yes girls, it's boring being God.

Chapter Three

Male Absorption
Fractured Families
Regurgitated Religion

1) Women look for god inside of themselves.
   Men look for God outside of themselves.

2) The concept of Male Spirituality is
   biologically, right-brainedly beyond the
   grasp of most women.

RELIGIOUS MEMES PERMEATE OUR our lives. Faith, Prudence, Fortitude and many other good human attributes owe their origins to the ravings of religion. I, for one, draw a sharp black line between religion and spirituality. They are not the same. In fact, they are exact opposites. Religion is a psychic swamp. Spirituality is beyond form and sound and words; it's not about ghosts, it's beyond ghosts. As Franciscan Father Richard Rohr says, religion is the safest place to avoid God because God teaches self-surrender and religion teaches self-control.[79]

Much of our everyday thinking comes of and through religion and, since we must start somewhere, let's begin with some simple

175

cultural observations and work toward the concept of a Male Spirituality.

A woman in jeans is not considered a transvestite but a man in a skirt is.[80] Interesting. Isn't that a curious slice of memetics at work? Men who dress like women are queer but women who dress like men are not – except for priests, who are queer anyway. Who is manipulating whom, into what? Can anyone tell? It's some kind of renegade meme. Absorption of the Male.

Even more insidious is a point made by Phyllis Schlafly that the women's liberationist is imprisoned by her own negative view of herself and her place in the world around her. Phyllis Schlafly is the woman women love to hate. Why? She takes on feminist hypocrisy. Says Schlafly, a N.O.W. advertisement in numerous newspapers, magazines, and TV spots showed a darling, curly-headed girl above the caption, "This healthy, normal baby has a handicap. She was born female." Is this "helping" women wonders Schlafly? Or shaming them? Or just getting them riled up about nothing?

I hope whoever wrote that ad has a guru by now. No one with the slightest spiritual inclination would permit themselves to wallow in that much self-pity. This is full blown mind-warp memetics, the spiritual impoverishment of the wealthiest class of people in the world: American women.

Says Schlafly:

> Men are philosophers and women are practical. Men may philosophize about how life began and where we are heading; women are concerned about feeding the kids today...Women do not take naturally to a search for the intangible or abstract.

In other words, since they do not function well in the abstract realms women will constantly draw our conversations back to some kind of pots and pans practicality. It is rare to find a woman who does not strive to manipulate the conversation into her own back yard. Probably the easiest way to identify a manhole is to determine whether he listens to what people are saying to him or whether he is just dropping what is being said into pre-existing slots in his brain – defending the ground of his female-generated psyche. Men are at home with mysteries and paradoxes, tracking strange creatures over uneven mental terrain, following a flash in the bushes or a quirky sound in a hollow. Women cannot stand a mystery that cannot be solved. It shrivels their circuits. They like to have all the furniture in their heads neatly arranged. They're the ones who keep the mystery writers in shoes. It would never have been a woman who discovered the earth was round, although talking long distance via geosynchronous satellite links is right up their groove.

Haragei is a term used by Japanese businessmen. Literally it means "bellytalk". For millennia the Orientals have located the "mind" in the belly. This is the umbilical connection to the mysteries of the universe, the source of wisdom and harmony, the fountain of intuition. Things that are good not only achieve the proper result but, just as importantly, they unfold harmoniously. I don't know if the Japanese practice what they preach anymore but traditionally the *hara*, or belly, has been a focal area in meditation precisely because that is where the diaphragm is located and, by slowing down your breathing, your emotions may be stilled. And when your emotions are stilled your mind is clear to receive messages from those rarefied zones we lump under the word intuition. Men are more prone to and adept at meditation and contemplation. Women and manholes prefer prayer and ritual, logicizing, or other devotional practices with verbal or physical vehicles.

Are we saying that women have no intuition at all? Apparently it has been shown that infant girls respond more readily to human faces, and a study by University of Pennsylvania brain researcher, Ruben Gur, showed that women easily read such emotions as anger, sadness and fear from photographs, whereas the only emotion men could distinguish regularly was disgust.[81] So, women appear to be more intuitive at reading human emotions from photographs. Men appear to be more intuitive at *everything else*. It's a man who spills coffee on his pants one morning and then comes up with the big idea to try selling Chinese typewriters in Venezuela. And it's his secretary who says, "In that case we better get to work"; then she starts calling shipping companies.

So what is the historical dynamic at work here? According to Margaret E. Hamilton marriage was instituted around 500,000 B.C. The primate societies consisting of baboons and Old World Monkeys do not utilize the pair bond. Monkeys don't get married. But, a division of labor based on cultural complexity implies an institutionalized pair bond – marriage. In other words, culture, and all its derivations, is a product of gender diversification.[82]

Patricia Draper says hunting and gathering societies remain mobile. They organize in nuclear groups where knowledge, skills, and decision-making are shared more closely. Women are more autonomous. But in agricultural societies sex roles are very marked, sexes are segregated and organized hierarchically. [The feminist meme.] In nomadic societies children do very little work, but in sedentary societies they are put to work (school) right away.[83]

Agriculturization was nothing less than the wholesale adoption of feminist memes 8000 years ago. Nomadic societies are looser and have less well-defined sex roles. But now, Helen Fisher of the American Museum of Natural History, opens the door on the magnificent schizophrenia of our era.

Says Fisher:
> Men and women are moving backwards to the kinds of roles they had on the grasslands of Africa millions of years ago. They don't earn their living on the "family farm", they go out to work in the concrete jungle. They meet people and fight over elevators and graze on fast food as if picking berries and nuts. They carry their babies around with them and have affairs, for wherever women are economically powerful, divorce rates go up.[84]

So there we have it. We inhabit a thoroughly feminized industrialized society and we are operating as nomads. We've cut down the forests to create toxic industrial hell holes and replaced berry picking with speedy grease-burgers. It's a feminist nightmare.

For 99% of human evolution we existed as hunter-gatherers, not farmers. Women in these cultures probably brought in the bulk of the staple foods and thereby enjoyed enormous clout. Isn't that really it? Power = food. You want power? Bring home a loaf of bread, put it on the table, and share it with everybody including your unemployed husband. And don't be stingy. Don't begrudge him. Don't shame him.

In the Creek (Muskogee) society of recent American history the women owned everything. Any time a man wanted anything he had to ask a woman. So, men had their freedom and women had a way of getting men to do things for them.

Sound familiar? It's like the world after divorce court except for one big difference: if the Creek man didn't need anything he didn't have to go to the woman. No one was holding a gun to his head. There was no court-ordered support to be made. The woman owned everything but she had to offer the man *something* to get him to come to her with the products of his chase. But now we've stripped men of everything and set up the courts as female enforcers. It's insane. It's slavery. People in America labor under this illusion that they are the freest country in the world and it's a crock. We don't enjoy the simplest human freedom: to see our kids without being manipulated by our wives and the courts. We can't raise chickens in our yards. We can't fish wherever we want. Ladies and gentlemen, THIS IS NOT FREEDOM WE HAVE HERE. The so-called oppressed people of the world enjoy vastly more simple human freedoms than we do. We all have termite-brain. Something is dry rotting up there. We are a society that is incapable of enforcing its own values. That's a recipe for extinction.

We have taken the worst of the nomadic and the agricultural ways of life and are building a world out of them. Unlike no-madic kids our kids are in school for twenty years starting as soon as they get out of diapers. They are not producing anything, they are an enormous drain on their parents, and they're not even having fun or learning basic values. Half of them are being raised without dads and have no notion whatever of the male modes of behavior.

And on top of that, all this nomadic grazing in the concrete jungle is directed toward amassing capital in the form of *material* objects and real property. We are nomads with 30-year mortgages! We do not allow ourselves the option of *not* owing things. We're in prison. Feminists are trying to tell us we need to be more nomadic so we can own more things. They want their freedom so they can own more property and have us pay for it. The only solution to this mess is the spiritual solution – don't buy into the Feminist Meme. It's deadly to human life.

That's precisely what Jesus was talking about in the Sermon on the Mount. He asked, who feeds the birds of the sky? Who clothes the flowers of the fields? He was not propounding a Christian Work Ethic. *There is no Christian Work Ethic.* That was made up by some womanized protestant farmers in Europe a few hundred years ago. We are not here to amass property. Jesus was telling us to live now, live like Creek Indian men, forget about ownership. Follow the Deer God – no ifs, ands, or Proverbs about it. Without exception, whenever I bring this topic up, people immediately start rationalizing and qualifying and interpreting it. 90% of the readers who made it this far will be doing that right now. Stop being defensive. Let this in. Christians wake up. Your God says get rid of the junk. Trust the Life Force. Do God's work. He was right then and He's right now. The way out of this feminized mess is to get rid of the junk. Follow Jesus. Follow the Deer God.

In medieval European art Jesus was depicted as the stag: the wild, cautious male deer, whose antlers died, and regrew – were resurrected – every year. The stag was the symbol of the Christ. The stag appears and disappears like a phantom. The stag shows up at Arthur's table and rises to heaven. The stag is the motif of mystery and gentle strength and regeneration.

And what is our Christ today? A bearded lady. A man who floats three inches off the ground as he wanders through settlements enforcing female values. We took God and made Him a woman. And we did it sometime in the past 1000 years. Our holy men are pathetically feminized. No wonder our families are such a mess.

Says George Gilder:

No institution has emerged that can replace the family in turning children into civilized human beings...Yet what is our leading social movement? *Cause celebre* of the intelligentsia? Why it's Women's Liberation, with a whole array of nostrums designed to emancipate us. From what? From the very institution that is most indispensable to overcoming our present social crisis: the family...And the movement is working politically because our sexuality is so confused, our masculinity so uncertain, and our families so beleaguered that no one knows what they are for and how they are sustained.[85]

We need to look at the family because that is the meeting point of the sexes. Without a family, men and women do not have much in common. The normal romantic entanglement that does not produce children lasts about two years. No big deal. The family spans generations.

Says Gilder:

A culture that deprives the elderly of prestigious positions – revered connections with children and grandchildren – is committing a form of sexual suicide, short-circuiting the extended patterns of family in which our sexuality organically unfolds. Children brought up by their peers and without frequent contact with venerable elders come to regard old age as a limbo of impotence. Men surrounded everywhere with cultural advertising of sex as a province of youthful and anonymous curves have trouble adjusting to the inevitable parabolas of their own lives and sexuality. Men who lack experience with fulfilled older people come to fear their own aging.[86]

They grasp frantically at illusions, treading emotions to keep their heads bobbing in the Cult of Youth that is being sold at us every time we turn on the TV. The family is, of course, an outgrowth of the institution of marriage. Lately marriage has come to be regarded as some kind of a contract.

Says Gilder:

To treat marriage as a contract is to destroy its *raison d'etre*. A marriage is a commitment of two people not to exchange products and services, *but to escape the psychology of exchange altogether*. Each person serves the other not in the expectation of specific gain, but in the course of serving the larger unit formed when they come together...Every time one conceives of the partner in terms of what he can do for you rather than who he is, one erodes the subjective sources of love. The marriage is slowly absorbed by the marketplace [*mater*ialism], until in divorce court it is entirely subsumed by a contract of barter.

We get married in church and divorced in court. We allow our most divine human institution to be degraded into motions and depositions, our most sacred bond to be secularized in the deadening logic of Feminist Memes.

That is why men have come all the way around to painting their faces and beating on drums. That is why we created rituals and initiation rites – to snap the logic and connect the initiates to the sacred ground of their psyches.

In marriage rites found in some primal cultures, a lamb is brought face-to-face with the bride-to-be. The girl is told that she is this lamb. Then the lamb is bludgeoned and stabbed and slaughtered. She cries. But she never forgets the message. The girl is dead so that now the woman may live.

Says Gilder:

During initiation rights found in hundreds of cultures men ritualistically reiterate the processes of childbirth. The boys are brought into a great womb-like structure; they are ministered blood, as if through an umbilicus; they are fed, as if from a mother's breast; all before being issued in great tumult of sound and movement into the world of men. The purpose of the ritual is to show that though women make babies, it takes men to turn boys into men. Because of their less-grounded sexuality, because men are not the fundamental unit of the human species, males must be incorporated in specific and exclusive tasks – not to accomplish the business of society, but to accomplish and affirm their own identities as males. If such roles are not given to them they disrupt the community or leave it.

There seems to be no point in entertaining the idea that women are going to flee the workplace and head back to the kitchen, but if men cannot be affirmed as men in their jobs then they need to begin looking into other areas for affirmation. Clearly the spiritual realm holds out such promise – not through the feminized religious institutions of our time – but through a vital, deeply intuitive penetration of the mysteries of creation. Men *need* spirituality to explain and survive life. Men used to inhabit – and nomadic men still do inhabit – a sacred world, where every rock, every tree, every animal was joined through myth to a timeless creation: what the aborigines still call "Dreamtime". In Dreamtime normal time is suspended and all myths, all stories, all legends happen *now*. Nothing may be moved or changed by man without affecting Dreamtime. The world was a sacred place and had to be respected as such. Changes made were recognized as changes made for all time.

And now we live in a man made world of glass and steel and nature shows on TV which inevitably end on some saccharin note about how pollution is devastating the habitat of the beaver, but never once reach deep into Dreamtime and pop out with the statement that the beaver is a sacred creature and when we kill it we are killing ourselves, we are killing our Dreamtime.

Says Gilder:

> We may find that the success or durability of a society is less dependent on how it organizes its money or how it produces its goods than on how it arranges its sexual patterns. The Industrial Revolution required a Draconian imposition on males that they relinquish their sexual freedom and spontaneous compulsiveness of masculinity in order to play their role as key providers. [A role formerly performed by women].[87]

* * *

Overnight, men were made to feel that their identities were not dependent on religious rituals or hunting parties but on work and responsibility for a wife and children, since the little lady didn't spend her time growing beans or canning tomatoes anymore. The price for continued participation in industrial society is ever increasing emasculation and alienation. We all know this. We've seen it in our dads' faces. We've suffered through it in our own divorces. But what do we do about it?

Some men turn violent. Rollo May asserts that violence is the result of impotence grown unbearable. The problem of violent men occurs in a society inadequately affirmative of masculinity: a society seduced by an obsessive rationalism and functionalism – a cult of efficiency and a fetish of statistical equality – which militate to eliminate many of the male affirmations employed throughout history.[88]

Having babies is more important to men than it is to women. That's right, *more important*. Men like to feel potent, but men need to have someone to nurture. Having a baby grounds a man. It allows his gentle side to emerge. It makes him get responsible. It gives him a reason to be. Men who have not been fathers are vastly less complete individuals than women who never became mothers. Nothing touches a man deeper in his heart than the birth of his first child. Nothing ever completes him as much.

Reproduction does not belong to women alone. Child rearing does not belong to women and their schools alone. Men need to be included in the raising of their children – if for no other reason than to coax the men away from becoming violent fuck-ups. We are not just beasts of burden assigned to work shit jobs and mail in our child support checks.

Men deserve automatic unequivocal rights to their children. In a divorce, two or more kids should be divided between both parents. Yes, that's right, forget all the noise about splitting up the kids. Too many women, on their lawyers' advice, automatically accuse the husband of child abuse so they can get custody of the kids. And too many judges, faced with believing the wife or believing the husband, reflexively side with the wife because that is the safer course. If the husband is right, only he gets hurt, but if the wife is right the kids might be hurt. Judges don't like to make decisions. You'd think that would go with the job description but the fact is that the last thing a judge wants to do is actually stick his neck out and make a decision. So he "sides with the kids" as they like to say. But the fact is that 95% of the time the wife is lying and just wants the guy out of the house and away from the kids so 95% of the time this seemingly high moral ground of hurting the man and not the kids is a *wrong* decision. It is much more damaging to the kids, and to the dad, and to society, for the kids to be removed from their dad rather than for the kids to be removed from their sibling rivals. Let the dads have half the kids.

Also, in this scenario, visitation trade-offs are insured, thus relieving the courts and fathers from unending hassles about visitation. Ex-wives won't be so likely to leave the state and thereby leave one of their kids behind. And the overall divorce rate is sure to nosedive as women begin honestly looking into marriage counseling as an alternative, rather than hastily filing for divorce when they get bored with the old man. Give the dads half the kids – automatically – without a court battle over it. Start from there. That should be the point where negotiations begin. Even if he's a junkie, or if she's a junkie, let the worried spouse take court action to have her opponent's rights to the child suspended. Some kids will get hurt, but not nearly as many as are being splayed and damaged for life by the divorce debacle. Fewer kids will get hurt when men have more rights to their kids. And fewer men will become raving maniacs and saboteurs of society when their God-given right to their children is protected rather than abused by the courts. Men are socialized into mainstream society by their children. Men are taught how to live by their children. Kids need men and men need kids. Is this headline news? What are we doing, wearing shoes on our ears?

Says Gilder:
What is happening in the US today is the steady erosion of male socialization. From the hospital, where the baby is abruptly taken from its mother; to early childhood, where he

may be carted off to daycare and placed in the care of a woman; to the home, where the husband is frequently absent or emasculated; to the school, where the boy is managed by female teachers and excelled by girls; possibly to college, where once again his training is scarcely differentiated by sex and he is often bludgeoned by feminist agendas; to a job, that is sexually indistinct; through all these stages the boy's sexuality is subverted and confused.

The man discovers that society offers him no distinctive roles. Society prohibits, restricts, or feminizes his purely male activities. It is increasingly difficult for him to hunt or fight or otherwise assert himself in a male way. Most jobs reward obedience, regularity and carefulness (female traits) more than physical strength and individual initiative. If man attempts to create rituals and institutions and secret societies like the ones used by similarly beleaguered men in primitive societies he finds them opened, by law, to women. If he fights he is sent to jail. If he is aggressive on the job he may be fired or accused of sexual abuse.

All the while women are castigating the "patriarchy" of the church and he is believing them, even though he knows in his gut there is nothing masculine to be found in the church. What's left? The religion of sports? Now there are female football announcers.

WHAT IS A MAN?

A buffalo hunter on a plain where the buffalo are gone.

A fisherman in a lake where all the fish have been poisoned.

A worshipper of gods whom others laugh at.

A feeler of powerful emotions that have no name.

A lover of women who wear jeans and talk smut.

A father of children who are trained to fear him.

A supporter of minority rights which has put him in the minority.

A seer across universes who is scorned by his own children.

A shaper of roads and buildings and jet planes who must be careful what words he uses around women.

A poet who is chastised for wearing the wrong colored socks.

A shaman who has surrendered his will to the Universe and is browbeaten at the dinner table.

A father whose children are legally removed from his influence at the age of six and placed in feminist fishtanks.

A lunar neural circuit imprisoned in solar time.

Someone who cries on the phone when he talks to his son and sings with laughter when he talks to his daughter.

Someone who endures rain and mud and paint fumes and tar and humiliation, who walks steel girders on the 122nd floor and dives in a bell compressing the nitrogen in his blood stream, looking for oil on the ocean floor – all for a fifteen minute blowjob at night.

Someone who has worked on the side of the road with a shovel while the faces on TV news have changed from men to women.

Someone betrayed by his lover, cuckolded by his wife, jeered by his children, and instructed by the court where to send the check.

A pterodactyl in an age of birds. A swan in a swamp of geese.

A creature who could make his way in the world with a blanket and a pocket knife, who has been preyed upon to buy his family a 3-bedroom house and a garage full of toys that they take for granted, and he paid for with his life.

A beast of burden moving rocks and shouting at eagles while women sit in climate controlled offices making appraisals, editing news, advocating policy, and complaining about men.

Lost is the hunter, lost on the plains, somewhere between the kitchen sink and the TV, stalking a moment of peace.

We live in a matriarchy. Female memes rule by law and by insinuation. It's a war out there.

Says Gilder:

As a general rule of history and anthropology man cannot be expected to remain an integral member of the family unit if his role is visibly inferior to that of woman. His [memes] require open subordination. In a matriarchy he will not endure this inferior status and will almost always leave.[89]

* * *

And if he doesn't leave he will be so despised by his spouse she will leave him. Men have been solicitous providers for women for millions of years. Men protect weak females. It's in their memes. Women do not protect weak males – they despise them. Women are not solicitous providers for their men. They don't have any idea what that role would be; historically, biologically, sociologically, memetically, they aren't equipped for it. *And that is why they will never lead this, or any other society*, until they can show that they are responsive to the genuine needs of their men. Right now, we're upholding their dignity while they squat peeing in our shoes.

The totality of what feminists are yearning for is acquisitiveness and selfishness. There is no higher motive in any of this. Any ruler, anyone who wants *power* the way Susan Faludi claims she wants it, must be kind to her subjects. If she isn't, she's beheaded. It's simple. It's happened plenty of times before. Without exception, self-seeking, would-be rulers with no appreciation for what their subjects want, do not get to hang out on the throne for very long. Even Hitler made his ascension by pandering to the greed and the fears of the German people of that time. Feminists haven't figured it out yet that rulers, whether they are rulers of the household or rulers of the corporation, are there to serve. Rulers serve. Empowerment is surrender.

Women have viewed men as their enemy for too long. It's a ready-made excuse for their own shortcomings and failures. Their enemy is their ego – as it is for all of us. The enemy of women is themselves. And the tragedy is that they're taking the rest of us down with them. What has happened in the ghetto is happening to American society at large. The Ghettoization of America – the Feminization of America.

Says Gilder:
  The only surprising thing about our ghetto tragedy is the way we doggedly refuse to understand it – and the ways we endlessly perpetuate it [by allowing this meme to infect our whole society]. It should be clear to any sentient observer that the worst parts of the ghetto present a rather typical pattern of female dominance, with women in charge of the

families and male gangs away on the hunt. Workable in primitive societies with garden and game this system brings unremitting tragedy in the tenements and on the streets of our modern cities.

In the absence of agricultural support the women and children become dependent on government. The Welfare bureaucracy supplants the matriarchal garden and the husband's game. In fact, the husband is not even supposed to bring the game back, by law, or the wife loses her welfare garden. With most of the available jobs [service jobs] dominated by women, he has trouble finding any legitimate manhood in the community at large. The women work the welfare and the women are the crossing guards. Black men need jobs. The greatest factor thwarting and sabotaging their entry into the work force is working white women. White women, far from riding the discrimination bus with the blacks, are in fact their usurpers.

Inevitably the black man turns to – or creates – a world of men: sports or music, if possible; crime, drugs, and pseudo-revolution more probably – but predictably and necessarily a realm where males command, where he can find external symbols of the necessities of his sex…it is a familiar drama fraught with violence, anger, and yearning, enacted on the black stage of the street, sung in a thousand blues voices, celebrated in a thousand "soul" rituals, proclaimed and transcended in the art of jazz.[90]

In any disintegrating society the family is reduced to the lowest terms of mother and child.

So says George Gilder in 1972. In 2000 it seems to me the whole country has moved the way of ghettoization. Women feel they are entitled to something from the government and the job market. Men are increasingly being made obsolete; their only purpose is to perform the menial labor jobs women don't want to do.

In response to that a male culture is forming – the main object of which will be the exclusion of women in any way possible. There must be sacred zones in which women are not permitted to mess with men's minds; where logicizing, prettifying, and analyzing are not tolerated, and intuition reigns; where men are safe from female memes. I'm not talking about playing drums in the woods, though there is nothing wrong with that. We need to recreate a male identity and women are not invited. They have feminized the churches and the government and the schools, and now we must carve out a sanctuary where they are not allowed or we will go mad. The government will never help us. The government is made up of manholes – guys who sucked up to feminism to get elected, knowing that more women than men bother to vote.

Says Gilder:
As long as the rest of society fails to see the need to reestablish the male, the government will continue to reinforce the matriarchy – thus ensuring anarchy and crime in the ghetto, alienation of men, and disintegration of society at large.

The Federal Government is useful for building interstate highways and keeping Cuba from invading us, and as far as I can tell that's just about it. We don't need them. What we need are real men in decision-making positions. The Chief of Police in Detroit told Gilder that the problem he faces is caused by young boys who never in their lives have seen an honest, dependable, successful male. The government can't fix that. Women can't fix that. Money won't fix that. The main beneficiaries of government programs are always women. They *always* feed female memes.

Men need to form a culture that is within the boundaries of the existing nations, but outside the control of the governments of those nations. Fuck nationalism. The next time we go to fight a war let's put the fat cats who want to fight it in a room together and see what they come up with. The thought of dying for their own oil wells – instead of sending someone else to do it – might put a different spin on the situation. We need to cast our minds outward toward forming a global male identity. Not sameness, but mutual regard – a global honor system like the kind we had when we were kids. **Yeah**, we had fights, but no one got killed. We must transcend *mater*ialism and *mater*nalism – the defensive she-bear mentality of protecting the cubs at any cost. The only dog I've ever seen kill another dog was a mother who ripped the throat out of a strange puppy who came to sniff her litter out of curiosity. Don't tell me women don't have their violent streak. Men are not that territorial. Men must be willing to extend their thoughts and their lives to partake of a global spiritual community where all men can be, if not brothers, at least allies and friends.

And what is the main impediment to this sort of cooperation? Women's programs.

Says Gilder:

The chief beneficiaries of the women's programs will be upper middle class white women, and the chief victims will be the upwardly mobile lower-class men, black, brown or white…and thus their families. The impact on black males will be exacerbated by the feminists increasing usurpation of the anti-discriminatory machinery of the federal and state governments and of many private corporations. The legal basis of anti-discriminatory litigation was fought out for a century by heroically tenacious civil rights lawyers and private citizens willing to risk jail to test and extend the rights of their people…Now the Women's Movement cruises in with claims of comparable grievances, which are positively obscene from the perspective of slavery and segregation. Companies that previously would respond to claims of discrimination by hiring black men now hire black women and dispose of two aggrieved categories at once. This aid to black women is a tragic misuse of government investigatory and enforcement powers that strengthens matriarchy and undermines society…Every cent of unemployment money should be spent on males. [Fat chance][91]

We pride ourselves on living in a nation of laws but few people recognize the limitations of the law. No law can prevail against the dissolution of the social connections and personal motivations that sustain a civilized polity. Carl Jung pointed out that society can resist epidemics of physical disease, but it is defenseless against diseases of the mind. [Memes. Like Marxist/Feminism.]

Children thrive better in bad homes than in good institutions, says John Bowlby. But even retrenching feminists like Betty Friedan are advocating a national day care system. For what? So white women can have even more time on their hands at society's expense? Irving Kristol has written that the unintended effects of social policy are usually more important and *less agreeable* than the intended effects. That means that social engineering usually causes greater problems than it solves. Forty years ago slum high rises like Cabrini Green in Chicago were being held up by University of Chicago professors as the solution to the housing problems of the urban poor. Now they're the cave dwellings of gang bangers. The intentions and emotions and high expectations of the daycare movement are typical of all efforts at proffering government solutions to human problems. They have little to do with the real nature of the program or its probable impact on society. We are moving to a system where children will be raised entirely by the state (just what we despise about China). Gilder calls this the emerging Matriarchy Without Mothers. The state, at this point, becomes so feminized that it is actually usurping women's roles. The AFDC welfare program and divorce court have decided that a man could best support his family by being forced to leave them. Now we are cozying up to a national daycare system which is saying the same thing to women. Whose foot's on the gas?

Says Joseph Chilton Pearce:
Day care is profoundly more damaging than most people are aware. For one thing, there is no constant role model on which the child can base his or her worldviews.

The model has to be constant or infant-child consciousness fragments. And finding such a constant model in day care is a problem. In a two-year study of day care in the United States, blood samples of these children across the country showed dangerously high levels of adrenal steroids connected with stress and anxiety. When the young brain gets an overload of adrenal steroids, it goes into shock. This happens often when children under the age of four are separated from their mother for a period longer than two hours or so.

The next negative factor [in impeding brain development] is television. Studies compiled by Dr. Keith Buzzell, Jerry Mander, Mary Jane Healy, and others show that the damage of television has little to do with the content but rather with the pairing of imagery in synch with sound. This provides a synthetic counterfeit of what the brain is *supposed* to produce in response to language, as in storytelling. The child's mind becomes habituated to such sound-images, and the higher cortical structures simply shut down. Paul MacLean's work shows how in habituation the ancient reptilian brain takes over sensory processing and the rest of the brain idles along, doing nothing, because it's not needed. The brain uses the same neural structures every time the TV comes on, and very few of the higher structures are developed. They simply lie dormant, and no capacity for *creating* internal imagery develops...

There's a wonderful story about a little girl who said she loved the pictures on radio so much more than the pictures on TV because the pictures on radio were so much more beautiful.

In storytelling, the stimulus of words brings about the production of inner images, an extraordinary creative play involving the entire brain. Each new story requires a whole new set of neural connections and reorganizations of visual activity within – a major challenge for the brain. Television, by providing all that action synthetically, is handled by the same, limited number of neural structures regardless of programming, since the brain's work has already been done for it. This is habituation. So neural potential goes unrealized and development is impaired – unless storytelling and play are provided as well as TV, or preferably, *instead* of TV.

Then, also, television has all but eliminated radio as a story-telling medium, turning it into a mere music box. The other thing television did was to eliminate the play between parents and children in about 70% of American homes. It also eliminated table-talk and "grandmother tales". All of that has disappeared, and the extended family has all but disappeared...[And let's not forget that computers are really TVs.]

Organized games, like hide-and-seek or cops-and-robbers, begin in the seven-to-eleven age group. They are games where you choose up sides, and where you chase and hide. They are organized in a very loose way. A kid that age never wants to lose [giant ego]: even cops-and-robbers is really all just a chase, the excitement of hiding and getting found and trying to find. And the rules and regulations are very loose.

But at age eleven you have a different attitude towards games: the choosing of teams itself is important. A sense of justice and fair play become paramount. Kids may spend an hour just choosing up sides to make sure they're fair and equally distributed. They start playing and every five minutes they stop and argue passionately about infringements of the rules: "You're out!" "I was not!" "I touched you!" "You did not!" The emphasis is on setting up the rules, and then fiercely enforcing them and arguing their fairness or the fairness of their execution. [Since boys, by far, play more team sports, they are constantly grappling with moral issues and fairness. Girls are, by and large, untouched by these issues, and it shows.]

You find this haggling in street play, vacant lot football, and sand lot baseball. The challenge in this period is to put oneself through a kind of test, a trial or ordeal. Kids are driven by a desire to get out there and slug it out. Then, too, they must come to terms with giving up individual freedom and practice self-restraint on behalf of the needs of a larger social body – the team.

Today, however, there is often no longer room for kids to get together and play. Many of our planned communities do not even have sidewalks. Kids can't play out in the streets anymore; there are no sand lots. So we have "play areas" and "supervised play", in the planned communities and in

the cities: after-school organizations with adults coming in
with the rules and regulations [feminist memes] and insti-
tutionalizing play.

Then after World War II came Little League. Instead of
kids being out there on the sand lot passionately facing the
issue of giving up their individual freedom on behalf of their
larger group, we have a group of adults making every
decision, drawing up all the rules and regulations, umping,
while parents line the sidelines screaming, "Get him. Kill
him. Win at any cost." These poor, grim little children, eight-,
nine-, ten-year-olds, all decked out in their perfect uniforms
with advertisements on their backs, following adult orders.
Where now is the working-out of our social instincts and the
ability to get along as a group?[92]

Our school system is filling the kids' heads with rot and
drivel in an atmosphere where moral values are suspended.
Schools don't teach anybody anything about how to live. Neither
does Little League. They don't offer advice on how a marriage
is formed, or a mate selected, or a family sustained. They teach
you algebra and a corporate, rah rah version of history. Nowhere
do they offer a survey of religious mythologies or a curriculum
of spiritual training. You want to stop violence? Teach kids how
to meditate as well as teaching them ball tag. You want them to
be sensitive? Admit them to small discussion groups where they
can bare their feelings without being cut off by some prepackaged
"words of wisdom". You want them to feel secure? Give them
male teachers. And most of all, let them sort things out by
themselves by being "in" them. 90% of us come from dysfunctional and/or broken homes and the people in school are
teaching us verb conjugations and finger painting.

At least there is a light on the horizon. Some women are
quitting the career course and going back to raising children.

Says Gilder:

These women are discovering that the *mater*ial and
sensual rewards of modern society are meager compensation

indeed when one loses the ability for the profound fulfillment of biological sexuality.[93]

When you ask a woman why she works she will tell you some version of the theme of empowerment. If you ask a man why he works he shows you pictures of his wife and kids. Society will not find fulfillment in the Feminist meme of full female employment.

In his book *The Mountain People*, Colin Turnbull has written poignantly about the destruction of an African tribe – the Ik – when the process of male socialization broke down.

Says Gilder:
It had been a hunting and gathering tribe and the men had held an affirmative role. They were generous and cooperative with each other and solicitous toward children. Kinship ties and responsibilities were elaborately maintained.

Then the Uganda government banished them from their hunting area and turned it into a game preserve. The sudden change to a largely agricultural mode of life left the men with no crucial role and the tribe with little food. The result, described in excruciating detail by Turnbull, was a sexual suicide society: the destruction of all family ties, the expiration of compassion and cooperation, and the emergence of a completely predatory and opportunistic mode of existence, which was dominated by hatred and contempt for human life *and did not change when food became plentiful*...If man has any greatness it is surely to maintain the values of society...but that too involves choice and the Ik teach us that man can lose the will to make it...We pursue those trivial, idiotic, technological encumbrances and imagine them to be luxuries that make life worth living, and all the time we are losing our potential for social rather than individual survival.[94]

Recently I heard about a Catholic Bishop in the American Southwest who has been given a small airplane and 50,000 square miles of mostly Native American lands to minister to.

The biggest problem among his constituents is alcoholism and this Bishop is making a worthy and heartfelt effort to help these people. He claims that the only way he can get to the men is through the women and children. Once he interests the women and children in church – basically scaring the mothers that if their kids aren't baptized they'll burn in hell – he can induce the men to come around once in a while to attend baptisms and confirmations and such.

Do you get it? Do you see what's happening here? This feminized male representing a feminized institution is appealing through the women to get some influence with the men. Does it surprise anybody that this is not working?

And then, one day, Pope John Paul II blew into town fresh from eating pirogi in Warsaw. He threw on a buffalo robe, stuck some eagle feathers in his hair, and presented himself directly to the men of the tribe. He told the men that the Church needed *them* to *lead* it. Their job was to seize control and make it their own. Here, suddenly, was a man's man. Here was a window thrown open on male spirituality. Here was a spiritual leader who followed the Spirit wherever it chose to go. No, there is nothing inherently spiritual about eagle feathers or buffalo robes – once again we must heed the warning of not confusing the symbol with the message – but these items comprise the metaphysical language of a great nation of people. They are their holy words, their doorway into the realms beyond – and as such they claim the same respect as a Chalice or a Torah.

The well-intentioned bishop, instead of throwing the resources of the church behind a Native American spirituality whereby these psychically raped men could resuscitate their role as spiritual leaders, decided to cast his lot with the women. Very sad. Is the church ever going to realize that men need God more than women do? That men want God more than women do? That a healthy male spirituality can bestow miracles on any society? Women pray for *mater*ial rewards. Men pray to affirm their place in creation. Women seek immanence – finding god in little things. Men seek transcendence – they want to address the Thunder God. There is more spirituality in most Blues songs than there is in the entire church oratory. "Soul" is first and foremost male soul. That's the nature of our minds. That's the nature of our bodies. That's the nature of life as a human animal. Male Soul is as necessary to us as water.

Schools reward feminine behavior. Churches reward feminine behavior. Jobs reward feminine behavior. It's high time to create a new playing field for the male psyche, a kickoff tee to that world beyond sight and sound and words – the spiritual realm – what Native Americans call the Great Mystery.

Says Gilder:

The selection for femininity in schools is duplicated in the bureaucracies. Here again, sedentary fastidiousness and opportune blandishment are the lubricants of upward mobility. As a consequence, the entire society becomes a difficult and hostile place for the most masculine men. Some of them can be found at construction sites whispering "oppressively" at upper class feminist women as they amble by, their breasts jouncing loosely in their shirts. "Gee whiz, these brutes are treating us as sex objects!" say the feminists in their books and magazines and pamphlets and speeches. But it is difficult to see how a working man – doomed to a lifetime of tough and relatively unremunerative labor in support of his family – is the oppressor of women who seem to embody everything the world has denied him: life options, money, style, easy sex, freedom, clean work environments, tropical vacations. Anyway, the girls pass by onto their own frustrations; after a while, only the hats and the work of the men are hard.[95]

Robin Fox and Lionel Tiger, in their book *The Imperial Animal*, assert that human behavior of all kinds is ultimately shaped by chromosomal information selected and assembled during the millions of years we spent hunting on the African savannas. They draw an analogy to the recent theories of linguists. Linguists speculate that all speech formation is ruled by certain principles inherent in the human brain. Thus, even though possibilities for varied expression are immense, they all must follow certain patterns, and whole lost languages may be deduced from a few surviving particles. Tiger and Fox contend that human behavior is similarly systemic and governed by what they call "biogrammar". Just as attempts to contrive languages that do not accord with the universal principles will fail producing gibberish – so modes of human behavior that violate our deepest nature will produce "behavioral gibberish". Social disintegration will result.[96] (Maybe that's why Esperanto never caught on, and why communism failed; they're both circum-stantial gibberish.)

When reforming the roles of men and women we must always be careful to avoid behavioral gibberish – patterns of activity that so violate the inner constitution of the species that they cannot be integrated with our irreducible human natures. Says Gilder, the problem with many of the sweeping new concepts of women's liberation is that they are sexually unconstitutional. The androgynous society is behavioral gibberish. We still need to figure out what to do with the men.

Margaret Mead has observed, across cultures, that the worry that boys will not grow up to be men is far more widespread than the worry that girls will not grow up to be women. What is it about the making of a man that seems so much more volatile and less reliable than the making of a woman? Vitality of males seems to be a much shakier deal than vitality of women. So why-oh-why are we not protecting men from women?

Contrary to the usual images of the helpless and abandoned wife, the statistics show far greater evidence of helpless and traumatized husbands after divorce. A man has been convinced by everybody and everything around him that if he just does one thing very well, and brings in a big paycheck for it, his wife will handle all the details and everything will work out great. Suddenly he's divorced, she's still getting his money, and nobody is handling anything for him – but the court has based his ability to pay on a standard of performance that he only achieved for a short while during his peak lifetime period of physical health and moral enthusiasm: the early years with his family before the schools have stolen his kids' minds away from him. This is out and out abuse. In terms of mental and physical disease and life expectancy, divorce damages the man far more than the woman. Divorced men are more likely to show up in psychiatrists' offices and mental hospitals (hopelessly abandoned by the cloying feminist biases of the courts and the church) their minds wallpapered with dead animals.

Warren Farrell makes the point in the August 1993 issue of *Playboy* that women suffer more economically in the aftermath of divorce, and men suffer more emotionally. Women have less money. Men have less love. Although a man still has to come across with a check, there is rarely a reciprocal transmission of love forthcoming from his estranged family. Child support is a "right". Emotional support is not. And whereas society extends all sorts of financial safety nets for women – alimony, child support, AFDC – it provides no emotional safety nets for men! That's why men go looney. That's why men need to reform themselves in male groups where they can spiritually transcend their emotionally shattered lives. It's worked for 2.2 million years. And a feminized government comprised of manholes is not capable of doing it for us. We inhabit a zone outside the bureaucracy and our only true sustenance will come from God and our brothers.

Says Gilder:

Men are more prone to profess unhappiness. Between 35 and 65 they have a mortality rate 3 1/2 times higher than women and are six times more likely to have heart disease. Men are most likely to lose everything, including children, when love is lost.[97]

Churchgoers have sharply lower rates of illegitimacy and divorce. Without a strong religious culture, a secular bureaucracy, with its rationalizing ethic and moral relativity, erodes the very foundations of family life, and thus creates the moral chaos it is ostensibly there to combat. Asexual bureaucratic women have replaced asexual bureaucratic men as the molders and shapers of our day-to-day life – can anyone believe this is an improvement? [They don't even know who won the game last night. They don't even know who played.]

* * *

The effort to inculcate ethical behavior without religious faith seems to be one of the great fiascoes of the modern age.[98]

Peter Drucker has declared that we are busily unmaking one of the proudest social achievements of the nineteenth century, which was to take married women out of the work force so they could devote themselves to family and children. Women in Israeli kibbutzim have, in each generation, moved decisively toward traditional (at home) roles. Today kibbutzim show the most distinct role divisions in Israeli society.[99]

The capital that Marx forgot to include in his thinking was the metaphysical capital of family and faith. Social scientists have invented a religion of their own called "Humanism", a nice ring to that; but humanism manages to perpetuate itself, [its meme] without compelling visions of family, or of that "surrender of the ego" we call Faith. The humanist vision calls for a cooperative, communal, egalitarian, secular, non-sexist, non-hierarchical and rational society that C. S. Lewis calls nothing less than the abolition of human nature.[100]

All the major accomplishments of civilization spring from the obsessions of men the sociologists now disdain as "workaholics". Men must give their lives to unrelenting effort, day in and day out, focused on goals in the distant future. They must create new technologies faster than the world creates new challenges. They must struggle against scarcity and entropy and natural disaster. They must resist socialists, feminists, disease and temptation. They must die without achieving their ends but their sacrifices bring others closer to their goal. [They are all cells in the body of humanity.]

Nothing that has been written in the annals of feminism gives the slightest indication that this is a role that women want or are prepared to perform. The feminists demand liberation. The male role means bondage to the demands of the workplace and the needs of the family [and the Will of the Life Force. Women seek freedom. Men, according to Esther Vilar, actively seek to enslave themselves.]

Most of the research of sociologists complains that men's work is already too hard, too dangerous, too destructive of mental health and wholeness. It all too often leads to sickness and "worlds of pain", demoralization and early death. I don't see it mentioned anywhere where feminists want to relieve us of this. The men's role that feminists seek is not the real role of men, but the male role of the Marxist dream in which "society" does the work. [101]

So there we have it. "Society" is going to do the work, and women are going to make the decisions. The Wicked Witch of the West is gazing at the Supreme Court in her crystal ball while her flying monkey friends in the church look on and you, my friend, have your choice of working in the asbestos mines – tearing out cancer-causing ceilings; or pouring blacktop – ingesting petro chemicals through the pores of your skin. You've even got job security. NO women whatsoever are lined up to take those jobs away from you. Divide and conquer is a female meme.

Says Philip E. Slater in *The Pursuit of Loneliness*:
We are all so accustomed to living in a society which stresses individualism that we need to be reminded that "collectivism" in a broad sense has always been the common lot of mankind. Most people in most societies have been born into and died in stable communities in which the subordination of the individual to the welfare of the group was taken for granted, while the aggrandizement of the individual at the expense of his fellows was simply a crime. It has been said, with some truth, that we now live in networks, not families or communities. We are disengaged from our reservoir of values. We seek entertainment, not God. The same man who chuckles and sentimentalizes over a happy-go-lucky film hero would view his real-life counterpart as a frivolous and irresponsible bum. Suburbanites who philosophize over the back fence about what a dog-eat-dog world it is, how success-doesn't-make-you-happy, and you-can't-take-it-with-you, would be enraged

to hear their children pay any serious attention to such a viewpoint. Technology, individualism, and mobility erode identity and make the need for affirmation even more desperate.[102]

So that's why men are so looney! The more technology succeeds, the more dependent we become upon affirmation from women. We were willfully addicted to praise in our youth. We have moved away from our childhood friends and community and plugged into the evening news and mass culture – which, in case you're not sure, is *no* culture. It is the culture of the monoquestion: "How do I feel right now?" We married self-consumed women because they were more exciting. Then they got hooked on ambition and individualism and got uppity and left us, demolishing the affirmation of our self-worth which was so vital to our damaged psyches. We almost killed ourselves. We either found the Holy Spirit and began to live, or the alcohol spirit and began to die.

Individualism is behavioral gibberish. No, we're not all ants. But we are all part of a bigger thing. And where does individualism come from? Consumerism. *Mater*. The *mater*ial. The idea foisted on you every second of every day that you alone can own this car or own this house or possess this woman by wearing this special cologne. Nowhere in any of this do we find the concept of sharing. Sharing is anathema to advertising. Americans feel every family member should have his own room, TV, phone and car. We seek ever more privacy – and feel ever more alienated when we get it. The Consumer Meme. Behavioral gibberish. Too much *Mater*.

In other nations people are assigned to fill a variety of positions, from nuclear engineer to beggar. There is no shame in either position. We are all in this together. We all have a role to play. Americans call this primitive. We call it the caste system. We pity these poor people who go through their entire lives without shame, and without the concomitant overachievement that comes with trying to work off shame. In America we are all free to pursue exactly the same goals – house, car, career, family, retirement. How boring to live in such a one-dimensional society devoid of wandering gurus – who are arrested for loitering – and Gypsy wagoneers – who can't get permits for their vehicles. *Mater*. Over-regulation gone mad, depriving us of simple human pleasures. Recently I tried to sell an oil painting on the lake shore in the city of Chicago and I was told by the cops they would confiscate my painting because I was trying to sell something on Park District Property without a permit. Fuck the Park District. We have a crack cocaine crisis raging out of control and the cops are riding around on three-wheelers threatening artists. This has gone too far. We need a hippie revolution again. A Populist Revolt. We've got bleached brains. We need to loosen up this whole goddamned thing. It's suffocating us.

Male intuition has been freeze-dried and bottled and denied to us, even in our popular folk "wisdom". Men are rational. Women are creative. And airplanes run on jello. Every new law is a nail in our coffin. We need someone in charge of wiping out stupid laws and certainly busting artists for selling paintings in a park is one of them. Institutions, like women, make laws to cover worst case scenarios, and in doing so inhibit and castrate human freedom of action. That's why laws need to be interpreted; they are chronically too strict for most eventualities. Selling drugs in the park is bad; selling cars might be obnoxious; selling tacos might be a bit messy, but so what, put the garbage in a can. And selling art? That's not hurting anybody and it's exposing people to a wider vista of life. Making and enforcing laws against selling anything at all in a park is like putting out a match with a wet blanket. The USSR is taken off the map but it flourishes alive and well in most American cities. Why? Because we don't do anything about it.

Men are afraid to do things women don't like. We're afraid because most of the male affirmations we know derive from boyhood games. Our fathers weren't there. Our mothers controlled us with praise. And the elders were prevented, by women, from doing their job – the job of initiating us away from our mother's control and joining us to a greater reality, rather than a selfish *mater*ial dream.

Women and the bureaucracy and the church use affirmations as a means of manipulation and control. We do it their way, or else they make us miserable. And one thing I've learned, they're usually bluffing. There is usually not a goddamned thing they can do to enforce their manipulations with the exception of withholding praise. When 10 million fathers stop sending in their child support checks they aren't going to go after us, they're going to change the laws. The nature of the legal system is that it only wants to pass laws that it can enforce, so it doesn't look ridiculous. That's why we don't have laws against masturbation, or falling down in front of somebody else's house. Judges only want to try cases where they don't have to make a decision, where they can fall back on precedent, so they don't appear ridiculous. Well, it's high time for the men in robes to get some notion of just how ridiculous they are. Respect must be earned and the guys in dresses espousing women's values are not earning our respect. Women talk more so judges hear more from them and that is the main reason the laws have become so skewed in favor of women. Men are not suddenly going to start speaking 7000 words a day. Our thing is action. Let's act. Stop sending in the checks. Period. Now. All of us. I have. I'm living underground, just like the old Vietnam resistance days, and I'm not paying the freight for a feminized bureaucracy that has stolen my children away from me. That'd be like feeding a skunk in my kitchen. We don't need an organization – someone to hold our hands and tell us we're doing the right things. We just need to be men, and men act on our principles, even when it hurts, even when it's scary. Women don't, manholes don't; they always back down when things get tough.

On page 25 of the May 4, 1992 *Newsweek* we can see a photo of women carrying placards which state, "Our Bodies Our Business". And on page 41 of the same issue we can see a lineup of delinquent dads arrested for non-payment of child support. When is someone going to figure out that these photos represent one and the same thing. If women are allowed to assume the life and death responsibilities for reproduction, then they are obligated to assume all the responsibilities of reproduction. They can't have their cake and eat it too. They can't blithely edit men out of the pregnancy decision and then stick us with a bill when they're bored with living with us. Women have the same attitude toward children as they have toward jobs – the idea that a job or a child are supposed to be "fun", that a family should be liberating instead of a bondage. Marxist/ Feminism. And through some talky legerdemain they have managed to convince national politicians that the big problem is that the dads won't pay the money rather than that the dads are not being permitted to visit or nurture or initiate their children – and, on top of it, they have to sit by helplessly, handcuffed by the law, while their children are poisoned against them. Emotional abuse, perpetrated by a government that enforces only the female half of the law.

The courts are against us, our elders crapped out on us, the WW II "give me mine" generation has done enough damage to last this society 200 years. American men must relearn how to initiate themselves. We are compelled to reinvent civilization. Everyone else is walking around backwards, butt-first. Good thing we have the strength and resources of the Vietnam generation to help us through this. At least these guys came up in an era when everything was the opposite of what they had been told to expect. "We need a war to keep the economy going." Shooting women and children peasants in an Asian rice field is good for America. So is coddling to the sector of American society that outlives its adversary by eight years, that owns more than 50% of the real property, that enjoys specialized health benefits paid for by the other half, that dominates education, media, church and the courts through meme-invasion, and that claims all reproductive rights including instructing the ex-father where to send the check.

If there is such a thing as American culture – which I'm not at all sure of – but if there is such a thing, then there must be an American male initiation into this culture. But what is it? Getting your first car? Getting a varsity letter? Getting laid? Going into the army? These are all transformations of the psyche but none of them cut close enough to the bone to qualify as male initiation. We have to look deeper.

In a public lecture in Seattle, Washington Margaret Mead suggested that American men had been so effectively dom- esticated by their women that they had too little time and too little energy to engage in the national and communal tasks which needed doing – including the initiation of young men.

Territoriality is a female meme – a meme encompassing the possession of children as well as land. Men attempt to control territory *only* insofar as they endeavor to please the women that go with the land. If women did not express dominion over land, if they did not link their destiny with the land, then men would have no use for it. Male buffalo and male humans move with the herd of females. Wars are fought over land and it is ridiculous to lay the responsibilities for war on men's shoulders. The women are gonna fuck the local guys – the guys who are there on their turf – no matter if they just blew in from Mongolia, or if they've been there for 10,000 years. They don't care.

Women are committed to a particular plot of land and to their agenda for it. Men could give a shit. We fight wars over land. Women control the land. Men fight over the land to acquire the affirmations – including the vaginal affirmations – of the women who live there, the women who staked a claim to that land. Therefore, WOMEN ARE THE CAUSE OF WAR. The rape of the land – the invasion by the enemy – is a metaphor for the rape of the women who go with the land. Stags don't fight over barren mountaintops; they fight over valleys clustered with does.

99% of human history saw us as hunter/gatherers. Men were pack hunters with a definite memetic advantage going to those who insisted on hunting in all male groups:

1) There were no sexual distractions in this group.

2) Groups of men could move faster through rough terrain tracking game or chasing wounded animals.

3) They were not disrupted by menstrual cycles, subjected to wild mood swings, or held back by small children.

4) Women were not as strong or as capable of subduing large prey and might prove to be dangerous to companions in perilous situations, which is still one of the arguments against women in combat infantry – they might endanger their comrades who would expect them to perform maneuvers they cannot do. [Example: Former U.S. Navy regulations stated that a sailor must be physically capable of lifting one end of a twoman stretcher so he could speed wounded comrades through narrow ship corridors. That requirement was changed to allow two sailors at each end of the stretcher since female sailors couldn't lift the weight. The problem is: how do they speed through narrow corridors with two people on each end of the stretcher – standing outside rather than standing inside the stretcher handles. Men will die so women can be in the Navy?]

Does the pack mentality still hold true? Certainly if you're pouring concrete in a tunnel under San Francisco Bay or parachuting into Iraq at night it does. But hormones will have their say. Somehow, around forty, men enter a phase of separation, an aloneness, a dark night of the soul. They watch their wives charge out the door frothing with ambition over some career or business idea. They hear their kids repudiate them. And, no matter what success they have had, it turns to ashes in their mouths. The walls crumble. The pussy cat turns into a leopard; the house becomes a prison.

Men don't show emotion? You must be kidding. I watched General Norman Schwarzkopf cry on national TV during the Gulf War while being interviewed by Barbara Walters. He even said that he couldn't quite come to trust a man who couldn't cry. I have never seen Barbara Walters cry on national TV. In fact, she is the one who said that, of the three things a woman can have – husband, children and career – it is only possible to have *two of them at a time*. Like many she chose children and career and let the husband fend for himself.

Says Sam Keen:

Men have been trapped in extroversion. We have not spent the time to learn the nuances of our own soul. We have to tap our intuition and rediscover imagination, for unless we allow free play of our imagination we can never be realistic again.

Stephen Johnson of the Men's Center of Los Angeles says the Men's Movement is not so much a reaction to the women's movement as it is a reaction to having grown up without enough "fathering". He feels that what we are experiencing is not so much a men's movement, but a "movement within men". We are standing at the threshold of a vast spiritual awakening. We have set in motion the beginnings of a major shift in men's consciousness affecting the form of our interaction with each other and with our environment. It appears that life on this planet may be determined well into the 21st Century by what evolves from the present day Movement Within Men.

Chapter Four

Missing Memes:
Initiation

1) **Mothers are never going to willingly allow us to initiate *their* sons, even if they're *our* sons too**

2) **The WW II generation can't be trusted to initiate their own grandsons**

EVERY ENDURING CULTURE IN the history of the world has offered boys a male initiation ritual – death of the boy, birth of the man. Guess what's missing in our culture.

Says Robert Bly:
   The boys in our culture have a continuing need for initiation into male spirit, but old men generally don't offer it. The priest sometimes tries. [He puts the boy in a dress and has him recite some platitudes that please his mom.]
   Here is what the Hopis and other Native Americans do for their boys. The old men take the boy away from his mom at the age of twelve and bring him down into the all male area of the kiva. He stays down there for six weeks and does not see his mother again for a year and a half...
   The fault of the nuclear family isn't so much that it is crazy and full of double binds. The fault is that the old men

outside the nuclear family no longer offer an effective way for the son to break his link with his parents without doing harm to himself…The ancient societies believed that a boy becomes a man only through ritual and effort – only through the active intervention of the older men.

It is becoming clear to us that manhood does not happen by itself; it doesn't just happen because we eat Wheaties. The active intervention of the older men means that the older men welcome the younger men into the ancient, mythologized, instinctive, male world.[103]

Bly says that one of the best stories he's heard about this kind of welcoming is the one that takes place each year among the Kikuyu in Africa.

When a boy is old enough for initiation he is taken away from his mother and brought to a special place the men have set up some distance from the village. He fasts for three days. The third night he finds himself sitting in a circle around the fire with the older men. He is hungry, thirsty, alert and terrified. One of the older men takes up a knife, waves it ominously, then opens up a vein in his own arm and lets a little of his blood flow into a gourd. Each older man in the circle opens his arm with the same knife, as the gourd goes around, and lets some blood flow in. When the bowl arrives at the young man he is asked to drink it, to nourish himself from them, the elders.

In this ritual the boy learns a number of things. He learns that nourishment does not come only from his mother, but also from men. And he learns that the knife can be used for many purposes besides wounding others.

He is now welcome among the men and they begin to teach him the myths, stories, and songs that embody distinctive male values: not only competitive values, but spiritual ones as well.

Now that the old men don't consciously, ritually, welcome the boys, what happens? In the nineteenth century grandfathers and uncles still lived in the house and old men mingled frequently with boys. Through hunting parties and hay baling and through local sports older men spent much time with younger men and brought knowledge of male soul and spirit to them…Much of that chance for incidental mingling has ended. Men's clubs and societies have steadily disappeared. Grandfathers live in Phoenix or old people's homes, and many boys experience only the companionship of other boys their own age who, from the point of view of the old initiators, know nothing at all.

Now here's the killer.

Says Bly:
   During the sixties some young men drew strength from women who in turn had received some of their strength from the women's movement. One could say that many young men in the sixties tried to accept initiation from women. [Another twist on the old affirmation game.] But only men can initiate men as only women can initiate women. Boys need a second birth. A birth from men.

All the young men in this country are alienated. Alienated from society. Alienated from themselves. And how has the machine of civilization responded? By creating the "information revolution" – yet another computerized, feminized attempt to solve the problem by shoveling on more information. We are inundated with advice about drinking distilled water, or growing your own papayas, or eating Vitamin C, or avoiding fats; meanwhile, our younger men are slashing each other to bits, wallowing in a mindswamp of torment and confusion. Where's dad?

Dad's either at work or kicked out of the house. Even if he does show up for an hour or two in the evening it's clear he's exhausted, he's not there to perform, and anyway, the house is suffused with female values. Bly says that the father now loses his son five minutes after birth.

And what happens to the boys? Alexander Mitscherlich has written that if the son does not actually see what his father does during the day and through all seasons of the year, a hole will appear in the son's psyche, and the hole will fill with demons who tell him that his father's work is evil and his father is evil. These heart-wounds are compounded by a general assumption that every man in a position of power is corrupt, and that every woman in power is nurturing [a phantasmagoric feminist meme].[104]

Says Bly:
The Greeks recognized positive male authority. They called it Zeus energy, which encompasses intelligence, robust health, compassionate decisiveness, good will, generous leadership. Zeus energy is male authority accepted for the sake of the community. It's not "liberation", not self-serving, not elitist or segregationist. Zeus energy is bondage to family and community. It is possibly the hardest, most important quality for a man to learn how to perform gracefully and with dignity. [The sheer amount of abuse a Presidential candidate in this country endures in the media is a tremendous test of his Zeus energy. Will he cry? Will he resort to low blows? This is what the people in this country want to know about their leader before they elect him.] To endure abuse with dignity he will need the help of a god.

But Zeus energy has been steadily disintegrating in the United States. Instead of gods we have sit-com fathers who burn their socks in the toaster and never know what cold remedy to take. It's easy for TV wives to outwit them, for kids to teach them a lesson, or for girlfriends to save the whole town by themselves. Many young Hollywood writers, rather than confront their fathers in Kansas, take revenge on the remote father by making all men look like fools.

Continues Bly:
Carl Jung believed that when the son is introduced to feeling primarily by the mother he will learn the female attitude toward masculinity and take a female view of his own father and of his own masculinity. He will see his father through his mother's eyes. Since the father and the mother are in competition for the affection of the son, he's not going to get a straight picture of his father out of his mother, nor will he get a straight picture of his mother out of his father.

Some mothers send messages that civilization and culture and feeling and relationships are things which the mother and the daughter, or the mother and the sensitive son, share in common; whereas the father stands for and embodies what is stiff, brutal, unfeeling, obsessed, rationalistic, money-mad, uncompassionate. "Your father can't help it," she laments [while she, the helpless one, manipulates the macaroni out of him]. So the son grows up with a wounded image of his father – not brought about necessarily by the father's actions or words, but based on the mother's observations and interpretations of these words or actions.

By adolescence the kids know something is wrong. They don't know who to believe. Stewing in emotional confusion they withdraw and it becomes difficult to get more than a "yep" or a "nope" out of them. Initiation is intended to draw them out again. In its absence the hollow numbing pain, the hole in the heart, can go on for decades or until the end of their lives.

Says Bly:
     Somewhere around forty or forty-five a movement toward the father takes place naturally – a desire to see him more clearly and draw closer to him. This happens unexplainably, almost as if on a biological timetable. We are cultural animals equipped with psychological time capsules that move us toward the wisdom of the elderly just as our bodies are wearing out and we need to know more than brute strength and ambition to survive.

Not all men are good men, but women tend to be judgmental about masculine traits that are merely different or unexpected. Our brains work differently – thank goodness for that. The recurring interaction between intuition and logic is the lifeline of our species. And how do we preserve this interaction? Certainly not by abolishing the male half of the species. To preserve the human dynamic we must strive to make boys into men. Boys are born. Men are made. The process of this trans-formation historically has been called Initiation.

According to Mircea Eliade, editor of the University of Chicago Encyclopedia of Religion and cross-cultural scholar extraordinaire, Initiation is equivalent to a basic change in existential condition; the novice emerges from this ordeal endowed with a totally different being from that which he possessed before his initiation; he has become *another*.

Arnold van Geenep reports that in the Ojibway initiation the shamans kill all the participants, and resurrect them one after another. The death of the boy – the birth of the man. The Masonic Order performs a similar ritual. Sometimes, to mark this symbolic death the hair is cut, or the boy is given new clothes. *Always* he is removed from home and familiar surroundings and meddling manipulating mothers. Initiation that is overseen by mothers is not initiation.

In the Poro Bush Society of West Africa a bladder filled with chicken blood is tied under the boy's shirt and then he is ceremonially killed with spears thrown by masked dancers which puncture the bladder. He falls over and pretends to be dead. Often the boy is provided with a new name. When he returns to his village, everyone pretends they don't recognize him.

In the movie *The Emerald Forest* a white boy is taken into a tribe of Amazon Indians. He is raised amidst them and when he starts taking interest in a young girl the chief announces that he must die. The chief's wife asks, "Must he die?" "Yes." We fear the worst. He is tortured by the other men and tied up to be eaten alive by a horde of ants.

But in the morning he is still breathing and is bathed in the river by the older men. The chief raises his voice and says, "The boy is dead and the man is born!" He gets the girl. A death, the death of the boy ego, is a necessary part of any initiation ritual.

The salient point about primitive initiations is this: they work. They do what they're supposed to do. They turn boys into men. A boy who goes through the test has a heightened sense of self-worth (less shame). He doesn't need to "prove himself" by driving 120 mph on his motorcycle or breaking his knees in football. Plus, he is welcomed, formally, into the world of men. He can do what men do in that society. He is part of it. According to Margaret Mead, the primitive world has no room for unplaced persons who have yet to come to terms with their society. We will soon see that this is not strictly true. Most societies have a "space" for struggling or grieving or transitional comrades. And yet, the thrust of every culture is to raise adult males endowed with Zeus energy.

Unfortunately for us, Confirmations and Bar Mitzvahs are lacking in some of the main elements of initiation, which include separation from family (especially mom) and a transitional hazing. You read from the Great Book, somebody gives you a gold fountain pen which you promptly lose, and then you go back to school the next day and sit behind Sally. But you've made mom happy, or if not actually happy, relieved that she has completed her obligations to her religious peers. It's pretty empty stuff. Nothing risked, nothing gained. Mom has taken over male initiation. Dad knows it's a joke. He can't wait to take you hunting and get you "lost" in the woods so he can find out if you panic. Dads are good for those kinds of gut-level tests.

And what about the army? They cut your hair and take away your clothes and start calling you a lady or give you a demeaning nickname.[105] Not bad. It's a start. It's one giant step down the road to annihilating your ego and surrendering your life in service, but the question is: in service to whom? God? Or the Pentagon? There is much to be said later in this text about making the transition from Plain Warrior to Spiritual Warrior. Many of the qualities of the warrior are important to everyday male existence – such as a fixation on transcendent values and a delaying of gratification – but there is also room for great abuse of the warrior archetype when it is introduced in a climate of moral relativity – I kill therefore I am.

In pre-agricultural societies the warrior was first and foremost a hunter. Getting ready for a hunt takes a certain amount of spiritual attunement – cleansing yourself of body odor, painting your face with charcoal, meditating and/or praying to your totem animal, and the animal you will hunt, and to the Great Mystery behind it all. Deep in our heritage the consecration and incorporation of animal egos into our psyche played a significant role in connecting us to Life. We used animal metaphors and prototypes to propel us out of ourselves, our finite human egos.

Initiation is a bridge from one life-phase to another, from tadpole to frog, from nestling geek to resplendent falcon. To deny this transition, to imagine that an individual can step from one stage to another with no support or guidance, is asking too much, especially in a society that changes lifestyles every few years.

Says Ray Raphael:

Our pluralistic culture gives only a loose and pluralistic response to the problems faced by developing young men. And so it is that we have become a nation of makeshift males...But, the problem with traditional initiations is that they encourage an elitist, xenophobic, "us versus them" attitude, and we can ill afford this kind of tribalism today.

We need a Deep Male Spirituality on the order of a Deep Ecology. In fact, the two are the same order of phenomenon. No more *mater*ialism/nationalism. An initiation is nothing less than a "revelation of the sacred". This is where the street gangs and the army miss out. A group of men voided of their youth and programmed to do battle without obedience to a spiritual realm are dangerous to everybody. Roman soldiers killed Jesus. The Government of Athens ordered Socrates to kill himself. Had these men not endured these travesties of justice we would not have Christianity or Democracy today. They died for their beliefs – the ultimate battle for the Spiritual Warrior. Either of them could have avoided the penalty, and thereby negated their entire life's work and condemned their followers to extinction but, unlike their oppressors, they fought for a higher goal.

In midlife men arrive at a crisis that is another experience of initiation. Here we metamorphose into an entirely different idea of manhood. We distance ourselves from the female values that have made such inroads into our lives in the past 25 years, and we seek the Deep Masculine.

The midlife crisis, faced alone and in private, is a life-threatening experience for us uninitiated males. Hunter/gatherers were dead by forty. We've extended our lives in such a way that, in a great cyclical movement, we begin to pull back on ourselves. This midlife crisis is foremost a reaction to being trapped into enforcing female values for the past half of our lives. For men it is a second initiation, a time to look past *material* things and find deeper meanings. With the lack of cultural institutions and initiations and an agreed-upon value system to take us through this period, divorce has become the mechanism for kicking off the midlife crisis. Allan B. Chinen has described a life movement from heroic masculine in youth, to feminine in middle age, and then into what he calls Divine Masculine in later life. He detects this movement in the lives of the men in Homer's *Odyssey* and Dante's *Divine Comedy*. It sounds to me like some kind of literary testosterone curve – the place where our balls touch our dreams.

In all cultures dreaming is considered one of the primary functions of grown men. This is male intuition properly understood and exalted. It was the dreams of the shaman that told the people an ice age was coming and they had to move south. They didn't have the scientific equipment to deduce that. Their wives resisted them and openly revolted against moving the camp away from that handy blackberry patch. But male intuition was respected. They moved south and thereby survived the climatic shift and populated the middle Americas. Thomas Edison's intuition was respected and now we have the light bulb and the cinema and talking cars. Men who are not encouraged to dream are dead. Jefferson's dream was respected and so we had Democracy reborn, after 2000 years of hibernation (with the notable exception of Switzerland), on a continent unknown to Athens at the time of its conception. [And with the whole world ensnared in the soft machine of corporate colonialism it's time to dream about Democracy again. What it is. How we do it.] Our definition of the male image must revere this quality of intuition and, indeed, place it right at the top of the list of positive male attributes. Men are supremely, overwhelmingly, organically intuitive. Men's intuition is to women's intuition as the night sky full of galaxies is to a flashlight. The flashlight looks brighter because it is closer, but that is just an illusion. Competition is the game of boys. Dreaming is the game of men.

Historically the Trickster/Shaman/Magician represents the Divine Masculine. He is not robust but he is clever and he has hidden forces that he can call to his service. He lives in the paradox. Carlos Castenada's Don Juan is the figure nearest to this we have in our popular culture. Life is a goof, funny things happen. However Patrick Arnold in *Wildmen, Warriors and Kings* makes a good case for Moses and Jesus as being cultural vessels of this Trickster/Shaman/Magician energy.

Says Arnold:

Many modern men are appallingly unaware of the tremendous psychic potential that lies within them unused; educated in a left-brain/*mater*ialistic worldview, they insist that things are just what they appear, that what you see is what you get, and that any other viewpoint is just superstition and religious hocus-pocus. [Manholes.] Other men, however, in developing an interior prayer and meditation life, begin to conjure their inner Merlin and experience the enhanced ability to "know" through a sixth sense. We call this psychic function intuition, and it is involved in such phenomena as extrasensory perception and clairvoyance.

Intuition is a function just like thinking: it needs to be valued, developed, and practiced if it is to do anyone any good. Ancient hunters depended for their survival on intuition to a high degree; one still finds in primal cultures, such as the natives of Australia, amazing psychic perceptual powers. Much of this ability has been forgotten among modern men, but a number of training exercises exist that can develop it. Men who have begun to develop their inner Magician often report an increased ability to follow "hunches" that pay off in business, to detect subtle emotional changes in their spouses, or to notice how uncanny coincidences create "lucky" opportunities in their personal lives.

One way to read the account of the ten plagues (Ex. 7-11) is to assume that Moses created his own luck, intuited the onslaught of various natural disasters in Egypt, and magically presented them to Pharaoh as divine signs of Yahweh's wrath. But we can only guess this; a true Magician will never tell. [Likewise Jesus chose to remain evasive about his presumed divinity. He called himself the Son of Man. Yet he allowed others to call him the Son of God. Who was he? In answering that question he would have obscured the real question – what have you done today to dissolve your ego in the Heavenly Father? Truth without paradox is not truth. The paradox must be respected, for unless we lose ourselves in the mystery we remain prey to logicizing, feminizing and psychic shorthand.]

At the deepest level of all, the Magician is the archetype that connects us to the Deep Magic of the Universe, that subtle but persuasive Force that guides all creation – including ourselves – according to a provident plan... Christians call this Deep Magic *Grace*, a word whose Latin root means unmerited gift. Grace is God's unexpected and gratuitous help that, to uninitiated and unaware people, seems like blind luck or good fortune, but to Magicians it is the secret Force that unfolds our lives in love and wisdom.

Grace is the Deep Magic that Moses conjures up for the impossible deliverance of Israel from Egypt's dungeon. The Exodus story describes how Yahweh, the high Magician, teaches Moses the secrets of this force field, how to harmonize and align himself with it, how to respect its powers, and how to bring it into battle in the holy war of Israel's liberation.[106]

As Moses raises his magic staff, Israel passes through the waters of chaos, and once safely across the Reed Sea, the tides return, miring Pharaoh and his chariots and troops. Harmony, Intuition, Deep Magic.

Well, now we've done it. We've tipped over the ant farm and freed our first archetype. If we're not very careful, 9000 more of the beasties will escape the oblivion of unknowing and crowd the dead wood of our minds like so many hungry termites.

An archetype is a "brain picture" – a meme. All archetypes are memes but not all memes are archetypes. Archetypes are a type of symbol, though not all symbols are archetypes. The flag of the United States is not an archetype. An archetype is alive; it wants to merge your mind with another realm. An eagle is an archetype of vision, a fox of wile, a Witch of evil manipulations, a Black Hole of mysterious hidden forces, an amoeba of minute agendas. As you can see, there is no reason to limit our appreciation of archetypes to the current Euro-American bias of considering only humanoid forms. Indeed, "accessing" the Black Hole or the amoeba or the red fox within you can be easily as powerful as "accessing" the Warrior. ["Accessing" – here we have a little more computer-meme creeping into our understanding of our psyche – crazy.] And, in the remaining pages of this book, as we tip-toe deeper and deeper into this psychic swamp of archetypes, it is important to understand three things:

1) "Accessing" an archetype has never cured anybody of anything. No one has ever discovered their inner shaman and stopped doing drugs. Quite the opposite. At times I've been filled with the indignation of Jesus kicking the merchants out of the temple when I've witnessed very confused and hurting people blindly perpetuating their miasma of pain and insanity by jumping their minds and their egos through a carnival of archetypes on the costly advice of a self-styled "Jungian" analyst. Imagining yourself as a warrior or a magician is easy. Surrendering your ego to the hidden agenda of the Life Force is a power of ten harder to accomplish, and a power of one hundred more rehabilitative.

2) Carl Jung, creator of the archetype meme, said that if someone has to explain an archetype to you then it's not an archetype. An archetype is a "brain picture" that strikes you with immediate meaning. It needs no explanation. Does this give you a bit of a warning about the current spate of archetypal "Men's Movement For Sale"

psychobabble that is proliferating around us like a bunch of bunny rabbits?

3) Carl Jung, whom I greatly admire, also said, on his deathbed, that his life's journey had been one of climbing down ten thousand ladders in order, at last, to shake hands with the lump of clay that he was. So his was a lifetime of unlearning. Unlearning what? Why, the European culture – by far the most feminized, *mater*ialistic, rationalistic, sense-oriented culture the world has ever produced. That's why the history of Europe is the history of warfare – too many people chasing too many *mater*ialistic dreams. And just look at what they did to Christianity. They took the words of a wandering, ascetic, desert guru, and turned them into the biggest business, the largest landowner, the most sense-oriented pageant of archetypes – of virgins and saints and theological-babble – the world has ever seen. Have you talked to a Frenchman lately? Most of them have the brain pattern of a Rubic's cube. A German? A Swiss? A Dutchman? Rigid. Formulaic. Fretful. Chipmunks playing checkers. They need a little Black Elk or B.B. King in their lives…So, Freud and Jung discovered the insidious extent of the female meme's penetration into European Culture, but they couldn't figure out what to do about it. They didn't have the tools we have: the rattlesnake, the bald eagle, The Doors, The Blues.

But even with these great and inspiring memes it is essential to take care lest we get horribly burned by imagining we will find psychological salvation by "accessing" archetypes. Remember the words of Ralph Waldo Emerson:

> Imagination cannot go above its model.
> The imitator dooms himself,
> To hopeless mediocrity.

We were put here to enlarge life, not to imitate it. But there's danger at the other pole too. You are not God, you are here to serve God. You are not the Wildman, your job is to free him from his cage so he can help you. As Robert Bly said, Jack Kerouac thought he was the Wildman and ended up exploding his liver. So did Jim Morrison. Imagine what will explode when you try to replace God. My relentless propaganda blitz of beseeching you not to get caught in the psychic swamp – what Joseph Campbell called "confusing the Messenger with the Message" – will become much clearer toward the end of this book when we discuss the "greatest archetype of all". Yes, this is my humble attempt at "carrying the message", and "meme engineering". Whether Black Elk or Buddha or Jesus or Mohammed, the message is the same – surrender your ego, let go of the past and let go of the future, go to work for God. Pick up a shovel and report in to the Life Force every morning. Its Will, will be done. Your job – Magicians, Dreamers, red foxes, mocking birds, old men and young men – is to ride the wave, surf for your life, sense the harmony and move with it. We, as dreamers and poets, and as men, have been working at this for a long time.

Says Allan B. Chinen:

Dr. Herbert Kuhn, who visited the cave of Trois Frères in southern France in 1926, wrote of his passage into this Paleolithic Cathedral:

> Once inside the cave there comes a very low tunnel. We placed our lamp on the ground and pushed into the hole…The tunnel is not much broader than my shoulders, nor higher. I can hear the others before me groaning and see how very slowly their lamps push on. With our arms pressed close to our sides we wriggle forward on our stomachs, like snakes. The passage, in places, is hardly a foot high, so that you have to lay your face right on the earth. I felt as though I were creeping through a coffin. You cannot lift your head; you cannot breathe…And so, yard by yard, one struggles on: some forty yards in all…It is terrible to have the roof so

close to one's head...And then, suddenly we are through!
Everyone breathes. It is like a redemption.

The hall in which we are now standing is gigantic. We let
the light of the lamps run along the ceiling and walls: a
majestic room – and there, finally, are the pictures: mammoth,
rhinoceros, bison, wild horse, bear, wild ass, reindeer,
wolverine, musk ox.[107]

Clearly, this cave was utilized in such a way as to lead the
initiate through the claustrophobic and suffocating birth canal
into the vast interior of a ritual chamber. However:

Says Richard Behrens:
Nearby, fifteen feet off the ground in a dark apse, in a
remote position not easily discerned from the ritual ground
of the cavern below, is depicted the most powerful image of
Trois Frères, and certainly the most controversial. It is a
tiny creature, no more than two and a half feet high, with the
ears of a stag, the eyes of an owl, the beard of an old man,
the tail of a wolf, the paws of a bear, and the legs of a dancing
shaman. Known as the Sorcerer of Trois Frères, clearly this
is not a man dressed in the hide of a beast, nor is it a mere
addition to the parade of fauna below.[108]

Here is the Deep Male. He was alive and well in Stone Age
Europe.

Says Behrens:

Generations of young boys were led by torch light down
the meandering corridors, crawling on their bellies through
suffocating tunnels, and then being brought into the awesome
sanctuary where the secrets of the hunt were revealed to
them with great solemnity, in a womb-like underworld appropriate for their death and rebirth as men.

Here we have the creation of a profound ritual space, a
timeless zone, whose images are "no less than the stone age
mass, the food of the gods, the herds of eternity...Only in the
province of our own dreams can we feel the awe that no longer
moves us in a world where the secret places have been measured,
catalogued, carbon-dated, copied and modeled in life-size, set
up as exhibits in museums and photographed in all-revealing
light." Count Begouen's son, the boy – one of the Three Brothers
(Trois Frères) – who crawled into this enlarged "rabbit hole"
on July 20, 1914, entered "the very fount of conjuration, a place
of deep magic and dreams that gives nourishment to the
imagination. It matters little that he couldn't 'read' the pictures
on the walls. They spoke to him beyond words, welcoming him
as their first initiate after one hundred and twenty centuries of
silence."

So once upon a time Europe had soul, now it has the bearded
lady. Like to guess whose agenda effected this transformation?
Europe, if you haven't been there, is a big park. There isn't a
spot of wild ground left. When an Englishman talks of going
out into nature, he is talking about taking a walk on a farm.
God help us to stop that from happening here.

Initiation for men, for the past 50,000 years until very
recently, has meant our submersion in the Deep Male. It's our
guided tour of the wound in the earth, Our Father, the male
womb, the dark place underground, where we learned not to
Fear, where we learned of our covenant with nature – we kill
and eat plants and animals; and plants and animals kill and eat
us – and that is Good. That is the physical and spiritual meaning
of Life. Protoplasm eating protoplasm, as Joseph Campbell said.
Through our wounds, and our acceptance and understanding of

them, do we grow and evolve. In *To Be a Man* Keith Thompson has made an hypothesis that each wound that a man receives at any point in his life is but a localized instance of the One Male Wound.[109]

Essential to every man is his wound. All men are wounded. Some manage to spend their lifetime dissembling, avoiding the admission. But the only way to spiritual growth is to crawl right through the wound. Who cares about spiritual growth? Anyone who is in a lot of pain – who wants to transcend his agony of mind or body – cares about spiritual growth. According to Joseph Campbell, the wound is the hole where the soul enters the body. The wound is the doorway into our souls, and without it we are just boys with guns – potential villains. Knowing our wound is knowing our openness, our humanness.

Our myths, our poetry, our literature, our religion are supposed to teach us how to experience our wound. Do they do that? Yes, to some extent. Blues music has always been my doorway into the Wound. Just knowing that other men have been there, have put up with that much shit, makes it all a lot less frightening and a lot easier to take. You need plenty of courage to sing about your pain and that's what the bluesmen do. Drugs kill the pain, but mask the problem. An uninitiated man is a prime candidate for drug abuse. We don't want to be sissies complaining about our wounds, and yet there are equal risks in not speaking the wounds and thereby allowing them to steer us blindly through our emotional lives. A man who is not allowed the humanizing experience of failure and defeat becomes a prisoner of perfectionism – an ignorant perpetrator of his own shame. And shame is the most all-pervasive wound in American society.

Says Francis Weller:
Shame is a bodily-based archetypal response to experiences that rupture a man's sense of adequacy and worthiness. When we experience a failure of bridging with the father, for example, we feel shame; what's more we feel we are to blame for the failure. What is wrong with me that

my father is not closer to me, does not touch me, does not love me?

Three shifts are necessary to initiate healing. First we must move from feeling worthless [shamed] to seeing ourselves as wounded. We must move from feeling contempt for the self to feeling compassion. And we must move from concealing our shame in silence to revealing ourselves in sharing.

Or else, you can just get rid of your ego. The only thing that ever hurts when you are hurting inside, is your ego. Shame is ego in reverse. It's making a big deal out of the fact that you're not a big deal.

Says Carl Jung:

There appears to be a conscience in mankind which severely punishes the man who does not swallow his pride [shrink his ego] and admit that he is fallible and human. As we heal our isolation we experience a connectedness that exposes the sacredness of all life. Thus healing our shame becomes not just a personal challenge but a transpersonal challenge. When the cloak of shame drops we find we are all men of soul.

Women seem to have very little desire to know their woundedness, and even less to do anything about it. This is not true of all women, but what we are talking about in this book are tendencies that shape up along sexual lines. Women like to chatter, they like to complain, they like to criticize and judge. But their very facility with language often operates as a barrier which prevents them from getting *down* into themselves. They don't take naturally to spelunking: exploring the caves of Father Earth or their own psyches.

Women have a life form which is almost identical in every society on earth. They are the basic unit of the species. They are tradition and stubbornness and defensiveness and resistance to change. In a decadent society the bravest, smartest women don't reproduce. Guess what we are? Men, however, have very little in common, outwardly, from culture to culture. What all men seem to share in their creative, intuitive, risk-filled sorties through life are the soul wounds, the injuries that accrue to the emotional body, that come from living life on the edge. These are readily transcribed from culture to culture through art and poetry. Men who eat octopus can easily understand men who eat mung beans when they sing about these wounds. Herein lies my precarious hope for a global male culture.

Women regard life as a bunch of foolishness. Men are the patron saints of the foolishness. It can't be any different. It takes a lot of poetry and fascination and risk-taking to break down a woman's logical armor and get her pregnant, especially in the age of birth control. We are the *animus* that punctures their organized, defensive shell; and the nature of this game of life is that we will *always be* that *animus* if babies are to be made and human life to go on. Given the opportunity, women will organize human life into sterility. That's their tendency. They will deride every goofy leap of the imagination that ventures near them. They have an opinion about everything, and anything that has not already been proven to them is adjudged as just so much foolishness. They are brutal on the male psyche. It is against *our* natures to let them so sterilize our minds.

Robert Moore says that if you are a young man who is not being admired by an older man you are being hurt. This is the norm that we have created for our boys pursuant to a 60% divorce rate. Bly adds that not seeing your father when you are small, never being with him, having a remote father, an absent father, an alcoholic father, is an injury. Having a critical, judgmental (deeply shamed) father hurts too. One way or another some blow usually comes from the father. It is a wound the boy remembers for years. It can only be removed by other men.[110]

From the mother, says Bly, the boy receives a baptism of shame. She keeps pouring the water of shame over his head to make sure it sinks in. She can turn on the fountain of praise or leave him drooling with shame. It took me 43 years to confront my own mother with her relentless psychic brutality. Every time she sat in her rocking chair telling me, her son, a grown man, the right way to hang a towel, or the right way to cook an egg, she was shaming me, making me feel worthless and incompetent. And why? So that she, the control freak, alive and well in her 2000 square foot bubble of existence, could feel useful and valuable. That's psychic rape. For 43 years she passed on her shame to me and *never once* dealt with any of the issues of her own limitations and fallibility. My mother is 300 pounds overweight, a compulsive over-eater. But rather than deal with the emotional issues behind her eating she'll just pass on her shame to her kids. This is obscene. We've let them go too far with this. Even the supposedly preliberated women that Esther Vilar pointed her cannons at are psychic monsters.

That's why boys must be separated from their mothers before they get too far into adulthood. This is not cruelty. It is the bread of life to a young man. A boy is simply too beholden to his mother; and mothers, with their vast insensitivity to the male brain, relentlessly take advantage of this privileged access and carry on their agendas with an air of ignorant bliss. Or, if confronted about their machinations, they reply simply that they don't know what you are talking about – and *they don't*, they're women! They are utterly ignorant of the psychic damage they are doing to their sons – of the prisons of shame, and dysfunction, and self-hatred they are creating – of the future failures they are setting their sons up for. Men have known about this for 50,000 years and for 50,000 years we've done something about it – remove the boys from their mothers!

But what do young men do today? They attach themselves to some young woman who immediately starts manipulating the macaroni out of them. They haven't been initiated by men to avoid this trap. They haven't broken out of the psychic swamp of praise and shame that their mothers nourished them on. It's not their fault; nor is it the fault of the young women, *per se* – they're just women doing what women do best: manipulating men. It is a failure of the elders, the old men, not to slam down their fists and stand up against the courts and the schools and the churches and choke this Feminist Meme that is operating against 2,200,000 years of human evolution by depriving men of their right to nurture their children and their children's children. Mothers teach their boys to get good grades and become doctors. Fathers teach their sons how to survive the many wounds that will come and thereby they create a continuity, a sustainability, that is crucial to any successful life. The mother has taught her son, "the doctor", absolutely nothing about how to survive the pain of his own divorce. In fact, she has made matters worse by setting him up for this defeat by nurturing his shame and feelings of inadequacy. This is vicious stuff we are dealing with here. The Jewish Mother, who is fast becoming the archetype of the American Mother, is not cute and quirky. The feisty, opinionated '90s woman is not just independent and effective and lovable for being so. These creatures are both grotesque manifestations of the hidden agenda of the Demon Goddess. They breed like maggots devouring male soul. They eat their husbands. We can't blithely allow ourselves and our sons to be choked of our very existence by these obscenely willful creatures. It's time to draw a line in the sand. It's time to take our boys back.

The critical moment in the *Iron John* story, as told by Robert Bly, is when the boy steals the key from under his mother's pillow. (If you haven't read it, please read it.) The story cannot begin until he steals it. It may take ten years or thirty, but the boy, to retrieve his golden ball from the cage of the Wild Man, must steal the key to the cage from under his mother's pillow and open the lock himself. No mother is ever going to do it for him, or even give him permission to do it. Not on your life. Her nature is to shield him from the wound.

The wounded man, in this case Iron John, knows something or is something, but why won't he talk about it? Bly said, in a conference with Deborah Tannen, that unless a man feels he can contain his feelings, he won't express them.[111] This is pretty deep stuff. Men are liable to fits of rage, and fits of poetry, and fits of love, and unless they can find a vessel to carry them, they will hold these emotions in a deep dark place. That's what we're taught as boys. Part of this is a very ancient psyche at work. You can't afford to wax poetic when you are stalking an elephant, and you can't afford to panic when a lion is stalking you. That's probably where this male meme finds its origin, but there is something more going on here. As we saw in Chapter One, through two million years of human evolution something biological has emerged to reinforce this meme and to facilitate the psychology underlying it.

Never being welcomed into the male world by older men is a wound in the chest. Being lied to by older men is an even worse wound. The young men who arrived in Vietnam to find out they'd been lied to received immeasurably deep wounds, says Bly. A wounded man fears he cannot contain his rage and therefore stuffs all his feelings within him. They are there. They are so very *there* they incapacitate him. Maybe he snorts heroin to get rid of the pain.

Or maybe he just drinks beer to loosen up and talks shit to his friends until some sweet young thing winks at him and immediately he's off and running to get some desperately needed praise and affirmation. Having no soul union with other men can be the worst wound of all, says Bly.

The circumcision, the tattoo, the scar, the chipped tooth, are all wounds given in the initiation. The initiation shows the boy how to deal with and live through all wounds, old and new.

Addiction is the fastest growing state in the United States, says Bly. When people identify themselves with their wounded child, or remain children, the whole culture goes to pieces. We are all in the emergency ward. The recovery of some form of initiation is essential to our culture. When the key remains under the mother's pillow we will end up in treatment sooner or later. We require the appearance of the "male mother", the mentor, who introduces us to that mythic, preconscious meme Bly calls the Wild Man – who is *not* inside us. Let me repeat that for the benefit of those of us who spent years of our lives lost in the psychic swamp of New Age memes. That mythic force called the Wild Man is *outside* of us. When we make the mistake of believing he is inside of us we explode our livers, or worse. This is God-power we are tapping into here. Doing God's will is not the same thing as being God. Sure, we are part god. But there is one-trillionth-billionth part *inside* of us and a trillion billion parts *outside* of us. We must never forget the scale of difference. We have a cellular scanner that allows us to resonate with the Life Force, to know its frequency. In the radio analogy, we are the receiver and the Life Force is the transmitter.

We are, to God, like a drop of water in the ocean. Sure, we are the ocean and the ocean is in us, but we would be tragically egocentric to ignore the power and depths and vastness of this thing we are part of. We contribute to the Ocean of God, but it is much greater than we are.

So, we submit to the mentor and trust that he is not the kind of guy who is going to have us spraying Agent Orange in Nam or poisoning lakes and streams with dioxin. The young man investigates or experiences his wound – father wound, mother wound, shaming wound – with the help of the mentor, in the presence of this independent, timeless, mythological, initiatory being – the Deer God, the Sorcerer of Trois Frères. If the young man steals the key from under his mother's pillow and climbs onto the Wild Man's shoulders, the wound, rather than being regarded as bad luck, will be seen as a gift – a carrier, a vessel – and that is the point of addressing the wound – not to wallow in it as on a psychologist's couch, but to be lifted up and carried away on it. The wound is not something to be cured of, or rid of; it's a spaceship of the psyche. What do singers sing about? Their wound. What do painters paint about, and writers write about? The wound.

David Steindl-Rast says that most people expect to get happy and then become grateful for their happiness. This makes perfect logical sense, but it's completely backwards. That's not how the spiritual path works. The empowerment (read surrender) of your life, is to *become grateful first*, and then happiness follows. Only someone who has visited his wound can *know* this. Be grateful first, and then comes happiness. It works every time. As Bede Griffiths has said, the solutions to human problems are not solvable on the human level. This is where the Deep Magic comes in. Be grateful for everything – every tragedy, every monstrosity, every abuse of the laws of God and man – so you can find the inner peace to go on. It's not that the shit is good. But it is good that *we are here* to have this shit happen to us.

Mircea Eliade says that the puberty initiation represents, above all, the revelation of the sacred. Before initiation boys do not yet share fully in the human condition precisely because they do not yet have access to the religious life. Bly says that religion here does not mean doctrine or piety or purity or belief. It means a willingness to be a fish in the holy water, to be fished for by Dionysus or Jesus or one of the other great fishermen, to bow the head and eat grief as the fish gulps water and lives. It means simply being there in the middle of all the pain, with no mother's little helpers, and it even means being grateful to be there. These things don't make any logical sense or *materi*al sense. We wouldn't look at the dirt in our soup and be happy about it. But we are not just a stew of chemicals. There is something about us that is outside of all that, and that place is what is touched by spiritual work. Be grateful for the pain of the wound, grateful for the pain of the circumcision, or the tattoo or the scar, grateful to be there, in a circle of men, where there is pain, and where the pain is overcome. Where the deep wounds are shaken loose, and like celestial horses, they pull the chariot of our soul upwards into the limitless black night sky.

Denial, says Bly, stands for amnesia, forgetfulness, sleep, dreaming, oblivion, enchantment. An ocean of oblivion sweeps over a child when he is shamed. Denial means we have been entranced. We live for years in a trance. And what are myths and fairy stories for? Snapping people out of their trances, or at least showing them that this happens. The girl kisses the frog prince and dispels his trance. That's the fairy tale we've pinned our hopes on. Good luck. I just got re-entranced with a feminist agenda.

The modern word for enchantment is Denial. Breaking denial, breaking a spell, breaking free of childhood shame or failure or divorce or abuse requires a conversation with the Wild Man. Mom can't help. Sally can soothe you but she is merely a balm, she won't get to it. It won't come from watching TV. That's another balm that keeps you from getting down into the wound. The wound is the hole where the soul enters the body. It is our way out of our ego and into the Unified Whole of Creation. We take the ride down, not to wallow in the pain, but because the

older men have taught us that for every descent there is an ascent
– we have to go down before we can go up – and we trust that
they are right.

Those with no wounds are the unluckiest of all, says Bly.
Where a man's wound is, that is where his genius will be.
Whether the wound stems from a shaming mother or an abusive
wife, or from isolation or alienation or disease, that is precisely
the place where he will give his major gift to humanity. The
human survival meme has learned that this is the most important
thing for any man to know. Through his wound he contacts the
source of creation and brings back the good news, the new idea,
the fire to heat the cave to survive the Ice Age, the telescope to
map the cosmos.

In initiation rituals, from ancient Greece, to the kiva used by
Native Americans, and all the way back to the cave painters of
Trois Frères, men entered the earth and made it theirs. Mother
Earth became Father Earth through male ministrations. The
mother is the nurturing ground, but the male seed is the source
of creation. In pre-scientific times it was felt that the female
was the vessel for the male seed. Then scientists discovered that
females possess the egg while males only provide the lowly
sperm. And yet, what has changed? Without the active penetration of the female entity by the male entity the egg dies and is
washed away in a river of blood. Men interfere with the female
penchant for closedness and containment and because of this
disruption human life gets reproduced. Men were designed to
disrupt women. That's how this things works.

Our job is not to get along with the Goddess. Our job is to
fuck the Goddess. The earth is male, the sea and waters are
male, the sky is male, the trees and birds and animals and flowers
are male. They're also female, but let us for once be sure to
emphasize that they are *male*. Maleness, activity, movement,
can be seen in clouds and pollen and just under the surface of a
perfectly still pond. The planets, the solar system, the cosmos,
are movement, are male.

Bly says that when the human being takes action, the soul
takes action. To bring the soul to life takes movement. If you
light a fire it chops wood. If you come to the mountain, the

mountain comes to you. If you hide her diaphragm, she gets pregnant. Mysterious forces, as yet beyond our comprehension, are waiting out there for us. What we don't yet know about the universe is as significant as what men didn't know about the sky when they assumed the earth was flat. When we move toward these forces, they move toward us. When we plant the seed, the magic of growth occurs – somehow. We can analyze the shit out of it, but which scientist can state with authority what causes this. We observe it. What more can we ask? Men love to drag their nets through the night skies, bringing up odd fish and shards of new understanding. Women couldn't care less.

Hazrat Inayat Khan says that on the surface all things appear to be different, distinct. But as we settle through each inner plane everything draws closer together; mammals seem more like fish, they both have two eyes and breathe oxygen; birds seem more like rocks, their skeletons have a mineral matrix. Until, at the innermost plane, everything is unified, everything is included in one grand energy vibration. We are all particles of matter seeking the anti-matter that we lost back there in the Big Bang.[112]

Nuclear physicists have discovered that all matter is energy that got separated from its mate in the Big Bang, 20,000,000, 000 years ago. Out of every billion and one particles created, one billion found its anti-matter mate and disappeared again into a realm that we can't track. The one-billionth particle left over became us, our world. We are a rip in the fabric of the universe, a colossal disruption. The electrons pumping through the wires of my typewriter right now have been around for 20 billion years, since the Big Bang. Do we want to call this Soul? It doesn't matter to me one way or the other except to recognize that this phenomenon is observable. Electrons last an eternity. Our bodies don't. Something big is going on outside the reach of our senses.

Hazrat Inayat Khan goes on to say that any disruption of the surface events disturbs the cosmic harmony all the way through to the innermost unity. He thinks that's bad. I think that in many instances that can be good. The Big Bang was, after all, a major disruption of something. On the surface men and women are different. At our innermost plane we are not only the same, we are one. When we bicker and feud we cause cosmic disgust; I agree with Khan wholeheartedly there. But when the opposites collide in a cataclysm of lovemaking again we rock the innermost core of creation – we fuse electrons, we bring another child into the world. We give love another chance to start afresh, without intimate memories of war and pestilence and abuse. Lovers create love.

People today labor under the misconception that men are hierarchical and women seek some sort of connectedness. That's because we haven't spent much time around chickens or cows. Women create a pecking order, a hierarchy, amongst themselves, and amongst the men they cause to fight over them. Women gossip, and through their gossip they disrupt harmony, they weave a basket of helplessness wherein solutions are never sought and nothing is ever really accomplished. Watch little girls play. They spend most of their energy excluding other little girls. Boys need bodies to make up a team. So what if Joey has a clubfoot? They'll put him on one team and Gordo on another team where their deficiencies will cancel out and at least *somebody* will be covering right field.

Women are swift to establish their place in the pecking order of whatever situation they enter. In fact, the Feminist Movement can be viewed as one grand assault to introduce a pecking order where none exists. The female business barracuda of today knows no moral limitations in her attempts to wrestle her way through the boardroom. She'll wear a wool suit, and wiggle her ass, and it's all the same. But men? Men work as a team. Manholes work for themselves – that is the evil side effect of corporate feminism – but real men, the guys who build the roads and bring up the oil, work as a team. Only the assholes want to be leaders because the leaders are the first to be shot, but if life demands it of him, any man will assume leadership.

We learn the intricacies of this stuff on the ball field. When someone hits a line drive there's no time to shout to Billy to get his mitt up, and even if there was, you wouldn't dare distract him by jerking him out of his right brain and into his left. By way of a nod or a lurch, Billy knows the ball is headed right at him, even if it's coming so fast he can't see it. Men think fast and they do it without words. They communicate deep meanings with glances. Hierarchy is something someone does on a battleship when nothing else is happening. These guys just want Billy to catch the ball right now.

And if he doesn't? Will they yell at him? Will they analyze what went wrong? No. They'll groan, and turn away, and spit at the ground and remember how they felt when they dropped an easy catch. 99% of the time life does not require verbal instructions and it is a feminist meme to believe that it does.

Before there was psychology there was mythology. Before we had buzzwords to describe intelligence in nature we had the Deer God, the Sorcerer. In other words, nature had a personality, or rather, many personalities, and these were entities that men trained themselves to relate to. Anyone can relate to a crying baby. It takes a little more finesse to relate to the Deer God. Subtlety, nuance, sitting quietly in the jungle for hours on end – this is how men developed contemplation. Right now, I'm on the Pacific coast of Mexico, where, in order to find the fish, the fishermen must be finely attuned to the nuances of the birds. They can't see the yellow fin tuna under the surface of the deep water. But where the birds go, and how they go there, tells the men where the tuna are chasing the baitfish from below. And so, in a vast expanse of ocean, they are able to locate the fish. After hours upon hours in the forest, or in the boat, the wind begins to talk, not in Hebrew or English, but in man-talk. Only if you are quiet and patient will you hear its message.

Says Bly, we assume that contemporary initiation is accomplished by being confirmed, or bar mitzvahed, or getting a driver's license. But to receive initiation truly means to expand sideways into the glory of oaks, mountains, glaciers, horses, lions, grasses, waterfalls, deer. We need wildness and extravagance. Working in the Green Peace office in San Francisco or Sydney is not enough. Whatever shuts a human being away from the waterfall or tiger will kill him: and that generally means his wife or his mommy or the slot feminized society has prepared for him. The Wild Man's job is to teach the young man how abundant, various and many-sided his manhood is. The boy's body inherits spiritual and soul powers developed centuries ago. There is a place for him among men, but he will not find it as long as he remains absorbed in feminist propaganda, nor will he find it in the militarist propaganda perpetuated by manholes who sit behind desks and send boys off to war.

Psychotherapists have been lying to us for 100 years. They tell us we are born without an ego and need to spend our lives building it up. For them empowerment is a matter of bolstering the ego, building self-esteem. This is straight-on feminist, *mater*ialist philosophy and indeed this is the diametric opposite of the truth. We are born with a humongous ego and spend our entire lives trying to rid ourselves of it. Our ego is so big when we are born that we are unable to differentiate ourselves from the world around us. Everything is "I" or "MY" and goes directly into our mouths. There is not the vaguest inkling that all this stuff might belong to someone who is not us. We cry when we're angry, we cry when we're confused, we cry when we want something, and we cry until someone figures out what we want and provides it for us. Then, a few years later, someone throws us a ball and we discover that if we just run around clutching the ball to our gut no one wants to play with us because there is no game unless someone else gets the ball part of the time. Along comes adolescence – the Age of Shame. Here the uninitiated experiences the ego-in-reverse that is shame. He pummels himself for not being something or someone he has seen in the movies, while simultaneously trying to cast off the shame that his parents have imbued in him – regarding sex, regarding freckles or skin color or whatever. What an awful time. No wonder traditional initiation was concocted to precede adolescence. And on we go, jettisoning our parental ego-bound shame just in time to invest our ego in a marriage partner and have that turn into a living hell within a couple of years – but by then we can insinuate our egos into our kids and repeat the mistakes of our parents and cripple *them* with shame. And then, hopefully, comes some catastrophe that causes us to wake up for the first time in our lives and get rid of our goddamn egos. Without this happy disaster, this "Good" Friday, we are doomed to spend the entire rest of our lives servicing the feminine meme, trying to control what cannot be controlled – Life!

The psychological meme that tells us we are born without an ego is about as valid as the perceptual meme that tells us the earth is flat. When we are born we think we are the world. New Agers get stuck right there; they spend their lives searching for the perfect beach to hang out on, slapping mosquitoes, and complaining. For tens of thousands of years spiritual adepts have been telling us to dump our egos if we want to be happy. For less than 100 years psychotherapists have been telling us to polish our egos if we want to be happy. Who do you want to believe?

Women like to get together in groups and talk about how horrible everything is. Men get together and joke about how stupid they used to be. A men's group is predicated upon smashing ego. Women are judgmental and critical. Men are goofy and accepting. Thank God for men.

Did you ever hang out in a group of homosexual men? As we saw in Chapter One, the emotional centers in their brains are built differently. I have a great number of homosexual friends and acquaintances. From my experience, their conversations consist primarily of degrading judgments or grandiose ego-building accolades – very little of Middle Earth, Father Earth, to be found there. That's not to say it's wrong or bad, but I certainly don't have to accept their feminized behavior as my standard, and you needn't do it either if you want to stay healthy in your own hetero head.

One time a gay guy told me that gays should be "put in charge of culture" since family men like me don't have time for it. I said, "Let me get this straight. A guy like me, who buys schoolbooks and soccer balls and winter coats for my kids, am going to have NO SAY in our cultural priorities? No vote in where this society focuses its thoughts and aspirations? That's cowshit...In fact, I think there should be a "childless tax", a "gay tax", an all-around "flake tax", for men and women over the age of 30 with no kids. Gay or straight. I supply my kids with the implements and services they need for 18 years or more of job training – while you sip expensive wines and vacation in

Bermuda – and then when you retire *my* kids will be working to pay *your* Social Security? That's a massive rip-off. You should be taxed, starting today, for refusing to accept any responsibility for continuing human existence...You can adopt some abandoned kid if you want to avoid the childless tax." He screamed – a woman's scream.

Here we have yet another feminized notion of "how life works" – we want rights without responsibilities. Give us jobs and don't discriminate against our lifestyle. But don't dare actually make us accountable for the Big Picture. This is just another rip-off of masculine energy. If gays want to get married and enjoy the financial benefits of that – fine with me. Let them pay a childless tax *to cover their own bills* when they get old. What is this? Kindergarten?

I've already gone on record as saying there's no shame in being gay. It's biology. However, I do not accept the idea that simply being gay is sufficient justification to pursue a selfish political agenda. You gotta make sense in the "grand scheme of things" guys – and gals. You gotta be looking out for someone besides your selves. That's what Life *is*. The gay movement can never realize its objectives until it assumes responsibilities along with rights; and until it effects a genuine rapprochement with hetero men...And until it stops sucking the tits of corporations and government. It's poison milk. Media corporations adore gays. Always good for a titter. Gay antics can be relied upon to light up the airwaves with a blowtorch aimed at the "stodgy" values borne by men, families and religion. Too bad the titter *always* comes at the expense of hetero men. It's pathetic. Can't you see you're sucking off corporations and stepping on your own dicks at the same time? You want a job with *whom*? You wanna be like Charlie Rose? Talking to celebrities about their toilet habits, and some book they once read? Good God. Wake up!

Modern media can most politely be described as a "celebrity suck-off". Let's get some famous person up here to tell an anecdote about what happened on a film set in Europe or something their daughter did. This is criminal misuse of *our* airwaves and *our* print space. *Playboy* magazine is notable for having the worst writing by the best authors around. If some literary light has something laying around under his bed he sends it to *Playboy*. Why not go out there and find some of the best writing by the least known authors? Don't tell me you don't have the time. You don't have the brains. You don't care. Your slant on publishing is to mount a monthly celebrity suck-off.

Why not tell me who General Electric is poisoning these days? What Franken-seeds Monsanto is selling in the Third World? Or tell me why *Playboy* is such a big contributor to feminist coffers? Feminist ideology is cowshit. Deadly to men. Your main readership. (Lookership?) The only thing feminists are right about is how *Playboy* trivializes women. So you try to buy off their only accurate criticism by supporting their whole bag of meaningless and misplaced priorities? Equality? My aching behind. *Playboy* wallows in billing itself as the vanguard of Sexual Liberation. But what about liberation of the male soul? What about liberation from corporate colonialism? What kind of pretentious crap will I glance over this month that has nothing to do with what's going on in the world? Asa Baber used to write some *great* men's columns, but somehow, lately, an invisible corporate hand of promotional politicking has eroded him. Maybe it has something to do with Hef's daughter taking over the magazine. Baber, sadly, has softened his bite…And the only reason I'm picking on *Playboy* is because of its rank hypocrisy in describing itself as the International Magazine for Men. The rest of the media doesn't even try. Doesn't even care. Let the corporations and their feminist hookers grab it all.

Whew! That's been waiting to explode out of me for a long long time. *Ahem*. Where were we?

The feminist biases in language are giving us a pathetically distorted idea of the human personality. We are raped with the propaganda that our feminine side is gentle and caring and considerate while our masculine side is incommunicative and aggressive. Cowshit. I have a feminine-induced *anima* that is strident and obnoxious and oozing with self-pity, which is generally called forth through exchanges with women. I have a masculine side that is silent and deep and patient with suffering, which is generally called forth in the company of men. The touchstone of inner peace for any male is to recognize when he is being overtaken by feminine mood, what Carl Jung called *anima*. To understand that you have a feminine nature is good for a man. But to act out of that feminine nature is emotional poison. Robert Johnson goes into this at great length in *HE*, drawing a sharp distinction between feeling and mood. Feeling is the ability to value, says Johnson. Mood is being overtaken by the inner feminine.[113]

To feel is the sublime art of having a value structure and a sense of meaning in life. For men, to *mood*, is to be in the grip of the feminine part of our nature. For a heterosexual man to be chatty, critical, or sarcastic means that he is in the grip of a feminine mood. For a heterosexual woman to be sharp, puncturing, challenging, or aggressive, means she is in the grip of a male mood; she is acting out of a poor quality of masculinity.

Often a man has to make a choice between feeling and mood. If he is engaging in one of these there is no room for the other, says Johnson. A mood prohibits true feeling, even though a mood may *appear to be* feeling. If a man is engaging in a mood – or, more accurately, if a mood is engaging in him – he automatically forfeits the ability for true feeling and thus for relationship and creativity. If he's mooding he won't hit the ball.

Consequently, no matter what just happened to a guy, his buddies will always tell him it's not so bad. They won't commiserate or feed his mood the way women will. They'll try to pop him out of it. That's a male meme – not to feed the mood, the resurgent *anima*. Says Johnson, a man overwhelmed by mood is a sundial in moonlight telling the wrong time. In the old language of mythology he has either seduced or been seduced by the inner feminine.

Notice this double-bind. Whether he seduces or is seduced, the outcome is the same. He cannot tame or trick his feminine side any more than he can tame or trick his wife or lover.

Depression and inflation are other names for mood. Both give one a sense of being overwhelmed by something that is not God. Moods turn one to other things or people for one's sense of value and meaning. *Materi*al things are valid in their own right, but when one asks them to carry an inner value they fail miserably. That is the intrinsic problem with hearth and home – no matter how tidy or well-painted the guy keeps them, they can never bring him inner peace – and no wonder, for the preoccupation with these objects demark the traditional limits of the feminine realm. Now women want jobs. Great. What they're talking about is glorified berry picking. They sure don't want to be diving to the floor of the Gulf of Mexico looking for oil to keep the microwave working.

Mythology describes the hero's battle with his internal self – his ego – as the encounter with the dragon, the overwhelming mood monster. That's why we have been bequeathed the image of St. George fighting the dragon – any grade schooler knows there were no dragons in medieval England. And that's why the Chinese parade a dragon through the streets at their big celebrations. Modern man has no fewer dragon battles than did his ancient counterparts.

Good moods are no less dangerous than somber ones, says Johnson. To demand happiness from one's environment is the sinister art of seducing the interior fair maiden. To be caught up in an exuberant mood is to be seduced by the inner woman. Ever do drugs? The Goddess wafts the seducer/seducee off to dizzying heights of inflation and then drops him into a depression. Drugs are *anima* in perhaps its cruelest and most direct expression. It is precisely to moderate mood swings that alcoholics and drug users employ chemicals to medicate themselves. They are trying to out-*anima anima*. To seduce the seducer. It doesn't work. Their lives are being run by unknown forces because they have never been exposed to the intricacies of initiation, and these forces are not of God. They are of the feminist meme. The meme that asserts life should be happy and comfortable. Not a painful quest for God.

Says Johnson, fate spends a lot of time bringing a man up from his depression or down from his inflation. This is the ground level which the ancient Chinese called the Tao, the middle way. It is here that the Holy Grail exists and happiness worthy of its name can be found. Enthusiasm, en-*theo*-ism, means being filled with God, filled with the Life Force. Asians, and Asian religions, have never wandered too far from the Grail Castle. They look at us westerners and ask, "What is the hurry and hunger in you people?" We have mingled our sex roles. We have men acting like women and women acting like men. We're experts at solving problems we don't have and fools at solving the problems we do have.

Someday we will all be living in space pods orbiting other suns in other solar systems and there will *still* be only two types of people – the ones who have slain the dragon of their ego, and the ones who haven't. Personally, I hope they put the egoists on a different space ship. Spaceship Earth, and American society in particular, are being tormented to extinction by these self-consumed individuals. Empowerment is an ego trip perpetuated under the auspices of deluded psychotherapists and New Age dilettantes – uninitiated novices messing around inside our minds. Dissolving your ego is a proven spiritual tool that has worked for 50,000 years and still counting. Don't believe uninitiated women – and there are very few initiated ones to be found – they don't know what they're talking about. There are some very beautiful women, like Mother Teresa and Peace Pilgrim, who have battled the dragon and surrendered their ego – more completely, by far, than any men, including myself, that I've ever met. But this is not part of the feminist currency, the female meme. These women transcended all that.

Says Bly:

A boy struggles against swaddling bands, fighting the narcissistic mother's desire to change him into what she wants. Says William Blake, when the boy fails to get free he learns to sulk "upon my mother's breast". How often has every adult man, when baffled by a woman's manipulations or her peculiar interpretation of his behavior – so different from his own – gone into a sulk. [He brings home the wild blackberries, that she's supposed to be gathering in the first place, and she starts complaining because he got the kitchen floor muddy.] In our twenties we can go into a sulk that can last for weeks. We can't explain ourselves to women so we don't even try. Screaming, shouting, kvetching never appear. They are too active. When a man sulks he becomes passive, deadened to his own hurts.[114]

The job of the initiator, whether man or woman, is to prove to the boy or girl that he or she is more than mere flesh and blood.[115]

A man is not just a machine for working. A woman is not just a machine for reproducing. We are all bags of salt water bent by fantastic spiritual yearnings to seek memes that give neuro-electrical charges to our lives. Children must not be wantonly abused or fed on false hope the way they are in the current school system. The most important thing in life is not recycling bottles and cans, the most important thing is recycling your soul. Why encourage 100 million kids to be marine biologists and scoff at waitresses and garbage men. Westerners deride the caste system, but in that system society has provided a way for the lowliest workers to do their jobs and live their lives with dignity. What are we preparing our children for? Sitting at computers all day? You must be kidding! At some point someone is going to have to pick up a shovel or a wrench and make something happen and we can't just relegate those jobs to Mexicans like they seem to do in California. Have you ever driven around California and looked out the window? The only people actually doing anything are Mexicans. No wonder their economy gets hit so hard during recessions. They're surfing atop wetbacks riding silicone waves.

Chances are, as you drive around the rest of America and look out your window, the people you see who are actually doing something are going to be men. Isn't it getting a little bit ridiculous to watch women operating the signs on the highway construction crews while the men do the actual work? Women want jobs? Let them do work, real work.

How many millions of people have you met, trained for some prestigious technical or creative vocation, who are working as cooks or salesmen? Is more education going to solve that? What are we doing to ourselves? Are we merely creating a society where women live longer, do easier work and less of it, dominate child rearing and education, and complain about their hardships all day long? Can anyone show me the society in which women are not caught up in bickering and complaining and self-pity?

We are a society intent on educating ourselves to scientific reality and completely ignoring our own emotional reality. We worship the mythology of science and its fantastic gorgons of black holes and electrons and ecology – and other mythic beasts which have never been seen; and we ignore the psychic memes which have for millennia permeated our emotional bodies. Can you picture the difference in the way Arthur was taught by Merlin, or Bilbo by Gandalf, and the way your sixth grader is eating it all up from Ms. Methodical? We were not put here to make money. We were put here to get rid of our egos.

But, cautions Bly:

Finding spiritual things too early and on your own can be damaging. This produces the "flying boys" – the *puer aeternus* or eternal boy. Giddily spiritual [read psychic] they do not inhabit their own bodies well, and are open to shocks of abandonment; they are unable to accept limitations and are averse to a certain boring quality native to human life. [They have been fed on feminist grade school fantasies and set loose in a competitive swamp more brutal than any caste system.] So the young ascenders often find themselves achieving spirit, but at the expense of life or their own grounding in masculine life.

Men and women alike once called on men to pierce the dangerous places, carry handfuls of courage to the waterfalls, dust the tails of wild boars. All knew that if men did this well the women and children could sleep safely. Now the boars have turned to pigs in the stockyard and the waterfall into the fountain in the courtyard of the Art Museum. [Feminization. The taming of life.] The activity men were once loved for is not required anymore.[116]

During the last thirty years men have been asked to go with the flow, to follow rather than lead, to be vulnerable, to adopt consensus decision making. Women want a tractable man, if they want one at all; the church wants a tamed man, the university wants a domesticated man, the corporation wants subservient men.

The main institutions in our society are entirely feminized. There is no need for women's liberation. The feminine value system already owns and operates everything and they, the oppressors, don't even have to get dirty or paint-splattered. That's for someone else to do. They just have to roll out of bed in the morning and turn on the TV to begin participating in the gossip of the day and pick up on the latest health tip – wash between your toes to prevent cancer. And the tiger and the waterfall are only seen on nature shows. How has it come to this? How did they get that much power? This is *entirely* a woman's world we live in. That's why they want the political accolades. That's why they want the recognition. They already run the whole show and now they just want us to formally acknowledge the fact.

And what does Man do? Sulk.

When no old men appear to break the hold of the sulking, the habit of passivity spreads to other parts of life. The men do what their families demand but they do so grudgingly and dragging their feet. The passive man skips over parenting, trundling the kids to soccer games, helping them to spell words, buying socks. He lets the wife do that. Chances are he'll do it wrong anyway and he doesn't need another argument with her over it. For her part she's afraid he'll realize how easy and exciting it is spending time and money on your kids. In that way, the whole concept of fathering is a threat to her.

Says Bly:

Along with passivity in men we are finding more and more naiveté. The naive man knows no boundaries. [For him the truth is relative. He follows the Tao when it corresponds with the desires of his ego and does not follow it when he wants specific results.] He doesn't see the dark side of people and is easily fooled and manipulated. Unaware of his boundaries he does not develop a good container for his soul.

The naive man tends to have an inappropriate relation to ecstasy. He longs for ecstasy at the wrong time or in the wrong place, and ignores all masculine sources of it. He wants ecstasy through the feminine, the Great Mother, the goddess, even though what may be grounding for the woman ungrounds him. He uses ecstasy to be separated from grounding or discipline.[117]

As I read this passage the word marijuana comes to mind. It is very possible that much of the passivity and confusion in men today is some manner of twice removed drug syndrome. I smoked pot for twenty years because I thought it was grounding me, bringing me closer to every flower and bee. I never thought pot was a drug until I stopped smoking it. Now I see clearly that it was not grounding me at all but accomplishing precisely the opposite. It was interfering with any transmissions from the earth or the sky or my mate or God. It snapped my life line to the Life Force in very subtle and ultimately insidious ways ...Sorry, potheads, but I call 'em like I see 'em.

Says Bly:
The naive man will sink into a mood as if into a big hole. If he feels hurt he identifies with the mood and everyone around him has to go down into the hole. The naive man doesn't know there is a being in him that wants him to remain sick. Inside each man and woman there is a sick person and a well person: and one needs to know which one is talking at any moment. But awareness of the sick being, and knowledge of how strong he is, is not part of the naive man's field of perceptions.
    There is something in the naive man that demands betrayal. The naive man will have a curious link to deceit, betrayal, and lies. When a woman lives with a truly naive man for awhile she feels personally impelled to betray him. When there is too much naiveté around, the universe has no choice but to crystallize out some betrayal.

The naive man thinks the U.S. judicial system works. He builds a house and puts the deed in his name only because his wife has put all her personal assets in her name only. He dumps great amounts of hard-earned money into it while his wife is separated from him and screwing around with her boyfriend who "understands" her so much better than he. Then, at divorce time, the naive man discovers that whereas his future-former wife gets to keep all her assets, he must give her half his money, half his house, and half of everything in it because they were still "married" during this episode of her self-seeking and betrayal. It's not all his fault. He believed in the system. And maybe now it's becoming clearer why a government of Men is not always worse than a government of laws. Men live and die behind the principles they stand on. Judges swirl their skirts and hide behind the law.

The naive man believes the court when it tells him they are going to assure him access to his divorced children, and three years later he owes $18,000 in unpaid child support and hasn't seen his kids once. Not even bankruptcy can free him of his support "obligations". No matter that his business went bust in the financial and emotional rape of divorce compounded by a sour economy. He's still supposed to pay according to the level of income he is "supposed" to make. But at the same time, no compensation whatsoever is owed him for three years of denied visitation. The ex-wife is off and running, scot free, to pursue her ego-driven dreams of success, and the dad and his kids have been deprived of the holiest, most nurturing experience in life for both of them. A feminized court system takes dads away from their kids. A vengeful ex-wife just has to stand up in court, with no proof whatsoever, and declare the former husband psychologically unbalanced, or better yet, a child abuser, and it will be years before even a saint of a father sees his kids again.

The naive man spends decades of his life building up capital and equity and real property – and emotional property – only to have them removed from him by some woman who has bound him to her by praise addiction. Men drink more than women because their lives are more horrible than women's – it's as simple as that.

A man's *real* life seems to consist of the amount of time he has managed to devote to avoiding the work that women –

mothers, wives and daughters – have tried to get him to do for them.

Romantic love is the single greatest energy system in the Western psyche, says Robert Johnson. In our culture it has supplanted religion as the arena in which men and women seek meaning, transcendence, wholeness, and ecstasy.[118]

What an awesome statement. Johnson is saying that we have thrown off male spiritual connectedness in favor of a feminine romantic mystique. We expect to find the fulfillment, the affirmation, in women, that we used to find in God. What a disaster. Vain as they may be women themselves will readily admit that they cannot fill that role in our lives. As Bly says, people who fart discreetly in elevators are not goddesses.

We have let them roll too far into our psyches. We must relocate the center of gravity of the human emotional personality far, far back onto the male end of the spectrum. According to the Hindus, we are living in the Age of Kali, the Age of the Goddess, right now! Kali yuga. Kali is the wife of Shiva. She wears a belt of human skulls and her hallmark is human degradation. According to the Hindus that's why we live in such a *mater*ialistic world – right now! The Age of the Goddess is not coming; it's on its way out. Women have been in control of our psyches for 8000 years. Now they want to work? Fine. Let them have some nice dirty jobs like growing the corn and making the pots which is what they're supposed to be doing anyway, and which, somehow, they tricked us into doing for them.

Mick Jagger sang about "Mother's Little Helpers" twenty years ago and now I watch my mother and my friends' mothers taking downers and watching TV all day and I know, in my soul, that this decadence is on its way out. It's all over but the shouting, and this book is about the shouting. The Female Meme has run its course. Women in America are creating mass decadence. No society can long endure which merely services its ego.

The females are the *mater*ialists. Males are territorial only insofar as they hope to screw the females who go with a certain verdant plain. To evolve as males we need to learn how to let the females come to us. We have to stop fighting with each other in order to please females on their terms. We have a great chance, a window of opportunity, to become something more than rutting bucks. Females don't know what's good for us, and worse, they don't really care. We cannot live our lives by acceding to their values.

So, the adoption of female values leads to naiveté. The naiveté leads to sulking. And the sulking, gone on long enough, causes an emotional numbness that grows like a cancer in the chest cavity of most men. Our feelings are so pained that our body responds by numbing them. Expressing our feelings may be the answer but expressing deep emotions, for men, cannot be done in words. We are not verbal creatures; our brains aren't made like that. Singing and chanting are good. It matters not what words are sung but it does matter what resonances they set up in the throat and chest to shake free the numbness. Silent contemplation is good. Sport is good. Helping other people is good. Watching TV is not good. It just drowns us in more feminist memes. We live in an era of feminist thought control. Observations that are unkind to women are simply not allowed on the national airwaves. We can bash men all day long but women are our sacred cows. Why not? We don't have God anymore.

It is generally acknowledged that the most successful men are the biggest assholes. Was this always true, or is it a recent phenomenon? My guess is that, since the dawn of agriculture, it's been almost always true. Why? Because the most successful men have always been able to play well in front of women. They produce what women really want, not what they say they want. They share money, not emotional secrets. They chatter about surface level feelings without ever diving below to controversial depths. Elected to public office they will lament the loss of the rain forests in Brazil and pass laws to monitor vitamins but ignore the fact that half of the kids in this country are growing up without dads due to the oppression of the legal system – and positively *run* from the fact that corporate money controls the agenda of government. Manholes. Feminized men. They are handsome and personable, not craggy and deep and challenging. Would you go to a handsome and personable shaman to crack open your soul pain? An unwounded smiley-face? Your ex-wife goes to a handsome and personable priest or rabbi or psychotherapist to get her biases manicured.

Says Bly, school teaches a lot about going up and nothing about going down. Throughout high school and college, teachers hint at the rough time you're going to have out there but no one offers the tiniest shred of soulful advice on how to survive the deflations. You go from worrying about the rain forest to worrying about the rent with nothing in between. Our high schools and universities are a pathetic rip off. Once again, the people who know nothing about education of soul and everything about tenure tracking – not taking risks – are the ones who have bludgeoned themselves to the top. The assholes. The manholes. The women.

Most people have heard about the "Peter Principle". That's the one about how you get promoted to the level of your incompetence: a superb college coach gets promoted to the pros where he is a disaster – that kind of thing. I hope no one is operating under the illusion that women in the work force are going to be immune to this one, or that the most successful women are not going to be the most successful assholes. To blindly believe in Salvation by Women is to know that your brain has been colonized by feminist memes.

The most important qualification for leadership is intimate knowledge of defeat – descent into the lower realm, annihilation of the ego – precisely what initiation teaches. Death and rebirth. Strident college girls screaming for more rights know nothing about descent – death of their little girl egos. Wait till they've worked some cowshit "career" for 15 years and want to have a baby but can't get pregnant – that's when they'll be equipped to negotiate living conditions for other people. We all have to go down and we have to learn how to go down gracefully, and even willingly. We need to know that after a certain point, the only way to go up is to go down. *Katabasis* the Greeks called it;

entering the earth, a normal and natural part of life – wretched but survivable, cleansing and ultimately inspiring. The *only* point of any education worthy of its claim is to teach people about this descent – but the subject is hardly ever broached in our schools and churches and synagogues.

Why this need for wretchedness? How many people have you met who say they "don't believe in suffering"? What exactly is being resisted here? The spiritual path has nothing to say about success and much to say about defeat and failure. It is all about arriving at the place where the special person no longer feels special. He is trashed, taking cold water bucket-showers, eating other people's leftovers. What has happened to him? His sense of self-importance, his self-esteem, has been peed on by life. His ego is smashed. His personality is capsized. And that's why this collapse has to happen. The person who doesn't unload his/her ego is stuck. He/she cannot grow and complete this life. He/she can never be trusted to lead others or to explain the meaning of life or to offer up goals to be pursued.

The descent. Here is Joseph being sold into slavery by his brothers, and put in a dungeon by a queen he won't make love to, so that one day he can rise above the turmoil and feed his starving clan from the granaries of Egypt. Here is Richard Nixon, who never admitted he was wrong, and Chuck Colson, fired from the White House, discharged by the nation, who did admit he was wrong and became "saved" – changed, reborn in this life and therefore able to do good things for other people. Here is divorce, and loss of your children, and loss of your job, the breaking of a leg or the breaking of a relationship. Here is where you have to rediscover your connection to a benevolent higher power, or spend the rest of your life in cynicism and regret. This is not optional knowledge. This isn't an extra credit course. The emotional tools for surviving calamity are the most important cultural items to be passed from generation to generation, and what do we have? Old men rhapsodizing about World War II while young boys without dads initiate themselves in crack distribution rings operating on the feminist meme that having enough money will solve all their problems.

This is not a compromise situation, not something that can be ameliorated or avoided, or that you can shield your children from. This is where the gray haze of moral relativity coagulates into deep shades of black and white. This is where you lose every shred of your "former art and life". Getting another degree doesn't solve the problem. We used to die around forty in the hard old days. Now we live longer than that, but only if we die to our egos. That's the price of admission to longer life – life everlasting. Death of the ego. That's what was really dying on the cross – Jesus' human identity – Jesus' ego.

In this century, says Bly, men have characteristically failed to notice their own suffering. We've called attention to the suffering of blacks and Chicanos and women, whales and snail darters and spotted owls, but white men are nowhere to be found on anyone's list of abused souls. For every job that a black or a chicano or a woman got, a white man lost one. That may or may not be fair in the scheme of things, but no matter how you look at it there was a loss of identity and suffering to be silently endured for every job lost. Who cares about the job – we're trying to zero in on the unaddressed suffering. This is precisely where the ego can be conquered if we are initiated to understand that that's what's going on.

The WW II guys didn't give up their jobs; they had seniority. The Vietnam warriors came back from the fighting in Da Nang or Toronto to find that wetbacks and women had moved into their jobs. Did the white boys complain? No. Not once. Inundated by feminist and civil rights memes they saw a kind of fairness in all this. But that nobility of heart did not lessen their grief at living in a society which expected them, historically, to work, but didn't have any jobs for them. What did they do? They got stoned.

Where were the old men? The initiators? Playing frisky games with the pert young chicks running around their offices. They have abandoned us, forgotten their hereditary roles. It started during Vietnam and hasn't stopped yet. I saw Dan Quayle on TV making a lot of noise about collecting child support from delinquent fathers and entirely *ignoring* the fact that half of the kids in this country are being *prevented* from seeing their dads.

Feminist memes. Manholes. Patriots who send other people to fight their wars.

We are wounded, and our wounds are the doorways into our soul. Women are not obligated to do, or not do, a single thing to heal us. Women are not kind, and caring, and sharing, and doing what is best for men – they are doing their utmost to manufacture a world that they can control, and we just happen to be one of their main tools. The old men have abandoned us. They think they're supposed to be playing golf or something. We have to come together in groups of guys we can trust and begin to heal ourselves. We have to take our children back somehow. We have to do it in the courts and we have to do it by civil disobedience and we have to refuse to pay child support if they don't let us have total access to the minds and bodies of our kids. They can't put us all in jail. Who'll dig the ditches and fly the planes?

Most of all, we have to initiate our children – girls and boys. We can't simply allow them to wallow in the gender suicide of feminist memes. We need to show them their intuitive home so that they can't be manipulated by machine values and *mater*ialist, *mater*nal, fix-it mentalities. The thing to fix is ourselves. The way to live is to live with less and find deeper meaning in that.

Says Bly, the way down and out seems to require a fall from status – from a human being to a spider, from a middle class mover and shaker to a derelict, from a quarterback to a parking lot attendant. In divorce, when a man's emotional safety net disintegrates, he can either walk backward through the door while looking at funny movies, or he can take in the true darkness of the door as he faces it. This is the Dark Night of the Soul of St. John of the Cross. This is the Divine Darkness of Christian and Hindu mysticism. This is where Carl Jung found his collective unconscious. This is where God is found – *in the darkness*. I'm not going to argue with the people who say God is light, but you don't find light by looking in the light, you find it by looking into the darkness. From that realm beyond archetype and astrology and psychobabble comes the stuff the shaman knew. The priests want light. Give me darkness.

To come to the pleasure you have not
   you must go by a way in which you enjoy not.
To come to the knowledge you have not
   you must go by a way in which you know not.
To come to the possession you have not
   you must go by a way in which you possess not.
To come to be what you are not
   you must go by a way in which you are not.

St. John of the Cross, I, 13, #10
The Ascent of Mt.
Carmel

We must be open enough to invite our lives to change in ways *we do not know*. That is the essence of male spirituality. Just as every Christian mystic has had to lock horns with the Mother Church, so every real man will lock horns with our *mater*nal Global/American culture. The ones who succeed in global culture are the betrayers, the manholes, the women, the phonies. Women and manholes woo the *mater*ial, men woo the divine darkness – the way they know not.

Divorce is a doorway into the darkness. Says Bly, it may have come about because of some particular childhood wound, or the marriage itself may have come about because of some childhood wound, but in either case the marriage's breakdown revives the wound. Now something can happen. An oft-quoted anecdote about Carl Jung claims that when someone came to him and said, "I just got promoted," he told them to "Stay calm. If we stick together we can get through this." But if they said, "I just got fired," he told them to celebrate, for surely, now "something important was about to happen."

Says Bly:
   Divorce feels, for most men, like a dishonorable discharge, as if one had been fired from the task taken on the day of the wedding. And the agony of separation from a substitute mother figure [to whom we were addicted by doses of praise like tubes of morphine], the sense of inadequacy among

demands for more money, the lack of grace in the new apartment or house, the felt rejection and isolation as the community withdraws some of its approval and support, the self-doubt the change evokes – all these add up to a new sort of loneliness. If the man refuses to be cheered up, and considers all of the discomforts to be cunning expressions of an isolating wound received early in childhood, then the man can use the divorce – like any other serious collapse – as an invitation to go through the door, accept *katabasis*, immerse himself in the wound, and exit from his old self through it.

[But only if he leaves his old ego back in his old life, otherwise he's a pig stuck in a pipe, doomed to repeat the same mistakes.]

One has the sense that some power in the psyche arranges a severe *katabasis* if the man does not know enough to go down on his own. Depression is a small *katabasis*. In depression we refuse to go down so a hand comes up and pulls us down. In grief we submit, we agree to go down. With initiators gone from our culture we do not receive instruction in how to go down on our own...[119]

On the way down one receives a little instruction about the dark side of God. The naive man may also receive a little instruction about the dark side of the Great Mother. Sooner or later the dark side of the Great Mother crystallizes out of the universe; the black darling has to appear, the one with the boar tusks hanging down from her lips. Perhaps she will appear in ordinary life as an enraged woman, a woman astounded by inconsistency or lack of control. The Angry Woman – the Rageful One, the Dark Side of the Moon, the Wretch who lives behind the furnace in the basement, the Ogre who lives on the back side of the moon with bat wings and ripped-apart birds.[120]

Women wear make-up and perfume and lovely dresses to conceal this creature from us. They decorate life and sweep it clean, wash its clothes, give us tender blowjobs, and for years we never pick up the scent of the beast. As Esther Vilar said earlier, women learn from a young age to camouflage their emotions, it becomes second nature, they do it unconsciously. They can talk all day long about how they feel and you still won't know a damn thing about how they feel. Sometimes you can see the pain in their eyes, in one of their "I don't want to talk about it" moods, when they really *do* want to talk about it, but they have trained themselves *never* to *really* talk about it. You can almost take it as a rule of thumb that whatever a woman *says* she is feeling, she is not feeling. This is not caring and sharing. We never know what they feel because they just lie about it. They lie to themselves, and in doing so, they lie to us.

Women turn emotions on and off like tap water. A woman can scream at her husband an hour after dinner and send him off to get drunk, watching TV in his room – then be ready to "give him some sex" a half hour later. These digital emotions belie how shallow the feelings are to begin with, and constitute a daily variety of emotional abuse. Men simply don't do this to each other. If you taunt the opposing pitcher, he'll throw you a beanball, not go off and get drunk in his room. We learn that in second grade. Women have ensconced vast cultural and judicial memes to prevent us from attacking them physically, but they think nothing of abusing us verbally and emotionally. Just before my ex filed for divorce, she was beating me, scratching me, kicking me, in the hopes she could prompt a violent response, call the cops, and file a police report against me. All this, on the advice of her manhole lawyer. When she failed to elicit a violent drubbing out of me she settled for calling the police and telling them I had threatened to "blow her head off", which I had. Great. She abused me verbally for fifteen years and when I respond to her physical abuse with one threat she calls the cops. What we've done, in this non-culture of ours, is erect one-way signs on a two-way street. Rightly or wrongly, abuse is answered by abuse. There is only so much abuse a man can take before he will respond forcefully. Women in other cultures know this; they operate their manipulation games within certain limits. Women in our culture – operating out of the vast, uninitiated, feminist meme – know nothing whatever of this two-way street. When women stop taunting and manipulating and abusing men the violence level will drop proportionally. When women stop flaunting sexuality there will be less rape. It is preposterous to watch pretty girls tease the hell out of men and then react with indignation when the men come-on to them. It bespeaks a deep sickness in our women that you don't find in Arab women or Chinese women or even European women – when they tease a man they know what to expect.

In India, the evil side of the great Mother is called Kali, and, as was just said, we are now living in her age, her era of *mater*ialism and *maya*, her meme – which is a time of being blinded by fascination with objects. In America, we don't have one single cultural archetype to represent and warn us off this type of behavior. Kali's life line runs the gamut from sexual conquest to utter human degradation. A worshipper of Kali might seduce a president or end up a junkie. Marilyn Monroe? Of course. But with all the evidence to the contrary we still want to believe the fairytale and never learn the lessons of the Blond Bombshell's dark side. We are only half a people. We think all women are good. The flowers around Kali's neck can change to human skulls and back to flowers in a fraction of a second. There's a lesson in this; they're trying to tell us something. If someone expects me to feel guilty and responsible because some black guy rapes a white girl coming out of a bar at 2:00 A.M. wearing two rubberbands and a cork then I want Gloria Steinem and Susan Faludi and all their followers to feel guilty and responsible for a 60% divorce rate and the fact that half of the kids in this country are growing up without dads. These self-appointed cops of our psyches have made a one-way street out of a two-way street and it's time to draw a line in the sand. Let's learn something from Marilyn. Let's have her be our Kali. Let's not let her life be wasted on a fairytale. She took drugs and fucked her way to the top and then killed herself, or got killed by people trying to protect Bobby Kennedy – that part of the story is still an unholy mystery. But that's Kali! An unholy mystery!

Only Shiva, a Hindu Wildman, can stand up to Kali. That is why, says Bly, that it is the Wildman who guides the initiation of young boys, not the palace priest. The Kennedy boys, with all their charisma, were hardly wildmen. The only way they could tame Kali was to off her. Not nice. And, not needed, once we understand the memes being played out here. The key is to transcend the *material*, transcend the ego, something the Kennedys, in their brief lives, never got a chance to learn. Let's learn something from them. Let's not allow them to have died in vain, these grand archetypes of our cultural era.

Says Bly:
> Descent is complete when [mom's soft tits and our girlfriend's slick ass] have been replaced by the boar-tusked, hog-bristled, fat-mouthed, skull necklaced, drugged, drooling, black hole [from which not even light escapes] of Baba Yaga, the evil side of the Great Mother.[121]
> Something wants us there, meeting the Black Queen, wants the boar to open its mouth, wants Grendel's pool to fill with blood, wants the sword to melt, wants the giantess to put the boy in the sack [wants the beauty queen to drown in her own whiskey-percodan vomit].

There is a witch in *every* woman. Our namby pamby do-gooder intelligentsia of limp-dicked social scientists have done a fabulously feminist job of educating us all to the idea that there are no such things as witches. Meanwhile, the witch-in-every-woman has flourished undetected, without the wisdom of a myth or a fairy tale or even a single article in *Psychology Today* to inform it. What are these people studying anyway? And who gives them all this money to publish all this useless garbage? If social science works why do we have a 60% divorce rate and a crack cocaine crisis? Who are these iguanas? What planet do they come from? Angry? You bet your ass I'm angry. I'm as angry as Jesus was when he kicked the merchants out of the temple, or when he said, "If you think I came to bring peace you've got your head up your butt. I came to bring the sword" – an ancient symbol that represents the severing of attachments and illusions.

A very young student once described a myth as a story that is not true on the outside, but is true on the inside. How much longer can we insist on rationalizing away the truth about our gender differences? How much longer can we tolerate the sheer amount of emotional pain of living in a feminist stronghold which is being presented to us as a "patriarchy"? Let's start calling it as it is. There are witches. There is a witch in every woman. Life demands that we confront this reality. We cannot trust a woman to become President who does not know that there is a side of her that is a stinking, festering, ego-driven ghoul – we'll just get Richard Nixon all over again.

Mythology stands ever ready to teach us. Circe, the temptress of Ulysses, turned men into pigs. Not four-footed, curly-tailed, garbage-eaters; but two-footed, lusty, foul-mouthed, gluttonous, squealing, female-serving, *anima*-cluttered, garbage-eaters. Women have the capacity for bringing out the mean, ego-driven worst in all of us. Without religion, *Male* religion, we don't have a chance. We don't have a center to retreat to when our wives are trying to convince us of their latest cowshit. You need the latest gadget she wants to purchase about as much as you need antlers. Go to the Deer God. Ask him.

Female religion teaches us to sing sweet songs. Male religion teaches us to eat ashes.

Says Bly:

Fairy tales preserve this awareness. A favorite character in Norwegian fairy tales is Askaladden (Ash Boy). For us there's Cinderella, the cinder girl, who tends the hearth of her evil step sisters. In folk tales tending the ashes always falls to the third son or third daughter; *i.e.*, the third life in this life. First comes childhood, then comes the vigor and success of the early adult years, then comes the ashes, the descent, the kitchenwork. Various cultures leave a time open for this hibernation or "ritual lethargy". In Norway boys who were working through emotional confusion actually slept in a raked area between the fire pit and the cinders, in the center of their long houses, sometimes for years.

* * *

In the South Seas a young man who does not want to work is fed and tolerated for months, or years, until the Life Force moves him into action again. This is just plain good mental health therapy. Why send a neurotic out in a small boat in huge waves to discombobulate everyone else in the boat? But our society does not allow or prepare us for these periods of regeneration. We are in one groove from second grade on and if we slip out of it we are lost forever, hammered with shame and a stigma of failure. How can anyone possibly decide what to make of his life in second grade? And no wonder the inevitable mid-life crisis is so severe. My son is doing everything in his power to please his mother and I'd hate to be married to him in thirty years when he finally snaps out of it.

Remember Ash Wednesday? Clearly this is an ancient and wonderful cultural connection between Christ's suffering during Holy Week and initiation rituals which took place more than 50,000 years ago. Hindus regularly apply ashes to their Third Eye. Why? To open it. The ash is the residue of failure that opens the eye of the soul.

Mircea Eliade recounts in his books the brilliant use made of ashes by old men initiators in Australia, Africa, the Near East, South America, and the Pacific. Initiation requires that before a boy becomes a man some infantile being in him must die. Ashes time is a time set aside for the death of the ego-bound boy. The boy, between eight and twelve years of age, having been *taken away from* the mother, passes into the hands of the old men guides who cover his face, and sometimes his whole body, with ashes to make him the color of dead people and to remind him of the inner death about to come. He may be put into the dark for hours or maybe days and there is introduced to the spirits of dead ancestors. He may crawl through a tunnel – a vagina – made of brush and branches. The old men are waiting for him at the birthing end of the hole, only now he has a new name. The mothers in some cultures feel so strongly about the importance of the ritual that when reunited with their sons they pretend not to recognize them and have to be reintroduced. Says Bly, the mothers participate joyfully in this initiation.

And how do American women react when you attempt to initiate your boy this way? With a gag order. With a restraining order. They file for divorce on grounds of insanity, withdraw visitation, and the *courts go along with it!* The boy is either going to walk the altar in his confirmation gown or you are going to walk the courtroom in front of a man wearing a dress. It's her way or the highway. This is America. It is so entirely feminine it baffles people all over the rest of the world and it is killing us off at an alarming rate. We fought and died to create this? Amazing.

Understanding ashes is understanding death. Ashes put on the face whiten it, as death does. But, says Bly, how can we get a look at the cinders side of things when society is determined to create a world of shopping malls [for women] and entertainment complexes [for kids] in which we are made to believe there is no death, disfigurement, illness, insanity, poverty, lethargy or misery. Disneyland means no ashes.

But around the age of 35 men begin to notice how many of their dreams have turned to ashes. They were going to write that novel, or marry that *Penthouse* Pet, or get famous, or save the whales or the rain forests or the hummingbirds or *something*, and they can see that an organization of strident young girls is already doing that. Rule by women is one big coffee klatch. No matter which of society's goals a man has pursued it is never satisfying because, essentially, it is a *mater*ialistic, feminist-approved goal; for if it wasn't, he would never have gotten anywhere performing it.

And, says Richard Rohr, even those who succeed in the system do not escape the ashes. What he calls the white male system (and what I call the manhole system) offers the illusion of power while holding back any real decision-making power. We are all free to do exactly the same things. This is why the system must offer illusions of success – promotions, paychecks, and other symbols of prestige – to men who know subconsciously that moving to another niche in the maze is no escape from the totally controlling game they are forced to play. A larger desk, a private office, a bigger house, a newer car, a more expensive vacation – such are the empty rewards men receive for surrendering their freedom to the [manhole] system [and for draining their masculine energy in the service of a feminized society rather than the Life Force].[122] They are being raped and abused. Men cannot serve both God and Mammon, and they are succumbing to Mammon – the Big Mammary in the sky. The dome of the Capitol. The star-spangled tit.

But, says Rohr, there is a way out of the system. In biblical language it is called salvation: being saved from the world and its false promises. And how is that accomplished? Historically the program was clear. The boy had to be separated from protective feminine energy and led into a ritual space where newness and maleness could be experienced as holy; the boy had to be ritually wounded and tested, had to experience bonding with other men and loyalty to tribal values. The pattern is so widely documented that one is amazed we have let go of it so easily, says Rohr.

That's cute. Apparently Father Rohr hasn't yet absorbed the significance of the fact that 85% of all teachers in this country are white women. We haven't "let go" of anything. We've been brain-washed, our minds have been edited by Marxist-Feminism, our teachers have skipped over the single most important character building moment in a man's life. A man cannot initiate his own son. For that he needs the united support of his community at large, and what is a boy's life but his school, the place where he is supposed to *learn everything* he needs to know to do well in life. What a sad joke.

Who will teach him if not his teachers? What kind of secular nightmare have we created for ourselves?

Says Rohr, now boys look to coaches, drill sergeants and gang leaders to give them what the church no longer gives them – and no wonder. The manholes are going to put him in a dress for confirmation and another dress for graduation.

Male initiation always had to do with hardness, difficulty, struggle and a respectful confrontation with the non-rational, the unconscious, the wild. It prepares the young man to deal with life in ways other than logic, managing, and problem solving – *i.e.*, all the stuff taught by mom at home and his surrogate mothers in school. Initiation prepares him for confrontation with the Spirit.[123]

"To organize is to destroy," said the Taoist poet Chang Tzu. He was talking about ancient China and modern America – both of them superpowers. We have organized ourselves to spiritual death. New diets, new pop singers, new authors are all ashes by the time we hit 35. Nothing works. The Fix-It-Philosophy is a bird flying around under water looking for a place to land. We haven't done the inner work. We don't even know what it is that we didn't do. There is nothing more to fix. There is only falling apart to do.

Says Bly:
Diminishment, falling apart, is a true and proper experience for men over thirty. A man who doesn't experience diminishment will retain his inflation and will continue to identify with externals: his sex drive, his mind, his refusal to commit himself, his addiction, his transcendence, his New Age cronies, his self-pity. Franklin Roosevelt found ashes in his polio; Anwar Sadat in prison, Solzhenitsyn in the gulag; John Steinbeck and William Faulkner found their ashes in the poverty of the Depression; [Mother Teresa as a young nun was shut out of Albania and never saw her mother or sister again – and never in anyone's memory, complained about it]; many pop performers find their ashes in drug and alcohol addiction.

But the lessons of the middle years are of a different order. "You only find happiness when you stop looking for it," says Chang Tzu. "Perfect joy is to be without joy. Perfect praise is to be without praise." This is not what our mothers and wives want us to believe. Once we do that, we are lost to them, lost to their manipulations.

Ashes work defies pigeonholing. Says Lao Tzu, "The Tao that can be named is not the eternal Tao." To do the work we must break with form, all form, but especially female form, female memes. Some have likened this work to looking for a dead body, our own dead body: the body of a shamed boy or a frozen intellectual or a feminized man. Says Bly, sometimes we have to slip through the enemy lines at night to find the corpse. Ashes work requires cunning and stealth. It requires the help of a god.[124]

> Says Father Rohr:
> By and large the church is no help. The western world has turned the church into another corporation, with corporate headquarters downtown in the bishop's office and company stores conveniently located all around the city and suburbs. In the fourth century, when Christians were first permitted to practice their faith openly, they allowed the church to be molded to the image of the Roman Empire instead of insisting that the Gospel of Jesus transform the crumbling imperial system. [The church was a crutch to prop up the empire.] Bishops and priests became the executives and managers of a vast new religious organization…By the fourth century, at the Council of Nicea, those parts of the Gospel that could be organized were kept in the church, and what could not be organized was left out.[125]

How can you organize a spiritual journey? To organize is to destroy. The Taoists organized their brilliant insights into a cult of demon and spirit worship which was alive and well in Singapore last time I was there; and which has absolutely no affinity to Lao Tzu's teachings. What happened? Women and Manholes happened.

How can you organize self-transformation and conversion? It's impossible, says Rohr. You can give guidance. You can provide a ritual climate conducive to shattering the ego's presuppositions. You can give hints and clues. You can offer assurance and encouragement. But you can't serve it up on a platter, which is what women and children demand. If religion were a restaurant what we have done is akin to throwing the menu out the window and serving only cheese pizza because that's what the kids and mom want. It's something they understand. We have demeaned the spiritual journey by serving up only its lowest common denominator. You can't organize and control spiritual development precisely because it's a matter of *spirit*, and you can't organize and control *spirit*.

And what else besides spirituality got organized in the fourth century? Clerical dress, says Rohr, which by now has become ludicrous. Men wear robes and dresses, and the higher up the hierarchy they climb the more ornate the gowns and jewelry they wear. This is the King, the Holy Roman Emperor, the Manhole. Do you suspect that this style of dress had any magical effect on drawing more women into the church? You bet your penis it did. The feminine style of dressing did not appear until the imperialization of the church began in the fourth century, and it's been with us ever since. I have no doubt that English and American judges adopted this style of dress to give themselves the same regal air. The king is the original manhole. So the king and the crown and the scepter all went together. As the feminine meme captured secular society 8000 years ago, so it captured the church 1600 years ago. Men dressed up as women espousing female values of organization and accumulation of wealth, and of gaining *currency* in heaven.

And now they want to be ordained. Why not? Anything less than that is just a profound deception. Esther Vilar already pointed that out. It can only speed us on our way. Men are unlikely to understand how desperately they need a rejuvenated male spirituality until they pop into church one Sunday and find a female priest spewing all the mumbo jumbo that manholes have been spewing for 1600 years. Once they hear it from out of the mouth of a woman, they will recognize it for what it is: psychic garbage – a spirituality that has been organized to death by female memes.

There is nothing at all wrong with female priests or rabbis. Ordaining women is simply a matter of calling a spade a spade. Personally, I want a priest who tears off his shirt and dances around the fire and howls at God. That's the kind of release my testosterone, my biology, is crying out for. I want a spiritual leader who touches the deep part of me that is not touched by words and meekness and nicey nicey. I don't need someone floating across the altar in a dress instilling guilt trips. Nor do I want to be wafted away on strains of New Age flute music. I want God and I want him now!

Now we're even trying to make God female. Great. Fuck the father hunger in our psyches, fuck the yearning in all of us for a benign and just Man who listens to us in our grief. Colonizing the schools and the government and the churches and the synagogues wasn't enough. What will they feminize next? Science? They're already doing a pretty good number on medicine and health care, and social science. I've yet to find a shelter for emotionally battered men. In fact, there is only one. It's called jail. So when we all get tossed in jail we can pray to God the Mother and that way the last remaining shred of masculine spiritual relief will be gone. Maybe we can get benefits for ejaculating into bottles and that way we can just stay in there, and the women can have the whole thing.

Apropos to what happens in jail Richard Rohr tells a poignant story which I'll simply repeat:

Father Hunger is sometimes called the Father Wound. Psychologists use that term to highlight the woundedness in a man's psyche that results from not having a father – whether it's because the father has died or left the family, because the father's work keeps him absent from the scene most of the time, or because the father keeps himself aloof from involvement with his children. In any event, the result is a deep hurt, a deprivation that leads to a poor sense of one's own center and boundaries, a mind that is disconnected from one's body and emotions, and the passivity of an unlit fire.

When I was giving a retreat in Peru a sister who ministers in Lima's central prison brought this lesson home to me. She described how, as Mother's Day was approaching during her first year there, the men in the prison kept asking her for Mother's Day cards. She kept bringing boxes and boxes of cards to the prisoners to send home to mama, but she never seemed to have enough. So, as Father's Day approached, she decided to prepare for the onslaught of requests by buying an entire case of Father's Day cards. That case, she told me, years later, is still sitting in her office. Not one man asked her for a Father's Day card. Not one man! She realized then – and as she told me the story I realized too – that most of the men were in jail because they had no fathers. Not that they were orphans, but they had never been around a healthy, sane, responsible man. They had never been fathered. They had never seen themselves as sons of men who admire them, they never had felt a deep, secure identity, they never had received that primal enthusiasm that comes from growing up in the company of a father.[126]

They had received all the love a mother can give, and for that they ended up in prison. Bad boys. Criminals. The situation is no different in America's prisons and Detox centers. American men have not been fathered, or grandfathered. The best that mom can do is not enough to keep her son out of prison. This is a fact of human life. It takes a man to make a man. Half of the kids in this country are growing up without dads. This is a *crisis* that makes the possibility of nuclear holocaust seem like a game of dueling water pistols. Some kids are really getting hurt here!

And for this reason, to fill this need, God the Father emerged in the midst of the feminist/agricultural revolution 2000 years ago. The archetype of God the Father is the only father some men, and women, will ever have. For most people, God the Mother is already alive and well, at home. God the Father is stern but just, and absolutely silent. He doesn't provide printouts of what you're supposed to be doing today. You know when you are doing the right thing or not. God the Father is everywhere. He is not yakking in your ear; he bids you to learn by making mistakes. The avatar Jesus – clearly at a loss to explain his own physical origin – referred to Him as *Abba*, which, in Aramaic, means "papa" or "daddy". Here was a boy who was a bit of a rebel, who didn't fit in, who didn't believe the crap he heard in the temple, who was adopted but not entirely "fathered" by Joseph; a boy who was a prime candidate for juvenile delinquency and a life of crime – who found his salvation in a spiritual Abba.

Can we afford to brutalize the psyches of our young men any further? God, the Life Force, is beyond color and form and sound and words. This is an acknowledged meeting point of Jewish, Christian, Buddhist, Hindu, Muslim and native American spirituality from way, way back. And yet, the first toe-print into those murky waters of "God" that many an addict or a prisoner makes, comes from testing the idea, just for a moment, that there is a loving Father out there somewhere. The notion that God the Father is loving, and not merely vengeful, like the alcoholic old man, the absent old man, is a tremendous psychic breakthrough for many a man, and woman, in Detox and jail.

Almost everyone has a loving mother. Almost no one has a loving father. And now the intellectual manholes are militating for "inclusive" language in yet another obscene attempt to cut the balls off God.

Says Patrick Arnold:

The devastation in the psyches of young people who grow up without a strong and involved father is apparent to anyone who has worked with juvenile delinquents, prisoners, and indeed, many kinds of wounded people from dysfunctional families. It is unfortunate that, at a time when millions of families so desperately need models and examples of father-involvement, religious intellectuals should argue for the annihilation of precisely the metaphor that most exemplifies and models masculine commitment and care – God the Father. Abba.[127]

It is clear to me that there is no end-point to female memetic incursions into our psyches – not in business, not in school, not in religion. Men were created to counter, to offset, to compensate for female memes; and we can only do that by drawing a line in the sand and asserting our position. That is done by holding your palm out in front of you and saying, "You can do what you want with your own life, but you will not invade my mind, or my children's minds, past this point."

Thousands of years ago men adopted female values and now the women are in a headlong rush to take over the positions of those men. Let them. It will only speed our journey. For 8000 years we've been flipping a coin that is tails on both sides.

Periodically attempts have been made to wrest spiritual authority away from the feminized church – early monastic movements come to mind. In St. Benedict's monastery, founded in the wake of the Council of Nicea, priests were welcome as guests – *only* if they didn't stay too long, or try to take over. Benedict started his community to get away from priests. Once a month the monks walked into town to go to Sunday mass and that was it. Says Rohr, as the church became more organized and systematized, individuals, and then groups of men and women, opted out of the system to try to live the Gospel in the desert or forest, on mountains, and in other places where they could be close to God and pursue spiritual development without outside interference. Soon enough, the church absorbed these movements and "organized" them. Nowadays more than half of the monks in a Benedictine monastery are priests and they hold mass every day so each can take a turn serving it. Also, the Abbot of a Benedictine community is required by Rome to be a priest. Awful. Originally a priest could scarcely be a guest in one! The forces of Marxist/Feminism are awesome and awful, and they never stop. There is no end point. There is nothing on earth they won't try to organize.

Says Patrick Arnold:

At the heart of masculinity is its resistance to the matriarchal world – life-giving, nurturing, and comfortable as it is. In the most basic sense, the masculine is defined by its opposition to, separation from, and contrast with, the feminine. From the first stages of fetal development the male differentiates himself from the feminine environment and the *mater*nal world…The male urge toward individuation creates in normal men psychic stress, anxiety, and guilt – a perpetual love/hate relationship with intimacy – as they feel compelled to protect their ego boundaries from *mater*nal influence.[128]

* * *

Their wife/lover eventually breaks down this barrier of mistrust with massive doses of sex, the one thing mom couldn't give. He opens his heart completely to this woman. Then she leaves him and he dies inside. But, being uninitiated and therefore having no notion of how to go down gracefully, he resists the fall with drugs and alcohol and crude amounts of willfulness. Consequently the descent is not complete and he is doomed to repeat the same mistake over and over again. If I thought women knew what they were doing to their sons and lovers (which I don't) I would be compelled to view this as a grotesque conspiracy to demolish men. The fact is, they're just oblivious. Willful and oblivious. The point is, we have to make the break from the world of mom, and for that we need help.

Says Bly:

We recall that most cultures describe the first stage of initiation as a sharp and clean break from the mother. The Queen Mother possesses the key to the Wild Man's cage under her pillow and she's not going to give it up. It must be taken from her. Old men simply go into the women's compound with spears one day when the boys are between 8 and 12 and take the boys away. Up to that point the boys have lived exclusively with the women. In New Guinea, to take one example, the initiated men live together in houses at the edge of the village. Mothers in New Guinea carefully refrain from telling the boys anything about the impending events retaining the element of surprise. As the men lead them away, the boys cry out, "Mommy! Save me, mommy, save me!" The mother's world looks wonderful all at once. The women put up a resistance but it does no good. The old men start to take the boys, say, to an island where the initiator's hut has been built. The mothers of the boys being abducted appear on the bridge with spears. "Here I am, mommy! Save me!" cry the boys, but the old men drive the mothers back. The mothers go home, have coffee, meet the other women, and say things like, "How did I do? Did I look fierce enough?" "You were great."[129]

* * *

When gender issues are well understood, the women do not oppose the initiatory work with the boys but participate enthusiastically, if wistfully, in the drama of it. This presupposes, of course, that the women want their boys to turn into men and not manholes, which these days is a faulty supposition. Most women will mouth allegiance to the virtues of having the father spend time with his son, and then do everything in their power to edit and control this contact. The women are not going to agree to the things that must be done. In this culture, getting mom's approval is paramount to surrendering your weapons before the first shot is fired. And, with the judges in their back pockets, it may be decades, if ever, that we can expect help from that quarter. Judges are men who wear dresses. And worse, the deceptions we are facing are becoming world wide.

Japan is considered a *samurai*, macho culture. Richard Rohr notes that Japanese women, assumed in the west to be docile and subservient, completely control the home, the raising of the children, and the money. Husbands hand over their entire paycheck to their wives and are rewarded with an allowance. Children hardly ever see their fathers because men gather in reinforcement groups to affirm each other thereby perpetuating the broken cycle of father-son bonding. This is how the Japanese achieve such a high degree of conformity in their society – the women control everything.[130]

Germany is much the same. Widely acknowledged as the most left-brained culture on earth we've been duped into believing that this is a macho, not a feminine, trait. Biology proves that wrong. Germany is a *mater*nal, *mater*ialistic culture. Black Elk and his kin have not been welcome there for thousands of years. More fucked up psychology has come out of Germany and Germanic cultures than from any other culture in the history of life on earth. And why? Because we've switched the metaphor. Women are left-brained. Women are the organizational *samurai*. Women demand rules and regulations and order.

As in the prior example of the supposed Judeo/Christian Patriarchy, the *actual control* in the most *mater*ialistic societies on this planet has been shrouded in veil upon veil of seduction and misdirection and mock subservience. The actual control has been wielded by women. Germany and Japan went to war because they wanted *more stuff*. And they didn't surrender until mama's farm was being bombed. I talked to an ex-Nazi woman, yes *woman* – I bet you were led to believe there wasn't such a thing – an ex-Nazi woman who heard Hitler speak many times. She told me she still remembers how "captivating" he was. *Captivating!* You bet your bra. He was feeding straight into the female meme, that same meme we're feeding today regarding women's "rights" to have more stuff, more control, more objects, more pride, more ego, more respect.

Female oppression is a lie. Women are not now, and never have been oppressed. They have never been required to fight in war or mine coal. Female greed and self-seeking is an historical reality. Female oppression is the biggest lie, as Esther Vilar said, in the societies where it is most highly and loudly touted. Europe, Japan, and America are female cultures. This is a hall of mirrors we've entered and we men pay with our health and sanity and shortened lives to take the walk through the Funny House of pop culture. We elect manholes to public office and then wonder why we get into wars. Mass insanity.

Will God Help?

Says Rohr, religion in our culture has become the province of the female, and spirituality has been feminized. American Christianity (and Judaism, and Buddhism, and Yoga, and Sufism) is more about belonging and consoling than doing, risking, confronting. No wonder men hate going to church. The institution is only servicing their *anima*, their feminine side, which is buried and which properly remains below the surface of life in the healthy male. Being aware of your *anima* is healthy. *Acting out of* your *anima*, for men, constitutes "mood". It's disjointed from our true selves. It's wearing our underpants on our heads.

Man has often seen the cloying part of himself as feminine, says Robert Johnson. And pushing it even further away he has turned it into the witch. Much of the cloying, insidious element rejected during the Middle Ages was construed as feminine – hence the burning of the witches. These were not a few isolated occurrences that gained unwarranted publicity; it has been estimated that more than *four million women* were burned at the stake during the height of the counterreformation in Europe.[131]

Why don't they teach us about *this* in fifth grade? This is the most incredible historical fact I have ever heard and I didn't hear about it until I was 43. Did our teachers think they were sparing us boys some guilt trip? Or were they afraid of giving us weird ideas? Is it another walk through this strange hall of mirrors to believe that everyone is better off not knowing the explosive and irrational ways men have reacted to real, or perceived, female spiritual oppression? What were these women killed for? Nothing? Four million women? I doubt it. Four million people are not burned at the stake in a public spectacle because they did nothing. Something had to have gone down. Some glorious rebellion or some insidious plot of some kind must have been afoot for society to spend its free time just collecting enough firewood to burn 4 million people. We've got better things to do with our time. So what's up? *Who* is hiding *what* from us now, regarding this outbreak of mass insanity? Who could possibly benefit from suppressing this information? The church, and the government – both feminist/*mater*ialist institutions? Something stinks.

I hate to think we are headed for another *real* gender war. Guns, knives, bonfires of insanity. That's why I'm writing this book. But how many boys can be torn away from their dads before society implodes and sets off another round of insanity equal to the above massacres? A society that executes four million of its women? I've never heard of such a thing. No wonder the Thais and the Indians and the Arabs consider us barbarians. Clearly something is wrong, but what is it? Europe has had a great history of famous and revered queens. The issue here is not political power. No one is going to off a woman for her economic/political aspirations – self-serving as they may be. But maybe history is muttering something in our ears in a deep gravelly voice: "Girls, keep your hands off male spirituality. It's none of your business."

We are all cells in the body of humanity – black, brown, white – red cells, white cells, bone cells. The human organism is the *whole* human organism, the whole thing, all of us together. We all constitute the human experiment. And just as our immune system is working constantly to remove cancers and kill amoebas, the human organism is striving to maintain some memetic equilibrium within itself. It is not "right" that four million women were burned at the stake, or that 12 million Russians died in WW II, but it is our evolutionary duty to try to understand the possible reasons for these disasters and diminish them in the future. Did Stalin's non-aggression pact with Hitler, which contradicted every socialist meme, set up Mother Russia for disaster? Did women's crab-clawed infiltration of male spirituality usher them into disaster? Who knows? But I do sense that women cannot govern male spirituality without killing it and thereby setting the Human Organism to devouring itself. Their intentions may be no more threatening than a whiff of pollen, but the Organism will throw the full weight of its immune system into battle against the incursion. To tame the beast we need old men.

Says Bly:
    Old men take the boy underground to meet the Earth Father, to handle the snake until their fear is gone. Mythologically, the snake resembles the Wild Man and other beings who lie in the water at the bottom of our psyches. [And girls don't like snakes.]
    When a man accepts the Descent, the ashes, as a way to move to the father's house, he learns to look at the death side of things, he glances down the rat hole where the snake feeds.

He trades in the bird of his youth for a black snake. Initiation asks the son to move his love energy away from mommy and warm milk and cookies to dad's cold steel shotgun bore and muddy boots. This is ashes work. When you learn this in puberty it's not so hard to accept ashes during life's later transitions when we are again expected to eat dust like a snake, increase our stomach for terrifying insights, widen our throats to swallow the evil facts of history and of our own betrayals, shudder as we detoxify from our addictions, burn deep with the molten heat of grief, navigate in the blackness without smacking the cave walls, using our intuition like the ultrasonic beeps of a bat – emptying ourselves of ourselves and being reborn, in total blackness, to the life of the Spirit within – and then, and only then, exiting the cave mouth, birthing into the light. Men find God in the blackness, not the light. Women, like moths, are attracted to light. Blackness is not evil, blackness is the ground of all creation. Look at the night sky. I'm not going to soft-pedal this any more by saying that without blackness you can't have light. The Blackness *is* the light! Blackness is the ground of male spirituality. From the Void of Buddha – best translated as a plenum, an empty space that is full; to the inner sanctum of a Hindu Temple – which is kept black; from the black hole of physics to the black hole of the kiva; from Zorro to Batman to St. John of the Cross and his dark night of the soul; from the belly of Jonah's whale, to the yang, of the yin and the yang – the deep male thing is always black. The Earth Father, who begets the Green Man, is black. The Soul Man is black. Black is beautiful.

And what is the soul journey we have carved out for the American male? Says Rohr, all his life man is engaged in what one would expect to be a typically female pursuit – fixing up the house. That's what we're good for – fixing up the house – an avocation which used to be performed by women. We have been seduced by our *anima* into believing that stability and meaning in life can be achieved by buying and maintaining a house. It cannot. A house is an object that sucks a preposterous amount of male energy into mortgages and taxes and insurance and repairs to satisfy essentially female needs for arranging furniture and hanging draperies. How many men do you know who have martyred their lives on the hearth of their fireplace? They can't quit a job they hate, they can't sail around the world, they can't go see the animals in Kenya, they're lucky if they can go fishing for one week in summer. And all for the false security of being a "property owner". Ever get divorced? First thing you lose is the house. And if they can get away with it they'll stick you with continuing to make the payments on it.

The modern American house is a black hole for money and energy. For 20,000 years Americans lived in tents. Now the Uniform Building Code, influenced by lobbyists from every conceivable building trade, have tripled the price of an average house. I've built four houses. I can build a perfectly adequate house for $30,000 – today, June, 2001. When the building and zoning departments get done with what I'm required to do to it, that house will cost $60,000, plus land. That means that instead of paying my house off in two years, like people in the rest of the world, I'll still be paying on it in 25 years. America, wake up. The feminist meme of serving only our comrades and "getting what is rightfully ours" has invaded the building trades big time. Why not? They're servicing and aggravating the boundless fears of women. You need a wall socket every ten feet like you need three intestines. You need an insulation inspector like you need nuclear acid in your granola. Other people in other countries don't live like this. To give one example, Florida has the toughest building codes, the most inspectors, and the worst quality construction in the United States. More inspectors and higher prices do not make for a better house. There's a building boom going on in America – but only if you're a contractor who builds expensive homes. Otherwise, forget it. Poor people can't find modest, starter homes because banks won't finance them. The Savings and Loan industry was destroyed due to bankers' greed and banks don't like to make a bunch of small loans when they can make a few big ones. So working people are left out.

All this propaganda we get about how happy and free we are here is a lot of whistling up your wazoo. Other people in other countries are not chained like dogs to 25-year mortgages. They sell some fish, they buy some cement, they get their brothers and uncles to help them, they pour some footings or lay some bricks, and in less than a year of sporadic labor the place is finished enough to move in the wife and kids. That's how this works!

And how do we do it? We create a whole paper-pushing class of women and manholes whose salaries we pay in order for them to tell us how we can build our own goddamned house and when it is finished enough to move in. No wonder there's a housing shortage in this country. We have organized ourselves right out of being able to provide basic shelter. Everyone has to be upper middle class, or there's no room for them. You are totally free to pay rent to somebody and, in two years, pay them what it would cost to build your own place. So what if your hand-built, third-world house would be small? It would be yours and it would be paid for! We don't even remember what freedom means anymore. It means: freedom from paying a goddamned mortgage.

Says Rohr, in the Greek city state men devoted their lives outward to the community. A freeman's day was spent on community service and community affairs. The women ran the house. Men who, due to domestic friction or incompetent wives, spent their lives divided between public action and their private world of personal concerns, were called *idios*, idiots.[132]

What has feminized American society made us into? Idiots. We make money during the week to meet our mortgage payments and then spend the weekend mowing the lawn and fixing the gutters. Idiots. Our cities are crumbling because masculine energy is not being spent in the public forum, it is mired in a feminine value system that refuses to look outside its own backyard. Our notions about ownership of property have gone completely off the scale of sane behavior. If our value system is such that we are only considerate of that which we own (a female meme) then our cities don't have a prayer of recovery. Where are we going to find the spiritual strength to extend ourselves, unselfishly, in the public forum, into the community? Probably not from the church.

Father Rohr says that if he were to name the virtues he was taught at the seminary he'd be sorely tempted to call them something like "company virtues". They're the kind of qualities that people at the top like to instill in people on the bottom so they don't rock the boat and so they keep the company's business running smoothly…in one sense, they can also be called feminine virtues.[133]

So there we have it. In one sentence Rohr corroborates everything I have been saying about the church, corporations, and women. They're the same. Their values are indistinguishable. Businessmen, priests and women operate off the same memes.

When the entire focus of the church or company or family is maintaining relationship and holding the center, something is sorely lacking – the masculine virtues of scouting new territory, mapping the frontier, feeding intuition, kindling creativity. Creativity is all about *breaking* old patterns of relationship. The memes our society runs on are militantly anti-creative, anti-intuitive, anti-male.

What Rohr calls the feminine virtues are humility, obedience, openness, receptivity, trust, forgiveness, patience, and long-suffering. Personally I do not know a single woman who displays any of these qualities except Mother Teresa. The women I know are vain, aggressive, defensive, willful, suspicious, grudge-bearing, impatient and quick-tempered. However, I do know a few men who display some of the above virtues. That's really the point of this book: men have absorbed female values to such an extent that the women are reacting by trying to take on male attributes. We're switching roles and we don't even recognize it. The Human Organism will have its agenda met, will strike its balance, one way or another. And so, men are acting out of their *anima* and women are acting out of their *animus* – we are all operating out of our weaker side.

Father Rohr, like all of us, has been caught up in the feminist whitewash of the past 25 years (if not 8000 years). He can't see that what he is really describing above are the attributes of feminized males and that women, by and large, don't fit those character descriptions any longer. He is right, however, when he says that these are the kinds of virtues a king wants his subjects to have. These are the attributes needed for holding the family, the company, the kingdom, or the Church together – but not for starting new families or churches or companies or kingdoms. It's a Vilarian world, the women have us doing *all* their work for them including keeping the families together. And we of the female virtues, the feminine meme, have no power to move in an outward direction.

What are the virtues needed to move in an outward direction? Says Rohr, they are self-possession, leadership, truthfulness, decisiveness, responsibility, closure, intelligence, inner authority, challenge, courage, risk-taking – *i.e.*, the virtues associated with the average warrior or saint. These are not traits associated with the "liberated woman" acting out of her *animus*, or weak male side. The poor quality of masculinity exhibited by these creatures includes *mater*ial orientation, trendiness, deceit, indecisiveness, irresponsibility, loose-endedness, ignorance, service to a *popular* "cause", obnoxiousness, cowardice, fault-finding, opaqueness and deviousness. We find this *animus* surrounding our lives at home, in business and even in church, but we never hear much about the true masculine virtues. They're bad for business. And that, says Rohr, is why it often took several hundred years for saints to be canonized – it took that long for the reality of their lives to wear off and for the Mother Church to domesticate their vision. St. Francis taking off his clothes in front of the bishop, and walking around talking to birds and cows? A little scary for any control-freaks to handle.

Has Rohr mentioned "intuition" anywhere in his list of male virtues? Hardly. He has the same blind spot almost all of us have regarding the true source of male aptitude. The male traits he's mentioned are the ones most easily mimicked by women, so let's have a look at that.

By "self-possession" Rohr means "the ability to be in touch with your clear center, your feelings and your motives." A self-possessed man knows his values and *acts upon them*. Do you know any men like this? Two? Pretty good. How about any women? That's what I thought. They seem to have an opinion about everything and act on none of them none of the time.

A "self-possessed" man has not been bought. He's not trying to please people or coddle their biases. But now we come to the real male part. Says Rohr, the "self-possessed" man seeks the will of God even against self-interest. Hurray for the thought, but does this sentence have any meaning? What sense does it make to say that the self-possessed man acts against his own self-interest? I apologize to Father Rohr, whom I greatly admire, for using his writing as an example of the kind of confused semantics, and the awkward thinking that goes along with it, that permeates male/female role conceptions in America. We need to get our thinking straight and to do that we need to get the words right. The real man, the initiated man (not the "self-possessed" man) is capable of reaching deep down into his well of intuition and acting against his own self-interest in favor of a greater good. Women, by and large, do not do this. That's why there are so many men out of work and so many women with jobs. Thank you to the Vietnam Generation for that bit of social grace. Men have been able to look *outside* their own interest toward a greater good. Women seem, in most cases, to be lined up squarely *behind* their own interests – the "special needs of women". They don't give a shit about what's good for society, they only give a shit about what's good for themselves. The manholes they fought to *get* their jobs were certainly not the guys who *gave up* their jobs. And before long the corporate manholes caught on that they could get away with paying women – along with blacks and wetbacks – less money, and a whole new arena of American economic exploitation opened up.

These developments were necessary and inevitable. I'll let you be the judge of whether they were justified or not; personally, I have no opinion on this issue. I couldn't care less who goes to work flipping burgers or selling real estate or making copper tubing. Men were not created to do that. That is not our destiny. Whoever wants to serve the *mater*ial beast, let them have at it. Let them be the idiots. Serving object-oriented domesticity is not the kind of masculine energy this world is going to need to marshal to survive the kinds of population explosions this globe is facing. By the time every Chinese gets a refrigerator the ozone layer will be gone and we won't be able to go outside without getting cancer. Maybe *all* the men need to lose their jobs to get their thinking straight on this one.

Women have to use less toilet paper, paper towels, napkins, and paper diapers and then maybe someone will stop cutting forests. Minorities have to fight to get off welfare – create their own economic communities like the Nation of Islam, rather than depending on government and corporations – stop sending half their paychecks back to Mexico, and provide strong male figures to initiate their boys. White men have to throw off the feminine memes of white women and generate an intuitive spirituality that takes them out of themselves and puts them back in touch with the ideals of working for the community. Says Rohr, the feminized corporate male cannot do what he believes is right because he's not even sure what he believes in. What's worse, if he ever figured out what he believed in he'd quit his job today. Or if he actually acted on what he believed in he'd get fired. "Primitive" man did not have to live out this schizophrenia. He worked with nature, not against it. We are idiots. We are manholes – feminized males at the top of society operating family and church and corporation *only* on the basis of *mater*ial perspectives. No wonder we are raping the planet. We, of the industrialized nations, are 25% of the people consuming 75% of the resources. We are not self-possessed. We are possessed by Marxist/Feminism – that uncanny ability to say one thing and do another.

Ask a judge to enforce child support collection and he has wage garnishment, access to your bank account, and various other means to employ. Ask him to enforce parental visitation and he has nothing to offer. He's wearing his underpants on his head. Possession is 90% of the law and that means that 90% of the law is dedicated to enforcing *mater*, the *mater*ial, the possession of objects. Our Constitution was written to enforce human freedom and our legal system is consumed by questions of ownership. We gotta pay the money but we can't see our kids – this coin is tails on both sides!

To continue Rohr's analysis:

The *truthful* man can step out of himself and view what is going on in the world apart from his emotional attachment to it. He is able to set aside his self-interest and seek the truth for all concerned.[134] This is what the initiation induces, the self-less state. Traditionally society has felt it was fine for girls and women to be self-seeking, the she-bear-protecting-her-cubs kind of thing. But it was vital that men transcend self-interest. The balance between these two poles of behavior is precisely what we have sacrificed by flooding the market place with feminine memes. Women and manholes in business do not serve purposes higher than themselves. This is the most severe ramification of deserting the masculine pole. This is the cause of war.

Says Rohr, *Responsibility* is *respond*-ability – the ability to size up a situation, see what has to be done, and do it.[135] If a man needs help he finds it. If he needs authorization he gets it. Something happens when the responsible person is on the set. You don't just get a bunch of talk about what other people are supposed to be doing – the cosmic "they". You get results.

Challenge, says Rohr, is meeting life on its own terms. Working with it. Interacting with it. Praying to it. Not bending it to your will. Bending your will to it.

Robert Bly has said that both Freud and Jung were mother-oriented (Germanic) so our modern psychology is mother-oriented. That fits. As we're seeing, so are all the other memes that inform our lives. He believes that at some point life requires a certain fierceness. Not violence, not aggression, not assault, but fierceness. The Taoists and all the other world religions, including the 12-Steppers, tell us to surrender to win. Are these memes contradictory? It certainly seems so. But hold on. Somewhere in here we find we are asking ourselves the most important question in life – "to will or not to will", that is the question. Herein lies the great paradox of our emotional lives on this planet. Yet we don't have to look far to find a point of confluence between the two.

Witness the halfback. The quarterback slams the ball in his gut and he charges upfield with locomotive fierceness. *But,* he must follow his blockers to make any progress at all, *and,* his art consists of evading, not confronting, would-be tacklers. An expert halfback is a good part Taoist. We are all born facing forward with a ball in our hands, propelling ourselves toward something, and the only way to get there is a subtle combination of fierceness and finesse – we move forward sidestepping tacklers. That is the art of life. Sure we get tackled, hard and often, that's part of the game. There wouldn't be a game without that. But we move the ball.

Closure, says Rohr, is the strength to make a decision when a decision has to be made. Most times we cannot find out a decision is wrong until it has been made. Nothing less than the courage to live with the results of your decisions serves here. The male trains himself to act instantly – jump off the cliff, or turn and fight the bear. There is no room for inner dialogue. Jump or fight. You can't call up your girlfriends or read about it in *Working Woman*. Jump or fight. It's an instinct call, an intuitive leap, that men have been making for 2.2 million years. Without this beautiful, paradoxical, combination of fierceness and surrender as pathways into our intuition we would not be here to talk about this. Men are "intuition in action". And we learn how this works from other men, not from women.

Robert Bly comments that over the past ten years he has heard it said in a hundred different ways that "there is not enough father."[136] This sentence implies that "father" is a substance like salt or ground water which, in earlier times, might have been in short supply but which now, in some areas, has simply disappeared.

According to Geoffrey Gorer, for a boy to become a man in the United States, the only thing he needs to do is reject his father. This is what the system requires, and mothers make this very easy. Many sons in this country view the father as an object of ridicule to be made fun of, as so often transpires in TV commercials, comic strips and sit coms. Clearly, says Bly, "father water" in the home has sunk below the reach of most wells.

When the father-table drops and there is too little father water what do the sons do? Drill for new father water, ration the father water, hoard it, distill mother water into father water?

Traditional cultures still in existence seem to have a good supply of father. In many of these cultures substitute fathers work with the young men. Uncles loosen the son up or tell him about women. Grandfathers give him stories. Old men teach ritual and soul – all of these men are honorary fathers.

Says Bly:
    Fathers and sons in most tribal cultures live in an amused tolerance of each other. The son has a lot to learn, and so the

father and son spend hours trying and failing to make arrowheads or spear bats or fool fish...When a father and son do spend long hours together, which some fathers and sons still do, we could say that a substance almost like food passes from the older body to the younger.

The contemporary mind might want to describe the exchange between father and son with some feminized verbal concept like bonding or miming or likening of attitude, but I think that a physical exchange takes place, as if some substance was passing directly into the cells. The son's body – not his mind – receives, and the father gives this food at a level far below consciousness. This is a meal of intuition served without words. The son does not receive a hands-on healing but a bodily resonance. His cells receive some knowledge of what a masculine body is. The younger body learns at what frequency the masculine body vibrates. It begins to grasp the song the adult male cells sing, and how the charming, elegant, lonely, courageous, half-shamed male molecules dance.[137]

Men are not more object-oriented than women. Women are the *mater*ialists. Men speak three and a half times fewer words than women and consequently a greater portion of their communication is done through gesture and nuance and body language that is beyond the scope of female apprehension. It bids you be quiet and observant to "hear" it, just as you must be quiet and observant in the woods or in a boat if you wish to hear a deer or find a fish. Men are not less nurturing than women; we nurture by moving and keeping still, by resonating a deep force that we call our children out to and up to. And often it is more painful for us than it is for them to be quiet and not shout out our fears and apprehensions.

I'll never forget the time in Little League my baby boy caught a fly ball with his face. He put his mitt up, kept his eye on the ball like I'm sure the coach had told him, forgot to move his mitt, and the ball whopped him right in the eye socket. I started to rush onto the field but I saw him shake it off and his coach got there before me so I stopped halfway. My heart flew out of my body to him, but he was not hurt and he was oh-so embarrassed. The last thing he wanted was his dad fawning over him in the middle of the field making him feel even more stupid. The mental pain, the embarrassment, hurt much more than the smack to his head. I cried inside, I wanted to hug him, to touch him, to love him, but he would have hated me for it. The coach nodded at me to communicate that everything was all right. He brushed my boy's hair, trotted off the field, and it was "on with the game". My son never mentioned a thing about it, but it was one of the roughest moments of my life. I had to let my baby boy decide what he wanted and not just shove my way into his pain to appease my own fear and distress. Was this a typically "cold" male response? On the surface it would seem so – but all I know is, at that moment, I kept my ego out of it and bowed to forces much greater than myself, including first and foremost, the wishes of my baby boy. He took the hit and called himself outside the pain to join a much bigger arena, and be recruited by a team that plays on a vast playing field – and all I could do was watch it happen.

Says Bly:

The son's early years are spent tuning to the mother's frequencies. How sharp a receiver his ear becomes for the upper and lower registers of mama's voice. He learns that, or dies.

But now, standing next to the father as they chip arrowheads, or repair plows, or climb on the roof, or wash pistons in gasoline, or care for birthing animals, the boy's body has a chance to retune. Slowly, over months or years, the son's body-strings begin to resonate to the harsh, sometimes demanding, testily humorous, irreverent, impatient, opinionated, forward-driving, safety-first, silence-loving, older masculine body.[138]

Sons who have not received this "retuning" will have "father hunger" all their lives. Such hungry sons hang around older men like the homeless around a soup kitchen. Like the homeless they feel shame over their condition, and it is a nameless, bitter, unexpungeable shame that drives so many of them to alcohol and addiction.

Women, no matter how much they sympathize with their starving sons or lovers, cannot replace that particular substance. Uninitiated men will try to seek this solace in women, but it is not to be found there.

Says Bly:
By the middle of the twentieth century in Europe and North America a massive change had taken place: the father was working, but the son could not see him work.

Throughout the ancient hunter societies, which apparently lasted hundreds of thousands of years, and throughout the hunter/gatherer societies that followed them, and the subsequent agricultural and craft societies, fathers and sons worked and lived together. As late as 1900 in the United States about ninety per cent of fathers were engaged in agriculture. In all these societies the son saw his father working at all times of the day and all seasons of the year. [Now junior's in school and dad is at the office or factory or on the road.]

When the son no longer sees dad what happens? A hole appears in the son's psyche – demons of suspicion enter. "Never trust anyone over thirty" were the watchwords of the sixties.[139]

During the sixties the older men were manipulated by the media to fantasize that Vietnam was some glorious throwback to WW II. The Gulf of Tonkin "incident", which NEVER happened, resurrected images of "slant-eyes" attacking American ships – Pearl Harbor all over again. I remember my father actually telling me that we needed a war to keep the economy moving. And I said, "Tens of thousands of American boys are supposed to go die in a swamp in Asia to keep the economy moving? Maybe there's something wrong with an economy that needs to be kept moving by burning up young male bodies." It was an explosive fight and he held fast to the position that that's how it "had always been". He was a union man, a capitalist water-boy caught up in communist rhetoric, stuck somewhere between two *materi*alist agendas, following orders from some mobsters who had taken the reins of his union. I saw it. I was there on the picket line, in the gray cold, outside some stinking plant in Chicago, when "Louie" drove up in his black Cadillac stretch limo and got out fiddling with his diamond tie clasp. "Hey Louie, what's happening?" the truckers shout. "We shot the tires out from under some scab at R. R. Donnelly," sez Louie.

It seemed perfectly "logical" to my dad that young boys had to die to gas the engines of money and property; after all, he heard it straight from Louie, or some other racist jackass in the coffee shop at work. What my dad *said* never made any sense to me and created an enormous gulf between us. What he did was get up every morning and go to work and provide an ample living for his wife and seven kids. I love him for what he did, and I forgive him for what he said, but it has taken me a long time to sort out these demons in my head.

And one day he actually apologized to me. That was a "first". One day, 25 years after the fact, my dad suddenly said, "McNamara lied." "What are you talking about?" I asked. "McNamara lied…There was no Gulf of Tonkin incident. It never happened. Some sailors shot up their own ship and tried to cover it up." [Lyndon Johnson squashed the truth and used that lie to justify massive troop build-ups in Vietnam.] There stood my dad. Veteran of the war in the Philippines. Drafted into combat after Pearl Harbor. Admitting they had played him for a sucker. Deceived him to get his support for Vietnam.

We looked at each other with tears in our eyes. For 25 years we had fought like dogs over what was ultimately a government lie. 25 years of trashed affection between father and son, pissed away on that! The bastards. We hugged and let it go. But I'll never trust government or their running dogs in corporate media. Nor should my children.

Says Bly:

In the next decade we can expect these demons of suspicion to cause more and more damage to men's and boys' vision of what a man is or what the masculine is. Almost half of American boys live in a home with no father [or a brainwashed father] and the demons have full permission to rage.

My ex-son distrusts me. His mother has convinced him that the meaning of life is for him to go to work as a doctor or lawyer or corporate clone and make lots of money. His brain was colonized by feminist propaganda before he even had a chance to grow hair around his pee pee. This is child abuse; there's no other way to view it.

My ex-wife makes sure that all my dreamy talk about male initiation and pursuing the deeper meaning of life is flushed down the cerebral toilet. My son looks at me like I'm a moonman when I try to bring these things up. He has no openness to the idea that I might know something about life his mom doesn't. This is a crime against human nature, a crime against all of human society. There is no other society on earth where sons are so cruelly poisoned against their fathers. This is the *real legacy* of "women's liberation". Destroy masculine values. Destroy family values. Throw the door wide open for female/corporate values.

St. Paul said, "When I am weak I am strong." When a Lakota Sun Dancer dances three days straight then pierces his body with hooks he is showing us that he is sustained by a superhuman power. He is so weak, he is strong – held up on his feet by an extra-human power, the power of the Great Mystery. When a man succeeds his ego increases, but when he fails he retreats to the protection of a Higher Power. We profess to be Christian or Buddhist or Jewish, and then lose sight of this basic teaching of our faiths. When we lose, we win – that is the seminal spiritual truth. What Richard Rohr calls the spirituality of subtraction. What E. F. Schumacher means by less is more.

America finally learned this in Vietnam. We lost, and we won. We got reborn as a nation. Our foreign policy has never been the same. Instead of getting beat up by Ho Chi Minh's we supported freedom fighters in Afghanistan. Then we stood by incredulous as our real super-terror, the Big Bad Bear, laid down its weapons in the grass. The USSR lost the cold war, and won a chance at a new life. [Too bad it got suckered into Corporate/ Cowboy Capitalism. No...Corporate/Capitalism does not have the answers. Time for all of us to die to that phony meme.] The alcoholic admits total defeat, and his life is reborn. The seed dies, and the plant is born. This is the wonder of life on earth – death brings birth – and we need to spend a little more time honoring that.

It's there, in our popular fiction, from *Rambo* to *Robocop* to *Star Wars*. The hero is abused and defeated and trashed and dies a million deaths; but then, through the help of a Deep Force that comes from *down* somewhere in the bat caves of his brain, he is rejuvenated, reborn – and he wins. He doesn't do it on his own. He may be the sole agent on the screen operating in the service of this invisible power – though typically some little kid or woman gives him the "clue" – but he dances the super-human dance of the Sun Dancer because he is hooked into "The Beyond". Death, of any kind, is our weakest human moment, and our strongest spiritual moment.

I used to tell my son that every team in his league, except one, was going to end the season with a loss. That is one of the great and sobering lessons of sport. It was one of the few good things I was able to pass on in my brief time with him.

Says Bly:
When a father, absent during the day, returns home at six, his children receive only his temperament, and not his teaching. The fragmentation of decision-making in corporate life, the massive effort that produces the corporate willingness to destroy the environment for the sake of profit, the prudence, even cowardice, that one learns in bureaucracy – who wants to teach this?

What the father brings home today is usually a touchy, irritable, and remote mood [*anima*], springing from powerlessness and despair mingled with longstanding shame and the numbness peculiar to those who hate their jobs. Fathers in earlier times could often break through their own humanly inadequate temperaments by teaching rope making, post-hole digging, grain cutting, drumming, brake repairing, animal husbandry, and especially singing and storytelling.[140]

But who's gonna listen to the old man now? There's homework, soccer practice, gymnastics class, Ronnie's birthday party, Sunday school – who has any time for dad? Just make sure the court tells him where to send the check.

The system we live in gives no honor to the male mode of feeling. What we inhabit is by no stretch of the imagination a Patriarchy. Women were the original manufacturers, turning the pots and weaving the cloth. Feminist memes induced men to automate these processes and then got us to do the work. What was the Industrial Revolution about if not machine-woven cloth and forged cooking utensils? More than anything our modern industrial society is a Matriarchy – the very worst kind of Matriarchy where prized male, and even female, modes of feeling have been swept away in the service of objects. Our separation from the metaphysical, from spirituality, from God, is precisely what has allowed this feminine aspect to gain such force.

Where is the female Martin Luther King, Jr., who is going to lead us out of this oppression? Surely there are women out there who are aware that operating out of their *animus* is not working. If women truly want power, if they truly want to be leaders, this might be the place to start. Less is more.

When the father becomes an object of ridicule the son has a problem. How does he picture his own life as a man? From books? From movies? From his goofy friends? From women?

Says Bly:
I count myself among the sons who have endured years of deprivation, disconnection from earth, thin air, the loneliness of the long-distance runner, in order to go high in the air and be seen, be noticed, be affirmed by society in the way I never was by the old man. He couldn't give it to me

because his old man never gave it to him. Such a son attempts to redeem the Darth Vader, the Dark Father, by becoming enlightened [instead of going down]. Society without the father produces these birdlike men, so intense, so charming, so sincere, so open to addiction, [so prone to be manipulated by women].[141]

And where are the priests during all this?

Says Rohr:
Although Catholic theology has for centuries been perceived as a man's preserve, the actual way that theologians went about their task was archetypically feminine. Since the days of Thomas Aquinas and other scholastics in the Middle Ages theology has been done by sitting and reading, thinking and reasoning, seeing the logical connections between ideas and drawing conclusions from them. This was a sedentary left brain, activity produced by less-masculine males that took place not in the world of action but in a secluded academic womb, be it a monastery, university, or seminary. That style produced volumes of books that could fill entire libraries, but very little of it touched the daily lives of people or had much effect on the world in which they lived.

As long as the world did not change, or did not change very rapidly, this sedentary theology was not exposed for its weakness. Today however, the world is changing faster than armchair theologians can keep up with it, and it is changing in many directions simultaneously. Science, technology, lifestyles, business, medicine, politics, economics, education, and transportation are continuously creating new opportunities and new problems. Unemployment, homelessness, overconsumption, militarism, pollution, debt, depletion of resources, drugs, abortions [and broken homes, and broken men] present crises that theology addresses too late and with too little impact. Theology is not perceived as relevant or important to the way most people live. In Italy, home of the Pope, only 3% of the people under age 35 consider the church an institution they identify with.[142]

* * *

Karl Rahner, the German theologian of our century, says that by the next century the only people left in the church will be mystics. I hope he's right. At least guys like me will have some place to go. But realistically, Europe never tolerated mystics – in the church or out of it. No Krishna, no Buddha, no Jesus, ever came out of Europe. Europeans are living out the pretence of some Higher Rationale that suffocated their indigenous soul millennia ago. The barbarity of WW II marked the end of rationalism and the "enlightenment" in Europe. The only thing Europe ever perfected was how to get men to think like women – *i.e.*, analytically – and then convince everyone that that's how men normally think! Preposterous. Reason – devoid of spiritual paradox – led directly to concentration camps, Jewish-German physicists, and the atom bomb. Female-inspired left-brainedness led directly to massive world war.

In America we still have the wonderful opportunity to participate in Native American traditions to deepen our contact with nature and enrich our spiritual life. I grew up on the prairies of Illinois but it wasn't until age 42, when I stepped out of a sweat lodge naked and dripping on a moonlit July night, that I felt connected, for the first time, to the heartbeat of that land, that big-sky prairie, that star-dome. And from a deep realm came the knowledge that people had been living in this place for 20 or 30 thousand years, doing this same thing – honoring the grasses, and the stars, and the four directions – and now I was finally one of them.

We need more of this kind of stuff in American churches and synagogues. The American Church is often run like an Irish-American social club; and most synagogues seem modeled on some WASP country club. When is someone gonna sweat and stink and show us God?

Says Rohr:

Although we like to think that the Catholic Church fostered spiritual development in the past, this is not entirely true. The Church promoted spirituality only for the small percentage of Catholics who were priests or members of religious orders. The homily to the laity was: pray, pay, obey. Furthermore, as we have seen, clerical and religious spirituality was feminine spirituality. Only the development of feminine virtues was considered important. Spiritual life in the past was therefore spiritual half-life.[143]

Male spirituality has been emasculated by the church. The honest priests will admit it. Feminized priests are arguing for yet more rights for women. It doesn't matter whether women get ordained or not, what matters is whether or not any *real* men get ordained. No longer will we, the parishioners, nod to the soft voices and squirm under the limp handshakes of men who have lived in the world as women. We demand a male spirituality. At this point we need it more than bread or water.

What's wrong with the older priests? They were taught by their moms, and then in the seminary, that it's a sin to make a mistake; therefore, it was better to do nothing than to make a mistake.

Says Rohr:

> This type of emasculated spirituality effectively cut out all risk taking from their lives. Although they prayed to God the Father in the mass, they were often more devoted to Mary and the rosary. As a result they never came into contact with the Father's masculine energy the way Jesus did. They never knew they had a wild man inside of them or if they did they thought it was the devil tempting them to make a mistake. [Fear of making mistakes is a feminine meme. Women evaluate, men act.] These priests were effectively castrated, not only in their relationship with women, but in their ability to act decisively in the world. By and large most priests have been company men, not wild men.

Lay people often fall into these constipated patterns if the only spirituality they know is a feminine spirituality. Communes dominated by women suffer visibly from toilet-face. Their daily goal is to have a pleasant time, never to reach into the unknown, never to extend themselves to help others in a way that might cause some burden to themselves. Whether Benedictine nuns or Sufi vamps the big question always seems to be: "And how do I feel today?" This is a psychic question, not a spiritual question. Might as well ask Jesus how good he felt carrying the cross, or Buddha if he had a nice time staring at a wall for four years.

Saints are codependent with the whole world. Saints give until it hurts. They do what the gospels say to do. They live the teachings of Jesus and Buddha and Krishna and Mohammed and Black Elk and Moses. That takes a lot of male energy.

Says Rohr:

Feminized males are the ones who want to get it all together before they start giving it away. They criticize from the sidelines but never risk getting into the action. They have all kinds of questions to ask and points to clarify but nothing to contribute. They never make anything happen. They have no masculine energy.[144]

Raising consciousness without service to others is a contradiction in terms. Unless there is some engagement in the world, some involvement in creating the kingdom of God, masculine spiritual energy dissipates. Male theology is something you do. Christianity is something you do. It doesn't matter if you believe Jesus was born of a virgin or resurrected after his crucifixion – or not. It matters whether you love your enemies and pray for those who persecute you.

Says Rohr:

If you only think about Jesus and never act like Jesus you are denying his life. The incarnation was the phallic insertion of God into humanity in the person of the man Jesus. Jesus told people what they needed to hear whether they liked it or not.

I like a priest who can talk about his gonads. Rohr has some interesting stuff to say about our often-fondled, little-thought-of, scrotum.

Says he:

Biologically speaking, masculine energy is not just phallic, but scrotal. It is important to recognize that most tender and protected part of a man, his testicles, as an essential part of his power. Otherwise, all men's nonphallic attributes are projected onto women and expected to be carried by women!

Our balls hang down there because, for some odd reason, sperm produced within the body at body temperature are not fertile. That's pretty strange. Maybe it has something to do with exposing the testes to a greater arena for genetic variation, but birds and reptiles don't have balls. It's not an absolute requirement for sexual reproduction.

Let's imagine our scrotal nature as our contemplative side. Thoroughly masculine, yet quiet and deep and cool, a hidden garden, a seed bag with billions of sprouts.

And with, Says Rohr:

A uniquely masculine capacity for containment and protection, patient ripening, rootedness, long-term endurance and nurturing. All of these are masculine qualities represented by the scrotum and testes in contrast to the overrated and infrequently hardened penis [and in contrast to the feminine memes that try to present growth and fertility as feminine attributes. Our cocks are limp most of the time. Face it. We think with our bean bags, not our dicks].

An exaggerated phallic energy, uninformed by scrotal energy, is the sign of an intrusive, domineering, exploitative [*anima*-driven] male. It is macho overcompensation rather than true masculine self-confidence. [The manhole], the driven businessman, the obsessive academic, the rigidity of the believer, the war games, the stabbing finger of the opinionated, the punishing inner father – these are all indications of the phallic [*anima*-driven] man, not the wild man. The true wild man has life for others and he *knows* he has life for others.

* * *

Exaggerated phallic energy, machismo, misdirected *anima*, are the hallmarks of the uninitiated man. Eastern religions are much more aware of the need for initiation than we are in the west. They know the father can't do it, he and the son are both in love with the same woman. When the time comes for a boy in the East to take his spiritual instruction seriously, he is given a mentor, a master, a guru – not so much that he can learn facts or doctrines from him, but so that he can pick up the energy of his teacher and begin to resonate with him.

That's how Jesus formed his disciples, says Rohr. He spent three long years exposing them to his energy. What he gave them was not so much his words but his example and energy. The Aramaic word for that energy was "spirit", better translated as "breath" or even *prana*, the breath of life. The Life rhythm.

Without spiritual fathering we become overly sensitive to feminine mood: the tendency to complain and worry and be judgmental. Feminine mood was *not* what Jesus passed on to his disciples. It took enormous masculine strength to preach love to a society immersed in vengeance and vendetta and political rebellion. It took great moral courage not to defend himself before his accusers. It took sweaty balls to drag his own cross up the hill. Some say he walked with a limp, a visible wound. He was not a dainty, soft-skinned, bearded lady floating six inches off the ground. He sweated and peed and limped through the dust back to his Father. Death of the ego.

So who initiates boys? Dads can't do it. I know of one guy named Richard Hohlstein, at the Abode of the Message, a Sufi retreat center in New Lebanon, New York, who has been working with boys in "ropes courses" for years, and who told me he is prepared to take a stab at recreating a male initiation. Richard's one compelling observation on this subject is that there must be a male culture to initiate these boys into. Right on! Here's a guy who is willing to risk putting an idea into action.

Other groups that have recreated a male initiation ritual are the Mankind Project (formerly New Warriors) and the Sterling Institute of Relationship. Both groups have gravitated toward putting on training "weekends" for middle age men – the guys who missed out on the real thing when they were young – guys like you and me. But they have begun designing certain weekends especially for young men. Good work guys!

I've done both "weekends". They're worth every penny and every ounce of effort it takes to do them – plus the Men will help you make it happen – financially, logistically, emotionally, spiritually. That's really what the weekends are about – men helping men accomplish something that's much more important than making money and much too big to pull off alone. Both weekends changed my life. I could tell you what's in them – but then I'd have to kill you. Some things are better kept a mystery until you experience them. Both the Mankind Project and the Sterling Institute of Relationship have web sites. They offer a rare chance to be "reborn" as a man. I recommend them to every man. How could you pass it up?

And what about girls? What is the substance of their initiation? Marriage is the axis of a woman's life; when a girl marries she now has her own man to work for her. But something is required for her to make her marriage succeed; something besides sex. In his book *She* Robert Johnson examines the Greek myth of Psyche as she endures her initiation ordeal.[145]

Psyche is "Mind". Thinking. Analyzing. Figuring out. Psychology, psychotherapy, psychic. The Greek word for "mind" identifies "mind" as the *essence* of female nature – an essence illuminated in the character of Psyche. But over the centuries so many men have taken up female occupations that now we attribute "thinking" to men. It's a crock. It's a phony meme. Women are the ones who are always "thinking". Mind, and its corollaries – reason, logic, analysis – are FEMALE. The ancients knew it. How did we forget it?

Hundreds of men have told me that they like this book, but they disagree with the thing about logic being female. I look at them with deep sadness. They have built a wall against understanding. They refuse to examine themselves. How do I gently explain that the problem is: they have too much *female* in their own persona! They spent much too much time listening to mommy. They think logic is masculine because they're men and hey!, they think "logically". What a mess. They have male bodies, but their brains are a black hole of female memes. It's like watching a carrot stand there trying to convince me it's really spinach. It's a massive problem. Forget about homosexuality. That's not a "problem". But this is: there's way too much female in the current model of the male brain. And that means all of us men – no one excluded. Psyche is Mind. Psyche is female. Therefore, Mind is female. Get the logic?

So…We begin the story where Psyche, a mortal woman, has, on the advice of an oracle, married Death. What does this mean? She has died to her maidenhood, her wedding is her funeral. She is not a little girl anymore. In some African weddings unless the bride arrives with scars and wounds it is not a valid wedding. In other ones a little white lamb is led up to the bride. The priest announces that this lamb is the girl child, then he slits its throat and makes her drink its blood. Women are not subtle and this is something they can understand. "Your girlhood is dead. Death of the girl, birth of the woman." Women who don't honor this death, experience fierce resentment to marriage months or years later. That's why our divorce rate is so high. That's *exactly* why our divorce rate is so high. Women arrive for their marriage wearing a white gown and when they leave the church they should not be wearing a white gown. The burning of the gown should be part of the ceremony. Someone needs to tell them that this marriage is a funeral. It means they can't hang out in bars anymore or get other guys to buy them things or take them on exciting adventures. American women don't get this. They think marriage is some way to have everything they have, plus get more. No. A marriage is a funeral.

After the wedding Psyche is led off to a lovely garden with a wonderful house where everything she needs is provided for her in lavish and idle luxury. In other words, every woman's dream. She has everything, and does nothing for it; is she going to be happy?

Every evening, when the lamp is put out, her husband arrives and she spends the night with him. He has given her only one rule: not to shine a light upon him, not to look upon him, but preserve his darkness. By day he is gone, by night he is a mystery.

Psyche's gossipy sisters (other parts of her own "psyche"), who are jealous of her good fortune, manage to convince her that her husband is actually a snake. Women love to accentuate the negative. The sisters convince her to expose him with a lamp and cut off his loathsome head. Great plan.

That night, after they've made love and he is asleep, she picks up a butcher knife, shines a light on him, and discovers he is Eros, god of Love, the most beautiful of gods. He wakes up, sees her hovering over him with a lamp and a knife, and splits.

So, the voices in her head which questioned love were the instrument of her losing love. The voices in her head betrayed her. She got nosy and meddlesome and *destroyed* her husband's business which, cinema propaganda to the contrary, happens much more often than its obverse – she gets nosy and meddlesome and *saves* her husband's business. I know dozens of men ruined by their wife's meddling and not one who was ever saved or improved by it. And remember, this guy is a god, his business is Love.

Psyche goes to visit her mother-in-law Aphrodite, who was against the whole thing from the beginning. Imagine, a god marrying a mere mortal! But Psyche, having pricked her finger on one of her husband's arrows that fateful night is now smitten with love.

Have you ever had to play out this game with your lovers? They take you for granted, snoop in your most private affairs, create problems out of thin air to satisfy their neediness for attention, and only fall in love with you again if you leave them! Nuts. And yet, very typical female behavior. Women don't seem to have a gauge connected to their brain to tell them when they have enough, or when what they have is good enough. As far as I can tell they're missing some circuitry. There is no end point to their cravings.

They are cheeky enough to imagine they can figure out the motivations and mind waves of you – a god. You are a passionate, intuitive wizard, an automobile alchemist, a star-gazer, a flying fish, a dream-carpenter, a water welder, oblivious to pain, responding to some voice that comes to you from over the horizon – and you are to be understood and controlled by a rationalist verbalist without the mental furniture to understand how to throw a football. Your extra-human flight will be reduced to words and phrases, slashed to bits with knives of linguistic precision, by a person who is afraid to bait a fishhook. The two "sisters" in her mind, Suspicion and Envy, will undermine anything her husband tries to create. Aphrodite will punish Psyche for listening to them.

Aphrodite promises to do what she can to woo Eros back if Psyche will simply perform a few – impossible – tasks. She throws together a huge pile of many different kinds of seeds and tells Psyche to sort them by nightfall or the penalty will be death.

What does Psyche do?

She starts crying and decides on suicide. What else? It's the only logical thing. There is no possible way she can accomplish the task by nightfall.

What a beautiful bit of symbolism, says Johnson. A pile of seeds to sort. "Mom, where's my other sock? Hon, where's the car wax? Mom, what's Uncle Ted's number?" What do women do in life? Sort. Sort socks, sort columns of numbers, sort words, sort information, sort, categorize, logicize, arrange, sort.

But she can't do it. Psyche can't possibly sort the seeds by nightfall. So what happens? An army of ants takes pity on her. They come along, and with great enterprise, they sort the seeds for her. What does this mean?

The ants are an archetype much more available than the Queen or the Princess or the Goddess. The ant-nature is primitive and earthy and organized in a mindless, selfless, repetitive manner. The ant-nature taps into woman's superiority in fine motor skills at a reflexive, almost meditative level. What man is not amazed to watch a woman crocheting while watching TV. Fine motor skills. Typing, filing, remembering, reporting – female skills. Sorting.

But, says Johnson, let's not overlook another dimension of the sorting process – the inner one. Just as much *material* comes from the unconscious demanding to be sorted as comes from our modern too-much-with-us outer world. It is the special provenance of a woman to sort in this inner dimension and protect herself and her family from the inner floods which are at least as damaging as the too-muchness of our outer world. Feelings, values, timing, boundaries – these are wonderful sorting grounds which produce such high values. And, says Johnson, they are special to women and femininity.

Robert Johnson has just jumped out of the cockpit holding a napkin for a parachute. This myth has been making the case that sorting is a feminine virtue. It has *not* been saying that feelings, values, timing and boundaries are feminine virtues. Johnson has been influenced by German psychology to see the world through the *animus/anima* duality, which, I am certain, Carl Jung himself set little store in. Jung said, "Learn everything you can about symbols then, when analyzing a dream, throw out everything you know." He was advising us to transcend archetypes.

Feelings, values, timing and boundaries *are not* specifically feminine dominions. Nor is this myth in any way implying that they are. When brilliant scholars like Robert Johnson represent the human personality with gender stereotypes they are doing a great disservice to men. Says Johnson, "When we speak of masculine and feminine, it must remain clear that we are not talking exclusively about male and female." Nothing could be less clear to me. Why tag a sexual connotation on something that is not sexual? Sloppy wording makes for sloppy thinking – and corrupted gender relations.

I happen to like Carl Jung quite a bit, but I don't like what has come to be called "Jungian" analysis. Jung was a deeply spiritual Catholic whose works have been reinterpreted by a bunch of secular humanists who can sell more books by currying to female sensibilities. Our sensitive side is not our female side, it is our *sensitive* side. Our sharing side is not our female side, it is our *sharing* side. You can't use sexually loaded language and then claim it has no sexual connotation. That's just plain stupid. Women are no more sensitive and no more generous than men. Period.

So far, this myth has been talking about one thing only: sorting. According to this ancient Greek story sorting is a feminine virtue. Psyche is developing her sorting-nature, her ant-nature. Have you ever watched a roomful of secretaries?

What are they doing? Sorting. Ever go through the check-out line in the supermarket? Ever watch how women shop? Right. Sorting. They must learn to tap into their sorting nature, but soon they do it as naturally as breathing.

The second of Psyche's tasks, arrogantly set forth by the non-sharing, non-caring, boundless, timeless Goddess Aphrodite, is for Psyche to go to a certain field across a river and gather some golden fleece from the rams which pasture there. She must be back by nightfall on pain of death. These rams are very fierce and the task is very dangerous. What does Psyche do?

Fall down and cry and contemplate suicide.

Then she decides that the best thing to do is to throw herself in the river which separates her from the field of rams. Great thinking. But a curious thing happens. The reeds on the bank speak to her and offer her advice.

They tell her not to go to the field when the rams are there but to wait until dusk when they have left, then she may go pluck some of the golden wool which has brushed off on the sticker bushes and tree branches. If she approached the rams directly she would be battered to death, so she is encouraged to take a circuitous route to her goal.

The ram is male. Very male. The reeds are telling her that when dealing with males she is best served by operating indirectly. Too much directness and pushiness out of her and they will butt her to death. Better to be non-confrontational. Devious? No. Psyche is bid to take what excess the male produces but not to ask for anything. She is to rely on her frugality and patience and she will accomplish her task. Deviousness is an over-extension, a perversion, of this female attribute. Essentially, what is being advocated in this passage are frugality and a non-confrontational style – two things that have dropped out of the vocabulary of modern women.

Says Johnson, the idea of taking the remnants, the scrapings of *logos*, the masculine rational scientific energy, off the boughs, may sound intolerable to a modern woman. And indeed it should…Wait a second! How, all of a sudden, has he injected *logos* and rationalism into a poem about rams and golden fleece?

Why this compulsive drive to associate the male with qualities which are primarily female? This is way too far afield and I'm going to have to smack Mr. Johnson's knuckles with a ruler this time.

Logos is feminine. Rationality is feminine. Woman the potter. Woman the planter. Woman the left-brained. Logical men are feminized men – even if they have pee pees between their legs. We don't understand this because we don't see how much our male nature has been subsumed and perverted by female values. Guys who sit around reading books and working on computers all day are feminized men. Guys who parade around in robes or suits, holding forth on law or religion are *feminized men*. Don't ever hire one to fix your car or get your stove working. Let's try once again to get this straight. Men who act out of their "logos", their "rational-scientific" side, are actually manholes operating out of their *anima*, their poor quality of femininity. Natural man is an intuitive right-brain dreamer – like Albert Einstein. Like Jim Morrison. Like Thomas Edison. Strident women, aggressive women, female business barracudas are acting out of their *animus*, their poor quality of masculinity. Natural woman is a logical, left-brain organizer, like ma on the farm, or Connie Chung on TV.

There is not the slightest hint of anything being logical or rational about the dangerous wild rams in this story and only a "Jungian" could find that in there. Show a scholar a snorting, stamping, stinking wild ram, and he interprets it as "science" and "logic". Has this guy ever smelled a wild animal? Boys, we have to stop doing this to ourselves. Let's just look at what's there, and not try to read any of it through feminized memes. What this story is telling us is that women may share the fruits of what we produce, our very hides as it were, as long as they're not cheeky or pushy. If they are, we will reject them, very firmly.

Men have ways to measure out power and pushiness. Big men, because they are intimidating to small guys, often have a quieter, gentler body language about them. Little guys are the big mouths. We have a male etiquette for dealing with power. We have linebackers, and safeties, and ends. We all play on the same team. We all want each other to stay in good playing condition.

No woman I know would dream of walking onto the playing field of 22 guys and saying, "OK, give me the ball." It isn't done. She doesn't really want the ball. Yet she thinks nothing of walking into the office and saying, "OK, give me the money." They don't get it...They *can* get it. They can get everything they need by being patient and non-confrontational – a second set of female attributes to add to their sorting nature.

Psyche collects the wool and the non-sharing, non-caring, Goddess of Love, Aphrodite, who by now is enraged and harbors suspicions about spies or treachery (classic female paranoia) decides to hand Psyche certain defeat. She instructs Psyche to fill a cup with water from the River Styx, the river that separates life and death. It is a circular stream, tumbling from a high mountain into hell, and then flowing upward onto the mountain again. Some sort of symbol of the cycle of life and death. It is guarded by monsters and impossible to reach.

True to form Psyche collapses and contemplates suicide. Then an eagle comes along, picks up the cup, fills it from the scary river, and hands it back to Psyche. What is this?

The eagle is the bird of Zeus, grandfather of all the gods, and father of her estranged husband, Eros. This is the third time in a row where all Psyche has had to do is surrender to fate and she has gotten mysterious help. Someone or something is watching out for her. As long as she doesn't do anything self-destructive or suicidal, as long as she waits, some kind of help shows up for her. This is one of the great lessons of "Mind" with deep spiritual implications.

She is now in possession of one cup of water from the River of Life and Death. This is a big deal. And all she had to do was wait. A man has to be made. A woman has only to wait and the River of Life will be brought to her.

An eagle is forward-looking and directed. He catches one fish at a time which he pin-points from a mile up. This is god-energy, Zeus-energy, male-energy that is available to a woman. It is given to her. She does not have to work for it. Imagine you are an eagle, flying perhaps 5000 feet above the earth; you can see across the whole state of Iowa, or maybe all the way to Athens. You see where the Ohio River joins with the Mississippi; you see the Grand Canyon and Niagara Falls and Old MacDonald's Farm. You circle downward, downward, spiraling, circling downward and pluck one single salmon out of one tiny pool. This is directedness. This is focus. From the overwhelming possibilities inherent in the panorama, to the selection of a single point. This is what feeds the eagle's family. Directedness. You cannot have your life scattered over three states, like so many women are prone to do.

So, if she sorts through things, if she is patient and non-confrontational and if she is directed, the River of Life will be brought to her.

And now comes Psyche's fourth task, the most important and difficult of all. It is the story of pregnancy and birth and the creation of family life.

Psyche is told to go to the underworld and ask Persephone – Goddess of the Underworld, the eternal maiden, the hidden female nature – for a cask of beauty ointment which she is then to deliver to Aphrodite. Psyche, seeing the impossibility of the task, goes up to a high tower so she can throw herself off it. Can you guess what the high tower is? A big pee pee.

The tower instructs Psyche to enter the breathing place of Hades and follow it down to the palace of Pluto, God of the Underworld. She is to carry two coins and two barley cakes. She must prepare herself mentally, for the journey into Hades is exhausting and she must harbor her strength. She must not stop to help other wayfarers in those realms.

Psyche finds the cave entrance and starts to go down. She passes a lame man with a lame donkey who drop their load of sticks, but she has been forbidden from helping them pick up the sticks. She moves on. She gives Charon, the boatman, one of her coins to ferry her across the River Styx. On the way they pass a drowning man who screams for help but she must preserve her strength and is forbidden from helping him. Selfish, necessary, *essential* feminine nature. Not good or bad, just a fact of life. But a fact of life that must be balanced by masculine selflessness and generosity.

Now comes a temptation that no woman I've ever met could pass up. Psyche passes three old women who are weaving the strands of Fate on a loom. They ask Psyche if she wants to help them weave the future, but she has been warned by the tower, the big pee pee of God, to pass by and not allow herself to be detained or she will never have the wherewithal to make it all the way down and all the way back up again. No meddling. Don't screw up your journey by trying to fine-tune Fate. Leave that to the "beings" assigned this task by a greater Authority.

Next Psyche encounters Cerberes, guardian of Hades, Hound of Hell, a monstrous three-headed dog. She throws one of the barley cakes to him and scurries past while his three heads are fighting over the cake.

Finally Psyche arrives in the hall of Persephone, the eternal maiden, the queen of mysteries. As the tower has warned her, Psyche refuses Persephone's lavish hospitality accepting only the simplest of food and sitting on the ground to eat. An old law of Greek etiquette binds you to any house where you have taken hospitality and so if Psyche accepts the luxury of Persephone she will be bound to her forever. But she doesn't. She rejects the Marilyn Monroe/Gloria Steinem single lifestyle. And she receives the cask of beauty ointment which contains a mysterious secret. She bows to Persephone and takes her leave. She feeds the second barley cake to the dog, gives the second coin to the boatman, and arrives where she can see the light at the end of the tunnel.

Home free. Almost.

What does she do now? What any woman would do.

She opens the cask to steal some of the beauty ointment for herself and immediately falls asleep.

Remember – this is a pregnancy test. Big thighs, big boobs, big belly, stretch marks – what do pregnant women complain about? Their looks. Their husbands think they look gorgeous and tell them that over and over again, but the wives snarl and accuse them of looking at other women. So Psyche's obsession with beauty has put her to sleep. A woman obsessed with beauty is not awake to life.

Who awakens her?

Why, her estranged husband, Eros, who has finally broken out of the psychic prison created for him by his mother, and comes to Psyche's rescue. They go off to heaven and have a big wedding where Zeus gives Psyche a pot of immortality (an omen of offspring) so she can properly wed a god. She drinks from the pot and this brings her both immortality and the promise that Eros will never depart from her again but will remain her everlasting husband. (When you give a man children, he hangs around long after your looks have faded.)

And the fourth task is consummated when Psyche bears a daughter whose name is Pleasure.

So what has happened here? Psyche, who disobeyed her husband, the God of Love, was compelled by her mother-in-law to learn four things. One: sort things out. Two: be patient and non-confrontational with male energy. Take only what you need. Three: out of the panorama of possibilities stay focused, stay directed, and the River of Life will be delivered to you. Four: listen to the Big Pee Pee, what Johnson calls the cultural legacy of our civilization, God the Father. He will tell you how to go into the deepest place within you. On that journey carry only what you need. Don't screw with fate – don't try and manipulate the future. Don't be codependent – don't get sucked into other people's problems. Feed the dog. Pay the ferryman. Be humble. Don't get enticed into the luxurious lifestyle of the eternal maiden, Persephone, Marilyn Monroe. Carry the secret cask and don't open it. Just carry it. Don't try to fool God the Father, your cultural legacy, or you will be put to sleep – entranced. Only your husband can dis-entrance you from these transgressions. Listen to him! If you'd listened to him in the first place you wouldn't have had any of these problems.

Obey all these strictures and you will obtain a god for a husband and you will achieve immortality through your children.

Psyche must honor the inner maiden, share food with the inner maiden, but not succumb to the enticements of the inner maiden. Few women who came up in the sixties ever got out of

Persephone's lap. Now, in their fifties, their beauty is faded, their marriages are ashes, their kids shun them, their jobs are a grind. They got everything their own way, and they've got nothing. They are drugged, like Marilyn. They are asleep to the meaning of life.

What was in the beauty cask? The stuff of gods, a divine mystery – nothing. Nothing is the deepest interior mystery. It must not be named or given a label. Here is some bold attempt to encourage women to break with words and verbalization – the landlords of their psyches – and just carry the mystery of the gods around with them. Carry nothing. What do words truly explain about being pregnant? Nothing. Where does the mystery of life come from? Nowhere. Life cannot be captured in words. Be content to carry nothing. To be the messenger transporting nothing from one goddess to another. Don't try to steal it or use it for yourself. Be the vessel of nothing – the Great Mystery. This is the essence of the spiritual path. Don't name it. Just serve it. Just carry it.

> Heaven does nothing
> Earth does nothing
> From the union of these
>   all things proceed
>   all things are made
>
> Heaven and Earth do nothing
> Yet there is nothing
> They do not do
>
> – Chang Tzu
> *translated by Thomas Merton*

Chapter Five

Legal Liverwurst
Media Chromosomes
Homicidal Health Care
Institutional Menopause

1) **Every woman is a whore except my mother who is a saint** — *Italian saying*

2) **You can't divorce your mother.**

THERE'S A LOT OF ANGER in these pages and I won't apologize for that. The notion that we're supposed to be polite and clean and discuss our feelings without getting angry is a female meme – a female control technique. I don't buy it. Anger is worse when I stuff it inside and it churns my stomach and numbs my guts. There's good anger and bad anger and women and manholes are not the ones to decide which is which. I'll be the judge of my own anger, thank you.

It's clear to me that anger is what wrote this book. Without that passion, that depth of feeling, I wouldn't have dropped everything I was doing for two years to research these gender topics. So it was a good thing. That anger. And in a big way my life and my writing have been about living with and defusing anger and resentments. Without some spiritual tools to dampen the dynamite, my brains would have blown out my ears long ago.

312

Lately, I've taken to saying a prayer that I gleaned from a story printed near the end of the *Big Book of Alcoholics Anonymous*.[146] I borrowed the book from a Spanish-speaking A.A. group in a small town in Mexico. The prayer is for ridding yourself of resentments and the point is to swallow your ego and redirect your willfulness and pray for those who persecute you – just like Jesus said. Only we never do it. We never actually do it. We nod our heads and say, oh yeah, that's great; but we don't DO it.

Well now I do it. In my case the prayer goes like this:

God bless my wives, my mother, and all willful women.
May they find health and prosperity and happiness.

I repeat it over and over like a mantra, when I'm walking up the hill in the dark, or sitting at the kitchen table, or watching the sun rise on the ocean, or lying with my eyes closed under my mosquito net.

The prescription says to take this medicine early and often for two weeks and then see what happens – but just after the tenth repetition I felt a great relief and lifting of my resentments. At first I choked on the words and couldn't pretend to take them seriously; but as my inner peace swelled I found that I could actually say them and mean them. I do not wish to visit pain or grief on any of these willful women – neither the ones I know nor the ones I don't. But I do think it's good for us, and good for them, to understand what they're doing to us. I feel that America, indeed all of Western Civilization, has reversed the natural sex roles and that both sexes are operating out of their weaker side, their wounded side. And I feel this is destroying the kids. But none of this in any way means that I wish to harm willful women. I'm out for understanding, not war. Male theology is something you do and I do this prayer.

God bless all willful women. May they find health and prosperity and happiness.

* * *

Now maybe we're prepared for some hard facts. We can start with Fred Hayward's Men's Rights Survey.

Q. What percent of Americans killed from hostilities in the Nuclear Age have been Women?

A. 1/100th of 1%.

Q. Which potential victim of rape is most likely to be attacked?

1) a young woman at home
2) a young woman in public
3) an older woman at home
4) a young girl
5) none of these

A. None of these. A young man in prison has the greatest chance of being raped.

Q. The most common child batterer is?

1) a middle class father
2) an uneducated father
3) a divorced father
4) a suburban father
5) none of these

A. None of these. Mothers are the most frequent child batterers. Their two-year-old sons the most frequent victims.

Q. Husband beating is a serious issue? T or F

A. True. Professor Susan Steinmetz (*Behind Closed Doors*) asserts the most unreported crime is not wife beating but husband beating.

Q. Men and women share equal rights regarding disposition of their children? T or F

A. False, obviously. Once a child is conceived a father has no right whatsoever to decide that it be aborted or not aborted. Should the mother choose to have the child and give it up for adoption the biological father may not adopt his own child. He may be required to pay child support even though permanently denied access to his child's life.

Q. What did John Lennon consider to be the most important thing in his life at the time of his death?

A. Raising his child.

Q. Employers are prohibited from practicing sex discrimination? T or F

A. False. Women can get parental leave but not men. The Supreme Court has ruled that the sex-discrimination law was enacted to protect women only!

Q. The American Constitution guarantees that a man is innocent until proven guilty. T or F

A. False. A man can be removed from his children and thrown out of his home on a simple unsubstantiated accusation of battering or molestation by his spouse. [This happens often. It was done to me. It's the easiest way to get you out of the house.]

Q. Last year how many men were denied their requests for full or joint custody?

A. Nobody knows! At the national, state, county and city levels there are hundreds of agencies and departments which research the problems and progress of women.

We know how many women applied to law school last year but not how many men filed custody suits.[147]

James Hillman says our culture is "overdetermined by women". Carl Jung said that American women are not happy with their husbands because they are not afraid of them.

Says Richard F. Doyle:
A "sacred cow" syndrome regarding women permeates our society. An example is the great concern in wars and disasters over the killing and maiming of women and children. The killing and maiming of men, even noncombatants, is of less, if any, importance. Men are treated like second-class citizens throughout the entire spectrum of crime, culpability and punishment. Affirmative action discriminates not only against white men, but against all men.[148]

Aaron Kipnis, in *Knights Without Armor*, wonders if the Vietnam War would have lasted ten years if we had watched thousands of robust, attractive, adolescent women getting blown to hamburger on TV every night.[149]

Says Doyle:
Objective examination demonstrates that over the past 30 years anti-male discrimination has become far greater, in scope, in degree, and in damage, than any which may exist against women. It takes the form of violations of law, decency, and common sense. It is most evident in the areas of domestic relations, employment, crime and punishment, and trashing of the male image itself.

The social repercussions are predictable and catastrophic. They include:

a. The male image is becoming that of "Jack the Ripper" or "Dagwood Bumstead".

b. The female image is emerging supreme, almost to the point of canonization.

c. Women and bureaucracies are usurping male roles and function in family and industry [and spirituality].

d. Sixty per cent of marriages end in divorce.

e. Half the kids are growing up without dads.

f. Defeated, emasculated men are matriculating to the flotsam and jetsam of skid row.

g. Immorality, neurotic instability, drug addiction, delinquency, crime, and other aberrations caused by a lack of male role models or leadership are being spawned at a disastrous rate.

h. The resultant welfare, corrections and mental institution burdens are becoming staggering and intolerable.

The roles of family provider, protector, disciplinarian and co-rearer of children, traditionally within the functions of husband and father, are being usurped by women, by the welfare department, by other agencies – including the current rash of child abuse watchdog agencies – and by the legal fraternity. The foregoing philosophies and more vicious anti-male attitudes have been assimilated by government offices. Government employees, from judges to Legal Aid lawyers, are like self-appointed Galahads who can't distinguish between ladies and women and who eagerly welcome the opportunity to rescue damsels in distress and enforce men's responsibilities. Men's rights may only be purchased by hiring expensive lawyers.

Probably the most extensive and outrageous manifestation of anti-male prejudice is in divorce. Divorce courts are like slaughterhouses, with about as much compassion and talent. They function as collection agencies for lawyer fees, however outrageous, stealing children and extorting money from men in blatantly unconstitutional ways. Men are regarded as mere guests in their own homes, evictable at any time on the whims of wives and judges.

Men are driven from home and children against their wills, then, when unable to stretch paychecks far enough to support two households, they are termed "runaway" fathers or "deadbeat dads". (Men in Father's Rights Groups now refer to themselves as "beat dead dads".) Contrary to all principles of justice and laws against debtors prison, men are thrown into prison for inability to pay alimony and support, however unreasonable or unfair the obligation.

In my case, after enduring surgery for a broken ankle – ten screws and a metal plate drilled into my bone – and watching my business go bankrupt because my future-former wife froze my business accounts, and being denied visitation with my kids for nine months because my ex bogusly accused me of abusing them, I was slapped with $350 per month child support based on an "anticipated" income of $1000 a month, which I didn't have, and couldn't make, and even if I could have hobbled my way around to doing that, how was I supposed to live on $650 per month?

In Florida, a single mother only has to apply for economic assistance and, even if she is rejected for that because she is too well off, she *automatically* qualifies for free legal counsel and representation in court by a state-paid attorney. So here's my future-former wife, heiress from a family of millionaires who owned the largest independent fuel oil company in Connecticut, getting free legal assistance.

I, who am unemployed and getting by on foodstamps, go to Legal Aid for help on Divorce Day. That's what they call it. Divorce Day. There are 35 fretful young girls, one 85-year-old man who got married to get laid one more time and now wants a divorce a week later – and me. I want to see my kids. I'm there to see my kids. After listening to self-consumed, uninitiated young women, who never died at their wedding, commiserating with each other for three hours I am finally ushered into a room. Across the desk from me sits a pimply-faced twerp, the Legal Aid attorney, who tells me in so many words, "You're not Black, you're not Chicano, you're not a woman. You're not supposed to be here; you're supposed to be out there making taxable income to pay *my* salary." He doesn't listen to a word I say about how I have been screwed out of seeing my kids for three years and that I have visitation rights according to my Final Divorce Decree *which are not being enforced.* He has me sign some paper that says they did all they could do for me at Legal Aid and that was that. I guarantee you, this legal system will not endure in its present form. There are too many guys like me who are going to continue wrestling with it until it changes.

God bless all willful women. May they find health and prosperity and happiness.

So, screw Legal Aid, I file my own motions. I file motions to have my visitation enforced and to have my support reduced to some workable portion of my income, which is at a low point because of injuries and a ruined business that can't begin to get rolling again in the middle of a building recession.

My motions are split between two courts. The HRS court, an enforcement division of the welfare bureaucracy, is going to hear about my money problems; the Circuit Court is going to hear about the visitation problems. We appear before the Circuit Court Judge, Judge Gallen, and he sends us to mediation. He doesn't want to make a decision. That's how he got to be a judge. My ex laughs into her tweed cuffs. Two more months wasted setting up appointments, breaking them, finally going to mediation and having my ex walk in and say to the mediator, "I don't have anything to talk about."

Meanwhile the other court threatens to put me in jail for not paying support. But they don't truly want to pay my living expenses. I am bankrupt, I don't have the money, I want to see my kids; at this point she's kept me from them for three years.

I set another hearing with Judge Gallen. Her attorney pulls a fast one. He moves the hearing date *forward*, gives me two days notice, and I can't attend. At that hearing, without me there, Judge Gallen, the guy I petitioned to enforce my visitation rights, *suspends* my visitation rights on the basis of accusations from my ex that I am mentally deranged. This the person who had nothing to talk about in mediation.

Fine. Months pass. I go to a psychiatrist. He writes a personal letter to the court saying that I should not be denied visitation with my children for any mental reason. This psychiatrist goes out on a limb for me. He certifies this. He puts it in a letter to the court. I set up another hearing with Judge Gallen. My ex's attorney gets it continued. Finally, Gallen sets a date but when we show up, he isn't there. He's in another part of the circuit. Smart guy. Judge number seven is sitting on the bench when they wheel in my cart piled chest-high with documents from five years of legal battling. I have no lawyer, I can't afford one. My ex *is* a lawyer, plus she has her free welfare lawyer.

I show the judge my psychiatrist's letter. My ex's attorney, without reading the letter, objects on the grounds that this is "circumstantial" evidence. The judge looks at his watch. I explain to the court that this psychiatrist has gone out on a limb for me to provide exactly what the court asked for, a clean bill of mental health. The judge looks at his watch again. I have reserved two hours hearing time. We are fifteen minutes into it. He can split an hour and forty-five minutes early. He upholds the objection, but then says he will put the letter in my file in case I want to appeal. He goes home early; I go three plus years without seeing my kids. These are the men who wear dresses. The last thing they want to do is make a decision. They want to follow precedent, fluff their egos, and go home early.

But I'm not done yet. I go to HRS court where my motion to reduce my support payments is still pending. I've written the judge a letter saying that I'm bringing my toothbrush in my pocket this time and I'm ready to go to jail. They don't whisper the word jail all day. My ex-wife's position, in this court, is that I'm a perfectly sane and healthy individual and I should be paying full support, even if I can't get a job. The judge listens to my spiel for an hour and a half. He decides that none of my injuries are permanent and irreversible. He decides that I am perfectly sane. Hence, I still owe support at the same level, plus I owe back support at the original level, based on the amount of money I *should* be making. Therefore, he tacks on an arrearage payment of so much a month effectively increasing my monthly obligation.

In Circuit Court I'm insane; I can't see my kids. In HRS court I'm healthy and sane and therefore I owe them lots of money. Let's not forget that the court gets a bite of the check every time any one of us sends a check in. This is having the fox guard the chickens to let these guys decide whether or not we owe them money.

So what has happened here? I asked the court to enforce my visitation rights and reduce my support obligations to some level that makes sense – my ex is a millionairess attorney, and I don't have a job. What does the court do? Suspend my visitation, and increase the amount of my support obligation. Our legal system is walking around butt first. This country needs a heart transplant. It needs to be shamanized.

How can I be sane in one court and insane in the other court? If I'm sane let me see my kids and come after me for support. If I'm insane don't let me see my kids but don't hassle me about support payments either. How is it possible to be sane in one court and insane in another court – based only on what makes it easer for the legal system! Do we try to make wine from asparagus? Why would we respect a legal system which is incapable of addressing our problems? This is the evil core of our Western legal system – it refuses to address the *whole* situation. It minces our lives into bits and pieces and makes schizophrenic rulings one "issue" at a time. Give me Solomon. Give me a MAN who is able to make a decision. Marriage is supposed to be a religious institution. Civil court should have no authority in marriage and divorce. That's a gross violation of the alleged separation of church and state. Let me get married and divorced by a priest or rabbi – someone who looks at the *whole* picture.

God bless all willful women. May they find health and prosperity and happiness.

Says Doyle:
    Dispel all notions that written "law" controls divorce. It has very little impact and few judges are even aware of statutory provisions.

I have personally sat in court and read the judge the statutes I felt applied to my visitation dispute. The judge stopped me and asked what I was doing. I told him I just wanted to be sure we were all playing by the same rules and he looked at me like I just got off the Good Ship Lollipop. Judicial whim, or what is politely called "discretion", is the actual basis on which decisions are made. The judges refuse to have one court deal with both visitation and support issues. If I'm not crazy let me see my kids. If I am crazy how can I owe you guys money when I'm not working?

It's been ten years since my visitation fiasco and something called the National Father's Initiative has exploded on the scene. It looks good at a glance – a movement to keep dads involved in the family. But the underlying rationale is mercenary and despicable. It all begins with the math. 95% of fathers who see their kids regularly pay full child support and pay it on time. Only 40% of dads who do not see their kids pay any support at all. So – goes the Washington logic – if we can keep dads involved with their kids we'll get more money. If the dad is around his wallet is around. Therefore we need to spend millions on a national "initiative" to encourage fathers to stay involved with their kids. This is a COMPLETE misreading of the situation. The problem is not that dads leave. The problem is that dads are kicked out of their kids' lives by vicious ex-wives. Automatic, assumed joint custody is the only solution to this mess. A woman going into court assuming that she is going to lose half of her kids – rather than assuming she is going to get the kids, the house and the money – is going to have a remarkable willingness to solve marital problems short of divorce. And if she still wants a divorce she loses half of the kids – automatically.

In custody disputes morality and fitness are insignificant. Sex-gender is the primary criteria. We do not start from the position that a man has completely equal rights to his children. We start from the position that he might get custody of one of his kids if he battles like hell for it and completely trashes the personality of his ex-wife in court.

Women are routinely awarded custody in 95% of the cases and this is wrong. No one has proven severe psychological repercussions when siblings are split up. Everyone has proven severe repercussions when kids are removed from their dads. If dads had automatic rights to their kids, fretful egocentric wives would think twice about filing for divorce. They wouldn't just preen and sneer their way through mediation. They would become part of the solution, instead of posing as the perennial accusers.

If you're baseball star Steve Garvey you can get your wife thrown in jail for a day for denying visitation. But here's what happens to most guys. *Chatelaine*[150] reports the case of a divorced father who cleaned and medicated his two-year-old daughter's vaginal rash, and was tossed into jail for sexual assault! His lawyer told him the fastest way to resume contact with his kids was to *plead guilty* and accept court-ordered treatment as a *sex offender*!!!

He got a female attorney who had the criminal charges thrown out four months later for lack of evidence. Meanwhile, the ex-wife took the kids to a psychiatrist. The father called the shrink but was never permitted to talk or meet with *her*. With his visitation still suspended the father was in court negotiating a new access agreement when charges were re-laid a month later. Those were eventually dismissed but a year later the man still had almost no access to his kids. They had to sneak over to his house if they wanted to see him. Having done her best to poison the kids against their dad the ex-wife was now suing for full custody.

My friend Dave B. told me a horrendous story of how his 8- and 10-year-old daughters walked through an Illinois cornfield on a cold October night with coyotes howling around them, avoiding the highways and the cops, in order to seek shelter at their father's house. Their mom was a drunken/doper/slut who made sure there was beer in the fridge – and nothing else. They had wanted to live with their dad for years and finally just took matters into their own little hands. Dave marched them, unannounced, into traffic court the next morning. The judge saw the kids and heard the story and immediately awarded Dave temporary custody. Is this a victory? How come these kids had to risk their lives to arrive at justice, fairness, a common sense solution? The mom wanted the kids so she could get the support payments so she could buy beer. And the courts went along with her. Criminal insanity. The judge who ruled in her favor should be thrown in jail.

If women really were the "sharing, caring" creatures we were brought up to believe, this visitation mess would be sorting itself out somehow. The truth is that this opportunity for women to demonstrate how philanthropic and benevolent they are is exposing them as the mean, selfish, willful creatures they are. Now hear this: women are NOT Morally Superior to men and there is no basis whatsoever for the feminized judges of our court systems to assume that they are.

Says Grace Wong[151], the fact remains that an allegation of abuse is particularly effective in keeping the accused away from the child. Abraham Worenklein states that in the 1960s the best way to get custody was to accuse the other parent of infidelity; in the '70s it was homosexuality; in the '80s and '90s it's sexual abuse. Nany Di Natale of the Catholic Children's Aid Society said 95% of the sexual abuse charges she encounters in divorce cases are unfounded.

Attorney G. Bertel Ljungstrom said that two-thirds of child abuse charges are false. These allegations buy the woman six to twelve months where she doesn't have to deal with the man, she can poison the kids against him, and she suffers no penalties for the deceit. This is America? This is what we fought for? This is the country of laws rather than the country of men? Give me back the country of men!

Judges are not making decisions. To protect or shield 5% of the kids they are destroying 95% of the families where the father has been falsely accused of abuse. I am not advocating child abuse; I am advocating fathers seeing their kids. Fine these women who bring false charges. Fine them heavily. Put them in jail. What we have done here is akin to making a law against peeing in somebody else's flower pots, without making any penalty whatsoever for doing so. Fine them. Jail them. American women, the most pampered creatures on the face of the planet, must begin being accountable for their outrages.

Carol Fetherson says it's impossible to have any sort of meaningful relationship with your children if you only see them two days a month.[152] She is President of Mothers Without Custody, and I cannot bring myself to gloat over the growth of this organization. Access to the children is the most important issue in divorce – many times more important than support payments. We cannot permit our feminized court system to value dollars and not relationships. We cannot allow the courts to separate the issues of visitation from support payments any longer.

Even the kids agree. I remember seeing a tearful young girl on an Oprah Winfrey show entitled "When Divorce Gets Ugly" telling the world that she didn't care about the money, they weren't suffering, and she just wanted to see her dad – who had been kept away from her for five years! "I just want to see my dad!" she cried. "For Christmas, for the summer…He used to take me and my sister fishing at least every weekend…without my dad a part of me is still missing. I want to see my dad!"

It's time to slam the door on the fingers of the feminist fantasy that has been creeping into our lives ever since Vietnam. Time to make some room for real men who really risked something for this country, whether dodging bullets or dodging the FBI. Politically correct means emotionally constipated. We cannot allow ourselves to think and feel only what women approve of.

George Weimer says that if we really want to have a revolution in America all we need to do is apply the same hiring practices to Pro Football as we do in industry – balance teams racially, and sexually: politically correct football. That way our sports can be as hobbled and non-competitive as our industrial performance.[153]

Come to think of it, we could apply the same guidelines to families. We can license families according to federal guidelines for age, sex and race – and remove the children from any family that does not meet the federal requirements. We've already got a good start on it. We're already doing it with the dads. That oughta solve a lot of problems. We don't need divorce anymore; we'll just have child removal.

Let's just take one case history, out of a million, to show how false sexual abuse charges were used to ruin one man's life. Ellen Hopkins reported this in an article called "Fathers on

Trial" and every divorced man with kids I know has been through some part of this scenario.[154]

Two months after Lucy Haines was born her parents separated. Roy saw his daughter frequently and when he filed for divorce in 1985 he sought joint custody. His wife, Sandra, responded by asking for $1,300 per week in temporary support payments. The judge awarded her $100 per week.

Shortly thereafter Roy had an argument with Sandra regarding visitation. She called Child Protective Services saying that Roy was abusing the child. The charges? That he was kissing his daughter's chest and putting medicine on her genital area. The child was then two and a half years old.

"That's the worst part about these allegations," says Roy. "On some level they're true. Of course I kiss my daughter. I love her. And Lucy was in diapers, she had a rash, so I put Desitin on her. The mother takes things any father would do for his child and makes them ugly. How am I supposed to fight innuendo?"

If his constitutional rights had been upheld, automatically upheld, Roy would have been in good shape. By law, he is innocent until proven guilty. Instead, for almost two years he bounced in and out of courts. He was only allowed to see his daughter under supervision. He paid $90,000 in legal fees, lost his business, and was investigated by the State Department and the IRS.

All the charges were dismissed a year later.

Within 24 hours of the dismissal Sandra claimed a more serious allegation: that Roy had held a knife to his child's mouth and chest. This supposedly occurred during one of the supervised visits! Roy's parental rights were promptly restricted. Then, a month later, Sandra remarked in passing that at some point Roy may have ejaculated in the child's face. She'd forgotten to mention it earlier.

God bless all willful women. May they find health and prosperity and happiness.

* * *

"How is it that charges so unsubstantiated have snowballed into a two-year ordeal?" asks Ellen Hopkins. The answer lies, at least in part, with Child Protective Services, the agency that provided "validator" Eileen Treacy.

Treacy has "validated" 400 cases of abuse and testified both in family court and criminal trials. Her *curriculum vitae* is impressive – eleven pages detailing the places she has trained, works published (including a book on sexual assault that Viking is negotiating for), courses taught, and positions held.

Her credentials though, are not quite as impressive as they seem. Under questioning by Roy's lawyer Treacy admitted that the last time she'd spoken to Viking was six years ago. While Treacy says she received "ongoing training" from two Columbia University professors in the field of child abuse, this instruction did not entail enrolling in a single accredited course. A postgraduate course in validation at St. Joseph College in Connecticut turned out to be a weekend seminar. Nevertheless, Treacy was allowed to testify as an expert witness.

Do you recall what I said earlier about overregulation in the construction industry? The states with the most regulations have the lowest quality construction. This is precisely what is happening in court. The offices with the most apparatus for preventing child abuse are the places where the most children are being abused. The "system", the feminized memes of the bureaucratic system, have become the oppressor.

To continue with Treacy: in an earlier case Judge Mark Epstein in New Jersey had ruled that abuse had not occurred and that the most damning witness against the plaintiff had been Eileen Treacy, who the judge felt had manipulated her questions in such a manner that she could induce children who hadn't been abused to say they had. Treacy's method of questioning:

Treacy:	Did you ever see (daddy's) pee pee?
Lucy:	Yeah.
Treacy:	Did he ever touch you with his pee pee?
Lucy:	Yeah.
Treacy:	Where did he touch?
Lucy:	I don't know.

* * *

According to Treacy's written report, "Lucy's behavior and statements are consistent with the Child Abuse Syndrome."

Treacy is not a psychiatrist or a licensed psychologist. This is a backyard business. Her professional cards identify her as a sex-abuse specialist. As a validator she gets $75 an hour for court appearances. If sexual abuse is not found she won't be hired to testify in court.

Who are these iguanas? Were they abused as kids and are they now trying to get back at the whole world? Does our feminized judicial system really have to be the mother that births such creatures in our midst? This woman has no business interposing herself between Roy and his daughter.

In another case Treacy concluded that two children had been abused on the basis of their "inappropriate" sexual knowledge. In court the mother admitted she brought home "anatomically correct" dolls for her children to play with. She also had shown them a video, *Better Safe Than Sorry*, which instructs children, "If daddy touches you, tell mommy."

Who are these people? The real sexual abuse, in both of these examples, was perpetrated by the mothers filling their kids' heads with fear and protosexual paranoia. When the father in the above example finally got to take his daughter on a vacation the girl announced, "Mommy said if you touch us call the Police." This is fear-mongering in a six-year-old child! This is driving a wedge between that girl and the wholesome trust in life that comes from being able to love and trust her father. This is child abuse and if this legal system was really interested in stopping child abuse it would have put this kid's mom in jail.

God bless all willful women. May they find health and prosperity and happiness.

Most lawyers who have taken cases of this nature will not do so again. Why? As soon as they say "My client is charged with molesting his child" they become courtroom pariahs. "How can you defend someone like that?" ask other lawyers who are defending murders, robbers, rapists.

And all it takes is one unsubstantiated accusation to set the whole machinery in gear. If you've had your brains turned on the past couple hundred pages you know by now that women are not given to telling the truth; they will say whatever sounds good to protect their interests or further their objectives. We cannot permit them to arbitrate what happens between kids and their dads. Lawyers estimate that 60% of all sex-abuse charges are unfounded and of the remainder most are greatly embellished. "Mommy said if you touch us call the Police!"

Judge Jeffery Gallet says, "I divest the accused parent of parental rights – without a trial, without a hearing. I'm forced to balance the constitutional rights of the accused against the best interests of the child." He is not "balancing" anything. He is wiping out the father's constitutional rights in order to play Galahad. The actual abuse is being perpetrated by the women and manholes – the system – not the dads. As we saw in Hayward's survey, most abuse is perpetrated by mothers against two-year-old boys. This judge is saying that 60% of the fathers charged with abuse are going to lose the most important, expensive, hard-won privilege in their lives – to be a father to their children. These children, growing up suspicious of men, hating men, as the demons of their psyche run wild, will waste billions of man hours and cost the system billions of dollars dealing with the psychological wreckage of this contrived situation; and all so that the few kids who actually get abused *can be removed from their families* and stuck in institutions. We already heard it said that the worst families are better than the best institutions. So who's gaining anything here? Galahad. The manhole in the white hat and black dress.

The latest scam in creating jobs for feminists is called "Supervised Visitation". That should be a good thing – creating centers where dads accused of some kind of "inappropriate" actions with their kids can at least SEE their kids while the courts sort things out. But it doesn't work like that. Visitation Centers have come to be utilized as a tool to displace actual fatherly rights. One Massachusetts father I know was slapped with bogus child abuse charges when he tried to stop the Brazilian mother of his kids from returning to her homeland with the children. It was a vengeful act on her part, pure and simple. The dad was only allowed "supervised visitation". On his daughter's 10th birthday he brought a cake to supervised visitation. The workers would not let him give the cake to the child because, "it might be poisoned". He's going to show up at supervised visitation and poison his own child??? As the dad left the center after a tearful visit with his daughter he told the workers they might as well eat the cake. They got out forks and dug in. Who are these ignuanas?

The court has no business deciding whether spanking my child or kissing my child is "appropriate behavior" or not. That's my ex's latest legal buzzword. I don't behave "appropriately" around my kids says she. Nobody wants children to be abused, but from where I stand they are being religiously abused every day they are compelled to attend a feminized school system which breeds neurotic behavior, devoid of moral guidance, and which causes the very problems it claims to be attempting to solve by completely removing kids from their dads. The only way my son and I could ever find the time to go fishing was when he took a Friday off school and I took a Friday off work. That was the only way we could get together and at least we did that. Family life? No. Cultural insanity.

After the divorce we couldn't even go fishing at all. And why?

Judith S. Wallerstein and Joan Berlin Kelly in *Surviving the Breakup: How Children and Parents Cope with Divorce* say one-half of divorced mothers were ambivalent or negative about visitation. They just divorced the bum. Why would they want their most precious possessions, their kids, to go see him? One-fifth saw no value in the father's continued contact with his kids and actively tried to sabotage the meetings by sending the children away just before the father's arrival, by insisting the child was ill or had pressing homework to do, or by making a scene. The mothers used "a thousand mischievous, mostly petty, devices designed to humiliate the visiting parent and to deprecate him in the eyes of his children."

In some states the law requires the custodial parent not only to *permit* visitation but to actively *encourage* it. That's like passing a law that people have to plant flowers along the highway. How do you enforce it? How do you make sure it happens? Everyone just drives around with a muddy gardening tool in their trunk and nothing ever happens. It sure makes the judges look good. They begin to look like they're really on top of the problem. Sorry. Judges *are* the problem. Judges have no business messing around inside people's personal and private lives. Give the fathers half the kids and be done with it because unless the custodial parent abides by the court order for visitation the other parent may never see his children.

We pretend this is a legal situation but there is no enforcement other than the voluntary compliance of the mother. No penalties are levied against her for deceit, perjury or non-compliance. "Enforcing a father's visitation rights when a mother won't give him access is often more difficult than winning sole custody for him," says New York attorney Carol Zimmerman. The first thing that happens when a father asks the court to enforce his court-ordered visitation rights is that he is required to go get a costly psychiatric examination.[155] His visitation rights are in effect, right now, according to the terms of his final decree; and the first thing that happens when he asks the court to do something is that they do nothing, and make him pay to go do something. He should be driven right from the courtroom to wherever his kids are – school, swim team, ballet, wherever, to effect his visitation; and if there is some question of his mental competence his ex can pay the money and set up an appointment and that silliness can be worked out while he is seeing his kids! Sometimes, as in my case, you get the exam, and you still can't see the kids. We are only enforcing one half of the law – the female half.

Daniel Molinoff, a lawyer who has many times tried to get an enforcement of visitation order for his male clients, says, "Temporary three-month orders of protection are given routinely, based on one-party testimony by women who, without a hearing, can and do have their husbands thrown out of the house or kept at a distance for allegedly abusing them or their children. But a man can almost never get an order of protection for denied visitation. Horrified judges say, 'You want the mother to spend a night in jail?' "

Yer goddamn right we do your honor. It's the least damaging solution to this whole quagmire. One night in jail has a way of straightening out most people's thinking. It don't cost much. It's much better than wrecking the lives of a father and his children for months or years or forever. Let it get around that women who fiddle with visitation spend a night in the pokey and suddenly there are going to be a lot less divorce disputes showing up on the courthouse steps.

It might even help to curb brainwashing. Experts believe that brainwashing – intensive, systematic indoctrination of the children over a certain time period – occurs in more than 15% of divorces. Subtle but vicious mind-bending occurs more frequently. With the kids in the background, on her end of the phone, I've had my ex ask me, "Do you have AIDS yet?" The next time I saw my kids they refused to touch me. This is child abuse.

Says one ex-father, "My kids have been so turned against me that if the judge gave me custody they would probably run away as soon as I took my eyes off them. When children have been brainwashed there's not much you can do."

New York cop Bob Ricci finally gave up and withdrew his petition for enforcement of visitation rights after his twenty-third court appearance. "How many times must a father be told by his own offspring to stay out of their lives before he starts to take it to heart?" he told the judge. "Abiding by the rules, paying my support, I expected my rights as a father would be equally respected and supported. It was an assumption I finally came to discover was false."

Ricci says he and his wife had been the Roy Rogers and Dale Evans of the Charismatic church renewal movement until one day she told him she hadn't loved him for years and asked him to leave the house immediately. How can she have the power to kick him out of his own house and remove his kids from him because she doesn't love him anymore? *What's love got to do with it?* He still loves his five kids. That's five times more love on his side of the scale if we are going to start basing legal pleas on emotionalism.

His wife informed him he should not see his children at all because he was not a good example for them. This guy is a cop, remember – the guy everybody else calls on to risk his life to solve *their* problems. Says Ricci, "Once when my three-year-old got in the car she blessed herself because mommy told her I was the devil."

In my case, my own daughter told me she was scared to visit me because she was afraid I was going to "steal" her. She got the notion from mom, and *from a videotape they show the kids in school!* As if school wasn't feminized enough now it has launched an offensive to instill kids with "fear of father". This is a crime. This is child abuse.

When Ricci tried to visit his kids his wife always made excuses for why they couldn't meet with him: they were sick, they had homework, they had a friend's party to go to, they had other plans, and finally, her work was done – they just didn't want to see him anymore. It seems clear the kids were sick and tired of being positioned at the axis of these manipulations and the least painful way for them to live was to avoid their father. This is child abuse.

God bless all willful women. May they find health and prosperity and happiness.

Ten years later, when I finally reconnected with my son, he told me, "Mom wasn't lying when she said we didn't want to see you. But the reason we didn't want to see you wasn't because we really didn't want to see you. It was because every time we got back from seeing you she put us through hours of inter-rogation and grief and misery. We were just tired of the pain and the hassle. It was easier just not to see you."

Ladies and gentlemen: this is child abuse. It even has a name: Parental Alienation Syndrome. One parent willfully turning the children against the other parent. Child abuse.

It so happens that Child Protective Services in Sarasota, Florida agrees with me. They want me to mount a test case against my ex-wife to pursue charges of child abuse based on evidence of Parental Alienation syndrome. They'll testify on my behalf that Parental Alienation Syndrome is *de facto* child abuse. I want to do it. I should do it. But when I told my son my intentions he said, "Don't do it or I'll be mad at you and you won't see my anymore. I'm tired of this endless battle."

So I won't do it. I'll do the "dad thing". I'll remove my ego. I'll snap the cycle of cowshit. I'll hold to the high moral ground. I'll enact my natural role as the spiritual leader of this family. I *will not* do what my ex did. I will not put my vengeance before the needs of my kids. That's dad's job: get bulldozed by evil, stand up, dust himself off, and keep going forward doing what's *really* best for his kids. But it's been ten years since I saw my daughter. She's still terrified of me. I'm afraid there's a world of pain eating her adolescent soul. God bless you Rebecca.

It has been found that children who do not see their fathers develop profound emotional and behavioral problems later in life. Does this surprise anybody? Children from single-mother households are at greater risk for: substance abuse, teen pregnancy, suicide, dropping out of school, and ending up in prison or a mental hospital. Both intact households and *single-father* households score higher in producing decent competent kids.

It's so much cheaper and healthier to enforce visitation. Yes, even by throwing mothers in jail for a night on the say-so of the ex-husband – just as fathers are removed from their houses on the say-so of their wives – than it is for society to pick up the tab for all the aberrant and criminal behavior spawned by lack of fathering.

Says John Munder Ross, clinical psychologist: we know now that father absence is associated with poor control of aggression and basic drives, impaired intellectual and academic functioning, and defects in gender identity. Says Dr. John Jacobs, professor of clinical psychiatry: kids who don't see their fathers tend to suffer from serious depressions over a long period of time and to have deep self-esteem problems.

Psychologists who counsel divorcing men agree that anguish over the loss of day-to-day contact with their children explains, in part, why some don't visit more often and why many stop visiting altogether. "Men who feel their guts are being ripped out of them when they are separated from their kids are not sick, effeminate, or stuck in some *mater*nal identification," says Jacobs. It's hard for a man to part from his children over and over again – so many goodbyes – and to suffer the diminishment of his parental role, which is some deep part of his biology and his psyche. Often the most devoted fathers can deal with the intense sadness only by withdrawal and fewer and fewer visits.

In Travis County, Texas, where visitation is as strictly policed as child support payments, the compliance rate for both is twice the national average. When visitation is enforced, compliance with child support orders is high. Illinois and Virginia both enacted Visitation Enforcement legislation. It's like a traffic ticket. Deny visitation – get a $100 fine. Do it three times – go to jail. Simple stuff that works. Judges feared the courts would get clogged. The fact is, court dockets have *decreased* because ex-wives don't like paying out money to advocate their own bogus charges. If it's free they'll take advantage of it. But if it costs money they only deny visitation if there really is a serious problem to be addressed. And the bottom line is more kids are seeing their dads.

It is estimated that 100,000 kids are kidnapped each year by non-custodial parents. But no one is keeping statistics on children removed by custodial parents, as if this was somehow acceptable. The mother just decides to move 2000 miles away with her new boyfriend and that's that for dad and his kids? This is legalized kidnapping – yet another way that the courts are favoring women and blind to the grief of men.

Listen to the words of Judge Richard Huttner, a manhole if I ever heard one:

You have never seen a bigger pain in the ass than the divorced father who wants to get involved. He wants to meet the kid after school, take the kid out to dinner, have the kid on his own birthday, talk to the kid every evening on the phone, go to every open-school night, take the kid away for a whole weekend. [He wants to live with this kid, not just visit his kid!] This type of involved father is pathological.

For my dollar it is Judge Huttner who is pathological, a disease in our legal system. This father is only trying to do what he would have been able to do if his wife hadn't kicked him out of the house. I like making my kids breakfast and helping them pick out socks. I like sitting in the same room reading with them, when we are not talking, just interacting on the most primal levels of breathing, and being, and tuning to each other's vibes. We are simply there, together, not talking, and something like food is passing back and forth between our bodies.

I used to love driving in the car with my son in the front seat, not talking, while he was obviously thinking about something. Suddenly he would say to me, "Mom, how come so and so is like so and so." Sometimes he would catch himself and sometimes he wouldn't. (If he didn't my daughter would scream from the back seat, "He's not your mom!") But for a golden instant I had merged with "Mom" in his head and he was there with me, comfortable and trusting, all defenses turned off, and even asking for some advice or clarification.

In 1985 only 10% of the 12 million divorced children were in the custody of their fathers. This wasn't always so. Until the turn of this century fathers routinely got custody. This bears repeating. The norm, the human historical meme, has been that when a family breaks up, the kids, and the house, go with the father. Why? Because the man is the economic engine who can provide the support for the kids. This was not a law. This was a convention, a value system that civilization arrived at over hundreds of thousands of years. It worked. And now what have we done? We've given the kids and the house to the mother, and still stick the dad with a support obligation. It doesn't work.

And when, you ask, did this weirdness begin? In the 1880s the concept of "*mater*nal preference" took hold of the courts like a bulldog on the neck of a spaniel. This is a clear, identifiable, black and white instance, of the feminization of American law. Suddenly, after 2.2 million years of human evolution, the country of laws, not men, decided that giving custody to the mother was in the best interests of the children – and by the way, she doesn't work, so send dad the bill. We are 110 years into the "*mater*nal preference" doctrine and our divorce rate is 60%. Ladies and gentlemen, this does not work. Give the kids back to their dads – automatically. When parents with multiple children divorce, split the kids between both parents, at the very least.

A woman can be a psychotic, a prostitute, or an alcoholic, and still keep custody. Says Manhattan attorney Raoul Felder, "I had a case in which the mother kept custody even though she had been hospitalized for depression 13 times!"[156]

Although 90% of the children of divorce are in the custody of their mothers, women activists who favor custody decisions based on who is the "primary care-giver" are alarmed at what they see as a trend toward granting custody to men in half of the contested cases. They are concerned because more than 5% of the kids might end up with their dads? There is no self-governing factor, no end limit to female self-seeking. At divorce time every dad is informed by his own lawyer of the tremendous financial expense of seeking custody of his own kids. If you don't have $100,000 in disposable income you can't even contemplate suing for custody.

Once you are a non-custodial parent you are a non-parent, says Michael Diehl, an advocate of divorce-law reform. Non-custodial parents simply have no *enforceable* rights. We have made men the Disposable Parents, and we have done it in the last 100 years.

A panel headed by Margaret Campbell Haynes has recommended to Congress that they empower states to suspend men's professional licenses if they don't pay support. How does that sound? Would you take away a house painter's business license if he didn't send in the check? Maybe, maybe not. Would you take away a woman's Realtor's license or driver's license if she didn't permit visitation? Now we're getting somewhere. If the second query is absurd then so is the first one. If not, then it's not. How about if we finally start to enforce both halves of the support/custody laws. The feminist fantasy is over. Men will tolerate no less than fair and equal treatment in this arena.

* * *

How did human society stray so far from common sense and traditional knowledge? How did survival of the fittest – battling egos – become the standard architecture of marriage? How many tens of millions of kids have to grow up without dads before we revert to something that works? How did marriage become so perverted? How? Through the wacky ministrations of another toxic American Myth – separation of Church and State. Our political hacks and media watchdogs have rigorously kept religion out of government, but they've done NOTHING to keep government out of religion.

For 10,000+ years marriage was a religious institution – holy matrimony. Marriage was a covenant with God that superseded civil law. Even today a person is not obligated to testify against their spouse in court. Marriage and divorce were administered by church law not government. It never occurred to our Founding Fathers that marriage and divorce could end up in civil court. Those were religious matters; they were to be kept separate. King Henry VIII had to start an entirely new church, the Church of England, so he could get divorced – because the Catholic Church would not allow divorce. And this guy was the KING. He had TOTAL control of the government. But a willful attempt to override religious law might have caused so much civil unrest it could have toppled him from the throne – so outlandish was the proposition that government could claim control over the religious institution of marriage. King Henry's only option was to start a whole new church that permitted divorce.

But the wall between church and state vanished about 150 years ago around the time of the American Civil War – in the very country that prides itself on the separation of church and state. Two court rulings and an administrative procedure broke down the barriers that kept government out of religion. The first court ruling prohibited Mormon men (any men) from taking more than one wife. This was not government's business! It is not the government's job to act as Moral Enforcer. But there you go. They cracked the egg and dribbled it on our dicks. No man can have more than one wife. If your wife metamorphosed into a screaming harpy you couldn't marry someone else to keep her in line. You had to put up with her crap until she divorced you, or ran off, or you finally kicked her out. By banning polygamy the marriage dynamic was rattled; the balance of power leveraged onto the female seat of the marriage seesaw.

Mormon men could look back on 3000 years of Judeo/Christian tradition to justify their religious heritage. Mormon women made a free choice to become the second or third wife of a man they wished to be with. Polygamy was a religious institution and the Supreme Court had NO authority whatsoever to breach this wall between Church and State. No one was being forced to participate in polygamy. The intent of the Constitution clearly opposed this type of religious interference. There was no moral justification for this meddling. In fact, Mormon men of the State of Utah were among the very first men to amend their State Constitution to grant women the right to vote. They beat out Eastern states by a decade. But Mormons were a cultish minority, so our esteemed political pundits stood back and let their religious rights get trashed. Thus government emerged as a Moral Enforcer – erasing separation of Church and State – ordaining itself with a misappropriated authority which muzzles us today. Our government has rendered opinions about everything from abortion to gay rights to women's rights to children's rights to No Fault Divorce – and NONE of them lie within the mandate to govern which WE CEDED to the government. Government has no business meddling in our moral affairs. They've put judges in our pulpits.

The administrative procedure which wrested marriage from religious jurisdiction and placed it within government jurisdiction was a seemingly innocuous, well-intentioned effort to protect freed black slaves. On occasion, before the Civil War, slaves were set free by their masters. They were permitted to marry other freed slaves. The problem came in where both freed slaves possessed documents attesting to their Free status – but their children did not. Therefore, a legal administrative procedure was put in place whereby freed slaves could *register* their marriage and thereby convey documents to their children certifying them as free also. Prior to this blacks without documents were arrested as escaped slaves. The children of freed blacks fell into this crack, and frequently back into chains. Thus marriage registration provided protection for the children of free blacks. So far so good.

But government, being government, soon realized it could make a few bucks by registering ALL marriages. State laws were enacted requiring marriages to be registered. A direct violation of the supposed separation of Church and State. And everyone today assumes that marriage registration is normal. It's not. It's hideous and insidious in a country which prides itself on separation of Church and State.

Separation of Church and State is another toxic American Myth, another phony meme, another one-way street. Government has invaded religion. I can believe whatever I want to believe – as long as I don't act on my beliefs – because then I become subject to law. Here's another example of the "feminization" of society – where opinions are separated from actions – like women's gossip circles. Where beliefs are severed from reality – like fat TV psychics talking about love. Sure, I've got freedom of religion. I can believe it's OK to have five wives. But if I act on my belief I go to jail. This is moral insanity proliferating within an ever-enlarging feminized worldview – ideas divorced from action. Think whatever you want, but don't act on it, or the state inquisitors will make you suffer. This is fundamental erosion of Male Soul. Government pissing on our masculine birthright.

And suddenly, in the wake of marriage registration, divorce disputes were removed from the Pastor's study and the Rabbi's office and thrust into the court of law. But our courts had no legal mechanisms in place to litigate divorce – none whatsoever – divorce did not fall within the purview of "law". So . . . cracking egg upon egg . . . the U.S. courts began importing sections of British Ecclesiastical Law, British CHURCH LAW!, into American civil jurisprudence. Preposterous! We should have had a revolution over this! Old King Henry finally got his way. Divorce was administered in civil court, and the wall between religion and government was laid waste.

By the late 1800s the logjam of litigation in civil court had become so ponderous that the State Supreme Court of South Carolina ruled that neither the legislature nor the judiciary of that state had any jurisdiction at all over marriage and divorce. These were not legal issues. They were religious issues. And some people in South Carolina recognized this obvious Constitutional violation. Some people – not surprisingly from a southern state that had just endured the battering of the Civil War – were trying to revert to strict separation of church and state as envisioned by the Founding Fathers. They won the battle but lost the war. Over time their sagacity was swept aside by a new secular agenda that was gaining control over the American psyche – allegiance not to church but to government.

If government could harness the will of the people – and if corporations could harness the will of government – then corporations could direct the activities of the whole nation. How could corporations accomplish that? By cloaking themselves in civil rights rhetoric. Emancipation of slaves and voting rights for women got perverted through the court system into an agenda for vastly expanding corporate power. The dislocations of the Civil War gave rise to the Robber Barons – commandeering huge tracts of land, gouging the earth, building railroads and factories, shipping over "slave" labor from Ireland and Italy and Slovakia. After one hundred years of anti-corporate Democracy based on Thomas Jefferson's warning that we should, "…crush in its infancy the aristocracy of our moneyed corporations," the genie was let out of the bottle. A praiseworthy social cause – granting additional freedoms to slaves and women – got twisted into a legal heyday for corporations.

The second legal decision that utterly trivialized the influence of religion was a ruling made by the Supreme Court in 1886 [Santa Clara County v. Southern Pacific Railroad] that a private corporation was a natural "person" under the U.S. Constitution. Henceforth corporations would be sheltered by the Bill of Rights and the 14th Amendment (which had been added to the Constitution to protect freed slaves). Sixty years later Supreme Court Justice William O. Douglas wrote that "There was no history, logic or reason given to support that view". But the deed was done. Human civil rights had been perverted to include corporations. From then on corporations were legally regarded as "persons" and were thereby entitled to "rights" of free speech and ownership of property. Invisible corporate "persons" who do not eat, sleep, die, inhabit a body, feel anything, pay a fair share of taxes, or get drafted in time of war suddenly had "rights".

But probably worst of all, these "persons" do not pray. They have no spiritual, no non-*material* life. A non-*material* form, but not a non-*material* life. Preposterous. It's kind of like believing that algebra is "alive" and has "rights". Corporations do not look over the horizon seeking divine guidance. Their only guidance is profit. They have no moral or ethical center, no conscience. If these were human "persons" most of them would be arrested and thrown in jail for anti-social abuses – polluting our air and water, selling defective machines, killing people through premeditated negligence.

This legal hubris is beyond belief. The government has the power to create "people"? This is a perversion of everything sacred. We never gave our government the power to create "people". It's a fundamentally preposterous idea. And wait until some corporation creates a test tube person and wants to patent her. We've all fallen asleep at the switch.

On purely religious grounds, the notion that "we the people" cede authority to a government which blithely believes it has the power to create people is a monstrosity of mythic proportions. We deride older civilizations which separated humanity into "slave" and "free", but think nothing of the fact that we send elected representatives to Washington to negotiate the daily activities of invisible "persons". We laugh at people who worshipped Zeus, or burned sacrifices to Astarte – but what would these same primitive people say if they were transported 3000 years into the future to observe a civilization designed by and for invisible corporate "persons"? The dissonance in this politic makes the Bible read like a science textbook. How can we be so stupid? Our government cannot create people – and certainly not without creating problems bigger than we can handle. Which is just what has happened.

There is a Jewish folktale about the Golem. A humanoid helpmate created out of clay by an alchemist messing with forces bigger than he understood. At first the Golem was an obedient servant, but then he grew so big and powerful and willful that he killed his master. Maybe that's the best metaphor for corporations – big dumb clay monsters that will kill us if we don't get them under control. They will poison our air and water, enslave our productivity, kill some of us, and then sneak out of town at night and leave us to clean up their mess.

This legal monstrosity, the Corporate Person, is the most outrageous violation of the separation of Church and State to infect our nation since its inception. And as far as I can tell, this violation has gone virtually unacknowledged and unchallenged. Why don't they teach us about it in grade school for Christ sakes? Here's a new meme. Let it sink in. The way to attack corporations is to attack the legal doctrine that they are "persons". That legal doctrine is a direct violation of separation of church and state – an outrageous case of government overstepping the authority we grant it, and trampling our religious domain. Our religions, our highest belief systems, are quite capable of telling us who is a person and who is not. That's one of OUR rights. We may cede authority to government to build highways or equip a navy, but there is no way in heaven we can be expected to cede authority to a government so it can create people. That's a violation of my religion. That's a violation of *your* religion. Government kills people with abortion and creates people with corporations. We never gave them that power. That's going too far. Let's sue the bastards.

A "person" has feelings and thoughts and a soul and children. A person is a potential convert to a certain religious perspective. A person is wide-ranging and open-ended, possessing physical, emotional and spiritual needs. A corporation is NOT! I can't convert an elephant to Catholicism or a moth to Judaism – nor can I convert a corporation to either. A corporation is not human. A corporation is not a person. It is sacrilegious to treat them as such. It is a violation of your and my religious prerogatives.

We are heirs of Psyche, the Greek personification of feminine mind, sneaking a whiff of the mysterious beauty ointment of

Persephone, goddess of the underworld, which violation of a godly taboo puts us all to sleep.

So...due to the dislocations caused by the Civil War government emerged as a Moral Enforcer. First it told men they couldn't have more than one wife. Then it required that all marriages be registered. Then it began importing British Church Law into American Civil Law so government could begin administering marriage and divorce. Finally, like thieves in the night, corporations hijacked the zephyr of justice which had granted wider civil rights to emancipated slaves and women. Corporate lawyers snuck under the fence and grabbed the greatest share of these civil rights for their invisible masters by getting corporate golems legally identified as persons. This murky cesspool of overlapping agendas, whereby self-righteous "suffragettes" unwittingly sniff-out the legal trail to enlarge civil rights for corporations, has been spewing legal toxins in our face for a century – and we never talk about it!

The more "rights" women get, the more "rights" corporations get. Women can own property, corporations can own property. Women can participate in the political process, corporations can participate in the political process. Women can skip out on war, corporations can skip out on war. What a nightmare. We've kept religion out of government, but not government out of religion. First women became "free" and "equal" – trashing 4000 years of religious tradition that preserved balance in marriage. And now the government is creating "people"! Masculine religion has been systematically beat to death and only the corporate golems are laughing.

Then feminism came along and destroyed the family. And now our kids are being raised by TV. Family values have gone the way of the buffalo. We've been colonized by our own corporations. We are all slaves.

One of the most ridiculous choruses we hear from feminists is how men have power and women do not. Of the nearly 58,200 names of war dead carved into the Vietnam Memorial in Washington eight are women. This is not power, this is powerlessness.

Women live eight years longer than men. This is power; power over life.

Says Warren Farrell:
When a man is in the hospital for a coronary bypass operation caused by the stress of working two jobs to support his ex-kids, who his wife won't let him see, that is powerlessness. It is in the area of physical health and longevity that men's power – control over their own lives – begins to fall considerably short of women's power. There can be no greater loss of power than loss of life.

Our reaction to the fact that men die earlier than women might be viewed as the quietest response to genocide in the history of humankind. It might be called "androcide". More empathy is directed toward the widows who cannot find men than toward the men who have died.[157]

Other countries do it. We're going to have to do it too. I'm talking about a National Strike. I'm talking about a two-day walkout of every man, who is a man, who has been abused by the court's ill-conceived attempts to legislate morality. We'll soon see who the manholes are. It will be right before our eyes. We walk out for two days: stop the trains, stop the planes, stop the TV transmissions, and stop harvesting the lettuce. Two days should do it, but if that doesn't get their attention then we go for two weeks.

We have nothing to fear. The female critics and media meme-architects are not stupid. They just don't know how much we are hurting. When no bricks are being laid and no planes are landing and the boob tube goes blank they'll have plenty of time to figure this out.

And let's not coddle ourselves with the illusion that some national Men's Rights Group is going to steer us on our way. Have you ever called one of these services and had a woman answer the phone, get your address, and start sending you useless, hate-mongering, taped information, billed to you COD! With the exception of Fred Hayward's group in California and Stuart Miller of the American Fathers Coalition in Washington

D.C., the father's rights groups I contacted in my desperation were inevitably run by out-of-work lawyers trying to drum up business. They will give you a free consultation for a $100 donation. Manholes. If there is a legitimate Father's Rights Group out there besides the AFC I hope you sue me so at least I'll be able to get your address.

We don't need them. The fact is, if you have an operating value system you don't need to depend on a legal system. They can't put us all in jail.

Says Doyle, after divorce, the next largest area of male subordination is crime and punishment: from decision to arrest, amount of bail required, guilt or innocence in judgment, severity of sentences, physical conditions of imprisonment, to release on parole. Men are jailed on offenses for which women would be winked at. When 48% of the population is committing 94% of the crime it makes you wonder who has defined what constitutes crime. It's a crime to steal a car – *Mater*. It's not a crime to sabotage dad's visitation – human relationship.

Men receive stiffer fines than women for the same offenses. Women are murdering husbands and boyfriends and getting off scot-free by pleading "brutality". Men get thrown in jail for date rape where the victim sustains no physical injury. Camille Paglia has stated that rape is equivalent to getting beat up – and men get beat up all the time. If a man looks into a home where a women is undressing, he will be arrested for window peeping. Reverse the situation, with the woman looking in, and again the man will be arrested – this time for indecent exposure. Men get arrested for rape. Women do not get arrested for dressing like available sex-goddesses. They are torturing our primitive mammalian psyches.

Ross Virgin reports that 50% of junior high school students believe that a woman who walks alone at night in seductive clothing is asking to be raped.[158] He also says that male lust constitutes a medical problem that can be alleviated by free government-run prostitution. As insane as this sounds to the ear it is exactly the sort of free health service that is being provided to women by government and industry all around us every day.

How many men are in jail for trying to steal enough money to satisfy the boundless cravings of women? How many women want their men to get them drugs or alcohol or a car or an apartment if they want a fuck? Ross Virgin is sounding less insane every minute. How much crime and disaster could we avert by addressing men's medical problem of "lust"? How many men wouldn't be in jail if it wasn't somehow for a woman?

Women honestly don't know that their constant talking and compulsive advice-giving constitutes *verbal abuse and violence to our brains*. Women think in words, men don't. We don't live in the left half of our brains all, or even most of the time. We can't make a law against talking too much, although, other than feminine memes to the contrary, I don't know why not. But what we *can* do is introduce our own masculine meme that says: wives, mothers, lovers, and daughters, with all due respect and love, we demand equal time – equal time spent in silent observation or silent reflection or silent action, to that amount of time spent talking. We have a right to live in the right side of our brains, even when we are in the same room with you. It should not be necessary for us to vacate our living space just to have some moments of right-brain reverie or right-brain peace. We need this time of not talking. To ignore this heartfelt request is to abuse us as men and as human beings. You want us to talk to you, fine, we will. But you must also be prepared to share our silence. We need that from you.

Says Doyle:

The alleged discrimination against women in employment, abortion, and education is insignificant compared to that against men in crime and punishment, employment and domestic relations. Braying neo-feminists are cluttering the women's cause with emotional trash, non-issues, impractical solutions, and dangerous policies; and the press takes them seriously. The very term "feminists" is misleading since most adherents are attempting to destroy all traces of femininity [hence he calls them neo-feminists].[159]

* * *

What Anne Wilson Schaef calls the White Male Society or the Addictive Society, I call Marxist/Feminism or the Manhole Society. It's clear to me that men are at fault here for not being men, for pandering to female values. These White Men at the top of our society are the manholes, the men enforcing female memes. The era we are now entering could be called the Age of Institutional Menopause. The people making the loudest noise and the biggest impact on how our society should be run are menopausal women and their manhole enforcers. We are being led to view human life through the eyes of menopausal women. I am not a menopausal woman. Just about nothing menopausal women say makes any sense to me. Just about all of their namby pamby fix-it-solutions strike me as naive psychobabble – and I have a right to my opinion. When I talk about relocating the center of gravity of the human personality far, far back onto the male side of the spectrum, this is precisely what I am arguing for. They have a right to their position, and I have a right to mine. Balance. What we are missing is balance because we have ignored the Deep Masculine memes. What we are seeing is neo-feminists assailing, then absorbing, the female memes of their manhole enforcers. As Vilar said, women are drubbing the very aborted masculinity they created. We are not even allowing the Deep Masculine to come into play.

Says Doyle, government and industry, taking the line of least resistance, are giving women preference in hiring and promotion, regardless of qualification. Women attorneys now start out at salaries $2000 higher than men. More than 50% of managers are women. Less than 1% of bricklayers, painters, and roofers are women.

The joke goes that as job-seeking Mr. Jones takes a seat across from the bald-headed personnel director, he is told, "You're well qualified for the job, Mr. Jones, but seeing as our company doesn't discriminate by sex in hiring, we're looking for a woman to fill the position."

Says Otis Adams, the social trend of the last few decades has been restricted to unilateral liberation. Men are less free, Blacks are no freer, women are much freer.

Under the Married Women's Act (first passed into law in Mississippi in 1839) a woman was allowed to take on paid employment without her husband's consent. This was a law rammed through by cotton textile manufacturers, corporate manholes, who needed female workers to replace the soon-to-be-liberated slaves. Corporations and women in bed together.

The Nineteenth Amendment to the Constitution gave women the right to vote and WW I had them taking over the factories and offices while the men were "over there". Thus WW I consolidated the suffragette movement as later Vietnam consolidated Women's Liberation. War benefits women – and kills men.

Women want to work? Fine. Let them work. Let the dads stay home with the kids, or take them out fishing and hunting.

Women are using sex as a weapon and tying the law into knots with it. One of my favorite episodes of Institutional Menopause is reported by Aaron Kipnis in *Knights Without Armor*. A plant worker at the Monsanto Company in Hahnville, Louisiana, was recently awarded $60,000 in damages for anxiety attacks she suffered because her foreman cursed at her.[160] Imagine what would happen to a man if he tried to sue his foreman for swearing at him?

Three NFL players for the New England Patriots were fined $72,500 for the sexual harassment of a female sportscaster who was walking around in *their* locker room. Have male reporters ever entered female locker rooms, much less sued the female athletes for exposing themselves?

One of Kipnis' cohorts told how his secretary seduced him when he had just broken up with his wife. They were lovers for three years and then when they broke up she threatened a sexual harassment suit? He had to give her a big cash payoff to avoid a scandal that could have ruined his business during the years it would have taken to drag the thing through court to exonerate himself. They both got sex and she wants money for it. She is a whore. Prostitution is proliferating wildly under the aegis of feminism. Women who expect money or *mater*ial rewards for sex are whores, whether you are married to them or you meet them in a bar.

In 1989 Danielle Tyece Mast robbed five banks and pleaded before a Federal Judge that her lover influenced her to do it. (Ms. Mast got two years.) I believe her. But what the hell happens to all the men apprehended while trying to score cars or coke or cash for their "babes"? Do *they* get to plead in court that their girlfriend made them do it? When are we going to boot women off the Morally Superior pedestal? This is the Twisted Side of the Mother in one of its most gruesome and pervasive forms. The men, victims of "medical lust", need to get laid – need that female affirmation they were addicted to by their moms. They *can* get laid, by a seductive goddess, who will service their sexual need if they service her boundless *mater*ial cravings. Servicing feminine greed is culturally approved cruelty. It's a recipe for disaster imprinted on the minds of young boys who are not initiated away from it.

Says Kipnis, as for violence against women, it is important to remember that each year over 97% of *all* husbands *do not* resort to violence in their relationships. Considering the sheer amount of verbal abuse we withstand that statistic amazes me. Meanwhile, violence of *women* against men, other women, and children, is on the rise and frequently goes unreported. According to Suzanne Steinmetz, Murray Strauss and Richard Gelles, 52% of domestic violence is perpetrated by women against men. Plus, women, being smaller, tend to use more weapons in their attacks and cause greater physical harm. So why are there women's shelters and no men's shelters? It's called "Follow the Money". Feminists cook up phony statistics, declare a crisis, and then hound the government for money to "solve" the problem – when all it's really about is getting jobs for their feminist buddies. Jobs that don't involve shoveling or getting dirty.

Two women in El Dorado County, California, fired six bullets from a rifle, a pistol and a shotgun into their shared lover, killing him, of course. They claimed he was abusive. They were *not prosecuted!* A woman in San Francisco shot her husband five times as he lay sleeping in bed. She was sentenced to probation and advised to get counseling!

What we are witnessing here is a vicious pattern of collusion between the feminized legal apparatus and feminized media memes. Says Fred Hayward, in a survey of 1000 random advertisements 100% of the jerks singled out in male/female relationships were male. 100% of the ignorant, 100% of the incompetent ones, were male. 100% of the objects of rejection were male. The only flaw ever reported of women is that they "love too much". Kiss my cannon balls.

3M sells a Post-It line of male bashing stickers like, "The more I know about men the more I like my dog." A 3M spokesman added they have no intention of selling a similar anti-female product. Innuendo is one thing, outright verbal assault is another. They forgot about Psyche and the rams.

Hayward reports how droves of people have told him that divorce laws should be made harsher toward men because it is too easy for them to leave the family. When these people are informed that women initiate the overwhelming number of divorces, each one then concluded that men are so oppressive women are driven out of the marriage. Aren't we getting tired of always being wrong?

Carl Jung has said that usually men are more honest with themselves than women. Women don't face themselves. They blame other people and things. They refuse to shine the flashlight on their own soul. Someone else or something else is always at fault for their problems. Asa Baber concurs. He says feminists attack men much more than they examine themselves. They don't want to hear about the evil side of the Great Mother; they just want to talk about the evil side of God the Father.

In recent memory Imelda Marcos is the one who comes to mind when I think of someone who typifies the evil side of women. Yes, it's fun to laugh at her 6000 pairs of shoes, but this woman was a political animal, a mover and shaker. Her husband took the political flak, and died decades before she will, but each pair of her shoes represents a clip of rifle bullets fired by her "husband's" troops at their own countrymen to create the circumstances whereby she could afford her 6000 shoes. Women need to learn that their greed, their urge to possess, their "shopping", is connected to political oppression and bullets to the back of the head. "Shopping" is not something that just happens in malls. It is connected to the lives of men who live like burros mining copper in Peru to supply the electrical wiring for the two houses per family it now takes to shelter the American family, since more than half of these families seem incapable of getting it together under one roof anymore. It is connected to adolescent slavery in Thai sweatshops and miners dying in stinking holes in the ground extracting the minerals of South Africa. This is the meaning of "shopping". When too much emphasis is put on the purchase and possession of objects too many people suffer. Shopping is evil. But you won't hear women or corporations say that. They're in bed together.

Michael Meade says that man has lost his "dwelling place". We are set upon at work, we are set upon at home, we take refuge in the bottle and die all the faster. The feminized society we inhabit does not acknowledge the need for a dwelling place of the male soul. We are nomads, at home only in the sky-domed prairies inside our heads. We have no resting place in this life.

Women watch more TV in every time slot than men. Media is bent to serve them and their buying habits. In *Why Men Are The Way They Are*, Warren Farrell, drawing from thousands of print, radio and TV examples, makes a prodigious case for feminist meme invasions of our sexual stereotyping. Says he, biases against other races we call racism. Biases against women we call sexism. Biases against men we call humor.

Farrell has drawn complementary cartoons with the sex roles reversed to make his case. For example: a cartoon with a woman holding a leash attached to a man's throat is laughable. But a man holding a leash attached to a woman is barbaric. A cartoon where a future mother-in-law is asking a young man, "How do you plan to support my daughter emotionally?" is contraposed with a cartoon whereby a future father-in-law is asking the future wife, "How do you plan to support my son financially?" Or how about a woman seated at the kitchen table reading a book, *The Joy of Not Cooking*, while her husband serves her dinner, contraposed with a suited female executive who walks through the door and drops her briefcase while her husband sits at the table reading *The Joy of Not Working*? You can play this enlightening game yourself. Just flip open any magazine and read any cartoon where the sexes are represented and simply reverse the roles. Let Dagwood fold his arms across his chest while Blondie eats huge sandwiches and steps on the cat.

TV producers employ what they have dubbed the Jackass Formula: the man has an idea...his wife tells him it won't work...he tries it anyway...it doesn't work...she steps in and saves the day. The most amazing thing is that we still sit there and laugh at this stuff. And we buy the TVs that infect our families with this propaganda. Women are so smart, and women buy things. A marriage made in corporate hell.

For women – harkening back to Esther Vilar – image is everything. Try on these dating scenarios from Farrell:

Case 1: You are a single woman. Your friend wants you to meet a man who is tall, handsome, articulate, warm, tender; he listens carefully, understands you thoroughly, and expresses his feelings. He is a night watchman at the local junkyard. Will you go out with him?

Case 2: You are a single woman. Your friend wants you to meet a short friend of hers. He's black, he's had plastic surgery four times, often wears make-up and has a high squeaky voice. Some people suspect he's gay but your friend doesn't think so. He has some odd habits, keeps live panthers, has a glove fetish. Got accused of child molestation. Interested? Yes __ No __ His name is Michael Jackson.

There are courses taught by human relations consultants called "Marrying Up" and "Marrying Money". Men are welcome to attend but the instructor warns the lessons will not be applicable to them. Is there a course for the modern female business executive called "Marrying Down"? Heaven forbid.

The kind of man Ms. magazine expects you to marry makes over $140,000 a year and can afford to buy you the $20,000 engagement ring they advertise in their paean on self-reliance. And, you can still keep the ring when you've had enough of him and his dirty socks under the bed.

Farrell discovers Joan Collins selling a perfume to "light his fire" in *Vogue*? No, try *Working Woman*. Coty's Nuance perfume ads announce, "Nuance always says Yes. But you can always say No." This is criminality. It's called entrapment.

Robert Doyle reports that a typical 12-year-old boy masturbates up to four times a day. Sexual fantasies fly through his brain 20 times an hour. Men are the ones who get thrown in jail for rape after being driven insane by advertising. Meanwhile, 12-year-old girls are trained to say "No" with their mouths and "Yes" with their clothes. We sit by and allow our mass media to keep us aroused to a constant state of sexual frustration. Sex is great. But to be sexually stimulated and not get laid is just what keeps rutting bulls rutting. They only have to go through this one month a year and still some barely survive the scars and the battering of antlered duels. The media is not going to regulate itself and, apropos to feminist memes, which maintain that verbal or mental abuse remain outside the long arm of the law, we are stuck with a situation in which "acceptable" men are the ones who quash their sex urges in the face of overwhelming sexual stimulation. We bombard men with sexual stimulation and when they act on it we throw them in jail. This is known as emasculation. Mass emasculation. Would you starve your dog for three weeks, show it a bowl of food, and when it went after the food lock it in the basement? How can we let women and manholes manipulate us like this? We are set up to be starving dogs controlled by the sexual food fed us by our masters – women and corporations.

A UCLA study found that 54% of boys and 42% of girls felt it was OK to force a girl to have sex under certain circumstances. These are college students begging for an adult world to set some kind of parameters on human behavior, to provide some sort of value system that we can all agree upon. *Cosmo* magazine ran an article called, "Social Rape: When seduction turns to horror." How can *seduction* turn into rape? Are we having some language problem here? Or just a memetic problem? Seduction is the entrée to getting laid. I'm not a fan of censorship, but this miasma of mental abuse is beginning to make funding government-run brothels sound as sensible as eating a good breakfast.

Says Farrell:

Billions of dollars worth of advertising has been flashed into the prepubescent boy's unconscious before the "age of consent". At fourteen, the girls, who develop quicker, look like goddesses, and he's still a pimple-faced goofball shrimp writhing with insecurity. He has been trained to desire her – the Genetic Celebrity. The only way he can attract her is by becoming a football star or by making some money getting an after school job in a super market. He feels desperate. She has done nothing except sprout tits and buy some clothes to accentuate her plump mounds. The girl he has been trained to desire has *beauty power* before he has *performance* power. These girls – these Genetic Celebrities – demand perform-ance. So, she goes out with guys from older grades and he cries inside. (Shame.)

Farrell relates a revealing anecdote from his own youth of how girls use boys to polish their own prestige. When he was captain of a baseball team at summer camp he assigned himself the role of pitcher. His summer sweetheart cheered him from the bleachers. Midway through the game he traded places with the second baseman in a typically male expression of giving another guy a chance to pitch. After the game his girlfriend pouted. "The other girls thought it was great when you were pitching," she said. But what she *meant* was, I had more status with the other girls when you were pitching. Farrell says he remembers how, at the age of 11, he was torn between sustaining that camaraderie essential to preserving good morale on the team, and maintaining that look of admiration in her eyes. In our society, more often than not, all of us are forced to make this choice between our friends and our woman. In a healthy society women do not have to stroke their self-esteem by us, or through us, or even in spite of us. These realms are meant to remain separate and complementary. Why must the boy trash his team's pennant hopes in order to please his woman? Why must the man hobble his business and cripple his creativity in order to please his woman? Where is this goddamn goddess in their lives?

Says Farrell, once a guy loses his place on the football team you never see a cheerleader run off the field saying, "Wait, I'm still cheering for you. I love your openness and vulnerability." Should he lose his position his loved one will cheer his replaceable part. When affection fades he might very well turn to gambling or stealing or dealing to "make it big" and get her affection back. Though men are the ones most often arrested, the greed at the root of most crime belongs to women.

What is date rape? To the sincere boy, "no" means "no." He won't push himself on a girl who resists. But, reports Farrell, what do girls say? "Right after I said a clear 'no' I felt released from guilt and if a boy persisted he'd get somewhere with me." Do you hear what is being said here? She wants to make him responsible for her submission. She wants him to take on the full burden. She wants him to rape her, to push her, to take her with passion, forcefully, so she can always deny that she agreed to it. The CIA calls this "plausible deniability". That is: no means yes. The clearer the no, the clearer the yes. For most men this is confusing. Ask Mike Tyson. He's in jail over it.

I appeared on a Montel Williams TV show with a young man who had been accused of date rape. Also on stage was his teary-eyed accuser. The young woman had invited him into her house, got him drunk, took him to bed – and when he didn't call her the next day she concluded she had been raped. Rape is a serious crime that deserves severe penalties. But this is NOT rape. There's no way in hell this young man should be staring at five years in jail for going to this woman's room. The instant she invited him over the threshold into her bedroom, no matter what happened next, the specter of possible rape allegations should have vanished, legally vanished. Let's keep the government out of our bedrooms.

Women's publications have taken to objectifying men as dogs, worms, turkeys. This is the first stage of committing violence against them. But more than that, categorizing all men as losers provides women a 100% foolproof escape from looking inward at their own mental furniture. Whole sections of some bookstores are devoted to cards that put down men. Would this be tolerated against women?

12% of husbands are violent against wives and 12% of wives are violent against husbands – a ratio of 1 to 1. Suzanne Steinmetz reports that in virtually all categories: hitting, kicking, stabbing, women equaled men in the severity of violence inflicted.[161] Abused women's shelters abound. There are no shelters for abused men. Except jail.

Farrell points out that moviegoers hardly react to a man murdered on the silver screen, but when a woman is murdered their lust for retribution is almost boundless. The recent popularity of some horror genres has been their breaking of the taboo of violence against women. And finally, we're seeing a lot more female villains.

In 1980 in Florida, Betty King had beaten, slashed, stabbed, thrown acid on, and shot her husband. Eddie King had not sought prosecution when she slashed his face with a carpet knife nor when she left him in a parking lot with a blade in his back. Neither of these incidents ever made the police blotter. She was arrested only twice – when she stabbed him so severely in the back in a bar that the incidents had to be reported.

All these stabbings, shootings, and acid throwings happened during a four-year marriage. During a subsequent shouting match on a friend's porch Betty King once again reached into her purse and Eddie shot her. When an investigation led to a verdict of self-defense there was an outraged outcry from feminists and the media. Why? Woman-as-criminal has never registered with us, just as man-as-complainer never was in style. I once offered a free copy of my book through a Canadian Men's Magazine to anyone who could give me the dignified word to use for "a man who points out problems". No one won. There is no word. The closest one is "whiner". How can we conceptualize problems and offer solutions when the only word to describe what we're doing is "whiner"? Our language is deficient.

In post-Renaissance France a man who was caught being abused by his wife was ordered to wear women's clothes and paraded through the center of town riding backwards on a jackass.

Within minutes of birth 90% of boys are put to the knife or tied to a plastic bell to be circumcised. This fulfills some religious requirements, makes mommy's job easier keeping his pee pee clean, and completely negates any value of circumcision in male initiation. It's just another example of an important male rite of passage being absorbed by female/corporate collusion and fundamentally distorted so that the letter, and not the *spirit* of the law is fulfilled.

Says Farrell:
Women are the only "minority" group to be born into the upper class as frequently as men. The only minority group whose "unpaid labor" allows them to buy fifty billion dollars worth of cosmetics every year; whose members have more free time to read more romance novels and watch more television than men; whose members earn one-third what white men earn and yet out-spend them for all personal and health items combined. Women are the only minority group that is a majority.[162]

Item: Sun Up San Diego. Christmas 1984. The host Jerry G. Bishop, asks each woman in the audience "in the spirit of Christmas" to list the things she loves about men – or even just what is good about men. Not one woman comes up with one single thing.

Literally billions of trees have spent their life after death thinly sliced into a *Redbook, McCall's, New Woman, Ms., Vogue, Cosmopolitan,* or *Working Woman.* Each tells a woman that she is the fairest – that he is the problem; he with the fragile ego, the male pride, the threatened masculinity, the impotence, the fear of commitment. Blaming him gives her a temporary fix, but it keeps her continually anxious about attracting men. From the magazines' perspective it is necessary for her to retain her anxiety – diet products, make-up and deodorants would sell less without it. James Joyce, as we recall, said that any art form which creates desire is pornographic. Women's magazines are pure pornography.

Nathaniel Brandon, author of *The Psychology of Romantic Love*, has said, "a woman in love will do almost anything for a man except give up the desire to improve him." The idea that men must be changed or manipulated is bound up with the notion that a woman's well-being depends somehow on men, and if she can just get them to do it better, do it right, her happiness is assured. I do not know a single man who goes into a relationship with the idea of changing the woman; I do not know a single woman who goes into a relationship without the idea of changing the man. She still wants to be saved. She will train him to save her.

Sally wanted to change Ted. He changed. She upped the ante. He changed again. Unwilling or unable to apply spiritual tools to her frustration she left him and took their kids. Ted may never trust women again. Sound familiar?

Women say they want us to tell them our feelings. When we do, they tell us we're having the wrong feelings. We shouldn't feel that way. This is *shaming* us. They want us to have the feelings they feel we should have. By not telling them our feelings we are removing the key to our brainpans from their fists. Very rarely do women express their true feelings or even know what they are. If they did they would not be like Sally above, telling us to change to suit them and when we do, still not being happy. The purpose of life is not to be happy; it is to diminish our egos.

God bless all willful women. May they find health and prosperity and happiness.

Asks Farrell, why do we regard women as more giving than men? Because what they do is more visible. This goes back to what Bly said about the effects of the Industrial Revolution. When the man comes home he plops into a chair and hopefully his wife brings him a plate of food she has been cooking for half an hour. She is serving him. But all day long he has been down in a hole in the ground contracting black lung disease, or inhaling toxic welding fumes, or getting poison-treated sawdust down his pants, serving her, making the money she needs to run her life her way. He is *serving her* all day long in ways that are invidious to his own health – she breathes in spaghetti sauce and he breathes in coal dust, but no one sees what dad does.

Gregory Stone noted children at play in the following anecdote: A boy and girl were playing house. The girl kept sweeping, moving furniture, cooking, moving babies around. The boy would keep leaving on his bike, then return to the play area, go to sleep, then leave again. The girl had extensive knowledge of the mother's role. To the boy, the father was someone who disappeared and reappeared and slept *ad infinitum*. That's the main reason men grow up to be so nuts – they have no idea what they're supposed to be doing.

Says Doyle, this is not to imply that all the blame for our distress lies on the shoulders of women, judges, lawyers, and institutions. Men have shirked their responsibilities and abdicated their pants. Fuzzy-headed house males purporting to represent "men's liberation" denounce their masculinity at consciousness-raising groups and caution each other about what words to use around women.

Men's liberation means establishing men's right to be men, not liberating them *from* being men. New books by feminists and manhole Harvard psychologist William Pollock have finally recognized there's a problem with men. Their answer? Make men more like women. Beware: feminism has shifted gears. It's funding is drying up. Feminists are on the lookout for ways to get money administering programs for boys and men. Wrecking the family and enslaving women to the corporate workplace wasn't enough. Now they're after men.

In Great Britain the feminists have shoved aside dedicated, unpaid volunteers like George McAulay and Robert Whiston – who have been advocating men's issues for a decade – so they can grab government funding for men's and boy's programs. Under British Marxist/Feminism six times more young men than young women are unemployed. Great work girls. But we're not fooled. It's just another Stalinist power-grab. A corporate-style lunge for "market share". You got paid to create a problem and now you want to get paid to clean it up. We don't trust you. The cycle has got to be broken. Men raise men – not women and manholes.

Male dignity and men's rights must be restored, preserved and protected against the excesses of society, legalists, educators and bureaucrats. Just and competent administration of law must be implemented. And let's get a leg up on the homicidal mental health care we are being served up with our spaghetti. Psychology programs are replete with courses regarding women's concerns and devoid of male issues except for brain-bashing treatises on violence. From the beginning psychologists and psychiatrists focused a disproportionate amount of their attention on women. Most of the patients studied were female. Says Kipnis, the most popular test of gender specificity in psychology today still characterizes femininity as nurturing: helpful, expressive and empathetic – and masculinity as controlling: dominant, confident, and assertive. Colleges call themselves Alma *Mater*, Great Mother, Soul Mother. And, says Bly, the negative matter in *mater*ialism puts whole nations to sleep.

Our culture does not take seriously the damage caused by psychic incest between mother and son. Marie Sandoz in *These Were the Sioux* mentions that the Sioux boy, after the age of seven, never looked his mother in the eye. All requests were passed through his sister. "Would you ask mom to wash this shirt?" "Dumbo wants his shirt washed." And when the task was finished, the mother did not hand the shirt to the son saying, "Here is your shirt," but again the energy went through an intermediary. Says Bly, much sexual energy can be exchanged when the mother looks the son directly in the eyes and says, "Here is your T-shirt, all washed." See – you need your mom. This is the way mothers sexually abuse their children without even touching them.

The precautions the Sioux took to segregate mothers and sons seem absurd to us, and yet Sioux men, once grown, were famous for their lack of fear with women, their uninhibited conversations in their teepees, their ease of sexual talk with their wives, their freedom of action and their lack of shame. Sioux women were more aware of the possibilities of psychic incest between mother and sons than we are, and they themselves took precautions against it. Mothers today are oblivious to the extent to which they manipulate their sons, and to the damage they are causing by it. They actually believe that the more men there are with female values, the better off the world will be. They don't understand that that's what's wrong with the world right now!

Says Bly, American mothers sometimes confide details of their private lives to their small sons, details that might better go to adults their own age: money worries, abortion rights issues, shortcomings of the father. Frank disclosure is often no better than silence and it becomes positively harmful if the son feels he has to do something about it. The boy in many a kitchen gets drawn to his mother's side and says, in some form, those terrible words: "Mama, when I'm grown up I'm gonna have a big house for you and you'll never have to work again." When the mother hears this she should immediately march the boy off to a male psychologist who runs a sweat lodge on the weekends and then sign the kid up for football. But what does she do? She hugs him and washes his T-shirt. Ladies and gentlemen, this is child abuse. This is the unfair manipulation of a young mind by an aged mind. This is imbuing a young mind with Marxist/Feminist values. He's telling mom what she wants to hear: that he will take care of her *mater*ialistic worries. And she is telling him what he wants to hear: that if he does she will take care of his emotional worries. This is where the disease begins. This is why so many marriages fail – psychic incest between mother and son. We are permitting women, who have no self-governing principles of their own, to colonize the minds of our boys. Father Nature doesn't like it. He will have His say.

The sons are paying for the sins of the mothers, right now – willfulness, egocentricity, emotional self-consumption – and they are ending up in jails and Detox in record numbers. When are we going to recognize that it is the women who are *causing* this? They squirt out a little baby who has a pee pee between his legs and are immediately lit with the desire to make this infant male into her image of a perfect man. They can't leave men alone, and here is one they can mold from the cradle. She will make him learn to be kind to all women, kinder than his father ever was. In this way he will be the best "lover". But who will he love? Who will he impregnate? Will he be so kind that he thinks "no" means "no"? Who will he marry? Some sassy young tease in a miniskirt? Not according to mom, but while mom has spent so much energy making him into her little knight she has forgotten to notice that there are no more damsels in distress left out there; no one has done anything at all to tame the cravings of women. They march around in blue jeans with steel-reinforced bras waving their car keys in one hand and their diaphragms in the other and junior's got a big problem – he thinks "no" means "no". Who's gonna straighten him out?

Says Bly, hundreds of times one man or another has said to me that now, at forty or forty-five, he realizes that his life-task has been to be a substitute husband, lover and soul companion for his mother. How does he feel about men? He is likely to say, "I've never been able to trust them." He will not steal the key and leave with the Wildman. He will not write his novel or go to the moon.

The boy who is called on by his mother too early feels helpless – shamed – when he realizes that he is too small to do what is asked of him. His emotional energy is too fragmented to support his mother's needs or to replace his father. He feels like a failure – not able to help his mother, not able to supplant his father – a double failure. He is shamed right out of the gate. Good luck, kid.

Bly is quick to point out that the blame for this emotional dynamite does not rest solely on the mothers. They are responding to deep psychological imperatives, they are women, they have no sense of the Deep Masculine just as we have no sense of the Deep Feminine. What is missing in this scenario are the male initiators who tear the boy away from his mother's psychic incest and submerge him in the imperatives of being a man. But my point remains that in our feminized legal climate the male initiators would be thrown in jail if they attempted to perform this ritual service without the permission of the mothers. Men need mothers' permission to turn boys into men, and that permission is not forthcoming in our society.

When the elders don't call the boys away the Twisted Side of the Great Mother will start its imprisonment, even though the actual mother doesn't, for a second, want these negative holdings to take place. The mother doesn't see these things happening. But the boy does.

Out of shame over his inadequacy, and in some fear of being pulled over onto the mother's side before he has stabilized himself as a man, the boy finds in himself an inexplicable anger, a RAGE, that prevents the mother's dream of a dedicated man from becoming real. Thank God for teenage rebellion. This is the boy's struggle to become a man. In a world of uninitiated boys it is not something that can be edited out of the program by kindness and niceness as the proponents of Institutional Menopause would like us to believe. The boy, biologically, memetically, is craving the entrance of the Deep Male into his life. He'll talk ugly to his mom in the kitchen and blow her off with heavy metal or rap lyrics; he wants out of the anger, out of the rage, out of the Twisted Side of the Great Mother.

The Twisted Side of the Great Mother is outside the brain scan of far and away most women. We have God the Father versus Satan, another man, and the Great Mother versus whom? No one. Says Bly, an audience of alert women, when asked to describe the Great Mother come up with adjectives like: nourishing, earthy, gentle, supporting. Not one of them mentions "unconscious" or "twisted". They acknowledge no feminine evil. Consequently, they impute all negative qualities to the Patriarch! Wake up, women. The children you harm may be your own. You are asleep to your own dark side.

The Twisted Side of the Great Mother has a putrefying effect on the male soul. All the things that I knew in my youth to be superficial and a waste of time became the norm and benchmark of our family aspirations during 15 years of marriage. There was no time for art and creativity because the kids needed tennis lessons at the rich people's club so all the doctors' wives could say, "Gee Audrey, your son sure is a good tennis player." It wasn't my son playing tennis; it was my wife's ego playing tennis through his young male body. This is evil. Her ego incorporated every waking moment of my children's lives, from doing their homework for them so they'd get good grades, to ferrying them to soccer and gymnastics. I was simply there to provide the economic fuel for her egotistical assault on life. The tricks and deceits she used to undermine my credibility in their eyes were endless and awful and evil. It's time to draw a line in the sand. We can't permit them to do this to our children.

God bless Audrey, my mother, and all willful women. May they find health and prosperity and happiness.

So the adolescent male, beleaguered by psychic incest, deeply shamed by his incapacity to "be a man" who can solve his mom's problems, comes across the one idea wherein he thinks he can find salvation. Here is the way to prove his manhood. Here is the way to be somebody. It's simple. All he needs to do is get laid.

One-third of all high school football players sustain serious injuries. Why? Because they want to get laid. From there it's a short step to alcohol and drugs to kill the pain. Aaron Kipnis says that the problem with our culture is that every man is *playing hurt* to some degree.[163] We regard it as normal for men to be in pain. Indeed, war may finally end when society begins to hold the security and lives of men to be as sacred as those of women.

If men survive adolescent acts of bravado, sports abuse, ritual sacrifice in war, adolescent suicide, or overdose, they enter the work force and start Dying for Dollars by becoming injured, disabled, and killed at a much greater rate than women. Men die of work-related injuries at a rate of 20-1 over that of women. If 20 women were dying on the job for every man we would have a Federal Task Force investigating the outrage.

The reverse discrimination that men are facing due to Affirmative Action quotas is forcing them to seek even more dangerous work as women take the cushy jobs. Kipnis says that while he was writing his book a roofer fell off the second-story roof of their clinic. Every one of the workers up on the roof was male while virtually every one of the therapists and social workers in the air-conditioned offices below was female. And have a nice day.

Now, couple this occupational homicide with the "hero" myth which assumes that men don't need the same level of community support as women in terms of health care, health maintenance, preventative care education, psychological counseling, parenting education, social-welfare assistance, and advocacy against discrimination – and what we have arrived at is a situation in which most men live lives of inferior quality to most women. It's a fact Jack. Men, as distinct from women *and* children, account for 40% of the nation's poor with single men representing the fastest growing group of impoverished citizens during the past decade. (Unmask those tricky feminist statisticians who say that women *and* children comprise the largest segment of the nation's poor. That's true, but it's *two* groups!) The health of single men is generally poorer than that of women and they have vastly fewer programs to support or protect them in their clearly more hazardous work environments. More women are covered by private insurance than men and government insurance programs such as Medicaid cover twice as many women as men. 50% of the federal funding for AIDS care is spent on women and children who represent 10% of the victims. 80% of the nation's homeless are men.

Kipnis reports that a recent lawsuit in Contra Costa County, California, attempted to change a prohibition against single homeless men from receiving free emergency shelter at motels, a resource available to all other classes of the economically disadvantaged. 30% of the men, ineligible because they were men, were also Vietnam vets!

In another instance of institutionalized discrimination one man reported that, "The county social worker actually laughed at me when I asked her to try and get some money out of my working ex-wife, who has not contributed anything to the support of our sons since she left seven years ago."

Says Kipnis, at our local county mental health care facility there is a group for women with low self-esteem, a general women's group, a group for women who were recently divorced, a group for women who were survivors of childhood incest, a group for low-functioning women, and one for low-functioning men which has three members and is the only men's group; and this is in northern California which might be expected to be a little more progressive in addressing social neglect.

With a 60% divorce rate women have convinced a great number of men that the most important issue between the sexes is abortion. You better believe that if women were the ones dying on the job or really suffering from the aftermath of divorce that would be at the top of their agenda. Instead it's abortion.

Let there be no mistake about it, abortion is a raw power issue. As William Sloan Coffin has said, not even God plays God. Abortion has little to do with unborn fetuses and everything to do with giving women power over life and death. Power comes out of responsibility. When women are ready to assume full responsibility for their children, maybe then they can be granted full power over abortion.

Meanwhile, in the country of laws not men, a 1988 Supreme Court decision gave a man no right to block his wife's abortion. That means, if she wants to have a kid she can divorce me before it's even born and have me paying for 18 years. But if she doesn't want our kid then there's nothing I can do about it. I can't even adopt my own child if she decides to put it up for adoption. Where is the balance? If somebody can find the balance in any of this please let me know. We have created a system that services the cravings of women and allows them to play God with human life. Rape, incest, yes, of course. Birth control, power-tripping, playing God? You've got to be kidding.

Twenty years ago my future-former wife had an abortion. She made up some fantasy about how the child would be born crippled, started believing it herself, and edited me out of the decision entirely. She forgot about it the next day and I haven't forgotten about it yet. I spent that day staring at the sky wondering what life was all about and that feeling has never left me. Now the ex drives around with Pro Choice stickers on her bumper and argues with anybody as if this was the most important question facing human civilization. Maybe for the self-consumed feminist it is, but something is way out of whack here. Something is being disturbed deep down in my masculine spiritual home. Neo-feminists are agitating for the right to play God, and meanwhile, a recent survey has confirmed my belief that more men suffer long-term guilt and regret over abortion than women. Once you acknowledge the depth and vastness of male spirituality the last pieces of the puzzle drop into place and you wonder how the survey could possibly have come out any differently. Men don't play checkers with the Life Force. We let the Life Force play checkers with us. We are not pathological, homicidal control freaks. There is nothing that happens that we can't endure and learn from as long as we recognize the Life Force at work in it. We are here to dance this dance, whatever the rhythm, whatever the beat. We are not up on the stage telling the bandmaster what tunes to play. He plays, we dance, that's it.

God bless all willful women. May they find health and prosperity and happiness.

Women's health clubs are proud to announce, "We have no Men's Room." All-girl colleges chant, "Better dead than co-ed."

Almost all childcare workers who fill the gap for parents are women. In the field of education 75% of BAs and MAs and well over half of the PhDs are granted to women. Universities may have more male (manhole) professors but they often lack even a single course in men's studies. This is criminal neglect, and it is producing a steady stream of college-educated criminals. Ever see the film *Animal House*? What was that about if not male initiation performed in the absence of trusted elders? Is learning computer language really more important than learning the language of the male soul? What is college for anyway? Corporate job-prep?

Meanwhile, says Kipnis, the lack of health care information for men is indicative of the ways men's lives are held to be of lesser worth than women's. Publicly funded clinics spend your tax money giving women free breast and cervical cancer checkups. No one is offering you a free prostate checkup. Many health plans have provisions for gynecological and breast checkups, but no parallel provisions for testicular and prostate checkups. Gynecologists are considered primary care specialists.

Gynecologists do not treat men, nor is there any other specialist assigned to male-specific medical problems. There is no pee-pee-ologist. Urologists, the prognosticators of the male plumbing, are classed as surgical sub-specialists. You don't get easy, ready access to them unless you pay a lot of money up front or pay a lot of money into a super-insurance plan. Female-specific health care is free, male-specific health care costs big bucks. Is it any wonder they outlive us?

Women are educated how to conduct self-examination for breast cancer. Breasts are beautiful and rate a certain amount of care. Men are supposed to perform a self-exam for testicular cancer once a month but that is probably the best kept secret in the medical industry. I never heard about it until I was 44, past the age of most occurrences.

1 in 11 men can expect to contract prostate cancer, the most common cancer after lung cancer, which approximates the incidence of breast cancer in women. 30,000 men will die of it this year in the US and 100,000 new cases will be diagnosed. This type of cancer responds well to treatment when it is diagnosed early but most doctors would rather feel up some beautiful tits than stick a finger up some guy's asshole. And so, we'll die.

Early signs of prostate trouble are restricted flow of urine, change in frequency of urination, or pain in the prostate region or perineum (behind your nuts). Most men don't know enough to report these symptoms and end up only going to the doctor when their bladders are completely plugged and they're writhing in pain. Or they wait until they have sexual dysfunction and the disease is advanced. Every man over forty should get a prostate exam every three years and over fifty once a year. Rectal cancer is also very prevalent among men and suffers from the same lack of detection. We have a lot of anxiety about bending over and letting someone look up our ass. It isn't cool, says Kipnis. But then again, neither is slow painful disintegration and death.

What about sex? Women's magazines are full of advice for how to stimulate G spots or achieve multiple orgasms. How many men know that if they come too fast they should slow down or even just freeze in mid-stream? Women take too long to come but sometimes it's manly to serve them. And sometimes it's not. Let them use the hosed shower head.

Here's another great monstrosity on the subject of sex. One man's wife left him for another *woman*. She took the kids, the house and all his money, moved her girlfriend in, and castigated the ex-hubby for not being able to fulfill her needs. If homosexuality is biologically brain-based how can she get away with this? *He* can't live with his kids because she's a lesbian?

Warren Farrell calls the feminist movement Divorce Training. He should know. He served on the Board of the National Organization of Women.

48% of American men are now employed by the government, or the top ten corporations, who are in bed with the government. This is called Socialism. Corporate Socialism. This is not Capitalism. It is also called Marxist/Feminism. The reason why NOW lobbyists in Washington can lean on congressmen to pass legislation that favors women is that these manholes are brain-locked inside an incestuous web of female-control memes that are 8000 years old. We've forgotten what freedom means.

I'm a leftist anarchist. I despise big government *and* big corporations – which are the same thing in my head. I worked for the Green Party and the Ralph Nader presidency. I believe in these populist issues. All except for one. The problem started when I read the Green Party Manifesto. The manifesto was great. Opposing corporate domination of our lives, advocating campaign finance reform so corporations can't buy our politicians. Then I got to the place where they said they were "inspired by feminism". What cowshit. The National Organization of Women *opposes* campaign finance reform because they already have lots of politicians in their pockets. They don't want a change for fairness. They don't care if corporations dominate our elections. They don't care what outrages U.S. multinational corporations commit in Indonesia or Iran – so long as half the board members are female. Leftists wake up! Feminism is not progressive. Feminists are corporate whores. Feminists are big government whores. Feminism is not a grass roots organization of poor oppressed women – it's a multi-billion dollar a year "not-for-profit" corporate industry that's bleeding us to death.

In his essay, "The Arrogance of Humanism" (also read: Feminism) David Ehrenfeld has described the arrogance of the person-centered value system. Humanists are fond of attacking religion for its untestable assumptions, says he, but humanism (feminism) contains untestable assumptions of its own. These are the givens, the things that are unconsciously assumed and rarely or never debated. If they occurred in others, humanists (feminists) would call them superstitions. For example:

All problems are solvable by people
(the Fix-It-Philosophy)

Many problems are solvable by technology
(a dishwasher in every kitchen)

The rest are solvable by psychology
(shrinks know more than 5000 years of religion)

We make things better by figuring them out
(talk is more profound than silence)

Humanism is yet another guise for Marxist/Feminism. The assumption of both is that people who get enough to eat and enough power over their lives will be happy. That's like believing the earth is flat. Every spiritual insight of the past 50,000 years has warned us of the exact opposite. *Mater*ialism is destroying our planet, carving up our forests, and impoverishing our lives. The person-centered approach to life does not work. We are men. Our memes bid us to look Beyond.

Historian Will Durant said that it takes a great deal of spontaneous, creative male energy to kick off every new civilization; but as the decades wear on, the female values of order, method, and control (rules, regulations, bureaucracy) gradually permeate to the core of that once vibrant society and stultify it – deaden it – until life becomes so routine and oppressive it's time for another revolution. Guess what? It's time for another revolution. Our society has been organized to death by women and corporations.

Says Kipnis, much of the move toward so-called femininity is a product of shame (father-hunger). Uninitiated, confused men, who feel worthless and don't understand why, look to women for strength and guidance. Many women today complain that men aren't manly anymore – not robust, self-reliant (God reliant), rugged or courageous. Women cowed us and seduced us into accepting their agenda and now they despise us for it – just like Sally and Ted. They surrender to no God, thus they are yoked to no eternal values, thus they sputter and crackle in the hot oil of shame – and like Groucho Marx, they wouldn't join any club that would accept them as a member.

And they sure won't to stick it out with any man who loves them…He must be stupid, she thinks. How could he love me? I don't even "love myself?" There must be something wrong with him. I better get away…Good thinking. Women's approach to what they call "relationship" is to shame us into changing for them, and then despise us when we do.

And here's a thought: I cannot love myself. You cannot love yourself. She cannot lover herself. Love is a purely selfless act. How can I be "selfless with my self"? It's oxymoronic. It doesn't make any sense. People obsessed with "learning to love myself" are really people fried by shame who are trying desperately to be rid of it. The problem is: shame is pride in reverse. There's just as much ego in shame as there is in pride. So if you try to banish low self-esteem by cranking up high self-esteem you'll just end up yo-yo-ing. What goes up must come down. Ego up, ego down. The way to get rid of shame is not to build up self-love, but to destroy self-love, demolish your ego, dissolve it in God. This is simple spiritual stuff that women just can't seem to get. They're terrified of thoughts like this. They'd rather just put us down.

Robert Bly has called shame a "hot potato". A shamed person (who doesn't pray, doesn't surrender to God) can only get rid of her shame by passing it on to someone else – tossing it to someone else like a hot potato fresh out of the campfire. The only way she knows how to build herself up is to put someone else down.

This shaming has become institutional. Kipnis relates that one time, after he gave a talk to some psychology undergraduates, a young man came up to him and gushed, "I just want to thank you personally. This is the first time in over three years of college that I have heard anyone in any classroom say anything positive about men. I'm really tired of being made *ashamed* to be male." This poignant story comes from the hallowed halls of academia – a *college of psychology* no less.

Robert Bly has said therapists will have understood what they are doing when they insist on doing it with a cow in the room. Pretty good. But where do we start? How do we unbend the minds of the mind benders? How do we address Institutional Menopause?

I just had a strong morning. I caught a couple of tuna from a small boat off the Pacific Coast of Mexico. My sperm count is up. My Deep Masculine is hooked into my brain with a mental hand-line. And now it's time for me to "take on" one of the feminists just to show how it's done.

I've selected for my victim someone whose work I greatly admire. She's a brilliant extrapolator, a perceptive analyst, and a clear rational thinker. Had she not cluttered her work with debilitating misandry – man-hating – I would have no cause to harpoon her. Her name is Anne Wilson Schaef and the book I will sink my hooks into is titled *When Society Becomes an Addict.*

Schaef's brilliant extrapolation posits that all of American society has taken on the characteristics of an individual alcoholic/addict. Building off the co-dependency work of Sharon Wegscheider-Cruse which suggests that 96% of American people might be co-dependent, Schaef asserts that the American system has absorbed the character defects, the "stinking thinking", visible in an individual alcoholic/addict. These defects include systemic dishonesty, self-centeredness, dependency and the need to control.[164] So far so good. I think she is absolutely, gloriously right.

Then she identifies the Addictive System as the White Male System. Why? Dishonesty, self-centeredness, dependency and the need to control are clearly female traits, female memes. They have nothing whatsoever to do with a man who is acting out of the Deep Masculine. The preceding couple hundred pages of this book have made an arguably strong case for this. And as I said earlier, what she calls the White Male System is what I call Marxist/Feminism, the Manhole System, men acting like women. So what's the problem? Why the confusion? Who is refusing to own up to what?

We need to look again at what is meant by the Manhole System. A manhole is a human being with a pee pee between his legs who is acting out of his *anima*, his wounded side, his poor quality of femininity. The fact is that virtually all of our judges, our priests, our educators, and our politicians are manholes. Yes, Ms. Schaef, they are white males, but they are not men; they are manholes. They have gotten to where they have gotten by serving *Mater*, the female memes. They are the King's lackeys. Corporate water boys. They know nothing whatsoever of the Deep Male. They have devoted so much effort to the politicking and ass-kissing it takes to succeed in this feminized system that they have not had the opportunity to grow as human beings. They know how to get good grades, to get out the vote. But they don't know how to look deep into their souls. Thus, the people who are the least competent to function as human beings are the ones who succeed in the Marxist/Feminist/Manhole System. It's a shame that our country works like that, and it harms all of us. We are a nation without true leadership. Our society is being run by men who are acting like women.

There is surely a Deep Feminine, a strong quality of femaleness, which does not countenance dishonesty, self-centeredness, dependency and control, but that is not what these men are acting out of because they cannot. They are men. Wounded men. Uninitiated men. Men elected to serve female memes. Their only option is to act out of their wounded female side if they wish to remain in office. So let's begin a tour of *When Society Becomes an Addict* that we may come to some understanding of Institutional Menopause.

* * *

Ms. Schaef lends some support to my proposition that we are born with humongous egos and spend our entire lives trying to get rid of them. To the baby everything is "I" or "My" and goes directly into its mouth. It cannot distinguish itself from the world.

Says Schaef:
Another aspect of self-centeredness has to do with what clinical professionals call ego boundaries. Self-centered people do not know where they begin and end and anyone else begins and ends. Self-centered people cannot respect others, because they are literally unaware of them as separate entities.
Because there are no clear-cut boundaries two things happen: the self spreads out, and the world rushes in. Everything becomes ME, and everything starts coming at ME, and is perceived as either for or against ME.[165]

This is the self-centeredness of an Addictive Society that asserts what is good for America is good for the world. This is the self-centeredness of the she-bear protecting her cubs against the merest hint of danger or disorder. This is the self-centeredness of a manhole judge who demands that you respect a legal system that is abusing you, and if you don't he'll throw you in jail. This is the Us vs. Them elitist duality which maintains that if you are not for us, you are against us. The judge swirls his skirts making his grand entrance into the courtroom with all the aplomb and conceit of a King, the original manhole, the original feminine enforcer. The court will control your life as the woman controls her home as the she-bear controls the forest in her vicinity. Meanwhile dad is asleep under a tree after pounding nails all morning.

Says Schaef:
In the Addictive [White Male] System everyone tries to control everyone else.[166]

* * *

Look around anyone's living room. Dad is reading the paper, silently trying to intuit money out of thin air. Mom is controlling steam, pots, fire, water, dead plants and animals in the kitchen – all the while bellowing directions through the hallways to move this, get that, pick it up, put it away. The atmosphere she exudes is the atmosphere of control. The urge to control is a female meme. As we stated earlier, a woman will give up almost anything for a man except the urge to change him, to control him. Abortion is a feminine control issue. Feminist lobbyists are control commandos. There is no masculist lobby and I hope one never emerges because it will be spearheaded by manholes.

Thus control, an attribute of the "White Male System", finds its home in femininity.

Says Schaef, in the Emerging Female System [the feminine "answer" to the White Male System] the goal is personal power, and not power over anything. Here we have a bit more psychobabble. Personal power connotes controlling the will. Surrender means surrendering your will – surrendering your personal power. What we of the Deep Masculine seek is the power of the Life Force moving through us. We pray to the Deer God, we surrender to the Deer God, we do not seek personal power through the Deer God – and we hope only to come into harmony with God's agenda. The thing that died on the cross was Jesus' ego. The thing that died in Buddha after staring at a wall for four years was Buddha's ego. These people were not seeking power. Jesus made no attempt to wiggle out of his crucifixion by justifying himself to the Roman judges. As Gurudev says, if you want to empower yourself, give up trying to control the events of your life. This is real live surrender and not some half-baked psychobabble designed to appeal to women who still want to cling to control and power memes. Seeking personal power is primitive psychic hocus-pocus – burning a sheep to buy God's favor – bargaining with God – if you give me this I'll do that. Grow out of it girls. Acknowledging powerlessness is about acknowledging powerlessness, over God, over life, over people, places and things – over yourself. Grace, that moment of harmony with creation, is a gift. We cannot buy it. The most we can do is make ourselves open to receive it. And we do that by surrendering our wills. Personal power, power over ourselves or other people, is a legacy of the Addictive Marxist/Feminist System.

Says Schaef:

The God of the Addictive [White Male] System is God the Controller. It follows then that if it is possible to be God as defined by that system, one must try to control everything, and we do![167]

Through some kind of classically feminine word-association cerebral-patterning Schaef has made a mental leap by concluding that somehow, when you have a system where God is the Controller, it is then possible for us to play God. Again, it seems to me there is some kind of female meme at work here, something that manhole priests have picked up and run with for millennia. Native Americans pray to the Great Mystery and don't adopt control memes. East Indians pray to Vishnu or Shiva and don't adopt control memes. But that problem aside, I wonder if Ms. Schaef actually believes for one second that the goal of feminism is self-surrender? The abortion issue once again leaps to the forefront of my mind – control over life and death itself. Also, I have never ever heard one single feminist mention service to God, or any power higher than herself, as being worthy and able to decide what is good and right for her. Marxist/Feminism is nothing less than an attempt by women to play god. Its agenda is all about control over physical reality – *Mater*. Dominion over the earth, dominion over men.

Another attribute of the Addictive, White Male System, is dishonesty – lying. Does Ms. Schaef actually believe that women are more truthful than men? What planet did she grow up on? Esther Vilar has already said that women train themselves from a young age to lie, especially to themselves. That's the only way they can hold all of their conflicting verbal constructs in place. Women have made a high art form of the rationalization. They can convince themselves that the planet is getting warmer when it is actually getting colder. Have you looked at the orange groves around Orlando, Florida, recently? They're not there. Freezes hitherto unknown in this century have killed them off. So we have a 60% divorce rate and we're worried about global warming? The answer to global warming is to walk to the store and buy less stuff.

Women, because they use both sides of their brains to process language, wallow in a miasma of word pictures and word association games. Their brains are more active when they're asleep than ours are when we're solving a calculus problem. The word pictures in their heads do not necessarily attach to anything in the physical world. They pat themselves on the back for saving 59 cents on a tube of toothpaste and then blow $10,000 by moving out on their husband and setting up housekeeping with their boyfriend. To them they're being efficient and frugal and "getting their needs met". The maddening thing is not that they lie to us, but that they lie to themselves. They convince themselves that having some cowshit career is going to make them happy and independent of men and then there's no stopping them. They'll wreck their family and the lives of their kids and trash their husbands all in the pursuit of this chimera, and the worse it gets the more they'll blame men for their problems. Women are consummate liars.

Men are judged by other men on how well they keep their word. We live and die by our word. Manholes, politicians, thieves and lawyers will break their vows, but not a real man. Too much is at stake.

I just went through an incident whereby I set up a certain price and time to go out fishing with a local boat owner only to have his girlfriend show up on the beach at 5:30 in the morning and tell me I had to pay more. I had made no deal with her. And little did this woman know that I had made up my mind to give her boyfriend the present of a fishing rod which would have paid for this trip 20 times over. Real men, in real men's society, are generous with each other. We reserve the mental space to give and receive gifts from each other. Life is not a business to us. Look who's sitting there counting the change in any third world market – women. Business is a feminine meme. Men are not consumed with counting today's pennies and guarding our own stuff; we are working out of a deeper place. Giving and receiving gifts is a deep part of the male ethos.

This man was Mexican, his girlfriend English. He and I looked each other in the eye. His manhood was at stake. Then he said, "Let's just stick with the original deal and see what happens." It might seem at first that he kept his manhood, but just by allowing his girlfriend to bulldoze the situation and create bad feelings to see what she could get away with, he lost the gift. I still send other gringos to go out with them, but I'm out of it; I won't go fishing with them again. At the end of the day I gave him the fish I caught. He was pleased, and I had a chance to be generous; but because he allowed his woman to interfere a door slammed shut that may not open again. Now I go out with some guys who won't take money from me when I try to shove it into their hands. They don't want my money. I give them most of the fish I catch and they give me a free trip and we're both happy. In India when you give a beggar an alm, the beggar does *not* say "thank you" – you, the giver, say "thank you". You are happy that fortune has favored you in this life so that you have something you can give away. This is the Deep Masculine; this is where men live.

My future-former wife once flew into a rage that I wasn't being paid enough. She cut me off sexually and made my life miserable until I took her advice and fired my salesman. Within two weeks my business was ruined. I was stuck with six months' inventory of unsold merchandise and no one would deal with me because I had broken my agreement with the salesman. And why? All because my spouse had to stick her *Mater* into my business. You cannot run a business the way you run a household; it doesn't work. I have seen this time and time again – female control memes wrecking a perfectly functioning male scenario – and the more women who enter the workforce the more we see it every day in business. Business barracudas. Have you met any female lawyers yet? Hold onto your jockstraps. They think the law is a poem written to put money in their bras. Dishonesty, chiseling, and conniving are female memes.

* * *

Says Schaef:

Being "nice" is an insidious form of dishonesty. Niceness is a form of control.[168]

How many men have you met who were accused of being "nice"? Some gurus are "nice". They also control the shit out of you with their vibes. Politicians smile a lot and act nice – as they sell us down the river to corporations. Sometimes Satan comes as a man of peace, according to Bob Dylan. Women go to work on niceness like men go to work with a hammer or a shovel. Niceness, according to Schaef, is another attribute of White Male Society. And peanut butter comes from cows. Does she really believe that? How about it? The checkout girls are always so "nice" as they take our money. Newscasters are so "nice" as they report on famines in Africa and mining disasters in South America. Female radio psychologists are so "nice" when they tell us we shouldn't be angry. Feigned objectivity is a form of institutionalized "niceness" – a control meme.

Being nice is playing their game on their field with their ball and their referees. Forget it. Niceness flew out the window when I took on the emotional burden of writing this book. I enjoy this assault on Anne Wilson Schaef about as much as I'd enjoy beating the family cat to blood-mush with a sledgehammer. But damn it. Somebody has to do it. We have to rip into this neo-feminist cowshit; it's destroying our children's lives. We have no culture left other than the culture of Institutional Menopause. The culture of acting "nice" and buying things. The only time women aren't nice is when you tell them men are *not* the oppressors of women, and never have been, and women have it too easy. Then they fly into a shit-fit.

Says Schaef:

When we consider our advertising, our businesses, the quality of the *materi*als used in our bridges, and even what our parents tell us about the way life is, we cannot ignore the fact that we live in a system where dishonesty is the norm. We [in the White Male System] have systematized dishonesty and assumed it is normal.[169]

How about "no" means "yes"? Is that a little dishonesty at work? How about, the abortion issue concerns incest and rape victims and has nothing to do with female self-seeking or birth control? How about "only her hairdresser knows for sure"? How about the school system discriminates against women – even though more women than men enter college? Or men are the oppressors of women – even though women live 8 years longer and 19 out of 20 people who die on the job are men? Or men are *mater*ialistic and women are "spiritual" – even though women own 65% of America's wealth and make 80% of all buying decisions? Innuendo and deceit are feminine bread and butter. Feminists fan their media wings creating tornadoes of self-deception and naive men stand on the sidelines clapping. It's pathetic. It's laughable. Advertising is to blame? Advertising simply appeals to the basest part of female nature.

Like Esther Vilar said, women convinced men to behave like women and now they're complaining about it. Women demand men's jobs because men's jobs have become women's jobs. Women are being consumed by their own consumption. They've become wage-slaves in their own corporate fantasia. Women are being manipulated by their own manipulations! They've been at it forever. They wear a mini skirt and hiss at guys who ogle their legs. They blow a week's wages on a fancy dress and sneer at someone who bought a fancier dress. Women are screwed up by themselves, not men!

What I want to know is, why can't women ever apologize? Why can't they seem to spit out the simple words, "I'm sorry I hurt you"? My mother has never admitted a mistake in her life. Whenever I pin her down on one of her brain-fevers gone awry, she reverses the flow of the action. If I say, "You know I got bones growing in my ear lobes from eating all that calcium you told me to take," she'll say, "Well you know calcium has been proven essential in the diets of cats, dogs, and pregnant women." "Mom, I'm not a cat, dog or pregnant woman." "I never said you were." And on and on it goes, moving around and around the issue and never arriving on a finger pointing at her.

My future-former wife could never apologize for her affairs. They were just something she "had to do". Well that's fine. But they wrecked my mind and destroyed our family for months at a time. Everyone in town except me knew she was fucking someone else. And at the bottom of it all, she could have said, "It was just something I had to do. *And I'm sorry I hurt you.*" Very simple stuff. Most religions claim you can be forgiven for anything, even killing someone, as long as you apologize and mean it. You don't fold your hands to Jesus or Allah and say, "Well, killing that guy, it was just something I had to do." Maybe it was something you had to do, maybe it was war, but if you want to be free of it, you have to apologize for it, you have to humble yourself, you have to annihilate your ego so the pain goes away. You don't pin your eyes into lasers and say it was just something you had to do. That's fending off shame, not seeking forgiveness.

I just had a female friend visiting me who was always cutting off my sentences and finishing them in some absurd way. Finally I asked her to stop doing it and she stopped. The next day she told me that the reason she was cutting me off was because she is clairvoyant and she knows what people are going to say before they say it. I told her, "Kymber, that is not an apology. In fact, it's a load of crap, because you have not once finished off any of my sentences in the way I intended to finish them. If you had, it would have moved the conversation along and I wouldn't have been upset at all. You don't listen. You sit there filing what I say into pigeonholes in your brain. You are not listening to what I have to say. You are anticipating me and trying to outmaneuver me so the conversation stays within what you are prepared to hear. You are not interested in learning anything, about me, or about my worldview." She left the next day.

This is what women mean by "talking" and "sharing". Men listen to other people. That's how we learn – that's one of our great strengths – keeping our egos and our preconceptions out of it and hearing something new. It's a wonderful experience. I recommend it to any woman. Just listen! Not listening to people is a deep dishonesty and a deep control game. Just listen. Don't try to "heal" me, or get me talking your talk. Once in awhile I want to talk my talk. Just listen. It will open up new circuits in your brain.

Says Schaef:

The Addictive System is highly dependent on left-brain functions. It is founded on the worship of linear, rational, logical thinking. This kind of thinking supports the illusion of control by simplifying the world to such an extent that it seems possible to have control over it.[170]

Excellent. Left-brain functions lead to the illusion of control. This disease is endemic in our society. In Chapter One we went into great detail about how females are biologically disposed to left brain, rational, analytical thinking. Through extensive studies of finger and toe-tapping exercises, it was shown that females favor their right hands and feet which are wired to their left brains. So...the Addictive/White Male/Manhole System is dependent on female thinking. That's what I've been saying for 300 pages.

Says Schaef:

White Male System Myth #4 holds that it is possible to be totally logical, rational and objective.[171]

Ms. Schaef has just shot herself in the foot. Left-brainedness and linear thinking are female characteristics. Rene Descartes is a manhole. Cartesian logic is a female meme that has been running roughshod over Euro-American culture for almost 400 years. To anyone unfamiliar with the Manhole concept – the ascendancy of men who act like women – Schaef's cheap gender shot at white males contributes to a mindswamp of confusion. This feminist is arguing for the abolition of a female meme that captured western civilization 400 years ago. It's as if she's having a gut level reaction to the wrongness of a situation in which men have been set upon to propagate female memes – and she's right in her reaction. Let's identify linear thinking's proper home in the Female, and free men of the compulsion to try to be logical, rational and objective so women can "understand" us and critique us. The human experience is being trivialized by chopping up reality into soundbites that can be "understood" by women.

I'd like to call attention to the logical, rational, seed-sorting-of-the-psyche way Schaef is dissecting society. She has made one wrong assumption – confused women with men – and run on with it for 150 pages. Can anyone who has read this far in this book actually believe for a second that a world run by women is going to be less logical, less rational, less dishonest, and less control-obsessed than our present society – a society already colonized by female memes? Women's intuition is a toxic myth. According to Vilar it constitutes little more than perennial predictions of doom. Women don't just let things happen. Everything in their genetics and memetics screams out against it. Women are control freaks. So here, pinned to our dissecting table, we have a logical rational person arguing logically and rationally against logic and reason. Confused? So is the whole planet.

Says Schaef:
When we live in an Addictive [White Male] System we use our very good minds to make assumptions that justify what we feel we must do to support our addictions.[172]

That's right, once a woman feels she needs to have a career so she doesn't have to depend on men, she needs a dishwasher and paper diapers to make her work-life happen. If she feels she needs to attack men, then she comes up with some brain-goop called the White Male System to derogate men and thereby enhance her word-picture called the Emerging Female System. Make no mistake about it, *Feminism is an addiction*. On a daily basis women sabotage their families and destroy the lives of their children in order to service their addiction to Feminist memes. The social atrocities that I have mentioned *ad nauseam*, including divorce, abortion, and denied visitation are the products of assumptions women make to service their addiction to feminism. Feminism bows to no higher power than the invocation of female willfulness and the idolatry of women.

And by the way, what Schaef calls the Emerging Female System has most of the attributes of the Deep Masculine – which is not new – she did not discover it. It has been around for at least 50,000 years, buried in the psyches of men, and visible every Sunday on TV sport, or out in the field on the hunt – both non-linear, highly intuitive activities, played under the fixed rules of nature or a referee, and dependent upon a great amount of silent dignity and good fortune. Sport is the last remaining area that female memes have not invaded. Sport is non-linear, out of control, honest, team-centered and interdependent – *i.e.*, exactly the opposite of the Addictive Society and Marxist/Feminism. Notice that there is no feminist lobby trying to change the rules of football or hockey. It's one of the few things feminists have left alone. Why? Because it has not been colonized by female memes for them to analyze and "cliticize". They have no doorway into understanding it like they do with feminized politicians and corporate organization.

Ms. Schaef's Emerging Female System is yet another attempt by women to lay claim to memes that are deeply and essentially male. A world that is less logical, more honest, less self-centered, more interdependent and less controlled will not be a world run by Emerging Females – *it will be a world run by Men.*

According to Schaef:
The left brain, the logical, rational mind, has one basic emotion – panic. Whenever it is threatened with the loss of illusion of control it panics.[173]

Like to place any bets on which gender can lay claim to the most panic? Have you ever seen a quarterback panic? It happens. It's what we call an interception. Too many interceptions and he is set free to open a car dealership. Ever watch what happens when the roast burns in the oven? Panic is a female staple. It's what we kindly call their "emotionalism". Panic is the most ever-present female emotion. Over-reaction is the stepchild to panic. Using a broom to kill a spider is like using an F16 to shoot down a pheasant. Driving your kid to the emergency ward at 3:00 A.M. because he has an earache is like shipping the entire contents of your house to Italy for a two-week vacation. Spending $1,000 on a new refrigerator because you "heard a squeak" in the old one is like buying new uniforms for the entire

US Army because one soldier tore his shirt. Control-freaks panic. Men can't afford to panic – not when the lion charges, not when your kid gets sick, not when the bridge starts collapsing under you. With her brilliant correlation between logic and panic Schaef has provided yet more evidence for the left-brainedness of women. Panic is born when logic and literalness break down. Why is modern life so stressful? Because a world organized for the benefit of women is intrinsically designed to favor logic and literalness – which inevitably break down – breeding panic – and stress. The contours of our stressful modern society have been shaped by panicky control-freaks – women.

Says Schaef:
> We see understanding as a way to gain control. But since control is an illusion, our attempts to understand actually put us deeper into the Addictive [White Male] System.[174]

Men don't try to understand life, men DO life. Women are the ones who exhaust themselves in books and lectures and study groups and gossip and magazines and Oprah trying to understand: men, female politics, female rights. Magazine racks would become fruit stands – and the standing trees would love it – if women stopped reading. The information revolution, the computer age, networking, are all female/manhole memes. More information is not going to solve our malaise – more surrendering of willfulness will.

Says Schaef:
> I often tell my clients that important decisions are discovered, not made. Trying to understand does not work. Logical, rational thinking does not work. Trying to straighten things out does not work; that only feeds the illusion of control.[175]

This is the divergent thinking that E.F. Schumacher talks about in the Introduction of this book. You must live through the problems. Once again Schaef shows her brilliance. I'd like to paste those phrases on my ex's forehead. Every counseling session we ever attended became a power play to bend me to her will. The counselors and court-appointed mediators took me aside and said there's no use coming back until she shows some willingness to compromise and change. Straightening things out meant doing things her way – buying a new refrigerator to fix the squeak in her head.

Denial is a great province in our society. Denial that there is a problem and that *you* are part of the problem. An alcoholic denies he has a drinking problem. His wife has all kinds of ideas of how to fix him, but denies she has any compulsive behaviors to address in herself. Society wide we have Denial that our *material* lusts are raping the planet. We have Denial that sometimes a government of men is better than a government of laws – when it's clear that no one in our government is prepared to take a stand on anything important. We have Denial that female memes have invaded every sector of our lives. Denial that the problems of our society are not caused entirely by white males. Denial that our laws, our health care, and our media are skewed toward women. Denial that there is a Twisted Side to the Great Mother. Yes, we are an entire nation in Denial. Carl Jung believed that women were much less prone than men to look inside themselves. What he was talking about was Denial.

Says Schaef:
    Perfectionism is another attribute of the White Male System.[176]

That's cute. Have you ever watched a woman clean house? She sees dirt that doesn't even exist. Ever watch a woman dress, or preen or put on make-up? Do you know that more than 50% of managers are women and less than 1% of bricklayers and house painters are women? A man will wear his favorite shirt for a year straight if no one complains about the smell. Perfectionism is a female meme.

Says Schaef:
    I have come to believe that the Addictive [White Male] System cannot tolerate intimacy.[177]

Just as church is the best place to avoid spirituality, so talking about feelings is the best way to avoid feelings. Women love to chatter about feelings, but their talk rarely goes deeper than voluble complaining, and rarely leads them into the inner work. Propelled by the same busy memes as the manholes who govern us, they are too busy and too bothered to actually *do* any of the inner work. Besides, understanding themselves might make them vulnerable, might force them into an admission of error or, god forbid, an apology. How can a woman be honest with anyone else when she can't even be honest with herself? Conversations with women are abominably one-sided. We are supposed to adjust our raw perceptions to fit their mental precepts, their pigeon holes, their TV psychology buzz-words. It's like trying to talk to a gorilla about how to drive a car. If it isn't yellow and sweet like a banana he doesn't get the point.

It's maddening to "talk" to a woman. That's why a vast territory of intimacy is reserved for silence and sex. Sex is the main form of male intimacy. Why? Because it's action. It's something you *do*. I just got a massage which was a remarkable form of intimacy. Why? Because it was something she did. Men learned long ago that women's talk about feelings has nothing to do with intimacy and everything to do with control. Our male bodies are tough and our minds don't work in words. A firm handshake means a lot, a mushy handshake means you're dealing with a flake. A slap on the back is even better. It's a jolt of energy. Tossing verbal darts at each other's egos is another form of male intimacy. Men who spend too much time around women don't have much of a knack for any of these intimacies. Ever kid a woman about her hairdo? Ever kid around with a judge about the law? Have you ever seen women slap each other on the back? Have you ever gotten more than a two-fingered, limp-wristed wiggle out of a woman who condescended to shake your hand? Touch, sex, and ego-puncturing are staples of male intimacy.

Have you ever seen a wide receiver get torpedoed ass-over-eyeballs by a linebacker – and then watched him get up and slap the linebacker's shoulder, saying, "Nice hit"? He respected it. It "touched" him. Men touch each other. Women touch their kids, and, on a good night, their lovers. The most shocking adjustment for a new father is that, when his beautiful little baby is born, all the touch he used to get evaporates as mom cuddles her infant. The man feels cheated and lied to in a very physical way, which is a way that cuts to his bone. He demands sex and his wife provides perfunctory sex to appease him. He got more intimacy before he got married. He might even come to resent this kid who, at the same time, he loves so much. His eye begins to wander. This, very simply, is the reason male polygamy has been so common in mammals, and female polygamy so rare.

Thailand, an ancient culture that to this day has not known the conqueror's sword, solved this problem thousands of years ago. When things get too shitty at home the men go to prostitutes. It is culturally accepted that women have only so much physical intimacy to go around. Men – in order to address their biological needs for physical intimacy – must, at times, seek their intimacy elsewhere. It's the best way to remain men, to stay in harmony. Obviously, getting divorced and remarried nine months later leads to the same dilemma – so why wreck the family over this problem of "medical lust". Just go visit a whore. The fact that most American women today have affairs four years into their marriages is evidence for how bored they get with the perfunctory order of sex they are expected to perform for their husbands. When the husband gets some of his intimacy elsewhere and only gets it on with wife when she's truly prepared to enjoy it and participate in it, there's a chance everyone will be happier and there's even a chance the divorce rate will plummet.

Intimacy, to a man, means physical intimacy, not "talking". If there's anything our uptight WASP-influenced society could tolerate it's more physical intimacy. Not just sex. The pitfalls of "free" sex have bequeathed us a 60% divorce rate. We need men who aren't ashamed to hug each other. And women who can come across with a firm handshake or an occasional pat on the back. Intimacy means touching.

Says Schaef:
Dependency [fostered by the White Male System] destroys intimacy. The person being depended upon feels

sucked dry, and the person doing the depending comes to resent the other. Dependent people are "human vacuum cleaners".[178] (Emotional vampires.)

Very true. But certainly dependency is not now, and never has been, regarded as a male attribute. Women foster dependencies. Men function as a team. Men move down the field as a group of interdependent individuals. The quarterback wants the tackle to block the linebacker so he doesn't get smashed into the mud when he lifts his arm to pass. At the same time, in the same way, he wants his wife to take their daughter in for her shots. The quarterback cannot trade places with the tackle – he's not physically strong enough to do the job of blocking the linebacker – nor can he afford to miss practice to take his daughter in for her shots. Not unless his wife has agreed to let him quit his job and volunteered that she'll be the one to slap the paycheck on the kitchen table. Interdependence is what men know and understand and strive for. They rely on the tackle and their wife performing their assignments within the game plan. They expect to have their wife playing on the same team as they are and are shocked to find out that she's not, she's playing on her own team, but she still wants her name on the checking account. Men like to have all the bases covered because they know that's how you win the game. Then one day Ted turns around to find Sally has walked out and left center field wide open so she can go to a "consciousness raising meeting" or screw her boyfriend. He feels betrayed. An easy fly-out to center turns into a home run for the opposing team – the entropic world of chaos and disaster he has fought so hard to hold scoreless against the family.

A family with two full-time working parents does not function as a family. Something is missing. The *family* is missing. The modern American family is a pathological joke that will not endure. If the women want to work, fine, let the men take the kids for their shots and paint their paintings and work on their cars all day.

Dependency comes from an inability to understand interdependency. Boys learn about that in group sports. Girls don't seem to learn about it anywhere. They don't think it's "fair" that they've whomped their elbow throwing a block that springs the halfback and lets him score. *They* want to score the points. They don't understand team play. They only want to work for themselves. And so they view the dynamic relationships of interdependency as mere dependency and their fangs grow long in the dark nights of their soul and the Twisted Side of the Great Mother sets up a store and starts selling poison candy inside their heads. Dependency is a female meme. Interdependency is a male meme. Men know a lot more about relationships than women.

Says Schaef:
The Addictive [White Male] System operates out of a scarcity model, a model based on the assumption that there is not enough of anything to go around and that we better get as much as we can while we can.[179]

Men, real men, as in the Potlatch example, are disposed toward generosity. Men share what they have, after all, they're men; they can always go out and get more – more fish, more honey, more money. Women hoard for the future, their "intuition" always planning for disaster. Scarcity and hoarding are female memes that colonized us around the time of the first king and haven't left us yet. The king always worried about his wealth and never had enough of it. He overreacted to "border threats" the way we've been overreacting to Cuba since Fidel came into power. The scarcity model, women's intuition, doom-predictions, are female memes.

Says Schaef:
The White Male System operates out of a zero-sum model. When you have "it", I somehow have less of "it", and there is only so much of "it" to go around. But in the Emerging Female System power is perceived as limitless.[180]

Well, blow my bazooka. I've just mentioned the real men of the Pacific Northwest who gave away everything they had at the annual Potlatch Ceremony. I have never yet read, or heard mention, anywhere, of a society in which the women "gave away" anything at all. For them there is always a price. For them everything is always business. Being generous, and allowing others to be generous – a Deep Male meme – doesn't figure in. I want to quote from Schaef just to establish the depth of her self-delusion.

> Says Schaef:
> I have a group of friends with whom I meet periodically. We are all bright, creative, intelligent, competent people. One of the things I have started noticing is that there is seldom much rejoicing when a person in the group accomplishes something. Why? Because the whole group is operating out of a zero-sum model. If one of the *women* in it accomplishes something and gains recognition, the belief is that this somehow lessens the amount of recognition available to the other members of the group.
> This unfortunate perception has led to a lot of comparing, competing, resentment, and inability to celebrate individual achievements.[181]

Please note that the group Ms. Schaef is describing here is a group of *women*! Something she has tagged the White Male System is here being represented by a group of *women*. When will it sink in? Women are zero-sum. The zero-sum thinking that pervades our society is a female meme carried over from the king. Men give everything away and that is why divorce court has been able to take such brutal advantage of them. The attitude is: you can always get more, but your poor little ex-wife has to make her way all alone in this big brutal men's world. Yes, we can always get more. But since all we really need is a pocket knife and a blanket and a few bucks traveling money, we don't ever need to get that *much* of "it" again. And we certainly don't have to give it to her anymore. We don't work on Maggie's Farm no more.

Says Schaef, at the top of page 78, in *When Society Becomes An Addict*: "In the Living Process System [the Emerging Female

System] power comes from inside, not outside the self." At the bottom of the same page she says, "If you accept that it is possible to be God, as the White Male System does, then you are doomed to failure. If you believe that you can know and understand everything, then you are doomed to failure."

Either this is a glaring contradiction or dogs have feathers. Is God inside of you or is God outside of you? I want her to come clean on this point. Like most women she loves to dance around it. That's why we never let them in to see the Deer God in the first place. If the power is within you, is this power your power, your ego, your willfulness – or is it God's power? If the power within you is not your ego then, one must assume, God dwells within you. If God is inside of you, are you not assuming that you are, in some way, God?

Recovering people who look for God inside of them do not recover. That's a compelling fact proven 10 million times over in Alcoholics Anonymous. Addicts and alcoholics have spent their entire lives, prior to coming into the 12-step programs, relying on their own inner value system, *i.e.*, playing God. In fact, that is the very thing that made them addicts – they served only themselves. And this is precisely the glaring defect in Marxist/Feminism. It serves only itself. And that's the "healing" this deranged woman is advocating? Preposterous.

Anne Wilson Schaef doesn't seem to know if God is inside her or not. Well I do. He's NOT! This meteoric feminist made the *New York Times* bestseller list by trashing men for behaving the way women taught us to behave. Let's cut through the crap. Anne Wilson Schaef is trying to conquer female shame by building up women's self-esteem. Fuck self-esteem. Self-esteem is just another huge helping of ego.

Inner power is ego power, willpower; not surrender, not God power. Native Americans didn't look for the eagle or coyote inside them; they looked for themselves inside the eagle or coyote. No surviving culture has ever prayed to itself. In fact, until the Greeks came along with their cult of body-worship, God was never even thought of as a person. The whole point of the "God idea" is to create something outside of ourselves to worship – something that is not a man, and not a woman. A fundamental distinction between God and man must be maintained for that magic to work. Cave painters didn't paint men and women on the walls of their caves; they painted mysteries.

Real men look for God outside of them, and when they don't, they become addicts. It's as simple as that. I don't much care what women do or don't do to themselves. But I do care very much that the saleswomen of Institutional Menopause would try to re-impress upon men this female meme which is a certain recipe for disaster. When men look for God inside themselves, they die. The Female Addictive System thrives on self-esteem. But surrender means emptying yourself of yourself. Moving beyond self-esteem. Men require expansive male-flavored spirituality not ego-centered female religion.

Machismo, the Macho Man, is tied in knots over issues of self-esteem. He wants to be somebody and he can't stand the fact that essentially he's nobody. The macho man is an uninitiated man – raised by women – who has never been initiated into the Deep Masculine. Conniving, self-serving, egotistical, at times maniacal in his quest for attention – for self-esteem – he is acting out of his *anima*, not his Deep Male Soul. Self-aggrandizement and career questing is feminine based – an agenda formed under *mater*nal influence. Screw what your mom wants; she's brutalized your mind with psychic incest. She's trying to live her life through you.

Schaef, the addictions therapist, with her willy nilly dancing around the issue of ego-surrender, is feeding the Addictive (Marxist/Feminist) System with more confused, willful, addictive thinking – with more feminized memes. Therapists will have work for millennia to come if we continue to buy into this light-headedness. If Schaef were a fish she would be a surface feeder regaling in the kingdom of light – light bodies, light-headedness, enlightenment – a sailfish, a sardine, a dolphin. The swordfish, who cuts through illusion, the snapper who munches on the crabs of attachment, the grouper who gulps down grief whole, live in the depths, down in the cold male realms, far beneath the dazzling light of fame and success and whale-watching tours.

Well…I'm getting a little bored with Anne Wilson Schaef, so I'll try to speed through some of her other "points". I guess the thing to keep in mind is that when a feminist is attacking you, you can always throw it back in her face by telling her that what she's complaining about is the way *women* taught us to be. It's women's fault. Not ours. If we're dishonest, panicky or "thinking too analytically" it's because women made us that way. Those aren't guy-things. Women don't complain about men who are strong or forbearing or confident. They only complain about men who are violent or numb or overbearing. In other words, they only complain about men who are acting out of their *anima* – their poor quality of femininity – female memes.

Sez Schaef: Negativism and negative thinking are characteristic of an Addictive White Male System.[182]

Guess what? Negativity is female. Women are negative creatures – perpetually complaining – worried about everything. Women love to predict disaster. They call it "intuition". Men are en-*thus*-iastic. En-*theo*-astic. Filled with God. Watch 'em watching football.

Sez Schaef:
Consider how the Addictive White Male System goes about the process of analysis. When it examines something closely, it focuses on finding what is wrong with it and picking it apart. We are educated to be critical and judgmental. To be supportive and positive is viewed as being weak. This is especially evident in academia. It is very difficult for academics to consider something and respond to it without feeling that they must come up with something negative to say.[183]

Would Ms. Schaef have us assume that academics are MEN? Academics are mama's boys. Academics do not grow your food or fix your toilets. Academics do not hunt pheasants or pray to deer. Academics are a perfect example of a species of man who has become so feminized he is duck soup for women to attack because all the things she sees in him are the things she sees in herself. Does a woman attack fishing, or auto mechanics? No. She knows nothing about them. But how to run society? Well, now, here's something she knows *all* about…And off they go, tripping into the sunset, two people who don't know how to patch a tire, gonna solve everybody else's problems.

Education is feminized. Our educational system is not about seeking out the Deer God or the Deep Masculine. It's about reading and writing – sitting down talking about stuff. If men truly ran the educational system the kids would pile into a pickup truck twice a week and go see how farmers farm or firemen put out fires. Masculine education is something you DO. Not something you read about.

Our educational system – the corporate job-training it has devolved into – and most of the jobs in modern society – are hopelessly feminine. The soul-scarring and deep resentment this causes in men is almost beyond calculation. Real men said NO to the educational-corporate conglomerate during Vietnam. Physicists became carpenters and poets became house painters. We can do it again. We *must* do it again. There is no resting place for men in this life. We are cultural nomads. Women and manholes will constantly screw us out of our gains, whether love beads or ecology, and put them up for sale. Our job is to keep poking new holes in the system. We are men; that is what the Life Force bids us to do. Our educational system inevitably leads us straight back to enforcing female memes. As long as we travel light and keep moving, those ponderous corporate golems cannot keep up. Men's studies cannot be taught at a university, as much as I'd like to believe that that's a place to start – and maybe it is – but the real work will not happen there.

Sez Schaef: The White Male System breeds defensive people, and defensive people are insecure.[184]

Women have cornered the market on defensiveness and insecurity. They're constantly masked behind a false persona of niceness and solicitousness. The only thing I'm sure of is:

whatever a woman tells me – that's not what she means. If I *care* about her I'm supposed to *figure out* what she means. If I hear her say, "Boy do I look fat in this dress," I'm stuck. Sometimes I'm supposed to say, "No sweetheart. You look lovely." If she smiles it means I said the right thing; I petted her ego. If she frowns I know I missed the point. She wants a new dress. If I hear her say, "The kids had a great time in the Granger's pool last week," what I'm supposed to do is put down my fishing pole, go in the garage, get down the pool, pump it with air, and fill it with water. But I'm a guy. I have a choice. Sometimes I *choose* not to hear "right". So sometimes, when the fish are biting, my answer is, "Yeah, that's great. Gotta go."

Worried about rubbing me the wrong way and getting my dander up? You *ought* to be. You're trying to manipulate me to do something I don't want to do, when I don't want to do it, by painting it with pleasantness. You're liberated. Go get the goddamn pool down yourself. Woman, thy name is Deception. Thy art is Delusion.

And If I should say, "What's this $500 phone bill?" she'll say, "What? Can't I talk to my mom?"

A world run by women is a world steeped in defensiveness and insecurity – glossed over with smiles and pleasantries. It's a world where politicians never answer a question and corporations traffic in innuendo. Guess what we live in?

Insecure people serve no god except their own ego and their own demons of self-esteem. The opposite of defensiveness and insecurity is acceptance. The king-meme, the female meme, is all about defense – accumulating wealth and guarding it. The hunter prays to the Deer God and accepts what nature provides. The hunter goes out fishing for mahi mahi and comes back with red snapper. Finding the surface fish aren't biting, and sensing something different on the water, he ties on a heavy weight and baits his hook with live crabs and pulls up giant red snappers off the bottom. Secure people adjust. The hunter stays tuned to nature and accepts what nature provides.

Sez Schaef:

> Frozen feelings are a hallmark of the Addictive (White Male) System...

Our movies, newspapers, and television programs tell us that we must never show our feelings. Men in particular are taught not to show their feelings from a very early age, which is probably why they are better at it than women. This may be one reason why our society perceives men as superior beings.[185]

Okay, hold the phone. It's true that we have a big problem with frozen feelings in our society. But it's also true that women, being left-brained, are more prone to panic than men. And harkening back to Vilar, it's pretty clear that women are wizards at concealing emotion and lying to themselves. Men, being less prone to lie to themselves, display fewer feelings, but what they do feel runs much deeper than female surface chatter. That's where our art and music come from. The pseudo-mythology that women are "more emotional" than men must be trash-canned. It's only half right. Women make more noise, women make more panic; men make deeper incursions into their feelings.

And this is a painful ride. Bly has mentioned the numbness that grows in the chest of the uninitiated man, lost in a mindswamp of female memes. His feelings hurt too much; his body shuts them down. All men in our society suffer from this numbness; it's virtually a medical condition. We feel so much pain our bodies cut it off; it's too much to handle. Our feelings are not borne by words or serviced by psychoanalysis. A female/manhole therapist is not going to put you in touch with your Deep Masculine. A lot of times when analysts tell us we are not feeling anything we are actually feeling something very deeply but we can't express it other than by beating on a drum or belting out a blues tune.

I feel angry a lot and negative a lot and grateful a lot. I'm a Dead Head, one of the grateful dead – my way of being does not fit into American Society and I'm pissed off about that because we have created such a feminized, corporatized, defensive, control-oriented culture that we have all but extinguished artists. An artist is not supposed to make a million dollars working for a media corporation. An artist is supposed to talk to God, and tell everyone what he heard. An artist is a

magician and a shaman and a healer of our psyches. A predictor
of Ice Ages. A prognosticator of new paradigms. A referee of
injustice – who calls 'em as he sees 'em – even if it means
rebuking one half of the human race. To be accepted as an artist
in America you need to make money – *i.e.*, you need to be
absorbed into the corporate system. The first question everyone
asks a person who introduces himself as a writer is, "Are you
published?" Sheesh! They don't ask him what he writes about.
They don't ask him what's the meaning of life, or what he predicts
for the future. They want to know if a corporation has bought
him! And the same goes for painters – what galleries they've
shown – or musicians – what venues they've played? It's all
cowshit. In Europe artists make chalk paintings on the sidewalk
and passersby throw coins into hats so the artists can buy bread
and cheese and pay their rent. Here they want to know if you've
kissed someone's ass at Simon & Schuster or Warner. It's insane.

Art is all about poking a maniac's eyeball into the center of
the meaning of life and singing out a song of prophecy. When
corporations buy and sell art there IS NO ART – there are only
corporate promotions. They're blow-drying our souls. Freeze-
drying our feelings. This is the Garden of Eden after we bit the
apple. Corporations are the snake. They've been whispering in
our wives' ears, "You should have this and you should have
that. You have 'rights', you have 'needs'. No one should stop
you from taking what you deserve." I hear God's heavy footsteps
right now, thump, thump, thump, coming to find out what the
hell happened. We're all in deep shit.

The main reason I haven't chopped my feelings out of this
book is so the wool-suited, feminized, academic crowd – the
manholes in politics and business and university – can be
reminded what it FEELS like to be a man. They've forgotten.
They've eaten too many meals of female memes…[Houston,
we got a problem. The flight crew is full of beans. They're
farting up the ship and we can't even open a window up here or
we'll all die!]

The men who control the wealth of society are women with
pee pees. They forgot it's OK to be a man. To feel like a man.
To get dirt under your fingernails. To touch life and have it

"touch" you back like a 255-pound linebacker. Men are hurting and it is time for women and feminized manholes to get this picture engraved in their heads.

Academics inhabit a dry world beyond the senses. Gurus do the same. They are feminized men and we need not view them as masculine ideals. Jesus sweated and stunk and shit in his pants a few times. Krishna fucked 4000 milkmaids in one night. Buddha was a prince, the son of a king, who threw away all the feminized delights of his palace life and sat under a tree, in the heat, in the rain, getting bit by bugs, talking to passing cobras, until he was struck by a bolt of understanding. These guys weren't pussies or wimps living in air-conditioned offices selling us information for a price. They weren't yuppies or manholes or women. They were divinely inspired men who broke the chains of this great big feminized farm we inhabit and penetrated to the center of life, sweating and stinking and fishing and fucking their way through it.

Sez Schaef:
A concept that is key to understanding the Addictive [White Male] System and what it is doing to us is ethical deterioration, "spiritual bankruptcy".[186]

The object of this entire book is to point out the spiritual bankruptcy of feminism and of our feminized Western Civilization. Jesus, the Son of Man, was an outlaw who was crucified in the midst of a civil war between the control-freak Romans and the control-freak Hebrews. Need I mention again that I have never had the pleasure of encountering a single spiritual axiom endemic to feminism? Women are making a lot of noise about the Goddess to compensate for this glaring deficiency. The Goddess is them and they are the Goddess and it's all a bunch of psychic masturbation. They are not about to surrender their will and their life to the Goddess; the Goddess is there to serve their egos and nothing more. This is a mirror image of the lip service the government pays to God while it invades religion and tries to control the shit out of our lives to make us better corporate consumers. The Goddess and the government are twin phantoms masking female/corporate control memes. Women will serve the Goddess as long as she is doing what they want her to do. Once she shows her fangs and her putrescence and her Twisted Side, they will jump ship with their hands to their cheeks. They know nothing of Kali and her necklace of human skulls, and they don't want to. The Goddess is nurturing and oh-so nicey nicey. They know nothing of Yahweh who smashed his chosen people with Babylonian and Roman and Nazi and Russian invaders whenever they got a little bit too *mater*ialistic and forgot who they were supposed to be bending their knees to. Goddess religion is namby pamby ego tripping. In other words, spiritual bankruptcy.

Sez Schaef:

The Addictive [White Male] System is based on fear. We fear for our very survival, and our children grow up fearing for theirs. In a system that fosters violence and uncertainty, where confusion and self-centeredness are rampant, where the scarcity model dictates that there is not enough food, money, time, or energy [because of *actual* hoarding and female greed], healthy survival is a very real concern.[187]

Fear is lack of Faith. Fear is the firstborn child of lack of faith – resisting surrendering your will to a Higher Power. Fear is the badge of the spiritually bankrupt. Spiritually developed people fear not in fire or famine or bank failure.

Women suffer from more fears than it's possible for most men to imagine. Life is constantly wrong and there is constantly a problem with it and their "intuition" tells them to fear the worst. It gets pretty exhausting for a guy to come home from work every day and be served up the Fear of the Day. Fear is a female meme. Courage is a male meme. It's never been different. God gives us the peace to see above our fears. If you don't have Faith you are doomed to a life of fear and worry.

Sez Schaef:

Almost all of the characteristics of the Addictive [White Male] System are rooted in fear. The illusion of control, crisis-orientation, dishonesty, abnormal thinking processes, denial, dependency, negativism, defensiveness – each is born of fear.[188]

Men and women without God inhabit a fearful world. The god of feminism is feminism. Feminism will never, ever, alleviate female fear.

Sez Schaef:
   The Addictive [White Male] System is built on the process of the promise. There is very little (if any) difference between the two statements "I will quit drinking tomorrow" and "A chicken in every pot". Both keep us looking expectantly toward the future and not recognizing, owning, and dealing with the present.[189]

The promise of the church is that you will get salvation, the promise of advertising is that you will get laid, the promise of therapists is that you will get "healed", the promise of the government is that they will take care of you, the promise of mom, as she hands you your T-shirt, all washed, is that you will have all of the above if you just stick with her. Our whole feminized society is built on the process of the promise. Women are averse to living in the moment; they constantly have their eyes set on something in the future. Real men do the work in this moment that the future may take care of itself. The 12 Steps teach that by living well today one is creating a healthy and sane past and laying the ground for a healthy and sane future. Everything is now. The past and future move through this moment. Eternity is Now.

Sez Schaef:
   Another process the Addictive System uses to perpetuate itself is that of absorption. The pseudopodic ego of the system reaches out and totally absorbs another system until it becomes indistinguishable from the Addictive System. It is similar to colonization, a favorite practice of the Addictive [White Male] System down through history.[190]

* * *

Colonization is also precisely what female memes have been doing to male minds and male government and male spirituality for 8000 years. As male initiation became obsolete – and now that half of our kids are being raised without dads because, in our energy-fat society, mom can press a button and open the garage door or heat the house "herself" – our colonization by female memes has become almost complete. The Wild Man was driven out of Europe eons ago and now there is virtually no room left for him in America. *We* are the last buffalo. *We* are the last of the Apaches. *We* are the last Men. And they are killing off our families and heritage just as they did to the buffalo and the original inhabitants of this vast land. They are focused on the promise of some Emerging Female future, and we are being plowed under and paved with malls.

Sez Schaef:

I believe that the constructs (process) of the linear, rational, logical brain, while interesting, are almost completely unrelated to our experience of ourselves in the world. Yet, these are what we [in the White Male System] keep telling ourselves are real.

Hurray for Ms. Schaef! She just shot a bullet through the brains of feminism while assuming she was advancing some female agenda. She has done my work for me. The logical, rational, analytical world of women has almost nothing to do with reality. I rest my case.

Sez Schaef:

Since the White Male/Addictive System defines itself as reality, everything else is unreal by definition. Since its referent is the external referent, the internal referent is unreal and nonexistent by definition. The process of invalidating that which the system does not know, understand, cannot measure, and thereby cannot control is so extreme that large areas of perception and knowledge are lost. *We give the system the power to make the known unknown.*[191]

* * *

What a beautiful way to put it: the power to make the known unknown. This is deep and good. How about making male initiation unknown to men through the process of a female educational system? How about making the Deer God unknown to us through the control memes of a feminized theology? How about making hunter memes unknown to us through the process of agricultural dominion over the earth? How about making unknown the fact that there is a vast amount of male suffering in this "White Male Society". How about making fathers unknown to their children? I think Ms. Schaef has finally hit on it. Marxist/Feminism insists on making the Deep Masculine unknown to men. And this, in one sentence, is the crisis we face.

Sez Schaef:

Most of us [in the White Male System] are trained in dualistic thinking. Our education prepares us to think dualistically – either this or that, either right or wrong, either in or out, either off or on, either black or white, either good or evil, and so on *ad infinitum*. I believe that this kind of thinking serves many functions in this system. The first is to oversimplify a very complex world, thereby giving us the illusion of control over what is in fact a universe in process. When we think we can break something that has many complex facets into two clear dimensions, it feeds our illusion of control.

The process of dualistic thinking also sets up a situation in which, if one part of the dualism is affirmed, the opposite is automatically assumed to be false. It is like the old mother-son interaction: The son says, "I like the blue shirt," and the mother responds, "What's the matter, you don't like the red one?"[192]

The Taoists say, two things become ten thousand. They quite agree with Ms. Schaef's above statements. But they, like me, are dismayed that she has just spent 150 pages contrasting the White Male System with the Emerging Female System. Schaef acts like an alcoholic in extreme denial. She sees the truth in her head, but it doesn't come out her body. A bogus duality between White Males and Emerging Females has turned into 150 pages of definitions aimed at the wrong people. Virtually everything that Schaef accuses white men of doing or being may be attributed to the feminized memes that have been colonizing our society for 8000 years. The real problem is that there are too many women and too many female memes conspiring to make a known Deep Masculine unknown. Now hear this: The pendulum has hereby stopped. In this precise moment the pendulum of gender priorities begins its swing back to the opposite pole of the human spectrum. We will hereby begin relocating the center of gravity of the human personality far far back into the Deep Male.

I want to quote a real sage here, a real wise man, so we can begin living in the solution – so we can feel the pendulum begin its move back.

Bede Griffiths was an English monk, guru, sage and scholar who lived in India.

Says Bede:
Pleasure and pain are the dualities. Everybody is running after pleasure, everybody is trying to avoid pain. Until we get beyond these spontaneous reactions, we will never get any peace. Pleasure is followed by pain. It is the realm of endless opposition.[193]

Isn't that refreshing? Here Bede is commenting on a passage from the Bhagavad Gita. Here's a guy who lived what he preached. He actually did this stuff. He actually transcended dualities. It wasn't just something nice to say at the end of a book where you've just presented 6000 dualities. Women, get out of your heads, start to *do* some of this stuff! No matter how much pleasure you accrue you will arrive at displeasure. It is the realm of endless opposition.

And now, two pages later, as if she were a different person writing in a different century, Schaef propounds her Lincoln

Log Theory, the essence of which is that the issues that emerge in therapy come in pairs – dualisms. Fear comes up with control, shame comes up with perfectionism, just like the opposite grooved ends of a Lincoln Log. There may be some truth to this, it may be an interesting therapy tool, but the fact of the matter is that Schaef spends the next 20 pages of her book creating dualisms! Self-centeredness vs. nonexistence, self-centeredness vs. disrespectfulness, dishonesty vs. niceness, worthlessness vs. grandiosity, fear vs. anger. Enough already! Come on lady. Give up your ego and all that shit turns to smoke. For as often as Ms. Schaef *talks* about the 12 Steps it is clear to me she has never *done* the 12 Steps – just as, in the midst of 150 pages of dualisms, she talks about the harm of creating dualisms. People go to work on the 12 Steps the way roofers go to work stapling shingles. This is something you *do*, not something you talk about! And this is what drives men crazy about women. Their ideas are divorced from their actions. Rank hypocrisy. Devastation of Soul.

Sez Schaef:
   Any therapist who is not actively recovering from the Addictive System is perpetuating it.[194]

Clearly Schaef is in early recovery from the Marxist/Feminist Addictive System and should not be accepting any clients right now.

Sez Schaef:
   When I first became aware that the White Male System and the Addictive System are one and the same, I felt completely overwhelmed with elation. It happened while I was speaking at a wellness conference. The words tumbled out of my mouth, a hush fell over the audience, and then there was a spontaneous standing ovation.[195]

Booo! Hiss! Whose wellness? Fire the ump. Throw da bum out! There must not have been any MEN at this wellness conference. Wellness conferences are comprised of sick women staying sick. Here she is blaming white men for doing a bad job being women. What a mind fuck. Go home.

Krishnamurti says words are violent. They tear uniform reality to pieces. Men, being right-brained, shun words. Life strikes us as a differentiated whole, rather than as a collection of parts. Women mutilate life with words. Here is Anne Wilson Schaef on the importance of naming things.

Sez Schaef:
> Once we name something, we own it. [Here we have naming and ownership in the same breath!] Once we own it, it becomes ours, as does the power we formerly relinquished to it. Once we reclaim that personal power, we can begin to recover, and not until then. Remember, to name the system as an addict is not to condemn it: it is to offer it the possibility of recovery.

Right. And wiping your ass with tree bark is good for your skin. If the real problem with our system is that it is polluted with female memes, how is naming it as White Male going to help anything? This is Institutional Menopause in full swing. It offers a solution, based on a prejudice, that is a monument of self-deception. Ready for more confusion?

Sez Schaef:
> Paradoxically, the only way to reclaim our personal power is by admitting our powerlessness. The first part of Step One of the A.A. Twelve-Step Program reads, "We admitted we were powerless over alcohol." [1] It is important to recognize that admitting to powerlessness over an addiction is not the same as admitting to powerlessness as a person. [2] In fact, it can be very powerful to recognize the futility of the illusion of control.

Now do you know what woman-think is? This perfectly rational-sounding paragraph is going in six directions at once.

The last two sentences, which I've numbered [1] and [2], are sheer psychobabble. I'm going to scare the bats out of Ms. Schaef's brain and see what we really have here. Sentence number [1] is a perverted misrepresentation of A.A. recovery philosophy. Sentence number [2] is the pinnacle of spiritual wisdom, a paradox, a famous paradox. The problem here is the same problem I've been ranting about for hundreds of pages – women absolutely refuse to relinquish the notion of their personal power. They will not do it. Their brains rebel against it. It's why they lie to themselves; it's why they manipulate the shit out of everyone around them; it's why they stay sick when everyone around them is getting well. They're like squirrels digging nuts out of the ground and hanging them back up in the trees – pretending they're God. They're living backwards. They go through life butt first and expect us to applaud their sophistication. For Ms. Schaef to trumpet her own "power" over the vast array of forces happening right outside her window is a special kind of insanity.

Clearly, Ms. Schaef is a therapist who has seen so much remarkable recovery come out of the 12 Steps she is trying to get her foot in the door. I think she should hang around for a while. Sentence number [1], intimating that an addict is not powerless over herself, only over her addiction, contradicts the very spirit and fiber of Alcoholics Anonymous. A.A., in fact, teaches that we are powerless over people, places, and things, *including ourselves*, for no personal power the recovering person has ever been able to muster has been able to snuff out her addiction. This requires the help of a God, a Higher Power. Personal power has nothing to do with it. The only real power comes from surrender. If Ms. Schaef still believes addicts are "not powerless" she should not be accepting clients at this time.

Sentence number [2] is the height of spiritual wisdom. Truth without paradox is not truth, said Richard Rohr, and here we have a great example of that. Schaef says, in effect, that it can be very powerful to recognize that you are powerless. This is the essence of recovery; the essence of praying to the Deer God; the essence of the Deep Masculine. The instant we relinquish our power, we have more power, and more choices, than we ever imagined possible. But it's not *our* power, it's Higher Power. And at that point the only thing left to do is to serve: to serve man, to serve woman, to serve children, to serve God, to serve the earth, to do work without any expectation of reward. Life is not business. Life is service.

Well, that's enough of Ms. Schaef and *When Society Becomes an Addict*. Apart from its sexist tyranny, it's an important book and certainly worth reading. But I wonder if Ms. Schaef can gauge the reaction she would have gotten if she used the word "Nigger" everywhere she used the words "White Male". To paint all white men as accomplices in a system that is overwhelmingly made up of Marxist/Feminist memes verges on criminal insanity. And yet, there are lots of other criminally insane feminists relentlessly destroying our families with the blessings of the "system", and they're not being arraigned for it. They're being interviewed on TV.

In summary: everything feminist psychotherapist Anne Wilson Schaef blames on men are things women put in men. Fear, negativity, over-controlling, addictive behavior are female memes that have plagued human society for millennia. Until we recognize that the source of these debilitating behaviors is feminine, we don't have a chance of eradicating them. Until we recognize that war is caused by female *mater*ialistic greed, we don't have a chance of ending it. Until we recognize that corporations are dedicated to servicing female *mater*ialism, we don't have a prayer of constricting them. Until we acknowledge that big government grows bigger by passing legislation to calm the fears of women, we don't have a chance of shrinking it. Until we realize that religion has been designed to appeal to female psychic fantasies, we don't have a prayer of regenerating a vital spirituality. Until we admit that MOST of the problems of modern life are caused by women, we don't have a feather in a hurricane's chance of eliminating them. As long as we keep blaming everything on men we're wearing our underpants on our heads – and big corporations and big government will continue to colonize our minds and our lives. Psyche, feminine mind, has put us all to sleep.

* * *

Let's take a stab at making what was once known – then became unknown – known again. Warren Farrell has made a list of some of the best things about men. Here it is:

GENEROSITY: Men share everything they have with their friends and the people they love.

FAIRNESS: Men play fair, they learn that on the ball field.

NURTURING: Men are nurturing, they provide "financial wombs" for their families; they provide a calm emotional rallying point to dispel panic and withstand crises.

LEADERSHIP: Setting an example, not shouting out orders; slogging through the uncharted swamps of life on foot, ahead of the caravan of pots and pans and Legos.

OUTRAGEOUSNESS: Boys get noticed by *acting* on differences, not by holding different opinions. The Rolling Stones are outrageous. So were George Washington and Thomas Jefferson.

KEEPING EMOTIONS IN PERSPECTIVE: When someone is bleeding there is no time to faint until you've stopped the flow of blood. Most of the time postponing emotion is NOT a bad thing. Panic contributes nothing to life.

DETERMINATION: An ability to stay the course, and find a way through your fears.

SEPARATING THE ISSUE FROM THE FRIENDSHIP: Men can be good friends and disagree. Women think you betray them if you don't think the same as they do.

EXPRESSING ANGER: Grudges are not held when anger is released – a burst of yelling at each other and our heads go down for the next play.

KEEPING COMPLAINTS ABOUT THE RELATION-SHIP WITHIN THE RELATIONSHIP: Women love to complain about men. Men don't even like to talk about women.

SAVING HER LIFE AT THE RISK OF HIS OWN: Men die protecting the women they love from risks. Very rarely does it happen in reverse.

GIVING UP HIS LIFE FOR HIS BELIEFS OR TO SUPPORT HIS FAMILY: Men sacrifice themselves for the good of the whole human organism. Men are the white blood cells in the body of humanity.

MEN SORT OUT THEIR OWN GOALS: Men "think for themselves". They are less prone to peer pressure and more apt to serve a goal outside their own ego.

SELF-SUFFICIENCY: [God sufficiency is a better word for this.] Men, more disposed to reporting to work for the Deer God, appear to others to be more self-sufficient.

SELF-STARTING: A man does not expect to be discovered, like Cinderella, or awakened, like Sleeping Beauty. He has to put himself out there.

RISK TAKING: Men push the limits of physical reality. That's why there are gurus like St. Francis. That's why we've walked on the moon.

CHALLENGE AUTHORITY: We respect those who have proven themselves and are quick to puncture the egos of those who haven't.

INVENTION: Men are the inventors. By being right-brained and intuitive and unplanned in our approach to life, we stumble across more new things than women.

CREATIVE: Men are the creative half of our species. Liberated from the compulsion to verbalize we make more fresh associations and discover more hidden relationships.

DEVELOP IDENTITY: Women are born, men are made.

HUMILITY: Humility is freedom from ego-driven self-consumption. If we happen to do something well, somebody will notice, no sense tooting our trumpet.

RESPONSIBILITY: Says Farrell, male socialization is a recipe book of taking responsibility. Women offer advice and cook spaghetti for those around them. Men take *responsibility* for those around them. When the wolf is at the door, it's the man who picks up the shotgun.

DOING RATHER THAN COMPLAINING: Men can't tolerate much complaining, in women, or other men. They want to offer solutions, even if they're just "learn to live with it" or "get on with it."

PUSHING THE LIMITS OF ONE'S TALENTS: We push past the envelope and learn from our failures. Women, assailed by ego, are afraid to fail.

SENSE OF HUMOR: Men are quick to laugh at themselves. Women are quick to laugh at others. Another clear ego difference.

RESOURCEFULNESS: Has to do with fixing your bike fender with a piece of coat hanger until you can find a screw. Our right-brainedness bids us to look for certain shapes when we're in a jam, whether the problem is physical, strategic or emotional. Female generals would be great for getting the right amount of troops to the right place at the right time. But male generals, on the ground, figure out how to get the men across a flash-flooded arroyo using goat skin bladders and bamboo poles.

ENJOY WOMEN: Men love women; it's in our blood. We like them right now, without weighing their value as mates or getting caught up in futuristic fantasies.

PLAYING WITH KIDS ON KIDS' TERMS: Men like to roughhouse and play tiger or horsey down on the ground. When a man gets down on his knees or lies down on the carpet, the kids come around like ants at a picnic. The tiniest baby will stop being afraid of you if you get down lower than she is. It's like magic.

CHANGE WITHOUT BLAME: Men have not come up with statements like, "women perpetuate a matriarchy that sends men off to die in swamps while they sleep in comfy beds". Why? We are trained by our mothers not to attack women. Says Farrell, the "war between the sexes" might best be called "women's attack on men".[196]

Aaron Kipnis came up with a New Male Manifesto. I like it. Here it is:

THE NEW MALE MANIFESTO

I.   Men are beautiful.

II.   A man's value is not measured by what he produces.

III.   Men are not flawed by nature.

IV.   A man doesn't have to live up to any narrow societal image of man.

V.   Men do not need to become more like women to reconnect with soul.

VI.   Masculinity does not require the denial of deep feeling.

VII. Men are not only competitors, men are brothers.

VIII. Men deserve the same rights as women for custody of children, economic support, government aid, education, health care, and protection from abuse. Fatherhood is honorable. Fathers are equal to mothers in their ability to raise children.

IX. Men and women can be partners. [Like yin and yang can be partners.]

X. Sometimes men have the right to be wrong, irresponsible, unpredictable, silly, inconsistent, afraid, indecisive, experimental, insecure, visionary, lustful, lazy, fat, bald, old, playful, fierce, irreverent, magical, wild, impractical, unconventional, intuitive, dreamers – and other things we're not supposed to be in a culture that circumscribes our lives with rigid roles to perform.[197]

And here's my male manifesto:

LET THEM FIX THEIR OWN TOILETS!

Women have power over life, the most important power there is. They can have what's left of my backbreaking "good paying" job; I don't want it anymore. I want to live as long as they do, spend as much money as they do, work as little as they do, and spend as much time with my kids as they do. They can make the money; I want the leisure time to reflect and create – I've earned it.

This society has been trying to tame men for 8000 years and hasn't succeeded yet. I don't need to own land and mow grass and accumulate wealth. I just need a passport and a couple hundred bucks; a fishing pole, some typewriter ribbons, a song in my heart and a dream that's as sharp and wide as the Deer God's antlers.

God bless all willful people.
May they find health and
prosperity
and happiness.

Chapter Six

The Psychic Swamp

1) **Jesus is the Greatest Archetype of all.**

2) **Now are you becoming wary of archetypes?**

THIS CHAPTER IS GOING to be about archetypes, but before we launch into that, let's recapitulate the previous, pain-filled chapter, under the simple heading of Misandry. Here's Patrick Arnold's definition of misandry:

Mis / an / dry (mis'-an-dree) n. hatred of men. 1: the attribution of negative qualities to the entire male gender. 2: the claim that masculinity is the source of such human vices such as domination, violence, oppression, and racism. 3: a sexist assumption that (a) male genes, hormones, and physiology, or (b) male cultural nurturing produces war, rape and physical abuse. 4: the assignment of blame solely to men for humanity's historic evils without including women's responsibility or giving men credit for civilization's achievements. 5: the assumption that any male person is probably dominating, oppressive, violent, sexually abusive, and spiritually immature.[198]

In previous chapters we reviewed misandry in law, the media, education, and religion. The answer to how the meme-makers can get away with such pervasive cultural misandry is: "archetypes". They have us playing their archetype game. There is no Twisted Side to the Great Mother that we can bring forward into conversation or debate. There are few, if any, positive male archetypes to bring into the arena. Carl Sagan stated that the world is endangered by "testosterone poisoning". Little did this manhole realize he was right, for the wrong reasons. Our world is threatened by a surge of testosterone poisoning spewing feminist memes from the mouths of lesbian and/or menopausal women – masculized females. Feminism is a disease of willfulness, spread by memes, which travel like viruses from brain to brain.

Says Arnold:

The day must come when a male-bashing comment marks the speaker, not as "politically correct", but as bigoted. The day must come when the automatic elimination of a male from a job search is seen, not as an instance of affirmative action, but as a case of sexist job discrimination. The day must come when a misandrist policy is regarded as atavistic, as out of place in modern society as Jim Crow laws, anti-Semitism, Know-Nothing rhetoric, and misogyny. And the day must come when ministers and politicians [and pop scientists] look on men with empathy rather than antagonism.[199]

Menopausal women – whose testosterone has risen as their estrogen has receded – are redefining our world. And they are not being fair about it. Their verbal brain patterning has created an array of archetypes which denies the Deep Masculine, and they attempt to draw us into debates using only their archetypes. It's as if we were trying to have a game of chess with only black players on the board. Enough of that, let's introduce some white men into the game.

The feminized memeology of our culture has overlooked hundreds, if not thousands, of positive male archetypes and negative female archetypes. Right off the top of my head, I have come up with a dozen archetypes, or "brain pictures" that have no home in our culture. They are:

1) The Phallus
2) The Green Man/Father Nature
3) Failure
4) The Twisted Side of the Goddess
5) Grandfathers
6) Father Earth
7) The Cook
8) The Pilgrim
9) The Hunter
10) The Hermit
11) Technocracy – The Evil Corporation
12) The Man Who Has Slain His Ego

As I've stated before, I'm very hesitant to put another foot down into the muck of the archetype-swamp. I've never known anyone to get cured of anything by "accessing" an archetype. But let's suppose that I am 100% wrong about this, that there is some value in this kind of poetry *cum* social science, and that there is indeed something to be learned here.

Says Richard Rohr, archetypal fascinations would seem like psychobabble to me if I had not seen the power of stories, icons, biographies, pictures, movies, celebrities and heroes in people's lives. Archetypes are filled with power. They lead you into the "sacred space" where you "see" for the first time. When you are in the grip of an archetype you have a vision and a deep sense of meaning in your life.[200] It can be, and often is, a stupid vision, he admits; and you can become "possessed" by an archetype the way the desert fathers talked of being possessed by demons.

Personally, I think that's nearer the mark. I've seen too many mythopoetic men worrying about what "animal name" to pick rather than where the nearest A.A. meeting is being held. Too many young women concerned about what their favorite celebrity is up to this week rather than how to boot corporations out of our political process. Too often archetypes take us away from life rather than to the center of it. They're psychic swamp gas – just another escape.

That aside, the central masculine archetypes always seem to be about power. How power is good, how power is contained, how power is shared, how power is used for others, how power is selfish, how power is spiritual. And who is the guy who is all about power? The guy I love to hate. The King. So let's have a brief look at the King.

Robert Bly has identified three kings: the Inner King, the Political King, and the Sacred King. What about Martin Luther King, B.B. King, Elvis, the King of Rock and Roll? What about Burger King? Two things quickly become ten thousand when we start analyzing the King, but let me choke my biases once again so we can get on with this.

The Inner King is what Freud calls the Id. His Majesty the Baby, the Ego King. In my opinion, this king must be slain. He's the one who wants everything his way. He wants to control everything. He inhabits the realm of endless opposition.

The Political King or Earthly King emerged, according to Bly, around 2000 B.C. in the city-states of Mesopotamia. His name is Gilgamesh. He's the one who sent the temple prostitute to seduce Enkidu, the natural man, away from his animal friends, so Enkidu would come live with him in the castle. He's the first manhole. He is a demigod, a man/god, who is *supposed* to receive his authority directly from the Sacred King. People throng to see the Earthly King in order to receive his blessing, which somehow comes directly from God. I've seen it in Tonga. Their Monarch is a guy who tried to make a deal with the State of Washington to take all their used tires and burn them in an electrical generating plant located on a pristine coral-reefed atoll in his South Pacific kingdom – thus trashing one of the last remaining undersea wonderlands in the world. Also, in the United Nations, he laid claim to the last remaining 14 satellite orbits to service the communication needs of his yam and fish economy. His subjects flock to him to receive his blessings the way others flock to see the Pope or Jackie O – that way maybe some of his royalty and grace will rub off on them. Clearly an ego proposition. Powerful, moving, psychic stuff. The exact opposite of spiritual awareness.

The Sacred King lives in a mythological, eternal, luminous realm. He's out there with Dionysus and Thor and the Virgin Mary and Kali and Allah and Zeus and Athena. Bly warns us to keep the human layer separate from the god layer and I think that's good advice. We do not find the Sacred King within us any more than we find Thor or Athena within us.

The most valuable part of the King-metaphor is the part that implies service. We SERVE the King. We are not the King, and can never be the King. He is born to it, not elected to it. There is no shame involved in not being King because we are not born to the position. The most a commoner can aspire to is to be one of the closest servants of the King. Service means surrender of your ego, your will, to a greater power.

Can the King help us? Possibly, but let's start calling the King by his real name. The King is God. I know that's off-putting to some people but the only significant part of the King-metaphor is the transcendent part. The Inner King is Ego. The Earthly King is a bozo. The Sacred King is the Good Father is the Life Force is the Source of Creation – is God. God is not a man. God is the source of the force that unfolds all of life in this world. God is energy. Good energy. Harmonious energy. If it's easier for you to surrender your willfulness to the Sacred King than to God – do that. *But do it.* Don't just nod your head and talk about how trippy the metaphor is. This is about surrender.

I've read the book *Iron John* five times and it has had an enormous impact on my life. I believe Bly redefined non-fiction writing with this poetic opus. And yet I do not find one single mention of the human will, of willfulness, or the pitfalls of willfulness, or the recovery from willfulness anywhere in this book. Certainly the theme is there, throughout the tale, from when the boy steals off with the Wildman, to his kitchen-ashes work, to concealing his golden hair under his hat. Surrender of ego is probably the main teaching of this story and Bly never mentions it. The notion of "ashes-work" touches on the idea in an almost mechanistic way, as if we were all bugs in a jar that some sadistic kid keeps shaking – but the effect of will is missing. Ashes is humiliation. Humiliation is the opposite of humility. When we are not humble, we get humiliated, like when we open the fridge door, cold air comes out. The object of spiritual teaching is to show us that as we rid our lives of willfulness, we rid ourselves of humiliations. You can't embarrass a nudist by taking off your clothes. You can't be humiliated if your pride, your ego, is not there.

When we stop acting willfully the psychic forces attempting to manipulate us have nothing to grab onto. We're *not there*. That's why the spiritual traditions tell us to empty ourselves. They're advising us to turn our willfulness back on itself and thereby free ourselves from the psychic forces that bind us like grasshoppers, hopping madly in endless reaction to life. Turn the will against itself – a sublime paradox. That's the real meaning of *free* will and is, in fact, the only free choice we ever make. The choice to not be willful. The choice to choose God.

No posse of elders is going to ride into our lives and save us. Our job is to slay the Inner King, fend off the Earthly King, and surrender our will and our lives to the Sacred King – God – the Life Force. The sooner the better.

Joseph Campbell said that our current spiritual malaise has something to do with the fact that our mythology has not caught up with our science. I think that's backwards. Our mythology *is* our science. "Accessing" a Black Hole is much more meaningful to me, personally, than "accessing" the King. A black hole is so dense if you dropped a pellet of one it would fall right through the earth like the earth was air; so dense that not even visible light escapes it, and yet so rich and full of the energy that comprises our world. I don't get the same mental blast out of calling up the image of the King. Astrophysics is a mystical science, so far beyond "logic" that it's breathtaking. What we need right now are some poet-scientists to present its wonders to our brains.

For the Egyptians, and the Hebrews (who drew much of their mythology from them) in the beginning was the "word". For Hindus in the beginning was the breath – the breath that formed the word. Maybe the Big Bang was a Big Sneeze. We in the West are too dependent on words to conceptualize our lives.

Yes, I use words all the time, and maybe that's why I'm so acutely aware that there are vast parts of my mind that can't be reduced to words. For me language is too literal, too feminine...I look outside the cabin window at a crow stealing a piece of bread off the porch and everything about the flight of this black winged creature over the wood pile into the permeable wall of forest green lies outside the reach of words. I take my fly rod and stand knee deep in the river casting upstream for cutthroat trout, my line looping through the mist against the backdrop of a blue snow-capped peak, and every part of this scene is outside the reach of words. I stand in the bow as our sailboat pulls in to a crystal clear cove on a South Pacific atoll. A squawking horde of fruit bats swarm along the jungle shore. We drop some handlines and catch snapper off the bottom as the sunset explodes in purple and yellow, and every part of this scene is outside the reach of words.

You think I painted pictures in your mind? I didn't. You painted your own crow and your own mountain and your own atoll. Words can only suggest. Words can only hint. The most important parts of life are invisible – and silent.

The breath of God animates all of creation – from the Big Sneeze to a baby's sneeze to the electrons whirling inside a rock. This world bears His invisible fingerprints and harkens to His inaudible voice. He talks rock-talk and tree-talk and wind-talk and meteor-talk. The Big Sneeze was a guy-thing: loud, noisy, chaotic, irrepressible and profoundly creative.

God is male.

Corporations are female.

Government is female.

Now there's something for social psychologists to choke on. Government and corporations operate according to rules and policies and procedures – female memes. God doesn't. He gave us the "law" of gravity, which – since the universe is now expanding faster than it was before – is currently up for grabs. Plus he put in some open-ended options to foster genetic variation: sexuality, genetic mutation, and a few as-yet undiscovered Lamarckian feedback loops between biological creatures and the environments they inhabit. And that's about it. No bureaucracy, no control…Oh yeah. We're supposed to love Him and love one another. But when we drop the ball on that we're the big losers.

God set up a universe of constant creation in which we can choose or not choose Him. We don't get to choose our government. Republicans and Democrats are two sides of the same corporate coin. We don't get to choose our power com-panies. We don't get to choose how much of our tax money goes to General Electric so it can develop new weapons systems which it then sells for a profit to other countries – thereby creating the need for more tax dollars to develop newer weapons systems. Preposterous. General Electric also owns the NBC media conglomerate.

A handful of transnational corporations dominate our global media telling us what to think and how to think while the other arms of these corporate octopi, their "advertising sponsors", manufacture the weapons we will need to "make the world safe for democracy", plus deliver our food, and our cars, and sell us insurance and banking services. There is no competition at the highest levels of corporate capitalism. Corporate capitalism smashes competition, routinely using our tax dollars to do so. There's a word for this: Technocracy. Technocracy means: when technology itself becomes an overbearing political force. We live in a technocracy where the needs of Microsoft and General Electric have become more important than the needs of working people. Says Andrew Kimbrell, a society in which the government serves technology before the needs of the people can in no way be called a democracy.

Lots of people think the internet is a great democratizing force. On a small level it is. We can fly information back and forth between our friends and comrades. But big corporations use it too. And when they use it things happen: currencies are destroyed, mines shut down, forests leveled. Technocracy, rule by technology, is the great new feminine evil. Corporations listened to the snake so long they became the snake. Our society has arrived at an awful place. It will kill people and starve people and pen them in ghettos in order to finance the advance of "technology". Technocracy: rule by *mater*ialistic, over-controlling, defensive, panicky, fear mongering, solicitous, prettified, media-friendly, FEMALE corporations.

We gotta get some men back in the game. Manhole politicians are killing us.

A friend once told me that my writing style is "a collection of essays". I'm gonna swerve away from the archetypes for a few pages and insert a guest sermon I gave at a Unitarian Universalist Church in Stow, Massachusetts. I need to nail down the facts about this unknown female archetype: Technocracy – the Evil Corporation. Technocracy is devouring men just like the Great Goddess did in ages past. Technocracy IS the psychic swamp. The problem is caused by what we are *not* being told. Meme warfare. Baffle them with Bullshit. Control them with Cowshit.

* * *

News Flash

Men are NOT the oppressors of women. Men are the protectors and providers for women. I know this doesn't fit in your brain easily. It contradicts the current dogma on the topic. I know that for 30 years we've been hearing that men are the oppressors of women. But I believe there is some merit in entertaining the idea that men are the protectors and providers for women.

Throughout human history men have hunted the buffaloes and mined the coal and made the money to bring energy into the lives of their women. Food energy, heat energy, money energy. Throughout human history, men have fought the wars and plowed the fields to bring safety and sustenance into the lives of women.

Today women can become Senators and Supreme Court Justices and Secretaries of State without every having to register for the Military Draft to defend the very form of government which has allowed them these high privileges. Men still take care of military obligations – even when they really really don't want to.

Men are the protectors and providers for women. I believe it's a deep part of our biological programming – of evolution. Women get pregnant – and for a while they become vulnerable, and they need to be supported by men who protect and provide for them. But, in the past few decades men's role as the protector and provider for women has been trivialized. While men are still expected to perform as economic engines, four distinct phenomena have eroded our earning abilities.

One: In the past 30 years 30 million women have entered the American workforce. This has had a huge impact on men. Think of our economy as a big water balloon. Squeeze on one side and another side bulges out. Everything is interconnected here. Nothing happens in a vacuum.

The facts on Affirmative Action are in. According to the General Accounting Office, over the past 30 years, 40% more white women are working, 30% more black women are working, 10% fewer white men are working, and 20% fewer black men are working. The very guys who were supposed to get helped by Affirmative Action are the ones who got hurt – black men.

But the numbers of working women is NOT the only factor, not the only hand squeezing on this water balloon that is our economy.

The second major impact on working men is that, in the past 30 years, 30 million immigrants have come to live in America. Do immigrants only take jobs Americans don't want? Not from where I sit. Once in awhile I need to take carpentry jobs or house painting jobs or cooking jobs to keep bread in my belly. Up until ten years ago I could find these jobs at will. Now I cannot.

I just heard that computer companies lobbied successfully for a special exception to the immigration bill now in Congress which will allow 180,000 high tech workers to enter the United States next year because the computer industry is suffering from a lack of trained employees. Is that true? It seems unlikely to me. My guess is they want to pay Bombay wages in Boston. So much for "education" and hard work. Let's have the Indian government train high tech workers and ship them to Boston to undercut our workers. The perfect corporate gambit. Increase profits, skip out on costs.

And then – the third factor – there's that other kind of immigrant into our economy. The robot. Automation and mechanization have removed millions of U.S. jobs. Whether its pneumatic nail guns in construction, or welding robots in car plants, or massive farm machinery that only corporations can afford; machines are being hired and people are being fired. And, unlike the governments in Europe and Japan which have legislated social contracts to protect people against the agendas of huge corporations, the American people are being abandoned. Welfare is under attack. We are being cast off into a black pit of joblessness with little social support. Welfare? If there wasn't welfare there would be armed insurrection!

The facts are that the U.S. government spends about $40 billion dollars a year on welfare for people, and over $400 billion dollars a year on Corporate Welfare – special advantages for corporations – tax credits, price supports, subsidies, direct government contracts. Corporate Welfare.

People don't want welfare. People want real jobs. Earlier in this century men were shuttled off the farms into the factories because corporations could grow food more efficiently. Now our factory jobs and even our high tech jobs are being *deported* overseas.

Since 1980 the U.S. has lost 2.6 million manufacturing jobs.

In 1965, 31% of our labor force had manufacturing jobs. By 1997 only 15% of our labor force had manufacturing jobs. That was the smallest share since the 1800s.

Our manufacturing and industrial jobs – jobs most often performed by men – are being deported overseas. The jobs being created in their wake are service-type jobs, computer jobs, jobs that attract more women than men. We are losing $20 an hour manufacturing jobs and getting $7 an hour service jobs.

Recently a guy in Iowa was told that the U.S. economy created 280,000 jobs in the last quarter. He said, "I know. My wife and I have four of them."

We've been led to believe that working women only earn 70% of men performing the same job. Not true. Working women earn 70% of men performing DIFFERENT jobs. Men do the harder, dirtier, more dangerous jobs: construction, mining coal, drilling for oil. Men also take the riskier sales jobs which are paid by commission, not by a regular salary. Women tend to do more information jobs, service jobs, office jobs. So men and women are being paid different wages for different work.

The transition into a service economy has had a tremendous impact on men and women – men are being put out of work, women are accepting low paying jobs.

And here we have arrived at the Fourth Factor affecting working men – the real problem. The problem we can actually do something about. The global economy. The corporate conquest of America. Corporate feudalism. Corporate greed.

For 50 years we fought a Cold War. We sacrificed. We lived in fear of ballistic missile attacks and watched our taxes rise from 3% in the 1950s to 30% today so we could finance a confrontation with the Soviets. But did we fight the Cold War to make the world safe for democracy? Or did we fight it to make the world safe for global corporations?

The instant we won the Cold War our corporations stepped up the process of deporting our jobs overseas. Why not? They didn't have to fear communist revolutionaries any more. They didn't have to worry about socialists organizing labor unions or trying to get health and environmental standards enforced. The instant we won the Cold War, our corporations sold us out.

Isn't it odd that for all the rhetoric hurled against centralized economic planning by governments during the Cold War, transnational corporations now assume it is THEIR right to plan the dimensions of the global economy – behind closed doors

– with no input whatsoever from citizens anywhere? Would it be fair to characterize the Cold war as a battle between state socialism and corporate socialism? I think so. Welcome to the era of Corporate Socialism.

Here are some disturbing facts:

Of the 100 largest economies in the world 51 are now corporations and only 49 are countries. General Motors – the 22nd largest economy in the world – is larger than Denmark, Thailand, Hong Kong or Turkey. GM is now the largest private employer in Mexico. Wal-Mart stores is larger than Israel or Greece.

Right now in America corporations are legally regarded as "persons". Corporate persons. That means they have rights to free speech (which means they can overwhelm us with advertising – and spend huge amounts of money lobbying congress) and they have rights to ownership of property (which means they can buy up everything in sight).

Keep in mind that these corporate "persons" do not eat, sleep, or die. They do not breath or feel anything. They skip out on paying taxes. They can be in a thousand places at once. They are not drafted in time of war. They commit felonious acts against our government and are not imprisoned. If a human person commits a felony he loses the right to vote and hold office and may be put in prison. He is not, like a felonious corporation, invited to testify before congressional hearings or to advise the White House.

Corporations only want to be regarded as "persons" when it is to their advantage. If they get in a jam overseas, send in the U.S. Army. Otherwise, just leave them alone. They operate in the free market you know.

Corporations want our taxpayer funded military protection. But they don't want to pay taxes. They want to partake of our government sponsored research and development. But once they've developed new products they choose to produce them overseas – not here, where they could create jobs for the very people who subsidized their research. Corporations want to make risky Third World loans, and expect U.S. taxpayers to bail them out if things go sour. They want all kinds of things from U.S. citizens, but when we ask something of them their attitude is, "Who us? You must be kidding! We're part of the free market."

When corporations are legally regarded as persons, human persons lose control of government. Living persons become second-class citizens because we do not have the money to oppose corporate persons politically.

In actual fact, no matter what the law says, corporations are not "persons", they are not citizens, they are economic nations. As such, instead of giving them tax deferments and government contracts, our government should be negotiating trade agreements with them as it would be doing with any other economic nation of comparable size. Israel has ambassadors in Washington and so does General Electric – but we don't call GE's ambassadors by that name. We call them lobbyists, and as such they can make eye-popping campaign contributions to both the Democratic and Republican parties without anyone asking, "What's going on here?"

They buy our politicians and they buy our elections. We vote for candidates who appeal to our social conscience. But when our elected officials walk out on the House and Senate floor, they vote the way of their corporate sponsors – the way of corporate money. Democracy in America has disappeared. This thing that started 200 years ago, down the road in Lexington, has vanished. Corporations control our political agenda. These corporations are not American citizens. They have proven they have no loyalty to this country. We should not be treating them as persons, but as foreign nations operating on our soil.

Here are some more unfortunate facts:

Between 1972 and 1994, real wages of working Americans fell 19%, the longest slide in three centuries.

In the last decade alone the number of working *men* who earn ONLY a poverty wage has increased 100%.

Since 1966 the share of American men with jobs has fallen from 85% to 76%. One in four men are out of work. Don't believe those "official" unemployment figures. They ignore the chronically unemployed.

There is no Free Market and no Free Trade. These are mere advertising slogans designed to appeal to our American ideals about fairness and justice. What Free Trade really means is that huge blocks of money can enter any economy on earth, and do whatever they want, with no regard for people's lives.

A true free market would be a market where people are allowed to form unions and enforce mutually desired health and safety and environmental standards. A true free market, a democratic market, is not based upon wage slavery, or child labor – like Mexico, or using troops to intimidate unions – like Indonesia, or threatening to move to a different country if wage and health and environmental standards are ACTUALLY enforced – like here. If corporations want to do business here let them pay the price of being here – let them contribute fairly to the American experience, not just sell their stuff here.

Free Trade pits one country against another in a bidding war to see who will provide the lowest wage and regulatory standards. We call this "letting the market set the price of labor". But according to George Soros, a world-renowned commodity trader, the market is, "dumb as a post, the market has no conscience, and the market will destroy itself if it is not regulated internationally, because the market is motivated only by greed."

What happened to our mom and pop grocery stores? Mom and pop hardware stores? Mom and pop restaurants? What happened to our TV and auto industries? What is now happening to our computer industry? Why are our jobs being deported overseas? How come working wages have been stagnant for 20 years while rich people and corporations got richer? Is it possible we are on the verge of a worldwide populist uprising against the abuses and manipulations of transnational corporations?

I think so.

Women are "inward looking". They're concerned about what they have and what they can get. Men are "outward looking" – spiritually and politically. It is the responsibility of men to solve the problems of the global economy. We are the ones who fought in, or fought against, WW II, Korea, Vietnam, Grenada, Panama and Iraq. We are the ones called to fight when corporations get in a jam overseas. We are the ones who, willingly or not, have been drawn into an economic war with this global corporate menace. We are losing our businesses and losing our jobs. But we don't stand a chance of winning alone. We need help.

In summary, American working men are being squeezed from four sides:

1) by working women

2) by immigrants

3) by mechanization

4) by global corporations

I'd like to suggest it's time for the women's movement to give men a break. I'd like to suggest it's time for women to realize that men are not the enemy. I think it's time for women to stop fighting men, and blacks to stop fighting whites, and for all of us to start pointing our spears in the right direction – at global corporations. It's time for us to regulate our transactions with these corporations by recognizing them for what they are – economic nations, legally disguised as persons, operating in our midst. And may God help us and guide us in this confrontation.

* * *

The spiritual is political. We learned that in the Civil Rights Movement. That's why Jesus was crucified. That's why Martin

Luther King Jr. and Mohandas Gandhi were shot. A genuine spiritual stand – as opposed to corporate butt-sucking, right-wing Christianity – is a foot to the neck of corporate socialism. We're in a war guys. We need to dig deep to find out who we are and what we are and how we can fight it. We need to resuscitate the Deep Masculine. Bring it out of hibernation. So here's a start:

God is Male. Nature is masculine – not feminine – masculine. The Farm is a female invention. The Factory is a female invention. The Corporation is a female invention. Government is a female invention. The King is a man who wears a dress. Judges are men in dresses. But Nature is masculine. Trees, mountains, streams, are masculine. In the ancient Mesopotamian and Mediterranean cultures, all vegetation – flowers, grass, wheat, grapes, lettuce – were imagined to be masculine. Each year the sprouted wheat stalk shoves above the earth; it swells and unfurls and hardens and releases its seed – then shrivels to nothing, just like your pee pee. Nature is masculine.

Naturally, the corporate/government/religious establishment in those days, the Goddess, decided to harness and control this masculine energy. Some things never change. Manhole priests cut the balls off young boys and let them bleed to death on June 21 and again on December 21. This was a pretty clear signal to even the most thick-headed guy. You will be sacrificed to the Goddess. (You will be sacrificed to General Electric. You will be sacrificed to Monsanto. You will be sacrificed to "make the world safe for democracy".) You are here to serve Us. We know, better than you, how to feed you and give you a good life. Without us making your decisions for you there is nothing but anarchy, chaos and death.

The boy they sacrificed was an uninitiated young boy – an adolescent boy, like the ones we send to war. He had no resource comparable to the Great Mother to draw energy from. She lived and he died. Some things never change.

Abraham was the one who put an end to this sacrifice. He substituted a ram for his son Isaac. Elohim didn't need human sacrifice. At that time this was a big deal, a slap in the face of the Goddess Astarte. Sacrilegious. A religious revolution. The beginning of the "patriarchy" and the end of human sacrifice as practiced on young boys by the Goddess cults.

Meanwhile, the "primitive" Europeans came up with a better solution to the problem of female institutions devouring men – The Green Man. Says William Anderson, The Green Man is an image from the depths of prehistory, vastly pre-Christian, who found his way into the court of King Arthur and whose face is literally carved into the pillars and arches of hundreds of churches in France, England and Germany. In his first and oldest form, the Green Man is a male head formed out of a leaf mask – his hair, his skin, his beard, are all formed out of leaf. Today, every spring, in parts of England, there are still parades to honor the Green Man. The Green Man is a powerful male image which was once known, then became unknown, and is now becoming known again.[201]

The Green Man signifies irrepressible life. He is *not agriculture*, but the explosion of dead trees and dried bushes and cold earth with the powerful green rush of springtime. Life, growth, renewal is active male energy. Go outside and look around. Hidden power, spiritual power, is oozing from every leaf and insect. Nature is not organized; it's organic. Chaos plus order – "chaordic" – according to Dee Hock. It's Taoist. A plant growing next to a wall grows away from the wall to get more light. It's not stupid, not willful, but charged with irrepressible life – Tao – moving along with physical reality. The vitality of nature, the Green Man, is masculine.

And how, you ask, did this freak get his face carved into hundreds of churches in Europe? Simple. That's how the Catholic Church works; it absorbs everything. When you go to Guatemala, you will see the Quetzalcoatl bird carved into the pillars of the churches. This is a sign to the local Indians that their god has a home here and therefore his devotees are welcome here. Same with the Green Man. The church enticed these stinky, hairy foresters – these Vandals – out of Bavaria, and the Alps, and Wales, by carving their god right into the walls of the church. In time, he was absorbed and forgotten by the men who wear dresses. Oh well. Time to be remembered again.

The Green Man is powerful and immortal and honorable and bold. He is the Life Force, recreating life anew every spring with his sheer vigor. He is not Mother Nature. He is Father Nature – the deep fertile male energy. He is not nurturing; he is irrepressible, unstoppable. God didn't nurture the universe into existence. He made a Big Bang – a Big Sneeze. It was a guy thing. If we insist on utilizing the poetry of archetypes, the Green Man is probably the best one going to give meaning to the lives of men. Pick up any can of Jolly Green Giant corn – there he is! They've made a fool of him – put him to work as a corporate water boy – but so what? He's irrepressible. Just don't forget that this is not the Potato King. This is no god of agriculture and well-kept fields. This is every leaf and berry and blade of grass – the very Life Force that feeds the birds, the spawning fish, the hungry bear – the Source of the Force.

Mother Nature's face is not carved into any churches in Europe I've heard about. They pulled a fast one. They've been doing it for millennia. They keep making our gods into women!

The Green Man is Father Nature. Intermingled with the notion of Father Nature is Father Earth. The Vedic Purusha is the progenitor of the earth as is the Chinese Pan-ku. Does Pan-ku meander backwards to some common root with the Greek god Pan? I don't know. Dumuzi and Enki (Enkidu) were Sumerian earth gods, as was Ogun in Africa. Hephaestos, Vulcan, was lame. He was the blacksmith of the gods who worked the metals of the earth into magical shapes. Geb was an Egyptian earth god. Why an earth god? Why an earth father? The earth is constant and grounded, steady and at peace, like men. We're not breezy and batty and unfocused like you know who. Men are solid, like the earth. Men move about freely on the earth. Women stuff their fears in their backpacks and carry them along with them. Men are cool and still and unmoved, like the earth.

And what about the Man in the Moon? asks Kipnis. How did the moon ever get ascribed to the feminine? Osiris in Egypt was known as the lord of the moon. In Sumeria the Moon Father was worshipped as Nanna. In Serbia he was known as the Bald Uncle. He was worshipped in Greenland and India and Malaya and Australia. In Babylonia he was named Sinn, in Ireland Saint Luan. The Eskimos speak of Brother Moon.

Men are subject to cycles, too, just like women, just like the moon. We have our off-days, and our power days. We are sometimes luminous, sometimes half-on, and sometimes black and obscure. If we recognize masculinity as moonlike, we can accept and appreciate the biological waves and emotional currents that run through us. We don't always have to perform and we need not be ashamed by a poor performance.

Archetypes are like maps or symbols of certain sectors of the psyche, says Aaron Kipnis. Archetypal forces are bigger than our individual egos. In learning to work with archetypes, we have come to realize that, to a significant degree, we are all powerless. The forms of the gods are infinite in their variety and vast in their complexity. We cannot control them. Perhaps, through our attempts to know them, we will gain some insight into the myriad forces that move our lives from within and without.

Perhaps is the key word for me in the preceding sentence. Kipnis is doing a noble job of combining archetypes with 12 Step philosophy. If it works for you, use it. I happen to get a lot more insight about the myriad forces that move our lives from within and without by knowing that men have more right brain capacity than women; that men are more intuitive, and less verbal or rational than women; and that men perceive life in terms of actions, not words. To me, there is only one decision we ever make: to serve God, or not to serve God. Everything unfolds from there. Understanding Life matters much less than serving Life. Yes, we can capture all the fame and money our shamed egos crave by following the stuff that is not God, but we will never get happy. As high as we get is how low we will get. It is the realm of endless opposition.

We don't seem to understand this in America because we don't understand Failure. Failure is the most important thing that happens in life and we treat it like a bullet through the neck. No growth, no sloughing off of ego, ever happens in the glory of success. Every sage will tell you that the path to enlightenment is paved, not with success, but with Failure. Understanding comes from success, Wisdom comes from Failure. We must create room in our Western psyches for Failure. To Fail means you tried something and it didn't work. Welcome to the club! Humans are blessed with overactive imaginations and most of the things we try don't work.

Failure is the mortal enemy of the deeply shamed person and, because there are so many of us un-initiates in this society, we are plagued by Failure like hordes of flesh-devouring rats. We can't stand to fail. Abraham Lincoln went bankrupt twice then went on to save the Union. Albert Einstein discovered that everything is energy and that knowledge was used to blow the people of Hiroshima and Nagasaki to radioactive dust. Failure. It fried his brain.

We don't know enough to know what failure is and what it isn't. Joseph got sold into slavery by his brothers and was able to bail his family out of a famine 20 years later. The Dalai Lama gets kicked out of Tibet and spreads Tibetan Buddhism all over the face of the earth. *Anything* that does not harmonize with the designs of the Life Force will fail. And so what? The Life Force doesn't provide us a computer printout of what we're supposed to be doing down here. Our "job" is to try stuff, and see if it works. If it doesn't work, pull out the symbolic Tibetan *vajra* sword, cut your ego out of it, and go on to the next thing. Only an Addictive Society, as obsessed with "control" as we are, could fail to see the wondrous properties of Failure.

When you Fail, it hurts; and what hurts is your ego. Krishna tells us in the Bhagavad Gita that we must work, but we must *let go of the fruits of our labor*. It doesn't matter if what we do works or not. It matters that we try, and that we fail, and that we try again. Certainly success is the greatest ego-building proposition there is. Failure moves our psyches outside the realm of endless opposition to where we make an honest and conscious attempt to annihilate the yapping voices of our ego, serve the Life Force, and let go of the results. Failure is Wisdom. Success is short-lived. Success is a trap.

Look at Mahatma Gandhi. He kicked the British out of India and set an international standard for non-violent resistance. And in the wake of his achievements? We have a seemingly endless Hindu-Moslem bloodbath in northern India. Failure? Or Success? What we do matters not at all compared to how we do it. General Norman Schwarzkopf made a famous speech to his troops after the Gulf War in which he commended them for respecting the religion, morals, customs, and cultures of the countries they were ordered to occupy. This was a man who had taken the Failure of Vietnam deep into his heart and came up with something better. He learned something from that Disaster.

Don't be afraid to Fail. We are only human. We cannot imagine the good things that will come of our Failures.

Jesus was a famous Failure. Everything he touched turned to vinegar, including his church. He was so diplomatically inept, so politically incorrect, he was crucified for it.

Jesus was an attempt to ground God again, to bring Him down, down out of the night sky and walk the earth as a man. Jesus was an attempt to bring back the male earth god, the Earth Father, who was then missing in the Hebrew tradition and the Greek tradition.

And before Jesus, there was the Phoenix. The Phoenix was the bird that rose in the flames of the campfire, reaching its flashing wings into the night sky and then died in the ashes, only to be reborn again. The Phoenix is one of those universal myths that Joseph Campbell has talked about – from Egypt to Persia to India to China, to Japan, and down into Mexico we hear the story of this bird, born again from its own ashes. Clearly, this is a story speaking to us from across many millennia. It is talking about death and resurrection, and the meaning of life. Jesus is the humanoid form, the Greek form, of this powerful message of rebirth.

Another favored archetype of the Jungians is the Warrior. It is both the most useful archetype, and the most abused. In the Judeo/Christian tradition, the confusion starts with Yahweh.

Says Patrick Arnold:

The previous deity of the Hebrews was the sky god, Elohim, a wonderful, patriarchal old god who mythically ruled the world from his throne on the cosmic mountain. Then along came Moses who got his ten commandments from Yahweh, the warrior god, who had freed the Hebrews from Egyptian captivity. In the Canaanite hill country, the Yahweh preachers proclaimed a kind of late Bronze Age "good news" to the poor and oppressed Hebrews: Yahweh is Elohim! The great God of the universe is the same one who freed us from bondage.[202]

Robert Moore has emphasized that a true warrior's most important quality is that he surrenders his will to a purpose greater than himself – a Lord, a Higher Power. That distinction gets muddled when your god *is* a warrior. Witness Israel and its *mater*ialist progenitor, the USA. The highest purpose of these Corporate Socialist states is to serve themselves, the rationale being that all the goodness they embrace will go out of existence if these government/corporate golems entities cease to exist – female control memes.

Bly tells a Japanese story about a pond that had lost its king. Uncertain about what to do, the pond's inhabitants – frogs, fish, tadpoles – elect, as king, a heron (who, in Japan, is associated with the warrior). The heron eats everybody up. An empowered individual who is not in service to a Higher Power is a pox on society. It cannot be stated often enough that the danger of Marxist/Feminism is that its highest purpose is to serve itself. The Addictive Society, operating on Marxist/Feminist memes, plays right into the hands of the high priests of corporate culture.

The other important attribute of the Warrior is that he must never kill out of passion. Another Japanese tale relates how a samurai warrior was entrusted with the task of hunting down the man who assassinated his lord and patron. He tracked the assassin from province to province, the assassin constantly eluding him. At last, years later, he came face to face with the man walking on a road. The samurai raised his sword to kill. The assassin, unarmed, spit in the samurai's face. The samurai blustered, and grimaced – then dropped his sword and walked away. Why? The spit in his face infuriated him, and, to stay true to the code of the warrior, he must never kill in anger.

Women deride us for not exposing our feelings. Let them. In the place beyond feelings is where we do our service to God. Telling them our feelings is like selling Iraq the very weapons they use against us in a war two years later. Few women understand the depth of honor and dignity and goodness that comes out of the silent place – the Deep Masculine. "Talking about feelings" is a feminist meme. We have a right – even a duty and an obligation – not to talk about our feelings. Our feelings come from a place that is beyond words, and what we have said we are doing now is putting some white men back in the game. We don't need to talk about feelings, or even to have feelings that can be talked about. We have a right to our own mindspace. We have a right to honor and sustain the Deep Masculine.

The warrior's "job" in daily life is to warn us when someone intends to pass on some of her shame to us. There are people in our lives who – no matter what you show them, no matter what you tell them – they'll poke a hole in it. They're not *listening*. They're unloading their shame onto us. Advice-giving is a particularly prevalent form of shaming practiced by women and manholes. I have a brother who picked up this habit from his parents. When shown a painting I worked on for months, he'll say something like, "Don't you think that guy's lips are too big?" He's not looking at the painting; he's unloading shame onto me. According to John Bradshaw my response should be, "I choose not to be shamed by you today." Maybe the guy's lips *are* too big, maybe I want them big, maybe his hands are exquisite, or maybe the subject matter of the painting warrants some comment. But these things do not make it out of his mouth. He needs to unload shame and just talking to such a person, about anything, is a shaming encounter.

We are constantly being shamed and we are not consciously aware of it. It chokes us and makes us shrivel inside. My mother-in-law and her daughter were famous for their shame. It was impossible to have a conversation with them without feeling like you were run over by a road grader. How I dress, how I hold my fork, how I blow my nose – all major topics of conversation. Never anything about the meaning of life or the purpose of art. The Tibetans have an answer for such a problem. They call it the *vajra* sword. It's a sharp interior sword intended for our use in slicing away illusions and attachments – and shame. When you slash the *vajra* sword in front of your face, you can separate yourself from shame and stupidity. You can then say, "I choose not to shamed by you today." You can rest in your silent home in the Deep Masculine.

Recently I stumbled upon a shame-annihilating technique I call DNA. When someone says I'm stupid, I can either say, "You're right," "You're wrong," or "DNA" – Does Not Apply. That's the third option, the option our binary culture has relegated to mental oblivion. When someone is trying to shame you, just say "DNA", and watch them squirm. People hate it when they can't pass on their shame to you. DNA – Does Not Apply.

According to Forrest Carter's grandpa, women are born suspicious – and critical, and contentious. They like to fight. My feeling about that is – let them fight with each other. I don't have the time for it. My warrior is engaged in a holy war out here against the evil forces of corporate *mater*ialism. I don't need to be fighting with my spouse or lover. Women need deep passion and when the pleasures and excitement of sex wear off, they take to fighting – just so they can feel *something* deeply. Let them. We have a deeper purpose to serve. We fight when there's a war; we don't need to fight with the garbage men and the checkout women. Women are famous for winning the battle and losing the war. Their right brains do not afford them the "big picture" that we enjoy.

"My father never stood up to my mother and I'm angry about that," hundreds of men have told Robert Bly. With the power women wield in divorce court and as praise-givers, it's easy to see how this can happen. My house was the same. Everyone's house is the same. Those of you who grew up with dominating fathers are quite the exception. Rock star Jim Morrison said that his dad, who was the captain of a US Navy aircraft carrier with thousands of men under his command, used to come home on shore leave and silently endure his wife screaming at him to take out the garbage and wash the dishes. Morrison, the greatest American poet, seethed with rebellion against female memes. In his Miami concert, he said, "You are all slaves!"

The opposite of praise is shame. We are addicted to praise at a young age, and when that praise is withheld, we automatically experience shame. We are praise junkies, just withhold the drug and we go into *delirium tremens* – D.T.s. When the battle to shame us has gone on long enough, it's important to bring out the *vajra* sword and just say, "Enough!" And mean it. That is the warrior. The spiritual warrior. The Deep Masculine. The soldier of peace. Peace through strength.

Another favorite archetype is the Trickster. The Trickster does not go with the flow, he reverses it. The Trickster is a master of "two-wayness" says Kipnis. He's good and bad, yin and yang, desert and lake, full of contradictions – just like us. He's fearless and willing to expend great effort to confound us.

The Trickster is present in all world cultures. He is around to take on the humorless ones, the ones who are so certain of their human perceptions. In Japan, he is called *Tanuki San*, a badger-like creature with big balls who carries around a bundle of useless I.O.U.s to hand out to unsuspecting shopkeepers. I've been on the wrong side of this one and it's not much fun, but it sure is eye-opening. Tricksters are as capricious as life. They will save your farm from a flood and then get your daughter pregnant. They are not nice guys, but we can only be hurt by them when we let our ego or our greed step out ahead of us. Tricksters are beyond logic. Jung called them god/man/ animal, all at once. A Trickster will even take on the gods, so convinced is he of his cunning. And when his self-centered manipulations blow up in his face, we laugh, not at him, but at ourselves. Feminists need a female Trickster more than they need a female president.

The Trickster teaches what Wes Niker calls Crazy Wisdom. Conventional wisdom is the habitual, the unexamined – 'a stitch

in time saves nine' kind of thing. Crazy Wisdom is – if you see
the Buddha in the road, kill him! This punctures our bubble of
complacency, it makes us think, it drops us out the airplane
window into the paradox.

Coyote is the premier Native American trickster. His favorite
medium of creation is dung – a shit into gold kind of thing –
alchemizing adversity. People think they are fooling him and
then BLAM!, they're caught in their own trap.

In the Pacific Northwest the Trickster is raven; for Eskimos
it is crow. Raven created light while fooling around with
blackness when he was a kid.

In Africa, they have Ashanti, and Kaggen, and Legba and
Eshu, who likes to stir things up. One story has him wearing a
hat painted a different color on each side as he walks through a
field. When he gets to the end of the field, he reverses the hat
and walks back. The people on each side of the field get into a
fight that night over what color hat he was wearing. The Trickster
tricks us into realizing that there are things we cannot know
from where we sit. Similarly, Zen instructors give their students
koans, paradoxical poems that are designed to wear down their
rational minds, free them from logic, which is the first step on
the path to enlightenment.

The Trickster is an outlaw. Clint Eastwood is one in the
spaghetti westerns. Bob Dylan is one, and the Rolling Stones
and Willie Nelson. We need outlaws sometimes to keep us honest.
When the principal is fucking the English teacher on his desk
it's time for some freshman to put a burning bag of shit outside
the principal's door and ring the bell. Every system rots from
within. Our freely elected congressmen turn into corporate
bagmen and the time has come for us to put a burning bag of
shit on the Capitol steps and ring *their* bell. Robin Hood becomes
the Sheriff and then the Trickster pays him a visit.

Says Kipnis, Brer Rabbit is a fun Trickster. He gets his
captors to punish him by throwing him into the briar patch – his
home. A turtle in Aesop gets banished to a lake – his home. The
Trickster often operates by allowing other people to think they

are tricking or controlling him when in fact he is getting them to do his bidding.

The defenses against the Trickster are humility and honesty, some of the most praised and least practiced human qualities. Honest people can't be tricked. When you think you're screwing the piss out of the guy who is selling you a Mercedes for $200 'cause he "needs the cash, man," you better check the number on the title against the number on the engine block. The Trickster will out-ego your ego and out-greed your greed every time. Street hustlers are 9/10ths Brer Rabbit – quick mind, sharp nose, big ears – look out.

Says Kipnis, overheated, polarized arguments are often improved by the entrance of the Trickster. The Trickster is a force that deflates pomposity. He is melded into the personas of our political leaders. He's there when Saddam Hussein proclaims he won the Gulf War. He's there in Tricky Dick Nixon, who made a catastrophe out of our whole political system. Here the trickster tricked himself right out of office. He's there as a ragged bum gnawing on a tit of salami on the steps of the hotel where Gloria Steinem and Patricia Ireland are holding their press conference. He's there all the time, but we don't see him.

The Trickster reminds us that on the quest for masculine soul there is much we do not understand. Life is a paradox. What appears to be solid matter is but a whiff of energy. The surest structures, of mind or matter, collapse under entropy. The only certainty is change. The Trickster is there to remind us that there is always an imp in the shadows, gnawing on salami, who, once released into our lives and minds, is quick to restore balance. In modern science, we know the Trickster as Chaos Theory – Complexity Theory – stable systems move toward instability and unstable systems move toward stability. Why? Who knows? But it's a fact as observable as gravity. The Trickster is Chaos. He is the reason why we inhabit a universe of variety rather than a homogeneous blob.

Says Bly, a whole community of beings is what we call a grown man, and one of these beings is the Mythologist, or Cook. The Cook controls animal and vegetable, fire and water. He can peel an apple or fillet a fish. He employs "secret" herbs and spices to bring forth flavor. The Cook knows how long cooking should go on and how to move from one stage to another. Sauces meld, yeasts rise, there's no way to rush it without burning it. Cooks know the parameters of physical and mental reality. The Cook takes things that are raw and gooey and turns them into platters that look and smell and taste divine. He knows not to mix too many different spices and just how much salt.

Cooking is not learned by talking about it, but by doing it. Women are great cooks, but the best cooks, the chefs, are men. Would women have us believe that this is yet another example of us "holding back" their creativity? Come on. Let's call it like it is. Men are naturally more creative, and it shows in cooking, or fabric design, the same way it shows in arts or business.

Cooks love to have a lot of implements – garlic crushers, sushi rollers – but they can make a feast with some damp wood, a rusty knife, and something they hit on the road.

Cooking enough food for 200 people is hard work. Kitchens are hot and dangerous – sharp knives, flame broilers, boiling kettles that take two men to handle – one slip and someone gets burned.

Mythologists are the cooks of the psyche. They perform their alchemy with different flavored words and tasty insights and delicious images. They start with the raw vegetables of our daydreams and the butchered meat of our hearts, mix in some spicy nightmares, a few tablespoons of lust, throw it all into a boiling pot of grief, and what do you get? The Virgin Mary, maybe. Or Marilyn Monroe. The Green Man come to cut off his head (his ego) right in front of you – like he did at Arthur's Court – and challenge you to do the same. Or Parsifal, the Grail Quester, who spent forty years without ever asking the right question. Or maybe even the Beatles, wagging their happy heads.

What'll it be tonight? Some Huevos Marilyn Monroe? Or Marinated Mary? Stir Fried Green Man? Or Deep Fried Parsifal? Or maybe even a little Barbecued Beatles with a side dish of Cold Turkey to keep you up all night. Or maybe we should whip up some Anarchist Egg Rolls for Jack Welch, CEO of General Electric, or some Conscience Cookies for the corporate boot-lickers in the U.S. Senate.

Cooking is knowing how food works. Mythology is knowing how life works. I find it meaningful to divide the world into the people who know how to clean a fish, and the people who don't. Here I find a sharp distinction. People who can clean a fish know what blood is and what guts are, and what they are for. They are not afraid to slip their hands into the slimy goo of life. They know that food comes directly from God – Father Nature – fish being one of the few foods that are not planted or shepherded or husbanded (except for some salmon and catfish and prawns). God gives free food if you are persistent and patient enough to go out and get it. That's a wonderful thing to know.

Little boys seem to know it in their bones. Little boys are natural hunters, like little kitties. That's what they like to do: chase bugs, throw stones at birds, pick up fallen branches and toss them like imaginary spears. The baseball pitch is essentially a spear-throwing motion – a hard follow-through, close to the body, for maximum aiming ability. Sitting at computer terminals is woman's work.

The Fisherman is the Hunter of Fish. Mythologically, fishing has always been a metaphor for delving into the subconscious mind. Fishing – as represented by the Fisher King of the Parsifal Legend – is about lowering a thin line and a small hook into your subconscious to see if you can pull something up – up from the obscure depths of your psyche, from a realm your vision cannot penetrate, but which you know, intuitively, is thriving with life and drama and activity.

Fishing and hunting operate on pure intuition – no logic is required, no talking is required. In fact, logic and talking only get in the way of the action. The fish and birds are never where you think they are, but sometimes they are somewhere close. I've gone snorkeling in ponds and lakes and oceans, and found thousands of places where I would hang out if I were a fish – but there were no fish there. Geese don't hang out in the cornfields where there are piles of food; they hang out on the golf course down the street because they know you can't shoot them there.

I believe in something called Fish Mythology whereby fish teach each other what kinds of baits the fishermen are using this year – and not to bite on them. Old standby lures of five years ago don't work anymore. Old fish know, just like old men.

The Hunter has a great reverence for nature and a great reverence for life. He is the original conservationist, the original Earth-Firster. He wants there to *always* be wild land and wild water. He sneers at civilization, and he worships the god who feeds him. Pheasant hunters love pheasants. They love seeing them. They love seeing their tracks. They love showing them to their kids – in all seasons. And the same goes for deer hunters, I'm sure.

The Hunter knows when to shoot, and when *not to shoot*. A wounded animal that runs away and dies in a cave makes him sick to his stomach.

Nets dropped in the ocean by commercial fishermen killing everything that comes along, make him sick to his stomach. Paper mills churning out paper diapers and newsprint and computer paper, that pollute trout streams and poison walleye lakes, make him sick to his stomach. Suburban sprawl that destroys the pheasant fields make him sick to his stomach. Herbicides and pesticides and petro chemicals dumped on farmers' fields that weaken the shells of bird eggs, any bird eggs, make him sick to his stomach. Genetically modified plants that wipe out butterflies make him sick to his stomach.

Mushroom hunting and berry picking are other great forms of hunting – seeking out the food that God has given – for body and spirit. The Hunter is the oldest archetype in the human psyche. Before Krishna or Astarte or Yahweh, was the Hunter. It is the Hunter's memes, more than any other, that graze on the vast neural plains of our minds. The Hunter kills only for food and never in anger. The Hunter is *not* a soldier nor even the prototype of the soldier. The Hunter does not kill men. The Hunter is not protecting a castle full of jewels or silk-shrouded maidens. All that is the King's doing. The Hunter prays to his prey – get it; it's the same word. It is only with an indescribable mixture of reverence and sadness and joy that he takes the life of the god that feeds him, the prey he loves so much.

Well, you say, he could always raise pheasants in his back yard. I've done that. It's not the same. The neighborhood dogs break in and eat them like candy. And anyway, hunting is something you do, it's a place you go to, it's not something you just talk about.

A deep, intuitive, exciting door opens in your brain when you shove off in a small boat in the dark, or step away from the jeep at dawn on the top of a mountain. Something happens. Something ancient and beautiful clicks on. If you see a bird or a fish, great. If you bag something, great. If you don't, it doesn't matter. You were there, in the right place with the right stuff, ready, and God wasn't ready. That, too, is a lesson. You can't make this happen. You can only be ready and be in the right place and wait. It's like Grace. You can't have Grace. You can only be ready and wait to receive it.

For me fishing is a metaphor for the meaning of life. You prepare your hooks and lines, you put yourself out there in God's country, and you wait. You learn your prayers, you say your prayers, and you wait. You do everything you can to be ready, and you wait for Grace to find you. That's what we're all doing down here – fishing.

And anyway, you left all your worries back there with the microwave and the leaky sink and the calendar hung on the kitchen wall. There is NO TIME on the hunt. 2.2 million years of human history are compressed into an instant and that instant is NOW. Raising vegetables is important work, but going hunting is forever. Hunting is not about killing, it's about living.

You wanna access a big time archetype? Go fishing or hunting. It's automatic. It's fresh fish for your soul – the kind of food that will sustain you through this corporate world war. A mental meal that will remind you what freedom is.

As long as we're talking about guns, let's talk about dicks. Eugene Monick has noted that when men are not connected to *Phallus*, everything is feminine. Phallus is archetypal earth-based masculinity; Monick's warning is exactly the point of this book.

Everything is feminine: the government, the schools, the churches, and the job. When men experience life solely through women, castration has begun. In America, castration has begun. We are offered, in a choice between two political candidates, two female enforcers, two corporate bagmen. Al Gore comes out in favor of women's rights, *and* saving the environment. That's a disconnect, a stark contradiction in policies. Women want to have jobs and buy more stuff, and the more they succeed the more wasted the environment gets. Feminists are corporate whores. Let's see Gore come out against paper diapers, then we'll have something.

Says Kipnis, in cultures without initiation rites boys are in danger of entering a son-lover-victim relationship with the Goddess. In other words, "Jewish mothers" emasculate boys. We see pictures of breasts everywhere but no penises. Are penises evil? Ask your Jewish Mother. Ask your Christian Mother.

We live in a society permeated by Fear of Phallus. I can walk into any convenience store and buy a sex magazine that shows two women eating each other's cunts – utter perversion – or sucking some guy's cock – group sex – but if that magazine were to show one single penis doing what a penis was designed to do it would be yanked off the shelf and put in a special XXX store. Why are we afraid of phalluses? Yes, our big skyscrapers represent phalluses, but the dome on the Capitol is a Big Tit! If we were truly a Patriarchy, we would not house our Congress in a Big Tit. If we were truly a Patriarchy we would be worshipping penises, not concealing their generative power. Instead, we worship breasts…And corporations and feminists flock to Washington to suck off the

Big Tit

Penises show up frequently throughout world art in all cultures except the Judeo/Christian – yet more overwhelming evidence of the feminization of western culture. Cave paintings in France from 15,000 B.C. show engravings of phalluses – notably the Sorcerer of Trois Frères. Icons of the earth-bull-father god sporting an erect penis are found in Hungary, Mesopotamia, India, Sumeria, Egypt, Crete and Greece. Bronze Age stone phalli are found in Denmark, Norway and Sweden, and there is a wooden image of a phallic god in Copenhagen which dates back to the Celtic Iron Age.

Kipnis reports that one of the earliest Japanese myths tells about the magic power of the phallus to prevent agricultural disaster and cure disease. There are remains of phallic standing stones all over England. Yes, these big dicks sticking up out of the earth signify something, from Stonehenge to the Sears Tower what we're seeing is the Big Pee Pee of the Earth Father standing erect and virile and full of creative power, pricking the belly of the sky.

Does the Judeo/Christian meme have any icons that represent the Big Dick? Of course. The spires of cathedrals harken back to the cult of the Earth Father. In fact, the great cathedrals of Europe were built by members of the original Masonic Guild who trace their guild all the way back to Egypt in the time of the Pharaohs, where they also built the pyramids, the Big Pee Pees of the Earth Father of the Nile Valley.

Female memes have prevented us from associating the spires of our churches with God's Penis, but what else could they represent? The Earth Father himself is unashamedly displaying the erect power and the life-giving force offered to us through His church. This is God the Father. This is male spirituality. And how do we honor it? We have sexless men parading around in dresses waving incense and singing sweet songs. It's like a perpetual funeral for the Earth Father. But still the Deep Masculine persists. It is something that was once known, and became unknown, and is now erupting into our minds, our memes, to become known again.

In the pre-Columbian Americas, Aztecs and Mayans erected entire temples devoted to the phallus. Hindus today still make offerings to the lingam, a vertical lump of clay, which is a two-fold symbol: 1) of the penis, 2) of the formless God, the God beyond shape and beyond apprehension by the senses. The Hebrew God is both male, and without form – the same paradox, the same idea.

Says Kipnis, it is very clear that for thousands of years in many different cultures, the cock was holy. We, in the west, are almost alone in how we have debased this symbol as a representation of violence and aggression rather than of fertility and healing. Our native Americans erected totem poles, Big Pee Pees, embossed with the animal archetypes that gave strength and meaning to their lives. I want to see Phallic Art reemerge in the West, and not only the lusty, sensual kind produced by pornographers and smirking homosexuals. We need real Phallic Art that penetrates the mysteries and inseminates our minds with the memes of the Deep Masculine. We need Male Phallic

Art to reform our psyches. It's essential. Men don't work in words. We work through our right brains, in silence, with visuo-spatial relationships, not verbal relationships. That's why art has always been important to men, that's why men have always been the best artists, and that's why we need Phallic Art.

Robert Bly has observed that there are no good fathers in Greek Mythology. Cronos ate his own kids. Zeus was a phil-anderer and cowardly about facing up to his own wife. Yahshua – who the Greeks dubbed "Jesus" – was resurrected in the wake of this Greek Mythology of people *cum* gods. He was born "illegitimately" and spent his whole life looking for his invisible Father. King Arthur radiates generosity like a kind uncle, but he is no father figure. Buddha was a father, but not a memorable one. He named his son "Impediment". Phallus has been taking a beating for the last 8000 years from Greece to China.

Meanwhile, the Polynesians had Maui, who went fishing one day, got his hook stuck on the floor of the Pacific Ocean, and yanked up the Hawaiian Islands. Here is a good look at the kind of Phallus that used to inform our lives before we got "civilized". Hawaiian men embody the widest spectrum of male attributes, from heartiness to gentleness, of any society I have yet encountered – and we only found out they were there 200 years ago. Kilauea Volcano is still today an erupting phallus spewing molten semen and creating new land. The fiery, temperamental goddess Pele is caretaker of the big dick, but it's Maui's dick.

The Christians brought forward the image of God the Father – Jesus' *Abba*. This was not a Jewish thing. And that's probably why Christianity enjoyed such sudden acceptance amongst those "primitive" Green Man-worshipping Europeans, and Hawaiians, and other tribal peoples. Sophisticates like to bash Christian missionaries but when they got to Hawaii, King Kamehameha was slaughtering everybody he could get his hands on. That was quickly arrested. When the Christians got to Tonga the people were cannibals, a habit they had recently picked up in Fiji. God the Father would not sit still for that shit. Anyone who didn't want to be eaten quickly became Christian. God the Father is God the Phallus, and there is nothing obscene about that.

There is great healing power to be found in praying to a Deep Male Life Force.

The most neglected and ignored archetype in our society is God the Father's Father – Grandpa. A God who has no beginning and no end doesn't have a father. This, for me, is the big flaw in the Christian metaphor – they made the whole movie without Grandpa.

Says Rohr:
Grandfather energy is energy that is quiet and secure. It has been tested and it has not been found wanting. It does not need to prove itself any longer, and so it can approve the efforts of others who are not, as yet, sure of themselves. Children can feel secure in the presence of grandparents because, while mom and dad are still rushing to find their way through life's journey, grandpa and grandma can create a space where the journey has found its end and purpose.

Grandfathers can trust life deeply precisely because they have come to terms with death. They know that pain is not the enemy; the enemy is fear of pain. They have lived through enough of life to understand that, in the long run, life is stronger than death.[203]

Grandfathers recognize the surge of the divine spirit in the human situation. Because they trust that ultimately, God is in control, they can let go of the desire to control reality and bend others to their will. They can stop trying to force life, as they often did when they were younger men, and simply allow it to flow in the patterns which eventually – if not directly and immediately – lead to greater life.

Grandfathers are not naive. They know what death looks like even when it comes under the guise of false promises and clever rationalizations. They look beyond the ignorance of those who desire money and pleasure. They have heard enough politician's promises and advertiser's claims to know that they are largely empty. They know what's worth fighting for and what isn't. Grandfathers understand that every human decision inevitably mixes good and bad.

The proponents of the Fix-It-Philosophy don't seem to be able to get this straight. *Every* decision removes energy from one sphere and gives it to another. A female president is going to be just as beholden to special interests as any man, just as corrupted by the pathways to power, just as egotistical. To imagine otherwise is some kind of psychic fantasy.

Continues Rohr:
The courage of the grandfather is not to fight death but to affirm life. Grandfathers can trust life because they have seen more of it than younger men, and they can trust death because they are closer to it than younger men. Every moment is a gift from God. Death is not good, but it is part of life and life is good. The body is a lesson, and once we have learned the lesson, we can let go of it.

The soul of the grandfather is large enough to embrace the death of the ego and to affirm the life of God. He has come to realize that spiritual growth is not so much learning as unlearning. He understands that he does not so much grasp truth as let go of personal obstacles to truth. He is aware that people who strongly approve or disapprove of something have too much ego blocking their vision.

Perhaps, more than anything else, one becomes a grandfather in learning to deal with limits graciously. It has something to do with loss of strength and fleetness and balance and the passing of pets and friends. Becoming a grandfather takes skill and luck and perseverance. It is not something that just happens to you.

Grandfathers largely mistrust the world's definition of freedom. They have seen too many people manipulated, led off to the slaughter, by leaders who appealed to their right to have this or their freedom to do that.[204]

There's a good story about a guy who dies and goes to heaven. St. Peter gives him the tour of everything and then stops at a door. "And here," says St. Pete, "behind this door, are all the things that God had planned to give you." The man opens the door into a warehouse stocked with yachts and private jets, dancing girls, Nobel Prizes, a shelf of books authored by the man, money, medical cures discovered by the man, and even a small tropical island. The man wrings his hands and turns to St. Pete. "Why show me this stuff now? Why didn't you guys give it to me when I was down there, where I could have really used it?" "We wanted to," said St. Pete, "but you were too busy holding on to all your other stuff."

Freedom is surrender.

Success is Failure.

No culture has ever survived where the elders have been unable to pass on this logic-defying, experientially-acquired wisdom to its youth. Living in the paradox.

Our grandfathers were scared into loving security more than truth. That's *why* we had WW II. That's *why* we had Vietnam. They got that fear from their wives. I love my grandmothers, but they were the generation that got the vote. Suddenly politicians became a lot more handsome, a lot more charming, a lot more two-faced, and a lot more *mater*ially oriented. So we have sewers and roads and food stamps, but we have lost any notion of what Freedom is. It's important to realize that Feminism and Corporate Socialism – that bastardized agenda advocating centralized economic planning by corporations – blossomed in the same times in the same places in the same ways – serving the same memes. We could use one word, "*Mater*ism", to describe them both. Matriarchy is every bit as heartbreaking and soul-destroying as were the policies of the former USSR – and as the policies of the corporate-controlled West continue to be. All three are systems predicated on the idea that if we just get enough stuff we will be happy. And elk speak Chinese.

Women do not take naturally to the "surrender thing". They postpone gratification solely to get their larger cravings met. They'll iron your pants or cook your dinner, but when you want to move to Hawaii or buy an apple farm in Michigan, they bring out the big guns. Life, to women, is in great part deal-making, *i.e.* business. They keep everything in a place where they can control it. It's foolish for us to ignore this truth.

Grandfathers once had the sheer force of authority to wear them down and bend their wills into some kind of balance. That authority is gone, and I don't know how we will recover it. My own father has not seen my son, his only grandson, in ten years. He has been thwarted by the machinations of my ex and, so far, he has not been able to muster the sheer balls to "just do it", just make it happen. It would have taken the entire U.S. Army to keep my own grandfather from seeing me. So much has changed, in such a short time. How did this happen to our men? How did they so completely lose their balls? They fought in Iwo Jima and Normandy but they won't fight to see their own grand-children? That makes me pretty suspicious of just how much courage they had over there. Grandfathers used to *know* that they had something vital to pass on to young men. Now they're just cranky old men in TV sitcoms fending off the advice of their kids as they pursue foolish dreams.

Says Rohr:

The Grandfather knows his boundaries and knows his center but does not need to protect either of them. And without their wisdom, the naive men of our times will continue to move toward psychobabble and New Age shapelessness [and trippy archetypes] precisely in order to avoid all boundaries and surrenders.[205]

And this is really the point: by relying on corporate/socialist/ humanist/feminist values we are not going to reach the wisdom – the point of knowing – that ego-surrender is not a capitulation, but the most thoroughly graceful act a human is capable of performing. Surrendering your ego – your will – is kissing eternity on the lips.

Is my father surrendering his will by neglecting to visit his only grandson? Hardly. He is staying within the safe, secure patterns of his own life. He's unwilling to be rattled. He's not serving the will of a Higher Power, he's serving the will of my ex. And this is precisely where the issue of will becomes so sticky. In our society, if we do nothing, we are serving the will of women, of feminist memes. The spiritual path is not one of avoiding responsibility, not one of taking the easy way out. The spiritual path requires us to dig down into the Deep Masculine – and do what's right. It's not my dad's place to be arguing with my ex on a weekly basis, but once in ten years it's worth taking her on. He just sent her a letter *asking* if he can visit. We'll see what happens. If this were a Patriarchy, he would simply fly to Florida and see his grandson and that would be that. [And now, months later, I find out that my dad's letter was never answered. His visitation request was not denied; it was simply ignored. In the absence of forthright male action – getting on a plane and going there – the female agenda churns on with the blessings of the legal system. My ex, the lawyer, would not be so foolish as to put it in writing that my dad can't come for a visit. And so, my dad goes ten plus years without seeing his only grandson.]

Says Rohr:

I cannot imagine a grandfather who is not a contemplative. A contemplative is someone who doesn't talk a lot. A contemplative is someone who lives out of, and returns to, the center within himself, *and yet knows that the Center is not himself.* Meister Eckhardt said, "The eye by which I see God is the same eye by which God sees me."

Here's a poem about that vision:

MEDITATION ON GOD'S EYE

It was a dark wall,
a wall of silence,
with too many contours to count.
It had no birdsong, no poetry,
no light-choked imagery,
no encyclopedia of explanation.

It was a black wall,
beyond sight and sound,
beyond chattering monkeys of metaphor.

No mind.

Not cold but warm,
not frightening but inviting.
Midnight of the soul.

It had a tiny black hole,
inward umbilicus,
peeking out the center of it.
And when I got on my knees,
and put my eye to that calm black hole
what did I see?
but the same eye
looking right back at me.

That's the eye ideal grandfathers see with. But, says Rohr, needless to say, we are not mass-producing elders in American society today. It takes a wildman to call forth a wildman. My own dad never met his grandfather, who was abandoned somewhere back there in the war-torn states of central Europe – thus, he doesn't really know *how* to be a grandfather. He was very devoted to his mother, who was a raging control-freak, and he's a deeply spiritual man, but his spirituality never quite seems to translate into action.

Says Rohr:
    A masculine spirituality would emphasize action over theory, service rather than religious discussions, speaking the truth over social graces, and doing justice over looking nice. Without a complementary masculine side, spirituality becomes overly feminine.
    Much of the modern sophisticated church [and synagogue] is swirling in the feminine. It is one of the main reasons that doers, movers, shakers, change agents have largely given up on church people and church groups. A false feminine spirituality is the trap of those with lots of leisure, luxury, and liberal ideas. They have the option *not*

to do – not to do anything that makes them feel uncomfortable or doesn't give them an ego reward. Their very liberalism becomes an inoculation against the radical teachings of the Gospel [or Koran, or Bhagavad Gita, or Dharma, or Tao].

The opposite of corporate manholes and female business barracudas are the saints. Forget all the crap you've heard about saints. Saints are simply men and women who have lived the teachings. Saints, mensches, boddhisattvas, shamans are honored in every religious tradition. The biggest problem with our own elders is that they have lost touch with these people.

Says Rohr:
Saints are people who do not need monogrammed underwear. They know who they work for. A saint's identity is settled and secure. By surrendering his ego he has been awarded early possession of his soul and does not give it up lightly to corporations, armies, nation-states or *mater*ialist power blocs.

Saints are people who are whole. They trust their masculine soul because they have met the Father [addressed the father-wound]. He taught them about anger, passion, power and clarity. He told them to go all the way through and pay the price for it. He shared with them his decisive word and his illuminating Spirit.

Saints are comfortable knowing, and they are comfortable *not* knowing. They can care and not care without guilt. They can act with success because they have named their Fear of Failure. They know the worst that can happen to them and they are not afraid of it. They are not attached to the results of their actions. They do not need to affirm or deny, judge or ignore, but they are free to do them all with impunity.

The fundamental reason why men and women have failed to love and trust their masculine energy is that the vast majority of people in western civilization suffer from the father wound. Those who have this wound have never been touched by the human father. [They have spent their lives wallowing in the mindswamp of feminist memes.]

The reason Jesus spoke of God as Our Father is because that is precisely where most people are hurting, unfeeling, unbelieving, unwhole. Without facing the wound, praying into the wound, most people will continue to live lives of pseudomasculinity, machismo, self-seeking, pseudo-bravado – men *and women* alike. [Whether in pants or dresses these walking-wounded are a pox on our society worse than an invasion of brain-sucking moths from Madagascar.]

Call it Phallic Faith if you will – masculine spirituality does not doubt the seed within it. The spiritual man in mythology, in literature, and in the great world religions, has an excess of life, he *knows he has it*, he makes no apology for it, and he recognizes that he *does not need to protect it*, it is *meant to be given away* to others.

There is no way to masculinity. Masculinity *is* the way.[206]

A number of years ago I abruptly quit everything I was doing, I sold my car and my carpentry tools, scraped together what money I could, and flew to India to talk to a man I'd read about in a book. The man was Bede Griffiths. The book is *Dialogues with Scientists and Sages* by Rene Weber.[207] I left Maui, a tropical paradise, my heart throbbing with fear, to go into the filth and chaos of India, knowing no one, having only the barest hint from the book that Bede lived in an ashram somewhere near Tiruchirapalli in south India. It was crazy. I didn't know what I was doing.

Now I know what I was doing.

I was going on a Pilgrimage: a soul-searching expedition into the unknown – looking for God – that is as old as human culture.

Says Patrick Arnold:

Two archetypes symbolize the male drive for freedom: the Wildman, and the Pilgrim...Every ancient religion featured the practice of pilgrimage, the deliberate journey to a holy place in quest of special blessings. In acting out this sacred ritual over many days and across numerous miles, the Pilgrim sacramentally recreated the essentials of his own "hero journey". He has become the image in the psyche for all the leavings we must do in life, all the detaching and separation we must undergo in order to find our way again to new life, new challenges, and higher danger.[208]

The practice of pilgrimage once offered men a powerful experience in humility, trust in God, and prayer, acted out over days and weeks and extended over many miles. The devotion was strenuous and even dangerous, and the more meaningful for all that; as the hours and the miles slipped by and the body grew weary, the pilgrim really felt the cost of his commitment and paid the price of his search. It is an axiom of human nature that we most value the things that we really have to pay for; perhaps one reason prayer is so widely ignored is that it doesn't seem to cost us much personally.

The first ingredient of classical pilgrimage is a burning need, an insoluble problem, or an aching desire of life-altering dimensions that everyday prayer and ordinary devotion cannot solve. Great problems, vocational choices, life-threatening diseases, chronic faith-doubts, [having your kids stolen from you by a feminized legal system] require great solutions. Every pilgrim is, in effect, saying clearly to himself and to everyone else that he needs help; pilgrimage is never for the complacent.

The second component of the practice is the pilgrim's outlandish faith that an extravagant gesture of faith will yield overflowing grace – everything ventured, everything gained. Pilgrimage is not for the cautious, but it is a bold and spiritually risky business that requires a bit of the gambler in a man.

The third element in pilgrimage is a clear and concrete goal such as a famous shrine or holy place where prayers are answered and grace given – a Mecca or Lourdes or Benares [or Shantivanam]. Some people think that certain geographical places on earth offer focused spiritual energy that wakens the human heart and soul; whatever the cause of this phenomenon (and millions have felt it), true pilgrims know intuitively the feeling of clarity and excitement that attends their reaching their goal, the spiritual electricity around Jerusalem or the gentle love that suffuses the shrine of Guadalupe. Pilgrimage *is not an act of the rational mind*; it is a belief that God imbues certain places with a Deep Magic that heals and answers prayers. Pilgrimage is an act of high faith and is not to be taken lightly. The true pilgrim experiences vulnerability at every turn and feels often the need for food, safety, rest and companionship. He places all in God's hands. For this reason, pilgrimage is a sacrament of the "hero's journey", and one of the oldest religious metaphors for life. The experience tells a man that his whole life is a pilgrimage demanding heroism, goals, and an abiding knowledge that, through it all, God helps.[209]

Arnold goes on to say that the malaise of elders, the quiet despair that one has seen it all and expects no change for the better, might well be cured by a pilgrimage. Grandpa's house is all tidy and his Social Security checks are coming in, and he's not "giving anything back" to society because, after all, he fought in the Big One, *fifty fucking years ago*, and maybe it's time for him to get a little hungry and a little thirsty again, to have his shoes smeared with highway mud and his windshield splattered with bugs. Peace Pilgrim, that astounding woman, spent her sixties and seventies and into her eighties walking around America carrying only what fit in her small pockets, fasting until given food, walking until given shelter, spreading a message of peace. An American *sanyassin*.

There are sacred places in reach of your home; you don't need to go to Jerusalem. The Native Americans identified thousands of sacred places in North America imbued with spiritual power. To them this is a sacred land, and we, the interlopers, still look to Europe and the Mid East for guidance. To us, America is an idea embodied in our Constitution. We make pilgrimages to Washington and Jefferson's home hoping to find that idea. That's not it. America is a sacred land and it will never be a real country until we understand that and resurrect a manner of worship which comes of and through this sacredness. Father Nature is alive and well in America. Take your fishing

pole or your walking stick and go out and meet Him. And take
your grandson with you.

Perhaps the greatest story of Pilgrimage is embodied in the
Myth of Parsifal and the Quest for the Holy Grail. Once again,
as in the story of Psyche, we will rely on Robert Johnson to
"walk" us through this myth to unfold its deeper meanings and
its pertinence in our own lives. The pilgrimage of Parsifal is the
"hero's journey", the vision quest performed by every single
living man, whether he likes it or not. We will only touch on the
later part of the journey, but I think it's important for every man
to read *He* by Robert Johnson [210] to get the full story of the
journey *you will take*, like it or not. There are Deep Masculine
memes at work and though we might remain oblivious to them,
they *will* do their work.

For forty years of his life, it's almost impossible for a man
to avoid serving Mammon, *Mater*, Money – female/corporate
greed. And then something awful happens: middle age.

We enter the Grail Quest where Parsifal has just spent twenty
years serving King Arthur – the man who wears a dress – as a
Knight of the Round Table. He has risked his life and limbs
battling all manner of enemies, saving damsels, and defending
the "honor" of Arthur (the law). Is he happy and fulfilled? Far
from it. He's bitter and disillusioned, not getting along too hot
with his beloved Blanche Fleur, even forgetting why he's lugging
around this silly sword anyway. He carries on mechanically,
functioning with less and less understanding and joy. Sound
familiar? These are the dry years, when a man is apt to give an
evasive answer to the meaning of life. The midlife crisis. When
farmers become bankers and bankers become farmers, lusting
after that greener grass. No man, no matter how great his
successes in serving the Earthly King – the institutions of family
and company that have laid claim to him – the female memes
that suffuse our laws and lives – no man is immune to this
middle age crisis. There's a hot wind in his nostrils and a desert
in his bowels. He dreams of drowning and falling and running
away.

We used to be dead at this age. The normal life span of the hunter/gatherer was around 35 to 40. At forty, you were close to becoming a great grandfather. And since we don't die at that age anymore, what happens? You guessed it. Another death. Human Culture steps in to change the sparkplugs on our biological engines, but first we have to turn off the engine. Time to die and be reborn *again*. The glimpse of a higher life, of the Grail Castle that we visited once during a fleeting dream in our long-lost youth, is back to make another grab at us.

Parsifal, virtually paralyzed with despair, unable to move, is approached by a ragged band of pilgrims who say, "What the hell are you doing riding around in your armor on Good Friday? You should be coming with us to see the Hermit!" Parsifal awakens from his dark reverie and follows the pilgrims to the old hermit.

Says Johnson, the Hermit is the highly introverted part of one's nature which has been hiding and storing energy in a far-off corner of the psyche waiting for this moment. The Hermit was implanted in the man's psyche when he was initiated out of boyhood. That was the subtle *agenda* of the initiation. So here is the *second time* the initiation comes into play to rid us of *Mater*. The deepness and quietness of the Hermit were introduced in us by a man who is now long dead, and almost forgotten, and again remembered – known again.

Extroversion is usually dominant the first half of one's life and that is correct. But when one's extroversion has run its race and all four tires are flat and your brains are dripping out your ears, it's time to consult the Hermit, deep inside, for the next step. The eye you see God with is the same eye he sees you with.

A lot of us have never seen real live hermits. Hermits are skinny with bad teeth; they don't take baths, they wear Salvation Army rejects, they don't talk much, and they are a lot closer to God than you are. In other words, they look like you feel when you go to see them. They are another variety of God-energy to replace the lost radiance of the king – of your wife and business and all the *Mater* in your life. The King is dead, thank God, long live the Hermit King. The hermit must know something about life nobody else knows, otherwise, why the hell would he live like that?

Says Johnson:

In our culture, we are spiritually impoverished by our inability to consult the genius of our introverted nature. It frequently happens to a modern person that he is forced into his introversion by an illness or accident or paralyzing symptom of some other kind. The hermit is a noble figure and will serve you well if you can go to him with honor and dignity. There is little dignity left if one is dragged into his realm by accident or illness; but one way or the other he will have you – sometime about the middle of your journey – dignity or no dignity.

So, Parsifal meets the hermit. The hermit berates Parsifal for his long list of faults and failures, but his worst failure is hammered at him once again in this story. That was Parsifal's failure to "ask the right question" twenty years ago, in his youth, the first time he had been admitted to the Grail Castle. Parsifal had been instructed by a sage to ask this question but, following *the advice of his mother*, he didn't ask it! The question he failed to ask was the "God question", and by failing to ask it, Parsifal doomed himself to spend a meaningless life fighting Arthur's battles for him.

It turns out that the inhabitants of the Grail Castle wait in a suspended time, entranced, until one single person comes along and asks the right question! The wounded Fisher King drops a line into your subconscious every day and comes up with nothing. The handmaidens who bear the mysteries of the meaning of life stand around bored and petulant, manufacturing intrigues, irritating each other. Everyone is stuck until *someone* asks the right question. By failing to ask it the first time Parsifal was put to work for the King, the manhole, the *mater*ialist enforcer, instead of God, who lives behind the King, and who is the true source of radiance. What's the question? Just wait.

So, after berating him, the hermit grows gentle with Parsifal. He takes Parsifal out to the road and tells him to walk two blocks and take a left across the drawbridge. The Grail Castle is right there! It's always that close, but it's generally only at adolescence and middle age that it's that easy to find. If anyone is humble enough and of good heart, he can find the castle. Parsifal has had the arrogance beat out of him by twenty years of playing knight and now he is ready for his hermitage, his castle.

Parsifal was never initiated by men. He was raised by his mother in a forest because his father had been killed working as a knight and his mother, as mothers will, wanted to keep him away from such things as knights. But one day, while he was playing, a band of knights rode by and Parsifal thought they were angels. He ran off to follow them and his mother had a heart-spasm and died. Here we have a botched initiation where the mother holds the boy back and creates bigger problems for everyone in the long run. This is the way of women. They cannot be expected to logically arrive at the conclusion that they must let go of their sons – and then act on it. They can't do it. Their method is control. They create manholes, not whole men. Whole men have to take what is theirs from the women – and what is theirs are human adolescents with pee pees between their legs.

Back to the Grail Castle – second time around, middle age. Just down the road, left over the drawbridge, which snaps closed the instant you cross nicking your horse's hooves – you just squeezed through.

Inside Parsifal finds the same ceremonial procession going on he witnessed 20-odd years ago. In the Grail Castle everything has stayed in the same place waiting for Parsifal to be ready. When he strayed off the path God unfolded his lawn chair and sat down to wait for him, knowing that Parsifal would have to come back through this same exact spot.

Here comes a fair damsel carrying the sword that pierced the side of Christ; another one carries the plate from which the Last Supper was served; yet another maiden bears the Holy Grail itself, the cup that was used at the Last Supper. The wounded Fisher King lies groaning in his litter, poised between life and death – the *mater*ial world and the spiritual world.

Will he do it? Will he listen to his mom again or has the Hermit plus twenty years of suffering finally hammered something into his head?

Yes, he'll do it. He'll ask the freakin' question.

"Who does the Grail serve?" says Parsifal.

All the servers gasp.

Who does the Grail serve?

What a strange question, says Johnson. Hardly comprehensible to modern ears? In essence, the question is the most profound question one can ask: where is the center of gravity of the human personality? Or, where is the center of meaning in human life? Most people asked this question in understandable terms for our times would reply that *I* am the center of gravity, *I* work to improve my life; *I* am working toward my goals; *I* am making something of myself – or, most common of all – *I* am searching for happiness. All of which is to say that *I* want the Grail to serve *me*. We ask this great cornucopia of nature: forests, oceans, oil deposits; we ask the wealth of nations and of people and of religion; we ask that *all* the productivity of the world should serve *us*![211]

Insane.

And preposterously feminine.

But no sooner does Parsifal ask the question than the answer comes reverberating through the Grail Castle halls.

"The Grail serves the Grail King!!!"

Another puzzling proposition. Who is the Grail King? In the entire Grail Quest, he has not so much as been hinted at. But there it is. All the outpouring and activity of life serves Him. He is present in all things but somehow hidden from our senses. He is transcendent but immanent. He is a mystery. He is Atman or Allah or God the Father. He is the Green Man or Dharma or the Tao. He is what Jung called the Self (with a capital "S") – that Self that we are all a small part of, but which is much, much greater than ourselves.

Jung, in spite of all the brainless sycophants he spawned, has spoken brilliantly of the "life process" as consisting of relocating the center of gravity of the human personality from the ego to the Self – from ego to beyond ego. This is the essence of every spiritual message. Jung sees this relocation as the life work of every human being and the center of meaning of all human endeavor. I couldn't agree more. As long as we remain locked into a world that services female memes, we can never find the center of gravity of the human personality – the point where the drawbridge drops and, if we ask the right question, we tumble right into the cornucopia of God.

This is the whole point of this book and the whole point of the meaning of life: when Parsifal learns that he is no longer the center of the universe – not even of his own little fiefdom – he is free of his alienation and the Grail is no longer barred from him. Though he may come and go from the Grail Castle for the rest of his life, he will never again be alien to it.[212]

The Grail is "It". The "It" of Coke is *it*; *It's* Miller time; or give *it* to her. The Grail is the "It" we are all chasing – excitement, fulfillment, security, whatever. We can't possess *it*; we can't buy *it*; *it* doesn't serve us; we don't get *it* at a weekend seminar.

Finally, to end the story, the wounded Fisher King, the Ego King, rises, healed, and starts singing. He has transcended his *mater*ial wounds. He has made the transition into the spiritual realm. He is not dead. He is finally, completely, spiritually alive. And why? All because one adult child asked the right question.

Who does the Grail serve?

The Grail King is invisible and everywhere – like the Life Force. The object of life is not happiness, not sense or mind gratification, but to serve the Life Force. All the Grail quests are to serve the Life Force. If one understands this and drops her idiotic notion that the meaning of life is personal happiness, then one will find that elusive quality – happiness – immediately at hand.

Says Peace Pilgrim:
    Blessed are they who advance toward the spiritual path without the selfish motive of seeking inner peace, for they shall find it.[213]

Says Johnson:

One detail of this story cannot be emphasized too strongly. Parsifal need only ask the right question. That's all it takes. He doesn't need to begin to have any answers. He just needs to ask the question. The asking is the deliverance, the salvation, the entry of Grace. When one is discouraged and demoralized and certain he will never express the wherewithal to answer insoluble paradoxes, he can remember that he need only ask the right question. [The answer to the question is in the question, say the Sufis.] To ask well is virtually to answer.[214]

There is a wonderful goof on this in the *Hitchhiker's Guide to the Galaxy* by Douglas Adams. Some scientists commission a super-computer to answer the Ultimate Question: What is the meaning of life? The computer takes seven million years working at light speed to cough out an answer. The whole galaxy gathers to hear the answer. The answer is 42. The scientists and philosophers plotz. What is the meaning of this? 42? They ask. "You must not have understood the question," fires back the computer. A couple of super-intelligent mice deduce that the question was *how many roads does a man walk down*? They go off to become talk show sensations. How many of us ever really understand the question? The question is a paradox, a riddle. The answer is the Grace and harmony that enter our life from simply asking it.

Says Johnson:

If you ask the Grail to give you happiness, that very demand prevents happiness. But if you serve the Grail and the Grail King, you will find that what happens and happiness are the same thing. If you ask the wrong question, if you ask for the wrong stuff, you are putting roadblocks in the way of obtaining it.[215]

Let me repeat that when the Frenchman Alexis de Tocqueville came to America more than a century ago, he made the observation that we have a misleading idea at the very head of our Constitution: the pursuit of happiness. This has always been one of my closest held ideals. But one cannot pursue happiness, said de Tocqueville, for if she does, she obscures it. If she will proceed with the human task of life, the relocation of the center of gravity of the human personality out of the ego and onto something greater outside itself, happiness will be the outcome.[216]

That's just about the only fault I can find with the U.S. Constitution – but it's a big one. We cannot expect law to legislate morality and this is precisely why: because law cannot legislate happiness. Self-seeking does not lead to happiness, it's a fact as observable as gravity. And it's a meme that has colonized the minds of our women like a virus.

God bless all willful women. May they find health and prosperity and happiness.

As long as we are talking about the Grail let's talk about the earthly personage who employed it: Jesus. According to Father Bede Griffiths, Jesus was 100% Man. Says Bede, his story would have no meaning for us if it was simply the account of a god coming to earth, suffering for a few years, and then going back to being a god. Jesus was an archetype. For Jungians to ignore him in fear of alienating Jews and New Agers leaves a gap in their thinking as wide as the Atlantic Ocean. I'm as much Buddhist or Taoist as I am Christian, but I find it impossible to ignore the sheer power of the Jesus-archetype in the past 2000 years of human history. Was Jesus the Greatest Archetype of All? Let's check out the myth.

Was Jesus a King?

He was called the Prince of Peace. He was the first representative of God's Kingdom on earth.

Was he a Warrior?

He fought pitched ego-battles against Satan, the Hebrew priests and rebels, and the Roman authorities. During his forty days in the desert Satan tempted him with *Mater*: food, power, disproof of God's authority. Jesus refused to be tempted. He is quoted as saying, "Don't even think that I have come to bring peace on the earth! It is not peace I have come to bring, but a sword!" (Mt 10:34) The *vajra* sword? Jesus' memes have outlived the Roman Empire and the Pharisees. Rome eventually absorbed him in some attempt to retain its empire. Christianity, with its message of tolerance for the oppressed, has provided a womb for Judaism that has permitted it to flourish in a manner unknown in 2000 years. In the profoundest historical sense, Jesus was a Jewish messiah. He was a deliverer of Jews. And let us not forget his warrior nature booting the merchants out of the temple.

Was Jesus a Magician/Healer?

He fed hundreds of people on two fish, and walked on water. He caused lame men to walk and blind men to see. (Remember, this is a myth we're talking about. It doesn't matter whether or not you believe he did this stuff. Just like it doesn't matter whether you think Krishna impregnated 4000 milkmaids. The meaning of the myth is much deeper than that. The meaning is in the archetype.) And, says Arnold, let's be sure to recognize that Jesus did not nurture the sick or indulge the ill. He did not care for the diseased in the compassionate way of a mother caring for her child. Jesus heals, not by being nice, but by a show of pure masculine spiritual force and authority; he drives out sickening spirits with all the gentleness of a Marine Corps drill instructor.[217]

Was Jesus a Lover?

He loved everyone. He was co-dependent with the world.

Was he a Trickster?

He told some of the most befuddling parables in history. His whole life was a *trick* on the *mater*ialist way of thinking.

Was Jesus a Wildman?

I can't spend forty days alone in the desert. He had some deep connection to Father Nature.

Was Jesus a Green Man?

He exploded on that desert scene with a masculine vitality that is still with us 2000 years later. He turned water into wine.

Was he a failure?

Nothing he tried ever seemed to work down here. His dearest disciples betrayed him. He caused so much disruption the authorities crucified him for it – and out of that Failure came his church.

Was he a Pilgrim?

His whole life was a pilgrimage back to the Father.

Was he a Hermit?

He preached a radical masculine detachment from the world which, in my opinion, he got from encountering Buddhist/Hindu philosophies somewhere in his wanderings and/or his solitude. He did disappear for 18 years from ages 12 to 30, and he did spend long periods of time in the desert.

Was he a Cook?

He presided over a meal of bread and wine that is still going on today. If the *Joy of Cooking* lasts that long we can only imagine the proportion of the myths that will have grown up around Irma Rombauer.

Was he a Hunter?

He was the premier "fisher of men" and called on his disciples to be the same.

Was Jesus aware of Corporate Evil?

He told people to leave their businesses and follow him.

Was he a Phallus?

No.

Was he a Grandfather?

No.

Did he acknowledge the Twisted Side of the Great Mother?

No. Not according to the myth. And that's the problem I find regarding these last three archetypes. If Jesus was here to try out life as a man, he had to get laid. Our main human function is reproduction. Sexuality is the flashpoint of many of our obsessions and much of our "sinfulness" – our drift toward the sense pleasures of the world and away from God. One cannot understand the human being without understanding the gravitational pull of human sexuality. But during the period of the Gospels Jesus entirely avoided intimacy with women. Not a bad idea for a guy trying to get more spiritual and less *mater*ialistic – but what did he know or what had he learned about how women degrade male spirituality? Is it possible he'd had a wife? He could have gotten somebody pregnant during his 18-years off the record, and even been around long enough to experience the joy of becoming a grandfather. We know nothing of his life between ages 12 and 30.

And his classic argument with Satan over the Three Temptations of *Mater* shows that he was *aware* of the Twisted Side of the Great Mother. When he was fasting and delirious during 40 days in the desert Satan visited and promised him 1) bread, *i.e. mater*ial comfort; 2) control of all he could see, *i.e.* unlimited *power*; 3) a chance to test God by jumping off a high wall and seeing if God would save him – *i.e.* a chance to *play God* – *i.e.* a chance to rule over life and death – as in abortion. He rejected them all. No wonder there are no Christian feminists. No wonder feminists trash Christianity. No wonder American feminism was started by upper class Jewish women.

Our western myth-makers, a bunch of celibate priests enthralled with mother-worship, chose to entirely ignore these three vital archetypes – the Phallus, the Grandfather, and the Twisted Side of the Great Mother – so we have inherited a mythic system with a great part of its right brain blown off. If archetypes are of any value at all, we should have a deep look at these glaring omissions.

Finally, was Jesus a Man Who Has Slain His Ego?

I think he set the high water mark for that. True, he was human; he blew it by complaining to his dad at the last minute. But he did a divine job at this task. Listen to this:

> Unless a grain of wheat falls to the ground and dies,
>   It remains just a single grain;
> But if it dies,
>   It yields a rich harvest!
> Anyone who loves his life, loses it.
>
> *Jn* 12:24-25

Jesus' God-status has always given Christians a ready excuse for not being able to achieve his degree of ego-annihilation. But let us not forget St. Francis and Gandhi and Mother Teresa when we try to "but, but, but" our way around this one. There is some nameless guy in your town right now feeding homeless people or working with fatherless teenagers who is living out of this wisdom. Slaying our ego is the whole reason we were put here. Happiness and peace are the rewards of this work.

One day the famed teacher Mulla Nasrudin was out walking with his students when a duck flew over and dropped a shit in his eye. "Mulla," said the students, "this is terrible! We must get some toilet paper!" "Oh, don't bother, " Mulla said. "You couldn't catch him now."[218]

And:
God bless all willful women.
May they find health
and prosperity
and happiness.

Chapter Seven

Smothered in Mother

1) Mom died in the middle of making me a sandwich. If I knew it was gonna kill her, I never would have asked.

2) Women account for the use of over 70% of all prescribed minor tranquilizers and 80% of legal speed. They also use the majority of barbiturates and non-controlled narcotics. They renew their prescriptions more often than men and use them with more frequency.

WE LIVE IN AN Addictive Society and the source of those addictions are female memes. From addiction-to-praise, to addiction-to-money, to addiction-to-barbiturates, our societal disease is female-based. Let's take a brief recap of human history to support this bias.

According to Aaron Kipnis, far back in our human past we had an earth-based masculinity. From 2.2 million to 8000 B.C. the sacred image was hunter/dancer/healer, attention was turned toward the earth rather than the sky. Nomadic man did not accumulate *mater*ial wealth. The work of men and women was complementary and equally valued: half of our teeth are for grinding cereals and half are for cutting meat. Population was stable.

Then from 8000 to 3000 B.C. we have the emergence of farming and husbandry – the agricultural age. The hunter is perverted into a soldier to guard the grain. The great agricultural earth goddess takes predominance over the earth god and nature goddesses. Cultivation becomes more valued than hunting or gathering. Narcotics and alcohol are mass produced for the first time. Men become subservient to the Goddess – complacent agricultural workers. Boys' balls are slashed off twice a year in honor of the Goddess. Eventually, the scapegoat sacrifice of male animals, and the ritual sacrifices of a male dying god – Dionysus and Jesus – emerge. This is no less than the crucifixion of masculinity. This is the Goddess.

Says Kipnis, nature becomes increasingly subordinated as sacred male images become feminized and animalistic images become humanized. The wild bull is tamed. He plows the fields growing wealth to attract women. Partnership between men and women turns into consortship – men serving the Goddess. Female memes define human society.

During the agricultural transformation of the human psyche, Earth Father mystery cults decline; matriarchy rises. Attention moves skyward as farmers begin to worry about rain, and sun and the effects of seasons and "planets" on their crops. Population explodes. Once fertile valleys in Persia and Egypt are desertified by goats and by clearing the land of trees.

During the Copper, Bronze, and Iron Ages, from 4500 to 1000 B.C., Kings emerge – the men who wear dresses. They step-up the program of perverting hunters into soldiers, creating modern armies to protect their wealth from roving bands of horse-mounted marauders – the first eco-warriors – who are watching the wild herds dwindle. Thus, Patriarchy slithers into preeminence to halt the ritual slaughter of virgin boys while, at the same time, usurping the female/*mater*ialistic agenda of the Goddess. A fantastic artifice. Affirmative Action of the second millennium B.C. A program ostensibly designed to benefit disenfranchised men ends up serving the *mater*ial lusts of women. Female memes like "security" and the "accumulation of wealth" had become too imbedded in human society to be readily undone. So just mask them by calling them something else. Call them

Patriarchy! Make it look like the men are really running everything. That way women get the good life, and they never have to pick up a gun. Sound familiar? And anyway, more than enough virgin boys will die in war. They won't be openly sacrificed to the Goddess, they'll merely be sacrificed for the glorious goal of expanding female-friendly *mater*ialism. A scam that's still going on today. Feminized men killing young men to advance a female/*mater*ialist agenda.

Yes, you guessed it. Female values are the cause of war. Female memes are the cause of war. Men are not the cause of war. Women are the cause of war. Another phony meme bites the dust.

Civilized women don't like war, but they *do* like washing machines. They need fighting men to assure the supply of water and copper and iron and electricity and soap so they can continue to skip out on the drudgery of beating their clothes on rocks like their "sisters" in the undeveloped world. Don't tell me women will give up their washing machines to make life easier for their "sisters" in poor countries. The sun will ice over before that happens. "Progress" may be understood as the means by which certain women acquire more stuff than other women. And damn the torpedoes.

Patriarchy – feminized government run by manholes – arose to preserve this imperative. Men would now do things women's way, and call it Patriarchy. Preposterous. An Ice Age of duplicity crept over the planet and cooled the masculine soul. But at least guys didn't get their balls cut off any more. Not literally. Only their emotional balls got snipped. Only their brains got emasculated…And today we have a "free market" that's dominated by a handful of corporations. That's when all this double-talk began. Back when the "Patriarchy" was created.

"Free trade" is a way to dress up unrestrained corporate greed. Patriarchy is a way to dress up men to enforce female values. The very thing feminists rail against is the thing women and their manhole enforcers *invented* to co-opt men. Patriarchy, my aching behind. Patriarchy is just a fantastic ruse to harness male productivity by pretending to give men power. Our Patriarchy is, in fact, a Covert Matriarchy! We're wearing our underpants on our heads. If women were tyrannizing us like this we'd see right through it, but since it's men up there in front of the cameras we stay oblivious. Gosh. Men are in positions of power. I'm a man. I must be in a position of power. Why don't I feel like I have any power? Logic gone female.

The Patriarchy is female. Civilization is female. That's the only way it would have worked. The only way they could have pulled the wool over our eyes. Make us think we're the ones running the show. The only good thing about feminism is that the more female Secretaries of State we see sending us off to war, the more women we see on corporate boards, the less interested we will become in joining their government/corporate female-friendly nightmare. And the closer we will come to balls-to-the-walls revolution.

Finally, from 1000 B.C. to the present, the earth fathers were eradicated. The Green Man went underground. The Sky Father rules, safely up in heaven, while down here his son died on the cross. The cross is female. Remember this symbol? ♀ Female memes, the Age of Kali, are firmly in place on earth. Monotheism becomes the primary religion and nature is defiled. As *mater*ialism rises, men lose connection to soul and to the earth. Cities, those greenhouses of *mater*ialism, grow immense. Manhole-made environments where everything we see, touch, hear, smell and taste is made by humans. Humans begin to believe that they, indeed, do "make" everything of importance, and the sacred simplicity of life is lost in the stampede to possess more and more manhole-made things.

In the past 3000 years, alcohol and drugs were, for the first time, cultivated in huge amounts, and dispensed to the laborers to help kill the pain and keep them docile so they would continue to produce more than their individual needs required and thus support an extensive privileged class who didn't gather their own food or wash their own clothes. The *raison d'etre* of government became, not merely defending accumulated wealth, but fueling *mater*ial growth.

And recently, in the past 140 years, children have been entirely removed from their fathers and put in "free public schools" which are suffused with female/corporate memes of job-training and desk-learning and which, in the absence of Deep Male guidance, have deteriorated into ego-driven agendas of self-seeking, grading of human beings, and armed camps of belligerents who know something is wrong but don't know what to do about it except rebel. Mother has conquered all of human civilization and made it her kitchen. Dirty dishes go in the dishwasher, food goes in the garbage disposal, and our marching orders are posted on the refrigerator door. At the same time, we have deprived children of the love of Men.

John Wayne movies aside, the last resurgence of the Deep Masculine occurred about 800 years ago. King Arthur's Knights of the Round Table endeavored to fight the good fight (battle the ego), shun acquisition of wealth, serve the Grail King, and honor women (not seduce them or be seduced by them). This last principle is an important point emphasized by both Robert Johnson and Joseph Campbell – the knight must not be seduced by his *anima*, his female nature. He sleeps with the maiden but he doesn't pork her. She is part of his unconscious, but not part of his conscious. She is part of his unspoken world but not of his spoken world. He must act, *always*, out of his male nature, not his female nature.

And what happened? Guinevere, the wife of the King, seduced Lancelot and fucked the whole thing up. The flashing red lights and twittering alarm systems went off in our collective brains 800 years ago and how did we respond? We went to the fridge, got a glass of milk, and made a movie out of it. We refuse to acknowledge that there is a Twisted Side to all women.

Says Bly:
> Children feel grateful when a grownup reads witch stories to them because it proves to them they are not insane. The child, male or female, lives with the secret that his mom, whom everyone declares to be supportive and caring, has a witch face at times. The child knows this and knows he is too small to do anything about it. Mom, the witch, goes into an invisible bag everyone lugs around with him. [A bag Bly calls The Shadow.][219]

Some men let the mother carry the witch around their whole lives but most transfer it onto their new bride. While the bride and groom trade rings, another important exchange takes place in the basement of their psyches. An hour after the ceremony, the witch is firmly in place in the bride although nobody knows it yet. But after a few arguments, a few obstinacies, a few money fights, it occurs to the groom one day that there is something witch-like about his bride he hadn't noticed before. She herself feels more witchy, more greedy.

She says to her friends, "You know, before I was married I was quite a nice person, but now I've been married three years and I keep getting bitchier and bitchier. How can this be?" Meanwhile, the good son, the good husband, keeps getting sweeter and sweeter and that brings out her witchiness even more. She becomes compulsive, greedy, unfair, hostile, makes no sense at all, not even to herself, and blames all of it on him. What's the problem? He thinks she's his mom and he won't "lay down the law", set boundaries. That's why we used to send them to church. Church was invented to contain the endless cravings of women. Men, uninitiated men, don't seem to be able to do that. Carl Jung has said that the problem with American marriages is that the men do all their fighting at the office.

What can we do? Burn their wedding gowns. At the culmination of every wedding ceremony, the bride should retire momentarily to change into a plain dress and then return to the altar where she hands over her white wedding gown to her spouse. His first act as her husband should be to light a match and touch it to her gown, thus converting her virginal fantasies into a pile of ashes. There must come some moment in a woman's life where she is compelled to accept boundaries. By allowing women to substitute psychobabble for spiritual surrender, Goddess drivel for healing their father wounds, by not erecting a brick wall of principles and morals for them to smash their egos into, we are undermining the deepest layers of the human psyche – we are robbing them of a life.

Women love to give advice, but they hate to be responsible. Women are not evil, they're just not creative. They gossip about new ways to thaw food or recycle garbage or enter data in computers as if this had everything to do with being creative risk takers. Have you ever lived on a commune run by women? They have 6000 ways to prepare tofu and not a scrap of original poetry anywhere. Ever been in a men's commune? Song and poetry abound, and there are some scrapings of three-day-old spaghetti in the fridge.

The woman's perpetual question in life is, "How do I feel right now?"

And the only sensible answer is, "Who the fuck cares?" Men are here to live a life despite their broken ankles and money worries – to transcend their feelings. Women want to gab about their feelings. Do you think the guys in a football huddle get together to talk about how they're feeling? No. They just want to know what the next play is. The next time you flick on a light, the next time you open a water tap, thank a man. He went out at 2:00 A.M. in a thunderstorm, with a bandaged knee and a headache, to keep the damn thing running. And he didn't ask himself how he felt about it. He just did it.

We do not live in a patriarchy. We live in a covert matriarchy. All of the values that make up our society are female and have been for thousands of years.

Says Richard Haddad:

What kind of privilege is it that bestows men with a ten-year shorter life span than women, and a higher incidence of disease, crime, alcoholism and drug addiction? What kind of privilege is it that blesses men with the self-destructive need to achieve that breaks his knees on the football field and his heart muscle at the office? What kind of privilege is it that honors a man with the duty to spend a lifetime supporting others by showing up day in and day out for a pathetically unsatisfying job? Men are locked in a vocational death-dance trying to please women who mock them.

In the name of eliminating sex-stereotyping, feminism has labeled men as: predators, stalkers, base, insensitive, exploitative, untrustworthy, driven by uncontrolled animalistic urges. But Woman is: victim, noble, pure, caring, selfless, loving, sensitive, suffering, used, battered.

Cities are female. Flashy and trashy – just like women. The urban male has lost the most territory in the war of the sexes. Women whose closest neighbor is two miles away still feel better with a man around. Urban/suburban man has lost touch with masculine soul. He has forgotten how to initiate his own sons, who are raised primarily by women.

Uninitiated man has a hole in his heart. Says Kipnis, we believe we cannot be loved for who we are. We are amazed when anybody loves us, even for a while. And like ants drowning in a jar of honey, our love/fear precipitates a more cloying disaster. For unless a man is in touch with his own masculine depths, he becomes like a vampire, sucking energy out of women because he does not have the ability to nourish himself from his inexhaustible depths.[220]

The real problem is you can't initiate boys if there's nothing to initiate them into. We have no male community. We have no revered elders. We need to put more grandfathers in contact with more kids. It should be one of the stipulations of receiving Social Security that each old man has to spend three hours a week with some kid from a broken home. It should be a stipulation for receiving AFDC that every mother has to surrender her kids for three hours a week to some elder who at least got it together to receive Social Security. Whether the grandfathers like it or not, whether the kids' mothers like it or not, whether the kids like it or not. Retired people are entitled to a comfortable old age, but they are also obligated to give something back: time. The recent generation of grandfathers seem oblivious to the second half of the equation. Let's remind them of it at the voting booth – cut Social Security or start giving something back.

An incident from my days as a carpenter comes to mind. Once, during my divorce, when my own business was completely shut down, I took a job with a large construction company that built two hundred houses a year. I was sent around to answer a complaint at a house our firm had built seven years ago. I was met at the door by a feisty retiree who was warped with rage because some flecks of paint were peeling on the ceiling of his closet! He was so abusive to me, such a manhole of misunderstanding, berating me and blaming me for things that happened seven years before I came to work for this company, that I left without doing anything. He was flapping his arms like a vulture and spewing obscenities like a wounded warthog as I got into my car. I rolled down the window and told him to forget about his closet ceiling and go teach some black kid how to play baseball. To this day, I know in my heart, it would have done him a world of good.

In Hawaii, the kids call every adult male "uncle" and every adult female "auntie". The beauty of this is that every adult feels involved and responsible for the health and worldview and good sense of every child. This simple tribal custom makes for one of the most truly gentle, dignified and loving races on earth.

The very word "entitlement" implies that the receiver has done *something* to earn his stipend. We don't need more automobiles and dishwashers. We need more trout streams and bluegill ponds – and more old men and kids going fishing on their grassy shores.

This kind of contact over generations creates something we can think of as ritual space. Because we live in a culture that has lost the concept of ritual space, we tend to err in two extremes: either we avoid ritual space entirely, or we hang out in it for forty years. A friend of mine named Jamie George once said that art is what we do beyond mere survival. In America, we have made survival so complicated it's a full-time preoccupation. We need so many items to accomplish a minimum existence in this country – automobiles, insurance, mortgages, permits, fishing licenses – that our daily life becomes a horror of money worries. We get so worn out we come home, flop on the couch and flip on the tube. TV is the enemy of ritual space.

Ritual space is "heated". There is something more going on there than a priest raising a cup, or an old man and a boy going fishing. Deep things are working.

In India and Tibet, ritual space is set up for lovemaking. We do that here, too, with candles and incense and erotic music and intoxicants. Then we get lazy and ignore the magic of setting up the space and our sex gets boring and our wives seethe.

Says Bly, men returning from war need to enter a ritual space where they can be cleansed and welcomed and reintroduced to compassion – where they can try to remember how frustrating it is to some people when the phone doesn't work, or when they lose their favorite marble.

Initiation is certainly a ritual space. An Australian aborigine said something to the effect that he had been doing initiations for forty years and he was just beginning to "get it" himself. That's the whole point, really. Initiation is for boys and middle age men and old men. It's a ritual space where they all come together and explore the mysteries of being male, recharge their fuel cells, serve the Grail, and encounter a moment of deep meaning and deep peace.

According to Camille Paglia, Masculinity is aggressive, unstable, combustible. It is also the most creative cultural force in history. Society came about to protect women from men's excesses, including rape.[221] At first this meant creating and maintaining "protected zones" for women; now it has come to mean that all of society is supposed to conform to female memes. Mama's Kitchen.

I live near a nude beach in Mexico where European girls come to take off all their clothes, lay in the sun, and complain about the dangers of getting raped – while Mexican men gawk in disbelief from behind palm trees, confirming their suspicions that all white women are sluts. This is a clash of two different societies: repressed Aztec and feminized Europe. What these girls do in Europe is their own business. What they are doing here is fueling rape. It should not surprise anyone when one of these impossibly aroused men sneaks out of the shadows and perpetrates some nefarious deed. The male brain is sexually aroused by visual stimuli – sexy clothes, no clothes. What these women are doing to these men is a form of mental cruelty and abuse. It's like inviting a friend for dinner and eating lobster and drinking champagne, while you serve her boiled peas and tap water. None of the sense stimuli conform to the reality that is being served up. If women don't want to be raped, they should wear clothes. What is this? Kindergarten? The more women can train us *not* to respond to them sexually when they prance around with next to nothing on, the more deadened we become, the more abused we become, the less masculine we become.

Women cannot be allowed to determine the parameters of male society. When they do, we end up with pathetically uncreative, socialist societies like those of northern Europe or marketing extravaganzas like Wal-Mart. The only way to reconstruct macho men, uninitiated men, is to bring them into a men's society where they can use their enormous right brain, sexual, intuitive, creative capacity to pierce the veil of *mater*ialist illusions and miscues that invade our brains – and find God – find the Source of meaning in life.

Carl Jung said, we overlook the essential fact that the achievements society rewards are won at the cost of diminution of personality. That is, the more women can train us *not* to respond to their naked bodies, the more raped our minds become, the less creative force we have to offer up. There is a direct correlation between serving feminist, *mater*ialist memes, and becoming less vital and less creative.

Says Jung, in order to sustain his creed (society), contemporary man pays the price in a remarkable lack of introspection. He is blind to the fact that with all his rationality and efficiency, he is "possessed" by powers that are beyond his control. Modern man does not understand how his rationalism has put him at the mercy of a "psychic" underworld. He has freed himself from superstition, but in the process has lost his spiritual values to a life-threatening degree. Humans are not equipped to "understand" everything. An appreciation for spiritual – not psychic – things helps us to delve fearlessly into the unknown. Without some spiritual "key" to unlock the doors of our minds, we cannot even approach our innermost levels of being.

Says Jung, there is a strong empirical (scientific) reason why we should cultivate thoughts which can never be proved. It is that *they are known to be useful*. They help us live. Man positively *needs* abstract ideas and ethical convictions that will give meaning to his life and enable him to find a place in the universe. "Man does not live by bread alone."

Says Bly, what we need is a Hairy Christ. I think we had one until someone edited out 18 years of his life – his young manhood. It's completely gone, like a screwdriver dropped in the ocean. Let's make some of the once known, that became unknown, known again. Whether or not Jesus physically traveled to India, there can be little doubt that he made his hairy pilgrimage into Hindu philosophy. Neil Douglas-Klotz retranslated some of the Aramaic words of Jesus. For instance, where the King James Bible translates Matthew 5:3 as "Blessed are the poor in spirit for theirs is the Kingdom of Heaven", a more accurate translation would be, "Aligned with the One are those who find their home in the breathing; the design of the universe is rendered in their form."[222] Is this the same book? Hindu yoga teachers are saying these same words every day in parlors in New York and Sydney. Prana is the breath of life. Westerners translated it as "spirit" because we needed to work in all those Greek forest nymphs and archetypes and minor deities so that Christianity would appeal to the pagan Greeks of 2000 years ago. Do you see it? We had a Hairy Christ, a wandering pilgrim, and we turned him into a Greek ideal god. We converted prana, "breathing", into the head honcho of all the "spirits" and "spirit powers" – a bunch of psychic crap.

Cynthia Bourgealt points out that for the earliest Christians, Jesus was not a Savior, not a life-saver, but a life-giver. In the Aramaic of Jesus and his followers, there was no word for "salvation". Salvation was understood as a bestowal of life and to be "saved" was to be "made alive."[223] Then along came the Greeks with their Dionysian rituals of death and resurrection and their intricate linguistic notions of "salvation" and once again the oriental import to Jesus' speech and life became westernized, *mater*ialized, psychicized.

Says Jung, what was the "spirit" (breathing) is now identified with intellect, and thus ceases to be the Father of All. It has degenerated into the limited ego-thoughts of man; the immense emotional energy expressed in the image of Our Father vanishes into the sand of an intellectual desert.

Says Joseph Campbell in *The Inner Reaches of Outer Space*, let's look at the opening of the Lord's Prayer and really see what it means. The invocation, "Our Father", is metaphorical, since the designated subject is not, in fact, a male parent, nor even a human being; yet the import is psychological, since the phrase suggests a relationship and a system of human sentiments such as that of a child to its male parent. There is evident, also, a transcendent, or metaphysical connotation, in that the implied parent is not of this earth, and thus out of time and space, but of eternity, in "Heaven", which is our popular term for the morphogenic fields beyond the perception of our senses.

The next verses call for the "will" of the Life Force to be present in our lives; an entreaty to be fed; and then come the curious passages, "Forgive us our trespasses as we forgive those who trespass against us." In modern American English this would best be rendered as "Forgive us our willfulness as we forgive the willfulness of others against us." And finally, begging off of the temptation to do stupid things. It's a good prayer. Don't be ashamed to use it just because of what some jerks have done with it. That would be like refusing to drive in a car because when you were 13 you saw a squashed bunny rabbit on the road. If it takes you out of yourself, out of your ego, use it. I do.

Says Carlos Castaneda's shamanic sage Don Juan: a man of knowledge knows that his life will be over altogether too soon, that nothing is more important than anything else. He has no honor, no dignity, no family, no name, no country, no culture [no ego], but only one life to be lived, and under these circumstances his only tie to his fellow men is his controlled folly.

Sometimes it takes certifiably insane people to drive this home to us. We can't see the forest for the trees. We can't see God for all the psychic memes. But the mentally incompetent are just that – they couldn't be bothered that nothing makes sense. They're working on something else, something much more important.

Ron Jones is a basketball and track coach for a Special Olympics team. My sombrero goes off to Ron Jones. Here's a man who set out to "give something back" and just look what he got for it.

Says Ron Jones:

My first Special Olympics team I took down to Los Angeles to compete in the state tournament. I had five athletes; you're always counting to yourself – "one, two, three, four, five" – to make sure they're all there. On this particular adventure, I had Michael Rice, who stands about six-four. He's a giant of a man. He and I started talking about, "We're going to kill 'em." He picked that up right away. Mentally disabled people pick up a phrase that you've tossed off callously and they'll begin to use it over and over. So in the airplane he begins to say nothing but, "We're going to kill 'em, Mr. Jones. We're going to kill 'em."

Joey Azaro is another athlete. Now Joey's got palsied arms that are all stiff and a wonderful smile. He's sitting next to me in the airplane, just grinning at the word, "kill". He's so excited about playing basketball.

Audi Stansberry is Michael's best friend and Joey's best friend. Audi is a great rebounder, but he doesn't know where to shoot the ball so he's always shooting at the wrong basket. But he does it with such grace and style that you have to take him on your team.

Then I had Jimmy Powers. He probably reminded me of myself because he's about two-feet-two tall. A great long shot, but he sleeps a lot.

And then I had Eddie Carter, the team lawyer. Eddie was always worried about: "We can't kill 'em. We don't want to kill 'em." And, "What time is it? We won't get there in time." He's always bustling around.

Anyway, we get into Los Angeles and I get my five athletes into their brand new black uniforms. In our first game we get blown away, but Michael Rice throws up his famous hook shot and he scores the last basket of the game. So my team jumps up thinking for sure they've won the game. We made the last shot so there's no doubt about it: We are the champions, we killed 'em. My five athletes are jumping up and down doing their war chant. The actual score was like thirty-six to two. That was the first and only basket we made, but it didn't matter – it came at the appropriate time.

The next game we play in East L.A. with these red devil uniforms. This team is really outstanding. Jimmy Powers makes one shot from about twenty feet away and that saves us for the first half. I'm finding myself standing up and yelling at Michael Rice, the best player I have: "Michael Rice, you dribble the ball down and do this and do that." I know what I'm doing, I can see myself in the mirror and I know I'm being stupid, but I'm lost. I can't help it. I'm so into the game that I'm a total fool and calling time outs and trying my best to change a physical situation that can't be changed.

So at the end of this game – we again were trounced terribly – my team gets off the floor and says, "We were great. Jimmy Powers was tremendous!"

I say, "Yeah, that was a good shot."

"We killed 'em, right Mr. Jones?"

"Well, we didn't quite kill 'em, but it was close." We had actually lost by sixty or seventy points; we just got murdered.

Then the official of the whole tournament comes over and he says, "Well, coach, here's some participation ribbons for your team. It might make them feel better. By the way, where's your team now?" We look around and the team has already moved on to the next floor and they're chanting at the game in process: "You're next! You're next! You're next!"

The final game we play is against San Diego, and everything you've always dreamed about happens in slow motion. Michael Rice makes the very first basket, a tip-toe lay-up. Audi gets the ball and shoots at the right basket. Unbelievable. Eddie stops being a lawyer and decides to play basketball and steals the ball and actually goes down and

scores. It's like the floor tilting in your favor. It only happens
once in a season.

Before this game, Joey Azaro had never even caught the
ball because he can't make his arms come down. He just
runs up and down the floor like crazy, grinning, trying to
scare the opponents. I usually give him a big defensive
assignment: I put him on the tallest player and he just grins
at his belt and circles around him in a great war dance. In
this game the ball was bouncing free in the open court and I
saw Joey go after it and I thought, "Oh no, he's going to
dive." Sure enough, midway down the floor he leaps through
the air, belly to the ground, lands on the ball and bounces
about four times with the ball under his stomach and then
rolls out of bounds. The official realizes what's going on
and does a dramatic gesture: "Ball goes to the black team
for good effort!" Joey gets up and smacks the ball back in.
His first catch and his first throw. By now I've settled down
and I realize the victories in this game are measured in inches,
not in baskets, and they're measured in different kinds of
qualities altogether. I'm very satisfied seeing what I'm seeing.
Of course now we're winning. It's easier to be gracious when
you're winning.

Anyway, the game comes to its dramatic end and my
team is now jumping up because they've won. I go over to
the other coach – winning coaches do this – and I say, "Gee,
coach, I'm really sorry that I couldn't hold my team back
and make the game more even."

The coach said to me, "Are you kidding? Look at my
team." I looked over at the San Diego team and they were all
jumping up and down: "We killed 'em! We killed 'em!" None
of these teams could keep score, so it's absolutely irrelevant.
The fact is you've played, you've played well, and if you're
lucky enough, the ball might have gone in the basket.

Coaching the Special Olympics, I realized that the level
of native ability is lower than anything I'd ever imagined. It
went way off the scale – so far off the scale that a brand new
game had to be invented. How do you play with someone in
a wheelchair who can only move with the assistance of

someone else? Well, the opposing team has to part and let this person move down the floor. You could easily take the ball out of that person's hands, but will you actually do it? It's an unwritten law in our games – when Rose gets the ball in her wheelchair and she's moving down the floor, no one takes the ball out of her hands. All the teams that play us instinctively know this, both regular teams and other Special Olympics teams. It's fun to see that recognition. Somehow, people know that the human spirit is more important than anything else.

The way we play it's impossible to lose. We declare ourselves 45 and 0. That's part of our loudspeaker announcement before the games: "Welcome to the King Dome, where the R.C.H. Special Olympic team is undefeated, forty-five wins and no defeats." The other team goes, "What?" There's a moment when their faces drop, like maybe it's really true. Then they catch on. But in truth, we are 45 and O – we are wonderful and successful and happy. Because we believe it, it's true.

When these people say, "We are the champions", they are saying we are *all* champions. That's the big difference. They are not saying, "We are champions, we're number one and you're number eight." It's hard to explain, because that wasn't my experience. I grew up striving to be "numero uno". But when you can't keep score, that's when bravery takes over, and a whole set of virtues. Like Joey Azaro diving headlong onto a ball that's bouncing loose. I've seen Joey Azaro try to high jump. He never could figure out how to get his legs to go first, so he dived over the bar like an arrow going straight up in the air and then straight down. I thought, "He's going to break his neck." I've seen the same kid approach a ropes course real high off the ground. With his elbows, he climbed up to the top of these things and then just rolled his body down into the net – because he wanted the experience. That seems pretty brave to me.[224]

As if that wasn't inspiring enough, Ron Jones tells another story of his team that is so deep with meaning I have to end the body of this book on it.

Says Jones:

A common Special Olympics experience is what happens when you prepare the athletes to race. I had painted pink lines with a spray can down one of the streets where I work and was very excited about giving the kids a sense of a real track with lanes and a starting line and a finish line. We worked a lot on how to start and finish a race. I had everyone all lined up in their favorite stance and they were all jiggling around in anticipation of the race. I ran about fifty yards and strung a line across from a telephone pole to myself. I told them, "I'm going to say, 'on your mark, get set, go,' and when you hear me say 'go,' you run as fast as you can down to where I am and run through this line. Does everybody understand that?"

"Yeah, yeah."

"Okay. Don't start yet. Now…on your mark…get set…go!"

I look at this surge coming at me, running and stumbling, and lo and behold this one guy is breaking out in front and this other woman is breaking out and it looks like I've got two really fast athletes. I begin mentally to cheer for the winner – "Come on! Faster! Faster!" – and I even start coaching – "Pump those arms! Lean!" I've got someone fast, maybe the championship of the world. So I'm out there yelling encouragement and all of a sudden I realize that this champion I've been yelling at has come to a screeching halt about five feet from the finish line, thrown both arms skyward, and then turned back to the other racers coming towards him. As the others reach him, he hugs them and holds them, and together they wait for the final runner who's literally wobbling down towards them. Then all of them, eight of them, grab onto each other's arms and cross the finish line together. My first impulse was to tell them, "You're supposed to race to win." But what I was starting to understand was that it was a sharing of victory as opposed to getting a victory. The idea that you would share something with your friends was more important than listening to this frantic coach yelling about pumping your arms. Coaches like you and I, or athletes like you and I who think we know the game – there's another game being played out there.

May the Deer God feed your life with meaning.
May you always remember to be grateful.

And may God bless all willful women,
and help them find
health,
and prosperity,
and happiness.

Conclusions

WE ARE ENGAGED IN a global civil war against FEMALENESS – the feminine urge to organize and control everything. Feminism is merely the visible symptom of this disease – femaleness – which has infested every corner of human society.

Here's the answer to the question every guy wonders about:

Q. How come we live in a society that APPEARS to be run by men but FEELS like it's run by women?

A. Because, like viruses, female values, FEMALE MEMES, have invaded our psyches. Men's psyches, women's psyches, children's psyches. It's been going on for millennia. We live in a world designed by and for female values – female memes.

The Patriarchy is a Matriarchy. We do not live in a Patriarchy; we live in a Covert Matriarchy. Women and feminized men enforce female values, female memes.

It's time for a Backlash – not merely against feminism – but against FEMALENESS: that relentless and largely unchallenged presumption within ALL our institutions that life is better if it's organized and controlled. Feminism is an insignificant historical blip, a petty diversion into greed, women taking jobs from

493

feminized men. Femaleness is an historical force which has marched on uncontested for millennia. Femaleness is *materi-alism* with guns. Femaleness leads to wars and we're the ones stuck fighting them. We've gotta break free of the control-freaks.

Above all, we need protections against corporations. Corporations should no longer be legally recognized as "persons", but as foreign economic "nations" operating in our midst. We should realize we cannot shrink government without shrinking corporations because then we are just handing our heads to corporate golems, setting them loose to terrorize our lives. Our goals should be these, in this order:

1) make corporations smaller
2) make governments smaller
3) make schools smaller
4) make churches smaller

Then may we regain some of the spontaneity and independence so crucial to masculine soul. Then may we regain variety in life and reinvigorate our society with this elusive thing called "balance". The female urge is to control everything. The male urge is to pray to God – and let it ride. We don't need careers, we need jobs. We don't need factory schools, we need a few good teachers. We don't need massive churches, we need a few spiritual leaders who live the teachings. We don't need central government, we need local control. We don't need corporations, we need honest businessmen who stay responsible for their business activities – not try to skip town when they create a disaster.

If corporations were held legally and criminally responsible for their activities government regulatory agencies would dry up and blow away. They'd have nothing to do. Government would get smaller. Right now we're stuck in a pattern of letting corporations get away with murder – real murder. There is no ethical reason corporate managers should be permitted to make "business" decisions to pollute our lives and sell us bad products

– and then skip out on the damages. Fine them. Throw them in jail. Make the same rules for all of them.

Corporations are not "efficient", any more so than throwing your garbage out the window is more efficient than investing in a sewage system. They're throwing their garbage out the window and it's landing on our faces and in our lungs – and we call this good business? We proclaim to the world that the free market is "efficient"? We're wearing our underpants on our heads. We argue – liked trained parrots – that corporations are giving us jobs. Where? In Taiwan? God help us to wake up. Corporations are not people. But corporate managers are greedy, self-consumed people. Make them personally responsible for their misdeeds and both corporations and government will get smaller.

This issue is not right wing or left wing, Republican or Democrat, capitalist or socialist – both political agendas have failed us. That labeling system doesn't work any more. Neither offers a choice. They're both female systems dedicated to the proliferation of *mater*ialism. Our goal is Freedom. Freedom *from* things. Not freedom to *have* more things. Our goal is to be free of femaleness.

You don't need permission from anyone to start living as a free man today. You just need balls.

Do I hate women? Not at all. I don't hate tigers, and I don't hate women. But I'm putting myself in extreme danger if I don't understand a tiger's nature or a woman's nature. Yes, extreme danger. This is no game any more. Feminism isn't cute. Femaleness is rotting people's souls. There's too much history and too much mythology warning us that men need to hold themselves apart from women. I don't hate women. I just want half of life back. The masculine half. I don't think women should be controlling that.

Feminists are not the problem, they're just trying to get due credit for 8000 years of women manipulating human civilization. Feminists are being manipulated by their own female manipulations. Millennia ago women thrust men up onto the podium to engender a more *mater*ialistic society. Female leadership in the early days of agriculture was so oppressive that the Goddess was offed and male gods brought on stage. Female leadership at the dawn of industrialization would have been too obvious, too self-serving. So, once again, in a repeat of the duplicity that commandeered the age of agriculture, women enlisted feminized men to do their bidding – and drafted no-nothing boys to fight the inevitable wars spawned by *mater*ialist obsessions.

And now that they've created a society that's a monument to *mater*ialism, women want men's jobs. But only the management jobs, the power jobs, the control jobs – thank you. They don't want to be going out in ice storms to fix downed electric lines. They don't want to be pouring asphalt. Just give them the jobs they shoved feminized men into centuries ago: congressional aide, policy wonk, lawyer, office manager, decision maker, and hey!…while we're at it, why not congresswoman? It's all a transparent rip-off of real masculinity.

All the things women *blame* on men are the things women *put in men*. Fear, negativity, over-controlling, addictive behavior are female memes that have plagued human society for millennia. Until we recognize that the source of these debilitating behaviors is feminine, we don't have a chance of eradicating them. Until we recognize that war is caused by female *mater*ialistic greed, we don't have a chance of ending it. Until we recognize that corporations are dedicated to servicing female *mater*ialism, we don't have a prayer of constricting them. Until we acknowledge that big government grows bigger by passing legislation to calm the fears of women, we don't have a chance of shrinking it. Until we realize that religion has been designed to appeal to female psychic fantasies, we don't have a prayer of regenerating a vital spirituality. Until we admit that MOST of the problems of modern life are caused by women, we don't have a feather in a hurricane's chance of eliminating them. As long as we keep blaming everything on men we're wearing our underpants on our heads – and big corporations and big government will continue to colonize our minds and our lives. Psyche, "feminine mind", has put us all to sleep.

We've flashed back to the Garden of Eden. Corporations are the snake, whispering in our wives' ears: buy more stuff, you have "rights", don't let God tell you what to do. Our women are lost. They're hopeless. And they're dragging us down with them. For shame if we don't stand up to this Unbridled Femaleness – these servants of the corporate snake.

Feminized Government has invaded religion and produced feminized religion. Separation of Church and State is a hoax. We did a good job keeping religion out of government but not a good job keeping government out of religion. Time to regenerate male-flavored spirituality. It's the key to solving this whole mess.

WW III has begun. It's an electronic war being fought between corporate persons and human persons. And feminists are whoring for the enemy troops. They're after a big piece of the corporate pie. They want official recognition that agriculture and industrialization was all about them – making life better for women – at the expense of men.

Let's revisit where this book began and see if my contentions make more sense now…Now that a little of the once known, that became unknown, has become known again.

Feminists are corporate whores.

For over 30 years feminists have demonized men, undermined the family, and ridiculed religion. Male values, family values and religious values have been marginalized, made fun of, dismissed as passé. In the vacuum created by the hemorrhage of these historically cardinal values corporations rushed in and flooded our brains with their core values: wealth, celebrity, and the "free trade" smorgasbord of things to buy. But since, as their root strategy, corporations design themselves to appeal to the endemic shopping compulsions of women, what we are left with is an incestuous, self-perpetuating cycle of greed. Feminists feed corporations and corporations feed feminists. Feminists don't care if corporations ship our jobs overseas and build Third World sweat shops. They only care if there are equal numbers of women on the boards of directors. Feminism is not a grassroots movement of oppressed women. It's a multibillion dollar a year "INFORMATION INDUSTRY" that has infected our schools, government, factories and families with high-paid workers oozing an academic pus of wrong "facts", misplaced priorities, bad ideas and self-righteous rhetoric.

Ever since we were walking around in wet diapers all of us have been drenched in a never-ending rain of corporate propaganda – on the TV, in the papers, on the streets, everywhere we look, everywhere we listen. At the same time, thanks to the haughty drumbeat of feminist ideologues screeching at us from every available electronic soapbox, we have been deprived of the masculine values, family values and church values which could have balanced the seesaw of modern culture. Feminists sold our heads to huge corporations with a whistle and a blowjob. They got jobs. So what? The trade-off was that our lives are now being bought and sold by impersonal, non-accountable, corporate behemoths. We have lost all sense of what a man is, what a family is, and what Faith is. In other words, we have lost all sense of the Meaning of Life.

The solution is simple.

We need to regenerate a male-flavored spirituality.

We need to move men, families and Faith to a reinvigorated prominence in our lives. Forget feminist schemes, Forget corporate scams. And don't forget that big government means big business these days. The two are equivalent. Or, as Gerry Spence says, big government and big corporations are like two screwing dogs who got stuck together. When one pulls, the other follows. Crude. But sublimely accurate.

And what's the first step in recovering from this feminist/corporate/big government nightmare? We need to get our thinking straight. Right now we've got it all backwards.
Men and women have swapped mental roles. Men have become more like women. Women have become more like men.

Men are submitting to their "female" side. Women, to offset this vacuum of masculinity, have begun acting out of their "male" side. It's not good. In fact, it's a disaster. Men do not make good women and women do not make good men. We are both operating out of our weaker natures. Men have no aptitude for the finer nuances of domesticity. Women do not understand the finer nuances of the "hunt". We have crippled ourselves. We're eating soup with a fork. We've tied our families into knots.

The feminization of human society began 8000 years ago when we abandoned hunting and gathering for the joys of agriculture. The "King" was the first feminized man. He wore dresses, garnished himself with jewelry, perverted the hunters into soldiers to guard his castle full of stuff, and all in all, behaved just like a woman. He was rich and powerful – which women admire. And he set a feminized, *mater*ialistic standard for what men should be like.

Our lives are inside out. Here's what we got backwards:

Women are more *mater*ialistic than men. *Mater*, the Latin word for mother, is the root word of *mater*ialism. Women own 65% of America's wealth according to Forbes magazine. Seven times more retail space is allotted to women's personal items than to men's. Women make 80% of buying decisions. Women have naively entered into an unholy alliance with corporations to provide themselves with more jobs and more stuff. The corporate conquest, the *mater*ialist mindset of modern society, may be blamed directly on female greed, female self-seeking and female *mater*ialism.

Men are not the cause of war. Greed, *mater*ialism, and self-seeking are the causes of war. The 20th century witnessed an exponential increase in women' rights including the right to vote. And an exponential increase in war – two World Wars and hundreds of equally deadly lesser conflicts. These facts are NOT unrelated. Female greed, *mater*ialism, and self-seeking are the major causes of war. Men are obligated to fight war.

Women are not. But women adore the security, luxury and technical "time-saving" gadgetry produced in a military economy. Female values are the cause of war. **Women are the cause of war**.

Men are more spiritual than women. Every human society has acknowledged the Earth Mother and the Sky Father. Woman is down, into the earth, grounded, *mater*ialistic. Man is up, into the sky, dreamy, creative, spontaneous, seeking that invisible God. It is a travesty and oppression of male nature to claim women are more spiritual than men.

Women are not Morally Superior to men. Women are not always kind, caring, and sharing. Sometimes they're mean and conniving and manipulating. Psychological stereotyping has done a profound disservice to men by casting women as nurturing and men as aggressive. Female business barracudas and politicians are ruthless beyond belief to most men's way of thinking. My kind, caring, sharing side is not my female side; it's my kind, caring, sharing side! My mean, manipulative, aggressive side is not my masculine side; it's my mean, manipulative, aggressive side! Sadly, due to our societal blindness to the fact that women are not morally superior to men, women get away with perpetrating far more than their fair share of tragedies and outrages. If a man hits a woman we want to toss the bastard in jail. If a woman hits a man we want to know what he said to piss her off. Women think "Fidelity" is a city in Pennsylvania. Throughout human history women, being physically weaker, have honed their skills at lies, deceptions, and masquerades. But we, simple-minded saps that we are, succumbing to their smiley, solicitous mannerisms, have subconsciously elevated them onto a pedestal of Moral Superiority. It's a crock. Women know what other women are like. It's us dopes who deny the moral sliminess of women. We think we "need" some image of feminine purity. We crawl on our bellies through the grease pits of life clinging to some icon of "mom". Well chumps…here's the low-down. When it's a man's word against a woman's word, best to believe the man.

* * *

Men are more intuitive than women. Our art, our science, our mathematics – our entire society – is the product of male intuition. For millennia men have grabbed abstractions out of the sky and struggled to bring them into physical form – "intuiting" the possibilities. "Women's intuition" is little more than analytical extrapolations driven by negativity – perennial predictions of doom. Few women are spending any time thinking about why the universe is now expanding faster than it has been for the past 10 billion years. But every one of them can produce detailed scenarios of how "everything is going to get worse".

Women are more analytical than men. Women are more "logical" than men. Once you understand that logic is a bicycle sprocket with missing teeth, a cuckoo clock that can't keep time – because it keeps skipping over huge hunks of reality – it's clear that women, not men, are the logicians. Logic ALWAYS breaks down. Female thinking ALWAYS breaks down. It's obvious to anyone that women analyze the bejesus out of the tiniest details of every situation and, in doing so, they organize the creative chaos of life into sterility and do-nothing nihilism. Men take a wider view and see a larger, albeit foggier picture – and then run on the field and throw the ball.

Men are more skilled in relationships than women. Women talk a lot about relationships. Men DO relationships. Men are team players. That's how Columbus crossed the Atlantic. That's how men got on the moon. Watch a basketball game – darting, dribbling, signaling with a bobbed head, motioning with an eye-twitch, passing to the place where the guy is *supposed* to be – leaping, catching, shooting, scoring. Male relationship happens faster than the speed of talk.

Men have deeper feelings than women. Women have more emotions, men have deeper feelings. Women gush about this or wail about that. Men hold their feelings deep down inside them. Occasionally masculine feeling explodes into the open – virtually all of our art and music and literature are products of masculine feelings. But mostly men are afraid to show their feelings – afraid because they've been shamed. Shamed by the very women who claim they want men who are "not afraid" to express their feelings. But when men put caution aside and tell their women how they really feel, inevitably, in one way or another, the women respond with, "You shouldn't feel like that." *i.e.* "You shouldn't have those feelings." *i.e.* "Shame on you, you big lout". And it's all accomplished with such sharing, caring, solicitousness that, from a very young age, men learn to see this for what it is: another female manipulation. When you reveal your feelings to a woman she'll use them against you somehow. It's like we're always in court, and the opposing attorney is drilling us with a deposition while she's cooking us spaghetti. Scary. Who do you trust? Other men? You must be kidding.

"Equality" is meaningless. Is a bee equal to a sparrow? Is a whale equal to a squirrel? The term is meaningless. And anyway, feminism was never truthfully about Equality. Feminism was about MORE STUFF FOR WOMEN. Women don't want to mine coal or get drafted into war. That's too much Equality for them. Just let them have some office job so they can stay comfortable and buy more stuff. Forget that they live 8 years longer than us. Ignore the fact that 19 out of 20 people who die on the job are men. Or 4 out of 5 suicides are men. Or 80% of the homeless are men. That's the other side of Equality, and they don't want to hear about it.

"Programs for men? Men have everything – don't they? …Me?" she titters. "Sign up for the draft? Drill oil? You must be kidding. I'm not equipped for that. That's not the kind of Equality I mean."

Feminism is a disaster. For 8000 years the world has been becoming progressively more feminized. We've lost sight of our true gender natures. 100 years ago the feminists were trying to get women and kids out of the factories to make stronger families. The current feminist movement wants to put them *back in* – and destroy the family. Insidious. Misguided. Evil.

* * *

Men are not the oppressors of women. The simple proof of that is that **Women are not oppressed**. Women are not now, and never have been "oppressed". Women have the right to vote with NO concomitant obligation to be drafted in time of war to protect their right to vote. Personally, I don't see how they got the one without being forced to assume the other. They have power without responsibility. The only way Democracy got reborn in the modern world was because men fought and died battling the power of kings and their corporations to seize this right. But women gained it by fighting what? A "courageous" ideological struggle? It's Twinkies. Philosophical oatmeal.

Nor are women expected to perform heavy labor – laying bricks, pouring asphalt, fixing cars. They live in houses they don't build, drive cars they can't fix, eat food they don't grow. This is oppression? In fact, women are coddled, not oppressed. Women are strident and pushy and obnoxious in ways men never can be because we'd get punched or shamed or arrested, and they won't – since they're just women.

If someone came up to me tomorrow and said, "I got a great deal for you. You'll never have to fight in war or do heavy labor again…All you have to do is sign away your right to vote." I'd say, "Where do I sign?" That's all I NEED government for. Keeping me out of war and protecting me from oppressive labor conditions. I don't need to vote if those rights are guaranteed. That's fair. But apparently it's not fair enough for women. They can vote but they need not fight nor pour concrete. That's a perversion of the word Equality. The entire feminist movement is built on the phony proclamation that "women are oppressed". Pull that out from under them (as I have on various radio shows) and their naked ego and raw greed flap like pantyhose in the wind. And what do they do then? Scream. Scream like little girls. Try to shame me any way they can. **The Achilles' Heel of feminism is the unprovable proposition that women are oppressed.**

Feminism has, in fact, created an **Aristocracy of Women** – a select club of people who, by virtue of birth alone, do not have to fight in war or pound nails. And, as if that privilege wasn't enough, they've browbeat politicians into instituting government fast-tracks so they can attain the highest positions of power and authority in society – judges, senators, CEOs, media mavens.

Feminism is government by coffee klatch. Feminism, by its very nature, dissociates opinions from action. It's easy to vote boys into war, or write a column about how bridges should be repaired, as long as you never have to be the one to fight or do the work. Feminism divorces ideas from action. Feminism destroys masculine soul. **Feminism annihilates Love**.

Time to recapture our true natures. Time to bury the hatchet in the gender wars by rediscovering who we really are, where our true strengths lie, and what we honestly expect out of life. It's either that, or we'll each be permanently assigned to a corporation at birth. Destruction of the family – social disintegration, ethical collapse – leads directly to corporate colonialism – the usurpation of all money and media and education and government and means of production – all thoughts and dreams and aspirations – by huge economic entities, servicing the "needs" of women – which "needs" were put there by corporations in the first place! That amounts to *de facto* Economic Slavery. Soul murder. The Dark Ages again. A snake biting its own tail.

The unintended consequence of feminism, the feminization of human society – the destruction of the family – has been the corporate conquest of our brains and our bodies and our lives. **Corporate Colonialism**. No, that's not what the girls meant to have happen. But it happened. So let's call it a mistake. A big mistake. Forgive each other. Trash the whole thing. And move on. Our enemy is NOT women. It's Corporate Colonialism. But we can never win this war when one half of the human race is blindly selling out to the other side. We need the women to wake up. Feminists are frauds. In a society as crippled by stress and frustration as ours – after 30 years of women having things their way – it's clear that women don't have the answers. They don't have any inborn natural knowledge of what is good and what is right. Time to dig deeper. I'm tired of living in a "female friendly" world that has become oppressive to both men and women.

By destroying the family feminism threw the door open for the corporate conquest of our lives. By marginalizing family and church values, a vacuum was created whereby corporate values became unstoppable. Our kids' brains are boobed out.

Why did that happen? Because we kept religion out of government but not government out of religion. Here's a summation of recent American history that isn't being taught in school.

Due to the dislocations caused by the Civil War government emerged as a Moral Enforcer. First it told men they couldn't have more than one wife. Then it required that all marriages be registered. Then it began importing British Church Law into American Civil Law so government could begin administering marriage and divorce. Finally, like thieves in the night, corporations hijacked the zephyr of justice which had granted wider civil rights to emancipated slaves and women. Corporate lawyers snuck under the fence and grabbed the greatest share of these civil rights for their invisible masters by getting corporate golems legally identified as persons. This murky cesspool of overlapping agendas, whereby self-righteous "suffragettes" unwittingly sniff-out the legal trail to enlarge civil rights for corporations, has been spewing legal toxins in our face for a century – and we never talk about it!

The more "rights" women get, the more "rights" corporations get. Women can own property, corporations can own property. Women can participate in the political process, corporations can participate in the political process. Women can skip out on war, corporations can skip out on war. It's been estimated that around 80% of the Civil Rights litigation clogging our courts today adjudicates the rights of corporate persons, not human persons. What a nightmare. We've kept religion out of government, but not government out of religion. First women became "free" and "equal" – trashing 4000 years of religious tradition that preserved balance in marriage. And now the government is creating "people"! Masculine religion has been systematically beat to death and only the corporate golems are laughing.

Then feminism came along and destroyed the family. Now our kids are being raised by TV. Family values have gone the way of the buffalo. We've been colonized by our own corporations. We are all slaves.

Throughout world history the most decadent cultures have been too feminine, and the most dynamic cultures have been too masculine.

Says Wolfgang Lederer:
Woman has no use for freedom: she seeks not freedom but fulfillment. She does not mean to be a slave or unequal before the law, but she does require the presence of a man in her life strong enough to protect her from herself.[225]

That's the point I've been trying to make for several hundred pages. Women are lost in a psychic swamp, throwing words and ideas and pictures at each other trying to rearrange all the furniture in their heads to make sense. Without the presence of a genuine male spirituality somewhere around them, they cannot get out of themselves, they cannot quit serving their own egos – and that will never make them happy. Not ever.

Let's run through a condensed smattering of some of the facts we learned in this book just to reaffirm how wrongly we've been educated. For decades feminists claimed that, "men and women are exactly the same except for how they've been raised." That's a lie.

Men and women are not the same. Our brains are as physically and functionally different as our bodies because our brains are gonads – sex glands. Male brains are larger with less verbal and greater intuitive capacity. Women are verbal and literal – left-brained. Men are intuitive and dreamy – right-brained. Women are analytical, men are creative.

Men are not born, men are made; first of all by male hormones, then by the society of men they are raised into. The hypothalamus, the brain's basic emotional center, is built the same way in women and male homosexuals, and differently in heterosexual men. Men are turned on by visual sexual stimuli. Women are turned on by aural sexual stimuli. Male *Homo sapiens* has the longest, thickest erect penis of the 192 species of apes. The more women succeed in training men *not to* respond to visual sex stimuli, the less vital and creative we will be.

Memes are mental genes that spread from brain to brain like viruses, propagating our cultural values.

We live in a covert matriarchy. We're smothered in mother. Like coeds in jeans, female memes have cloaked themselves in male costumes – male absorption.

The "men" who run our society got where they got by enforcing female values – playing well to women. These men I call manholes, the opposite of whole men.

Our educational system is female.

Our churches and synagogues are female.

Our government is female.

Our corporations are female.

All of these are enforcers of female, *mater*ialist memes.

Mater, the Latin word for mother, is the root word of *mater*ialism.

"The Hunter" is the oldest male meme, the deepest male archetype.

"Work", the central preoccupation of modern society, is a crime against humanity and is directly responsible for the rape of the planet.

Men are the original hunters and priests. Women are the original farmers and manufacturers. For 8000 years, since the arrival of the Great Goddess, men have been seduced away from their hunting and praying, and taught to farm and work in factories. In other words, for 8000 years men have been educated to think of women's work as their own. For 8000 years women have been influencing men and machines to do their work. Men and machines gather the grains. Men and machines make the pots. Women haven't been bothered with that work in eons. This they label "progress".

The abandonment of the Hunter/Priest, the man who prayed to his prey, has dropped a bomb on male spirituality. Men don't bring their prayers to work anymore.

Women are not more intuitive and creative than men. Women are less intuitive and less creative than men. The greatest chefs and clothing designers, as well as the greatest artists and thinkers, are all men. It is the natural, normal tendency of women to employ a practical, verbal, literal, *material* approach to problems, thereby squashing intuition and creativity. In other words, women like to take over. Understand things on "their terms". Not reach into the unknown. In order to defend themselves from women, men, in every surviving human society, have created a male ritual space. They segregated themselves from women and initiated boys into this sacred, non-verbal space.

Men are addicted to praise by their mothers. They are manipulated by visual stimuli to crave sex. They are shot full of shame and lust and set loose in the female/industrial mindscape to find their way on their own. Businessmen are sexual psychopaths addicted to gratification. So are politicians. Says Esther Vilar, in a country where man is exploited as unscrupulously by woman as in the USA, a movement that fights for yet more rights for women is reactionary.

Women are trained not to feel emotion. Men are trained not to express emotion. Men feel things much more deeply than women. That's where our art and music come from – male emotion.

Female intuition is a euphemism for statistical probability based on perennial predictions of doom.

* * *

Feminist propaganda has painted woman as the nurturer, man as the destroyer.

Wars are fought to defend *mater*, the *mater*ial. The cravings of women cause wars.

Welfare dispenses economic power through women and emasculates men.

Working wives do not anticipate spending their income on the "bills". Their income is reserved for gifts and toys and vacations.

Our schools are geared for girls. First grade rewards you for sitting still and having good handwriting – a fine-motor skill that girls excel at. Boys feel dumb and sloppy and restless in school. School is a shaming experience for boys.

Men look for God outside themselves. Women look for God inside themselves. Women confuse psychic phenomena with spirituality. Male spirituality is beyond the grasp of most women.

The Men's Movement is a movement within men. Guys need guy friends to stay sane. Fishing buddies, football buddies – guy friends.

Priests and judges are manholes who wear dresses in some theatrical attempt to give themselves a regal air. The King was the original manhole. 8000 years ago in Sumeria Gilgamesh, the King, seduced the Wildman away from his herds by using a temple prostitute of Astarte – it's still going on today.

If American culture were a real culture, it would provide some sort of initiation rituals to bring young men into the company of revered elders.

Joe Campbell says that a wound is a hole where the soul enters the body. There is no question of going through life without being wounded – that would be an inhuman experience. We are born with humongous egos and spend our entire lives shrinking them. We are deeply shamed when our parents pass on their particular brand of shame to us, and working through this mindswamp of ego and shame is our job in this Life.

We require a reinvented male initiation into American culture. Our culture is so vast and amorphous – tribal thinking has gone the way of the passenger pigeon – that this is at once a tall order and an excellent cultural focal point for America. We are, after all, the inventors of the notion of a global culture.

Our church spires are emasculated dicks. The Washington monument is an emasculated dick. The real business of our government takes place within the White House and the dome of the Capitol, which is a big tit.

The agenda of our government, fostering *mater*ial growth – and then being forced to defend it – is an ancient female agenda, as ancient as making bread and shooing rats out of the pantry.

Why do men still love to hunt and fish? Because the Hunter meme hooks us into the deepest part of our psyche. It puts us back into the prayerful intuitive space we inhabited for 2.2 million years up until about 8000 years ago. The United States is a "new" country. In fact, it hasn't really become a country yet, it's just an idea. We have no culture other than the culture of buying things and talking about freedom. 400 years ago we were still living as hunters here. Hunting is gaining food without polluting the rivers and tearing up the earth. Men are the original conservationists. Women are the ones who love to plow things up and arrange them and put their stamp on them. Men are capable of living in harmony with the earth. Women, manholes, and their *mater*ial memes, taken to the extremes of the past 8000 years, clearly are not. Shopping *means* the rape of the earth.

Corporate, church, government and female values are identical. Control, manipulation, accumulation of wealth are precisely the opposite of the values enacted by the Native American man who gave away everything he had at the annual Potlatch ceremony. Why did he do it? Because he was a man. He was in harmony with his god. He could always go out and get more.

The old archetypes aren't working. The King is a man in a dress. The Warrior stepped on a mine in Nam. The Magician has wires and strings running up inside his sleeves. The Lover has AIDS. If you need to use archetypes, junk the European archetypes, and come alive to the idea that we live in a country where every mountain is a temple and every stream is sacred to the original inhabitants. We live in a sacred universe, not a constipated Freudian nightmare. Forget Europe. They haven't known what they were doing over there in 1000 years. Their art sucks. Their literature sucks. Their philosophers are manholes. Their governments wear dresses. The pope is a politician. They haven't produced any spiritual giants since St. Francis, and they won't, unless they rediscover the Green Man carved into their churches and recapture a sense of the sacred. Europe is the most feminized continent on earth. God is dead and culture is style. As Joseph Campbell says, we need a new myth for our times. The old ones aren't working. Physics offers us the mythology of black holes and quasars and virtual particles which hold forth spiritual promise for guided meditations on the wonder of it all. Welcome back to the place where science and spirituality hold hands.

It's time to turn away from all the signs and symbols and archetypes and psychic masturbation of the feminized world we inhabit and stare into the blackness. Black is beautiful. The black is the light. Our world emanates from a world that is beyond the reach of our senses and our measuring instruments. Particle physicists know this world is there, but we can't measure it, because our measuring devices are made of the stuff of this world. This appreciation for the unknown is in the touchstone of male spirituality and male creativity.

"Wellness conferences" are composed of sick women staying sick. All the health fads and exercise programs and pop culture psychobabble are recycled feminism – the Fix-It-Philosophy. "Healing" communities and workshops are mostly psychic masturbation. We're not here to get healed. We're here to die. We're here to kill our egos. Whatever it is that may or may not go on after we leave this life, it's not going to be our ego. That stays here. We aren't going to be sitting around in heaven eating spaghetti and watching football or discussing "relationships". That stuff stays here.

* * *

The female's initiation is her wedding. The groom should burn the bride's wedding gown *at the ceremony* to demonstrate to her that her girlhood is over. This is real. This is marriage. This is the death of the little girl ego.

James Joyce said that all art which creates desire is pornographic. Our media, our advertising, are pure pornography.

A man's constitutional right of being presumed innocent until proven guilty is shit upon the instant his spouse levels *unsubstantiated* accusations of abuse against him in a court of law. 95% of abuse accusations tendered during divorce are false. To "protect" 5% of children, we are destroying the most sacred bond there is between 95% of so-accused divorcing fathers and their kids.

The most frequent child batterers are women.

The most frequent victims are their two-year-old sons.

The most unreported crime is not wife beating but husband beating.

Men have no rights in abortion. They cannot even *adopt* their own child should the wife/girlfriend opt to give it up for adoption.

The Supreme Court has ruled that the sex discrimination law was enacted to protect women only.

Marriage has always been a religious institution, not a government program. The reason our divorce rate is so high is because government is incapable of administering marriage and divorce. We have kept religion out of government but not government out of religion. There is court machinery to collect child support but virtually none to enforce visitation. Mothers who deny fathers' court-ordered visitation with their children should go to jail.

Support and visitation disputes must be handled in the same court – not split between two courts as they currently are.

In divorce the children should *automatically* be split between both parents. This will curb divorce and steer the parties toward honest mediation, eliminate visitation disputes, and alleviate the "problem" of so called "runaway dads" – beat dead dads – guys who couldn't support one household on their income, much less two.

Our divorce rate is 60%. Half of the kids in this country are growing up without dads. The feminist agenda is destroying the family.

Studies show that kids raised without dads are neurotic and insecure. Unsubstantiated rumors warn us about similar effects when siblings are split up. "It's bad to split up the kids," they warn. It's worse to remove the dads.

Until the doctrine of "*mater*nal precedence" took hold of the courts 100 years ago, fathers routinely got custody of the kids in divorce.

The bane of our society is the self-consumed woman. Feminism has no self-governing factor, no end-game to its self-seeking. Feminism serves feminism. Any mythology will tell you that this is a psychological crime. As soon as one goal is accomplished, the rhetoric heats up for the next objective. There is no end-point. Isn't a 60% divorce rate enough of an end-point? Isn't the corporate conquest of our society enough of an end-point? Female greed has bottomed out. There's nothing more to get.

Women have power over life. They live 10%, eight years, longer than men do. That's the most important power there is in this plane of existence.

Men are right-brained and therefore more attuned to "relationship" than women. Male relationship happens faster than the speed of talk. We are less verbal about relationships because we are less verbal, period. Men speak 2000 words a day, women speak 7000. We are also less nosey, less controlling, less manipulating. But by no measure do we experience lesser feelings.

Who defines crime? Stealing a car is a crime – abusing the *mater*ial. Denying a dad's visitation is not a crime – abusing relationship. Wife beating is physical abuse – a crime. Female shaming is verbal abuse – not a crime. Possession is 90% of the law. 90% of the time the law is enforcing *mater*, the *mater*ial. That means 90% of the time the law is ignoring relationship – the Deep Male.

Most men are in jail for trying to score cars, cash or coke for their "babes", who offer them sex and praise, which they were trained to crave by mom and media. We were addicted to praise when we were still peeing in our pants and it's used to manipulate us throughout our lives. The only remedy is the sloughing off of shame – the annihilation of ego – that genuine spirituality provides.

Carl Jung has said that men are more honest with themselves than women. Women are quick to blame other people or things. Men strive to see their own part in a problem. *Women can't even have an honest relationship with themselves. How can they have an honest relationship with anyone else?* Women don't even know what a relationship is. It's taken me forty-five years to realize that the women in my life are not lying to me. By the time the lie gets to me, they're already believing it. They're lying to themselves, and I just happen to be in the way. The amount of confusion and misdirection women create in the lives of the people around them is awesome to behold if you are a person who is capable of being half-honest with yourself. My ex would have an affair, then try to get me to believe that she hadn't *really* had an affair because she only slept with the guy six times! Nothing in this life worth having can be gained through dishonesty. And now women are convincing themselves they are the "relationship" half of the species. Why? Because they talk four times more than we do? Marriage to a person who is incapable of self-honesty is a banana boat to Pluto.

Esther Vilar says that women train themselves from youth never to express their true feelings. Talking to women about how we're feeling constitutes little more than handing them the ammunition to shoot us in the back.

* * *

Men die of work-related injuries at a rate of 19 to 1 over women. Aaron Kipnis calls this Dying for Dollars. The reverse discrimination of Affirmative Action is forcing men to take even more dangerous jobs as women slide into the cushy ones. More than 52% of all managers are women. Less than 1% of house painters and roofers and masons are women.

In their dangerous occupations, men – instead of being targeted as the group that requires the greatest health benefits – receive virtually zero community support for health care, health maintenance, preventative care education, psychological counseling, social welfare assistance, parenting enforcement or advocacy against discrimination. Most men live lives of inferior quality to most women. That's why they get drunk.

Men, as distinct from women *and* children, comprise 40% of the nation's poor – the largest single bloc. 80% of the homeless are men.

More women are covered by private insurance, and government insurance covers twice as many women as men.

Public clinics offer free breast exams. No one is offering us free prostate exams. I've yet to meet a doctor who volunteers to stick his finger up my ass.

Female healthcare is free. Male healthcare costs big bucks. Is it any wonder they outlive us?

There are not nearly enough male studies courses. 85% of teachers are white women. College campuses are the province of manhole professors with soft hands and clean fingernails, who aren't disposed to pass up getting laid by a coed. It doesn't take courage to tout the agenda of feminist harpies, it takes courage to oppose them.

The so-called Patriarchy, the "White Male" System, is the Manhole System, is the Addictive Society, is the *Mater*ialist Society, is Corporate/Socialism – is Marxist/Feminism. Feminism means government/corporate control of our lives.

The traits of the Addictive Society, the Marxist/Feminist society, are the feminine traits of: negativity, fear of scarcity, control, manipulation, judgmentalism, egoism, finding god inside yourself, being "nice", being "objective", dishonesty, left-brainedness, prone to panic, rational, rationalizing, "understanding", denial (dishonesty with yourself), perfectionism, physically aloof, defensive, concealing feelings, psychic masturbation (spiritual bankruptcy), promise of future rewards, praise bestowing (more ego building), shaming, absorption of other people – meme invasion – colonization, forgetful of unpleasantness, the sleep of unknowing, dualistic thinking, and most of all – shooing the Deep Masculine off the steps to your brain with a frying pan or a hint of mascara.

Here are some good things about men. Men are: generous, fair, focused, nurturing, leaders, servants, silly, outrageous, not panicky, not controlled by emotion, determined, tolerant of different opinions, not grudge-holders, protective of weaker ones, willing to sacrifice, serve higher goals, spiritual – depend on an invisible Life Force – self-starting, risk-taking, quick to challenge authority, inventive, creative, humble, responsible, have a sense of efficacy – know "what works" – don't complain or gossip much, not afraid to fail, funny – quick to joke and laugh – adventurous, resourceful, enjoy women – right now – and love to play with kids on kids' terms.

Men are beautiful, not flawed by nature, not machines for work. Men are full of deep feeling. Men have the right to be wrong sometimes. Men must not depend on women for "spirituality" – or they'll get sucked into psychic goop – and lose all sense of who they really are.

The New Male Manifesto is easy to remember. It goes like this:

LET THEM FIX THEIR OWN TOILETS!

Women love to get men to work on their real estate for them. Especially divorced women. They scored some "land" or even a whole house in the break-up, and now they just need some sucker to build them a house or fix up the one they're in; and this fool doesn't realize that she can – and will – kick him out of it when she's bored with him, and he doesn't have a legal toothpick to stand on. Let them take care of their own real estate. We need to go fishing.

Feminism is a disease of willfulness spread by memes which travel from brain to brain like a virus. Feminism is an addiction.

Women obey rules and regulations. Men obey principles. Our legal system is a swamp of rules and regulations incapable of honoring or enforcing principles. It cannot dig up the truth for all the hard roots of precedent and technicality cluttering its soil.

In our culture, if we take no action, if we take no moral stand, we are automatically servicing female memes.

To those I can't dissuade from playing the mental macaroni of the archetype-game here are some missing archetypes to ponder: the Green Man, Father Nature, Failure, Phallus, the Twisted Side of the Goddess, Technocracy, the Evil Corporation, the Female Corporation, Grandfathers, Father Earth, the Cook, the Hunter, the Pilgrim, the Hermit, the Man Who Has Slain His Ego.

We live in a society permeated by Fear of Phallus. We can go into any convenience store and pick up a magazine that shows two lesbos eating each other's cunts, but if they show a penis doing what it was designed to do that magazine will be yanked from the racks and banished to a XXX store.

We need male phallic art. We can stop somewhere short of worshiping the penis, but we do need to bring it out of hiding. The penis is not ugly or evil. It's the male life force. Not a symbol of the male life force, but the male life force *itself*.

Machismo is *not* masculinity. It is the warped ego-aspiration of a deeply shamed, uninitiated man. A man raised by women. Real cultures don't stomach macho idiots. They're banished.

Saints are people who don't need to wear monogrammed underwear. They know who they work for and are not side-tracked by *mater*ialist machinations. They know the worst that can happen to them and they are not afraid of it. They are men and women who live the teachings.

Jesus Christ is a super-archetype. From Trickster to Green Man to Spiritual Warrior, he embodies elements of most other archetypes – which is why he was so readily accepted by culturally diverse tribes all over the Earth. Forget the Church, read the Sermon on the Mount. The guy knew how to live.

The Parsifal myth teaches us that we cannot pursue happiness. Happiness is given, like grace. We need only *ask the right question*. Who does the Grail serve? Who does Life serve? And happiness can be what happens. We live in an Addictive Society comprised of Corporate/Socialist values and Marxist/ Fem-inist memes – if we just get "enough stuff" we'll be happy. It's a lie. The female agenda which serves this lie is doomed. We don't have to go down with them.

There is a Twisted to Side to every woman.

Children are being removed from their fathers in a blatant offensive to emasculate Western culture and clear the way for corporate colonization.
Cities are feminine. Nature is masculine. Corporations are female. Government is female. God is male.

Old folks receiving Social Security should be required to spend three hours a week with some kid from a broken home.
Every adult is responsible for the health and good sense and worldview of every child. That's how human society works.

An uninitiated man is an emotional vampire sucking energy out of women – the same way women suck energy out of us – because he has no masculine spiritual depths to tap.

Carl Jung said, it's important for us to develop spiritual "tools" because we simply are not equipped to "know" everything.

The meaning of life, as shown us by Ron Jones' Special Olympians, is to "share the victory".

Probably the single most helpful suggestion to glue to your brain pan as you put down this book is to remember to separate psychic phenomena from spiritual phenomena. It's easy to tell them apart. The rule is: if you can see it or hear it, it's NOT real. Psychic stuff is all the words and ideas and images we float around inside our skulls. Spiritual stuff is beyond color and form and sound and words. Psychic stuff is what feminist harpies are always screaming about. Psychic stuff is what your wife devours live and in color when Oprah Winfrey plays psychotherapist in your living room. Psychic stuff is what's spooned out on corporate TV and dished out by government. God is invisible and silent – and everywhere, all the time.

What men seek is immunity from the psychic garbage that invades our minds and our lives. We seek immunity from the System that is poisoning our lives with *mater*ialist memes which, from every historical and spiritual perspective – humanity-wide, world-wide – conspire to persuade us to adopt an agenda for living which has failed a million times, and which has never, once, worked.

With this understanding, we should be able to recreate a genuine male pole of existence. We should be able to relocate the center of gravity of the human personality far, far back toward the male end of the spectrum. We should be able to stop raping the earth, and we should be able to stop ruining our children.

We don't need an army to do it. The government is not going to change, corporations are not going to change, the church is not going to change, media is not going to change. But we...we will change. And they will fall all over themselves trying to come up with new things to sell us – new formulas, new fads, new economic plans, new social panaceas – and none of this psychic noise will be able to reach us in the silent place that is our natural home. It will blow clear of our brains like smoke in the wind. The purpose of men's lives is not to get along with women. The purpose of our lives is to be men, and then, getting along with women will be what naturally happens.

God Bless all willful women.
May they find
health and prosperity and happiness.

Always remember to be grateful. And always remember:

ETERNITY IS NOW

Footnotes:

1)   Jerome Rothenberg; *Technicians of the Sacred*; New York: Anchor Books, 1969, p283

2)   E.F.Schumacher; *Small is Beautiful*; New York: Perennial Library/Harper and Row; 1973, pp 97-101

3)   Rainier Maria Rilke; *Letters to a Young Poet*; New York: Random House; 1984, p34

4)   Schumacher, pp 37-38

5)   Emery Kelen; *Dag Hammarskjold: A Biography*; NY: Meredith Press, 1969

6)   Joseph Chilton Pearce, *Parabola*, Summer 1992, p60

7)   *Science*; v253, p958

8)   Anne Moir and David Jessel; *Brain Sex*; NY: Carol, 1991, p91

9)   *Omni;* Oct 1990, p44

10) *Ibid*

11)   Dianne McGuiness; *Male-Female Differences;* ed. by
        Roberta Hall et al; New York: Praeger, 1985, p86

12)   Charlotte M. Otten; Hall et al

13)   *Omni*; Oct 1990 p44

14)   Sandra Witelson: *Psychoneuroendocrinology*: v16,
        p131, from TIME, 1/20/92, p44

15)   Charlotte M. Otten; from Hall et al

16)   James Doyle; *The Male Experience*; Dubuque: W.C.
        Brown Co., 1983

17)   Michael Hutchinson; The Plague of Intolerance; from
        New Age Journal; July/August 1990, p41

18)   Ruth Benedict, *Patterns of Culture*; NY: Mentor
        Books, 1934, p233

19)   Janet Saltzman Chafetz, *Male-Female Roles;* ed.
        Bruno Leone and M. Teresa O'Neill, St Paul MN:
        Greenhaven Press 1983, p24

20)   Patricia Cayo Sexton, *The Feminized Male*; NY:
        Random House, 1969, p4

21)   Sexton, p32

22)   Sexton, p101

23)   Sexton, p7

24)   Sexton, p104

25)   Sexton, p115

26)   Sexton, p116

27)   Sexton, p127

28)   Sexton, p6

29)   Sexton, p131

30)   Sexton, p201

31)   Esther Vilar, *The Manipulated Man;* NY: Farrar,
      Straus and Girous, 1972, p50

32)   Vilar, p52

33)   Vilar, p52

34)   Vilar, p53

35)   Vilar, p17

36)   Vilar, p18

37)   Vilar, p54

38)   Vilar, p55

39)   Bede Griffiths, *River of Compassion*; Warwick NY:
      Amity House, 1987, p74

40)   Eleanor E. Maccoby, *American Psychologist;* April
      1990, pp517-518

41)   Vilar, p76

42)   Vilar, p78

43)   George Gilder, *Sexual Suicide*; NY: Quadrangle,
      1973 p25

44)   Vilar, p78

45)   Vilar, p79

46)   Vilar, p83

47)   Vilar, p91

48)   Vilar, p96

49)   Vilar, p97

50)   Vilar, p97

51)   Vilar, p98

52)   Vilar, p109

53)   *US News and World Report*; Aug 8, 1988; Merrill
      and Mcloughlin et al, p56

54)   Vilar, pp110-111

55)   Vilar, pp112-113

56)   Vilar, p117

57)   Sam Keen, *Fire in the Belly*, NY: Bantam Books,
      1991, p23-24

58)   Vilar, p117-119

59)   Vilar, p121

60)   Vilar, p126

61)   *Male-Female Roles*, ed. Bruno Leone and M. Teresa
       O'Neill, St Paul: Greenhaven, 1983, p124

62)   *US News and World Report*, Aug 8, 1988

63)   Vilar, p131

64)   Vilar, p136-137

65)   Vilar, p148

66)   Vilar, p149

67)   Vilar, pp152-153

68)   Vilar, p160

69)   Vilar, p163

70)   Vilar, p165

71)   Vilar, pp166-172

72)   Vilar, pp175-176

73)   Vilar, pp177-178

74)   Vilar, pp180-181

75)   Sam Keen, Ibid, p199

76)   Keen, p203

77)   Vilar, pp181-183

78)   Vilar, p184

79)   Richard Rohr, OFM, *Simplicity*, NY: Crossroad,
       1992, p122

80)   *Male-Female Roles*, Ibid, p48

81)   *US News and World Report*, Aug 8, 1988, p56

82)   *Male-Female Differences*, Roberta Hall et al; NY:
       Praeger 1985, p48

83)   Hall et al, p7

84)   *US News and World Report*, Aug 8, 1988, p57

85)   George Gilder, *Ibid*, p6

86)   Gilder, p69

87)   Gilder, p85

88)   Gilder, p105

89)   Gilder, p107

90)   Gilder, p117

91)   Gilder, p123

92)   Joseph Chilton Pearce, *Parabola,* Summer 1992,
       pp57-59

93)   Gilder, p164

94)   Colin Turnbull, *The Mountain People*, NY: Simon
       and Schuster, 19723, pp290-295 [from Gilder,
       p181]

95)   Gilder, p229

96)   Robin Fox and Lionel Tiger, *The Imperial Animal*;
       NY: Holt, Rinehart and Winston, 1971; Delta
       paperback 1972, p7 and passim [from Gilder]

97)   George Gilder, *Men and Marriage*; Gretna: Pelican Publishing Co., 1986, pp66-67

98)   Gilder, *Men and Marriage*; p98

99)   Gilder, *Men and Marriage*; p147

100) Gilder, *Men and Marriage*; p163

101) Gilder, *Men and Marriage*; p173

102) Philip L. Slater, *The Pursuit of Loneliness*; Boston: Beacon Press, 1970, pp5-7

103) Robert Bly, *Iron John*; NY: Addison Wesley, 1990, p14

104) Bly, p21

105) Ray Raphael, *The Men from the Boys*; Lincoln: U. of Nebraska Press, 1988

106) Patrick Arnold, *Wildmen, Warriors and Kings*, NY: Crossroad, 1992, pp107-109

107) *Parabola*, Summer 1992, pp75-76

108) *Parabola*, Summer 1992, p77

109) Keith Thompson, *To Be a Man*, Los Angeles, Tarcher, 1991

110) Bly, p31

111) *Common Boundary*, January/February 1992, p32

112) Hazrat Inayat Khan, *The Mysticism of Sound;* Geneva: International Headquarters of the Sufi Movement, 1979, p22

113) Robert Johnson, *He*; NY: Harper and Row, 1989, p32

114) Bly, p61

115) Bly, p55

116) Bly, p60

117) Bly, p66

118) Robert Johnson, *We*; San Francisco: Harper and Row, 1983 p. xi

119) Bly, p75

120) Bly, p77

121) Bly, p78

122) Richard Rohr, *The Wildman's Journey,* Cincinnati: St. Anthony Messenger Press, 1992, p44

123) Rohr, *Wildman's Journey*, p50

124) Bly, p84

125) Rohr, *Wildman's Journey*, p75

126) Rohr, *Wildman's Journey*, pp85-86

127) Patrick Arnold, *Wildmen...* p214

128) Patrick Arnold, p34; from Carol Gilligan, *In A Different Voice;* Psychological Theory and Women's Development; Cambridge, MA: Harvard, 1982, pp5-8

129) Bly, p86

130)   Rohr, *Wildman's Journey*, p105

131)   Johnson, *We*; p65

132)   Rohr, *Wildman's Journey*, p127

133)   Rohr, *Wildman's Journey*, p131

134)   Rohr, *Wildman's Journey*, p135

135)   Rohr, *Wildman's Journey*, p136

136)   Bly, p92

137)   Bly, p93

138)   Bly, p94

139)   Bly, pp94-95

140)   Bly, p97

141)   Bly, p102

142)   Rohr, *Wildman's Journey,* pp155-156

143)   Rohr, *Wildman's Journey*, p157

144)   Rohr, *Wildman's Journey,* p158

145)   Robert Johnson, *She*; NY: Harper and Row, 1989

146)   *Alcoholics Anonymous Big Book*, Soft-cover portable edition, 1988, p552

147)   Fred Hayward's *Men's Rights Survey*: Men's Rights, PO Box 163180, Sacramento, California 95816

148)   Richard F. Doyle, *Male-Female Roles*, Bruno et al, p83

149) Aaron Kipnis, *Knights Without Armor*, Los Angeles: Tarcher, 1991, p28

150) *Chatelaine*; Feb 87, p49

151) *MacLean's*; Oct 31, 1988, p52

152) *Chatelaine*; Nov 88, p63

153) *Industry Week*; November 18, 1991, p70

154) Ellen Hopkins, *New York*; Jan 11, 1988, p45

155) Jane Young, *New York*; Nov 18, 1985, p55

156) Ibid

157) Warren Farrell, *Why Men Are the Way They Are*; NY: McGraw-Hill, 1986, p. xvii

158) *Chatelaine,* Dec 88, p88

159) Doyle, *Male-Female Roles*; Bruno et al, p85

160) Aaron Kipnis, *Knights Without Armor*, Los Angeles: Tarcher, 1991

161) Suzanne Steinmetz, *Victimology*, vol 2 1977-78, no. 3-4, pp 499-509

162) Warren Farrell, *Why Men Are the Way They Are*; NY: McGraw-Hill, 1986, p237

163) Aaron Kipnis, *Knights Without Armor*, p28

164) Anne Wilson Schaef, *When Society Becomes An Addict,* Harper San Francisco, 1987, p14

165) Schaef, p40

166)   Schaef, p41

167)   Schaef, p47

168)   Schaef, p58

169)   Schaef, p59

170)   Schaef, p61

171)   Schaef, p61

172)   Schaef, p63

173)   Schaef, p64

174)   Schaef, p65

175)   Schaef, p66

176)   Schaef, p68

177)   Schaef, p73

178)   Schaef, pp72-73

179)   Schaef, p75

180)   Schaef, p77

181)   Schaef, p75

182)   Schaef, p78

183)   Schaef, p79

184)   Schaef, p80

185)   Schaef, pp88-89

186)   Schaef, p90

187)   Schaef, p92

188)   Schaef, p93

189)   Schaef, p100

190)   Schaef, p102

191)   Schaef, p108

192)   Schaef, p112

193)   Bede Griffiths, *River of Compassion*; Warwick NY:
        Amity House, 1987, p37

194)   Schaef, p136

195)   Schaef, p137

196)   Warren Farrell, *Why Men Are the Way They Are*;
        NY: McGraw-Hill, 1986

197)   Aaron Kipnis, *Knights Without Armor*

198)   Patrick Arnold, *Wildmen, Warriors and Kings*, NY:
        Crossroad, 1992, p52

199)   Arnold, p63

200)   Richard Rohr, *The Wildman's Journey*, Cincinnati:
        St. Anthony Messenger Press, 1992, p199

201)   William Anderson, *The Green Man*, San Francisco:
        Harper Collins, 1990, p14

202)   Arnold, p99

203)   Richard Rohr, *The Wildman's Journey*, pp210-211

204)   Richard Rohr, *The Wildman's Journey*, pp211-213

205)   Richard Rohr, *The Wildman's Journey*, p216

206)   Richard Rohr, *The Wildman's Journey,* pp224-225

207)   Rene Weber, *Dialogues With Scientists and Sages,*
         NY: Routledge & Kegan Paul, 1986

208)   Arnold, p35

209)   Arnold, pp75-76

210)   Robert Johnson, *He*; NY: Harper and Row, 1989,
         p74

211)   Robert Johnson, *He*; NY: Harper and Row, 1989,
         p77

212)   Robert Johnson, *He*; NY: Harper and Row, 1989,
         p78

213)   Peace Pilgrim, *Steps Toward Inner Peace*; Friends of
         Peace Pilgrim, 43480 Cedar Ave, Hemet, CA,
         92544

214)   Robert Johnson, *He*; NY: Harper and Row, 1989,
         p79

215)   Robert Johnson, *He*; NY: Harper and Row, 1989,
         p80

216)   Robert Johnson, *He*; NY: Harper and Row, 1989,
         p82

217)   Arnold, p188

218)   Robert Bly, *A Little Book on the Human Shadow*;
         Harper San Francisco, 1988, p30

219) Bly, *ibid,*

220) Kipnis, *Knights Without Armor,*

221) Camille Paglia, *Sex, Art and American Culture*; Vintage Books, 1992; from Utne Reader, Jan/Feb 1993, pp64-65

222) Neil Douglas-Klotz, *Prayers of the Cosmos*; Meditations on the Aramaic Words of Jesus; Harper San Francisco, 1990, p47

223) Cynthia Bourgealt, *Parabola*, Summer 1989, p27

224) Ron Jones, B-Ball: *The Basketball Team That Never Lost a Game;* Ron Jones, 1201 Stanyan St., San Francisco, CA, 94117

225) Wolfgang Lederer, *To Be A Man*; Los Angeles: Tarcher, 1991, p153

Order Coupon

Tear this off and give it to a friend

To order *The Corporate Cult, Water People* or or gift copies of
What Men Know That Women Don't
contact:

Virtualbookworm.com
PO Box 9949
College Station, Texas 77842

at their website:
www.virtualbookworm.com

(click Bookstore, then Search, then type in Zubaty and click Search again)

or email:
orders@virtualbookworm.com

or toll free phone/fax:
1-877-376-4955

And if you still can't get 'em get me at:
richzubaty@hotmail.com
or
www.geocities.com/Athens/Oracle/5225/
or
1-888-347-4364

Rich Zubaty

It's OK to be a Man

Printed in the United States
97898LV00002B/341/A